I'D LIKE THE

WORLD

TO BUY A

COKE

The Life and Leadership of

ROBERTO GOIZUETA

David Greising

John Wiley & Sons, Inc.

New York • Chichester • Weinheim • Brisbane • Singapore • Toronto

Library of Congress Cataloging-in-Publication Data:
Greising, David, 1960–
   I'd like the world to buy a coke : the life and leadership of
Roberto Goizueta / David Greising.
      p.   cm.
   Includes index.
   ISBN 0-471-19408-5 (cloth : alk. paper)
    1. Goizueta, Roberto, 1931–1997. 2. Chief executive officers—
United States—Biography. 3. Coca-Cola Company. 4. Soft drink
industry—United States. I. Title.
HD9349.S632G74   1998
338.7′66362′092—dc21
[B]   97-49220

Printed in the United States of America.

10 9 8 7 6 5 4 3 2 1

In memory of Dad, who cautioned me against life as a writer, and of Mom, who didn't.

Preface

When I wrote Roberto Goizueta a letter asking him to cooperate with me in the preparation of this book, I used the word "biography" a total of five times. It was a word choice with consequences.

Goizueta agreed to meet with me to discuss the book before he even looked carefully at the letter, based on the recommendation of his public relations staff, who told me they favored my proposal. Now it was just a few days before our early February 1997 meeting, and Goizueta was finally focusing on the letter itself for the first time. He did not like what he saw. Taking a pen off his desk during a meeting with one of his public relations people, he circled the word "biography" every time it appeared. "Biographies," he told the staffer, "should not be written about people while they are alive."

It is, of course, a sad irony that Goizueta's words would prove so prophetic. Even though he ultimately decided not to cooperate with this book, Goizueta did not dismiss this project lightly. He tried, in his own way, to find a way to work with me so that the story of his career at Coke would be told accurately and well. In the end, though, he could not escape his own feelings about biographies, and his own discomfort at being the subject of a biography while he still was working at Coke.

Despite his misgivings about the nature of my project, Goizueta still kept his appointment with me. I spent much of our 45-minute meeting making a case that his education, life in Cuba and flight from Castro were an essential part of the story of his impact on Coke, because those events so strongly shaped his character. He carefully reviewed my preliminary outline for the book, and said he would be willing to field all questions, except those that sought to probe his life before Coca-Cola. As the discussion continued, he allowed that he might talk briefly about his personal life, but only as it directly related to his career at Coke. I told him I expected the book would begin with him answering a blind advertisement for the job at Coke, would flash back briefly to his early years, and then would develop almost entirely as a history of his career and his company. The book, I told him, was a business biography, not a biography in the classical sense of the word.

He agreed to proceed, and the last words he said to me were this: "I'm not going to tell Olguita." His wife Olguita in Goizueta's later years had grown increasingly protective of her husband's image, even trying to dissuade him from allowing newspapers and magazines to photograph him for stories they were publishing about him. Intensely private and conservative people, the Goizuetas had understood early that image management was one of the costs of running a high-profile global enterprise like Coke. He opened the veil at times when he wanted or needed to: when he first became president of Coke, during the New Coke debacle, and as he was preparing for a personally meaningful speech to a citizenship ceremony at Thomas Jefferson's Monticello on July 4, 1995. But in his later years, as his dark hair thinned and grayed, as his wiry frame took on weight, and, not incidentally, as his need to promote himself diminished because of the strength of his performance as Coke's chief executive for more than 15 years, Goizueta grew ever more reluctant to share his personal life and thoughts with the public.

Goizueta did, however, agree to cooperate with me. He allowed me to begin researching in Coke's archives, and gave an OK for his top lieutenants to speak with me. Even so, it was clear even at this early stage that he was having second thoughts. Try as I might, I could never get a firm appointment with any of Goizueta's top people. Interviews with those further down the chain of command were scheduled, then canceled without explanation. And after two initial research forays at the archives, Coke's corporate library became inexplicably busy, and Coke's archivist called to cancel an appointment, explaining there was too much activity for the time being.

Then two related events changed Goizueta's stance toward this book for good. *The Atlanta Journal-Constitution* published a story saying Goizueta was cooperating with a biography of himself. The six-paragraph story, which a Coke public relations staffer had leaked to the AJC, confirmed Goizueta's suspicions that the world would see this book as a biography, regardless of whatever I was calling it. The same day I had a telephone conversation with Goizueta's personal public relations assistant, who wanted to know what I would do if Roberto Goizueta's version of events differed from those of other sources I interviewed for the book. When I told her that I would first try to clear up any confusion, but ultimately would make a judgment based on the weight of the evidence, she told me that was unacceptable. "This is his biography," she said.

From that point on, Goizueta was not a participant in this book. In conversations with several people who worked for him and knew him, the thinking behind his actions has come through. He feared that a biography, scheduled for publication not long after he turned 66, would naturally raise questions about how much longer he could stay at Coke's helm. Coke's directors already had extended his tenure indefinitely beyond the company's mandatory retirement age of 65, and he quite clearly was not yet ready to step down. The concept of the celebrity CEO repulsed him, and he did not want to be seen as a chest thumper akin to Lee Iacocca. If he did work with a biographer, he wanted to make certain he had some editorial control over the outcome.

Once Goizueta decided against participating, he tried to stop the book from coming out at all. Randy Donaldson, his top public relations person, telephoned John Wiley & Sons and told my publisher that Roberto Goizueta "is a very private person and does not want this book to be published." He and a colleague flew to New York to meet with Jim Childs, publisher, and my editor, Ruth Mills, to reiterate Goizueta's opposition to the book and to learn what they could about our plans for it. It is to the great credit of Childs and Mills that they stuck with this project despite the pressure from Coca-Cola. I know of other authors working with other publishers who have seen their projects vanish when the subjects of the books let it be known they opposed the projects.

Once Coke put the word out that Goizueta did not want this book written, doors slammed shut all over Atlanta and throughout the Coca-Cola system worldwide. The company's public relations office refused such routine requests as providing press releases, earnings statements and other matters of public record. Former Coke executives canceled interviews, often without explanation. A secretary for one former executive, Sam Ayoub, said he had been called out of the country on business. When I phoned back a few minutes later and asked if he was in without identifying myself, she said he was on the phone. The secretary for former Coke executive Brian Dyson said he would not speak to me "because of the kind of book you are writing," even before I had an opportunity to tell Dyson or his assistant what kind of book I was in fact writing.

Despite this initial rough going, I did not give up and ultimately persuaded many of the people who had turned me down to grant interviews for the book. All told, I interviewed just more than 100 people, and tracked down notes from prior interviews with almost all of those who turned down interview requests because of Goizueta's noncooperation. By the time Roberto Goizueta died of complications from lung cancer on October 18, 1997, I had completed virtually all of my research and most of the writing for the book. Coke agreed after his death to help me to check facts in the book for accuracy, but after I sent Randy Donaldson a list of facts covering every chapter in the book in December, he never returned a phone call over the three weeks that remained before the book went to press. Even so, I was able to check the facts myself and stand by the book's accuracy in every respect.

His death was a grievous occasion for his family and a great loss for his company. But it also meant that some people who had declined to grant interviews because of Goizueta's stance might now come forward. I had a brief window in which I could reach out to a select few people before my publication deadline. Foremost among the few who did change their stance was Don Keough, once Goizueta's rival for the top job who went on to be his partner at the top of Coke for 13 of the 16 years of Goizueta's tenure. Don Keough made a principled decision that Goizueta's death had removed the chief reason for his noncooperation—his discomfort with a biography being published while he was still alive. He served the memory of his friend, and measurably improved this book, by helping to bring new insight and detail to the story of Roberto Goizueta's life and career.

Throughout this project, the comment from Brian Dyson's assistant about "the kind of book you are writing" has stayed in my head. The kind of book I have tried to write is one that presents Roberto Goizueta as the complex, three-dimensional character he was.

Goizueta's non-cooperation did not affect my view of him, or my reporting for the book, except to the extent it limited my direct contact with him and the people currently in his inner circle. He was a man of incredible drive and vision, someone who cared at least as much about his work as he did about anything else in his life. While aloof and independent, he also cared intensely about his public image, and the image of his company. He could be visionary and strategic at the same time he meddled in details or took sometimes petty swipes at his competitors. He was correctly regarded as one of the most imaginative and successful executives of this or any other time. This is his story.

THIS BOOK HAS BEEN AT ONCE THE MOST DIFFICULT AND MOST REwarding challenge of my career. I want, first, to thank Jim Childs, then publisher at John Wiley & Sons, Inc. for sticking with this project at the outset. I want to thank Jeff Brown, vice president of the Professional, Reference and Trade Division, for making the right call in giving me extra time after Goizueta's death to reach a few key sources who had previously not talked. My editor Ruth Mills, who brought the idea of a Goizueta biography to me just before the 1996 summer Olympics in Atlanta, stuck with the project and with me through all the challenges all the way through. I am grateful to her for that.

Robert Barker and Kevin Kelly proved, once again, that they are outstanding editors as well as incredible friends. As volunteer readers, they shared their expertise and effort in a way that dramatically improved the book. I want to thank Bob, a senior writer for *Business Week,* for not asking me to run the entire manuscript through my typewriter again, and Kevin, a journalist-cum-businessman, for his pointed and sometimes humorous comments about my various assaults on the English language.

Attorney Todd Musburger enthusiastically backed this project from the outset, provided wise counsel throughout, and represented my interests with the right mixture of accommodation and moral outrage. I thoroughly enjoy working with him.

My research assistants, Jennifer Rivera in Miami and Brad Wolverton in Atlanta, helped track down numerous people and stray facts that I never could have handled on my own. Jennifer, especially, succeeded in locating the help-wanted advertisement Roberto Goizueta answered when he took his first job at Coke, and the fine materials from the Belen yearbook that contribute mightily to the photo spread. Other colleagues generously offered their insights and, in some cases, notes from interviews they had done relating to the subject of this book. These include Mark Clifford and John Pearson of *Business Week* and Maria Mallory, my former Atlanta colleague now of *U.S. News & World Report.*

My research efforts at the Special Collections department of the Robert W. Woodruff Library at Emory University were aided immeasurably by the efforts of Linda M. Matthews, head of special collections, and her staff. Keith Nash, Kathy Shoemaker, and Beverly B. Allen guided me through the Woodruff papers, from which I drew much excellent material about Roberto Goizueta's early career. At Yale University, archivist Christine Weideman provided helpful guidance, and Julie Ann Ludwig followed through on a last-minute request for help.

While I could never persuade Roberto Goizueta to cooperate with me, my efforts to do so still benefited from the counsel and moral support of several people. Anthony Bianco of *Business Week* shared his success in persuading the reclusive Paul Reichman to cooperate in his book *The Reichmans,* and *Wall Street Journal* reporter Roger Lowenstein commiserated about his experience trying to persuade Warren Buffett to cooperate with his book, *Buffett: The Making of an American Capitalist.* Frederick Allen offered insight into the unique sociology and politics of The Coca-Cola Company, information he gleaned in his excellent history of the company, *Secret Formula.* Joel Koblenz of executive search firm Egon Zehnder International was a helpful sounding board in my effort to divine the various motivations that might drive a typical chief executive to extend or withhold cooperation.

In journalism, we do not often have an opportunity publicly to thank the people on whom we most directly rely for success in our work: the people we interview for our stories. Books do afford us that chance. Along with Keough, thanks go to Chaplin Tyler, who was there when Goizueta first started his trajectory in Atlanta, and filled in the details on a period that previously had never consumed more than a line or two of a resume in the numerous newspaper and magazine profiles of Goizueta's career. Richard Cook, Goizueta's Yale roommate, shared his recollections as well as some excellent photographs and the Goizuetas' wedding invitation. I also want to thank the many people at various levels inside Coke who took a risk by sharing their thoughts and information with me. You know who you are.

I could not have completed this book without the generous support of the people at *Business Week*. Editor-in-chief Stephen B. Shepard graciously allowed me a six-month leave of absence from my job as *Business Week*'s Atlanta bureau chief, proving again that he values the personal and professional development of his staff as much as he does a timely and memorable story. Former chief of correspondents Keith G. Felcyn arranged the leave, and his successor, James E. Ellis, welcomed me back with a host of good ideas that should strengthen our coverage of Coke and other companies as we move forward. When I reached dead ends in my research, chief librarian Jamie Russell and her staff offered timely advice. My Atlanta bureau colleague, correspondent Nicole Harris, worked to pick up the slack in my absence and shared her knowledge of Coke as well as insights from some fine work she did about the company in my absence.

Among the many people who helped in personally meaningful ways, I want to thank those who offered sustenance and security while I toiled into the wee hours at Peachtree Center in Atlanta. They include Bayo K. Brown, Kyong H. Lee, and Edward Lee, and night guard Larry Savoy.

There are events in life that strip away everything else from our relationships and lay bare their very essence. Book writing is one of them. Gradually over time, the book consumes more and more of the author's energy and attention, until at the very end it becomes a compulsion that uproots virtually everything else in the author's life. In times such as these, we know for certain whether we married well, whether our spouse is truly a life partner willing to devote almost everything to the success of something that is, in the end, a somewhat selfish undertaking. My wife, Cindy, is my life partner and so much more. She took charge of our children, our house, and our lives, patiently shared her attention in endless discussions of the book, put up with my late nights, and did it all so well that Wesley, Greta, and Claire barely noticed anything amiss. I dedicated my first book, "For Cindy, for everything." For this book, she did everything, and much more.

Timeline: Roberto C. Goizueta

1931	Born November 18, Havana, Cuba
⋮	
1936	Attends Colegio de Belen, Havana
⋮	
1948	Attends Cheshire Academy, Connecticut
⋮	
1949	Attends Yale University, Class of '53
⋮	
1953	June 14, marries Olguita Casteleiro
1954	Works for father in Cuba
	July 4, joins Coca-Cola in Havana
1959	Castro Revolution
1960	Spring, sends three children to Miami
	October, Roberto and Olguita leave Cuba
	Works in Coke's Bahamas office
⋮	
1964	Moves to Atlanta to redesign Coke's management systems
1966	Becomes Coke's youngest vice president (age 35)
1969	Becomes U.S. citizen
1970	December, four-year-old son Carlos dies of leukemia
1974	Learns "secret formula"
1979	Chairmanship fight
1980	May, becomes Coke president
	Fall, "Spanish Inquisition"
1981	March, becomes chairman and CEO
	April, Palm Springs conference
1982	January, buys Columbia Pictures
	August, launches Diet Coke
1983	August, sells wine business
1985	April 23, launches New Coke
	July 11, relaunches Coca-Cola Classic
1986	May, Coke Centennial
	November, Coca-Cola Enterprises spinoff
1987	Backs Olympics in Atlanta
1988	March, Warren Buffett discloses he owns 7.7% of Coke
1989	June, buys 41% of Coca-Cola Amatil
	September, sells Columbia to Sony
	November 10, Berlin Wall falls, Coke invades eastern Europe
1991	Receives $81 million bonus
1992	November, Coke overtakes Pepsi in eastern Europe
1993	January, launches Tab Clear
	February, "Always Coca-Cola" ads unveiled, makes a deal with China
	April, Don Keough retires
	July, Sergio Zyman returns
	October, recruits George M.C. Fisher to head Kodak
1994	April, extends his tenure as Coke CEO
	July, M. Douglas Ivester becomes president and COO
1995	July, first public discussion of Cuba
1996	July, Atlanta Summer Olympics
	August, purchases Venezuela bottler
	Goizueta Foundation ($38 million in stock) set up
1997	July, Coke's sponsorship of Boys & Girls Clubs
	October 18, Roberto Goizueta dies, six weeks after diagnosis of lung cancer

Contents

Prologue: The Song from the Mountaintop

He changed the formula.

Ever since he foisted New Coke on an unsuspecting and, as it turned out, an uncooperative world, his decision to change Coke's secret formula was the one part of Roberto C. Goizueta's story that had attracted universal notice. Quite clearly, we missed the point. While the rest of the world was transfixed by Coke's sweetness and fizz, Goizueta quietly and unrelentingly went far beyond changing the taste of the world's most popular soft drink. He changed the formula for how his company was run and, much more broadly, he changed the recipe for personal and corporate success in a global world.

Formulas were an important part of Goizueta's life from the time he was a small child growing up in Cuba in the 1930s. His grandfather, an immigrant from Spain who had made a fortune investing in sugar mills, filled his head with formulaic Spanish proverbs. "If your neighbor's beard is on fire, make certain yours is soaking wet," he would say. Or, "It is better to be the head of a mouse than the tail of a lion." Those truisms constantly popped out of Goizueta's mouth both in personal conversations and in his role as chairman and chief executive of The Coca-Cola Company.

As a student at Cuba's most prestigious school and then as a chemical engineering student at Yale University, Goizueta spent years memorizing formulas in textbooks. He expected to apply them while working at his father's sugar mill. But then Goizueta's life changed dramatically, in a way that altered both his future and the course of one of the world's great global enterprises. He took a job at Coca-Cola and, a few years later, Fidel Castro took control of Cuba. At age 29, Goizueta fled Havana with his family and, armed only with intellect, political skills, and a powerful ambition, eventually seized control of Coke in one of the most jarring boardroom cock fights in corporate history.

Coca-Cola, when he took control in 1980, was in a mess. On the strength of the Pepsi Challenge, Pepsi-Cola had seized leadership in the key category of supermarket sales. A corporate-wide ban on borrowing money had restrained Coke's ability to reinvest in its operations, and his predecessor's ill-advised effort to make Coke a conglomerate had run aground. Announcing there would be "no sacred cows" at Coke, Goizueta launched Diet Coke and bought a Hollywood studio. Then the New Coke fiasco seemed to open his eyes to the value hidden at the core of his company: the universal power of the Coca-Cola name.

His unique gift as an executive was his ability to change his own formula, to quickly understand his mistakes, adapt, and ultimately triumph. From New Coke forward, for Goizueta as for his company, Coke was it. He designed every move to increase his ability to pour that bubbly, slightly bitter, caramel concoction down the throats of more people every day. He unloaded Coke's bottling operation, figuring someone else should bear the cost of actually bottling his soft drink. He sold Columbia pictures, and reinvested the money in a push to knock Pepsi-Cola out of the old Soviet bloc countries as fast as the Lenin statues fell. Then he hooked up with strong multinational beverage companies, "anchor bottlers" he called them, and used the power of their capital to multiply Coke's own investment in developing markets. From that platform, he hoped to find nirvana in utterly underdeveloped markets that he called "Coca-Cola heaven."

Goizueta was single-minded about building Coca-Cola, but he was a multidimensional corporate strategist. He reinvented the way he ran his company and, on his tail, many executives around the world found new ways to run theirs. He used performance incentives to squeeze the most out of his executives, and personally benefited when Coke's runaway results netted him an $86 million pay day for 1991, and more than $1 billion in earnings for his career. He based strategic decisions on how much money he could earn, not how much things would cost. He turned the speedy transfer of information into a competitive advantage. Toward the end of his career, he cultivated a worthy successor at a time when his peers in other executive suites either ignored the issue, or badly botched their efforts. In an age when corporate complexity is often seen as a virtue, Goizueta simplified. As a result, Coke's stock price during his reign had perhaps the greatest unchecked run in the history of American business.

Consistently, he was a person of contradiction. An aristocratic billionaire, he always vacationed in a rented villa at Sea Island, Georgia, where he listened to country & western music and refused to take phone calls. His flight from Cuba, it turns out, was more harrowing than most people ever realized, but he almost never talked about it. He had a remarkable grasp of the minute details of Coke's business, but virtually never meddled in the mundane. Unforgiving about errors in grammar or math, he did not trust any manager until he saw them make a major strategic mistake. He was scrupulously courteous, but wrote biting letters to reporters or analysts who dared criticize Coke. Goizueta was reverent toward his elders, particularly the Coca-Cola legend Robert W. Woodruff, yet he consciously debunked virtually every precept by which his predecessors had run the company.

Roberto C. Goizueta changed the formula by which chief executives will be measured from this point forward. More than anything, he did it by taking lip service about serving shareholders and turning it into a life's creed. All his life, his most valued possession was the 100 shares of Coca-Cola stock he bought, with money borrowed from his father, just after he began working at Coke. And he spent his life, to his last labored breath, working to make those shares grow in value. When Goizueta called someone a share*owner*, he meant that he understood the tie between the lowliest widows and orphans who own Coke stock and the man at the top.

He did quite a job. By the time cancer abruptly ended his work and his life on October 18, 1997, The Coca-Cola Company during his 16 years as CEO had grown from a $4 billion company to $18 billion in sales. Goizueta broadened and deepened Coke's presence in almost every country on the planet. Coca-Cola's stock market value, the measure that mattered most to Goizueta, jumped from $4.3 billion in 1981 to $180 billion, a staggering 3,500 percent increase. Goizueta's early and earnest dedication to adding economic value to his company made millionaires out of thousands of Coca-Cola employees and shareholders, and boosted the billionaire status of Warren Buffett, the revered Omaha investor who became Coke's largest single shareowner and one of Goizueta's biggest boosters. Impressed by Goizueta's consistent excellence, Buffett dubbed him and Coke "The Inevitables."

He earned such praise by adopting a formula that was as simple as it gets. Goizueta invested every ounce of his energy, money, smarts, and guts into the drive to sell more Coca-Cola to more people in more places every day. He liked to talk about the jobs and investment capital that Coke brought with it when it expanded around the globe, but that is not what drove him. All Goizueta really cared about was boosting Coke's sales beyond the one billion eight-ounce servings the world drinks each day. When he died, his next target was the two-billion-drink day.

In the mid-1970s, as Goizueta maneuvered his way to the top, Coke aired an advertisement featuring a multi-ethnic group of young people standing on a hilltop. "I'd like to teach the world to sing, in perfect harmony," they sang. "I'd like to buy the world a Coke, and keep it company." It was classic advertising, and it caught the mood of a generation. But Goizueta never particularly liked the ad because it did not sell much Coke. For him, perhaps, the message was not quite right. He did not want to buy the world a Coke. Roberto C. Goizueta wanted the world to buy a Coke.

1

Cuba, Castro, and Coke

The young Cuban scrutinizing the pages of *Diario de La Marina* did not typically read the help-wanted section of Havana's oldest and most conservative newspaper. But on June 18, 1954, Roberto Crispulo Goizueta was trolling through the want ads. For the first time in his 22 years, he was looking for a job. Not just any job, for Roberto Goizueta was a man of expectations. After graduating at the top of his class from Cuba's most prestigious academy and earning a degree from Yale University, he was not about to make a false step at the start of his career. Roberto Goizueta's new job would have to do more than feed, clothe, and house his family. It must declare his independence from his father, fulfill the promise of his schooling, and give substance to his ambition. And with his young wife Olguita just pregnant with their first child, the job must befit the standing of a young couple starting life together on the top rung of Cuban society.

Alternatives abounded. For starters, Roberto could stay with his father's company. Crispulo Goizueta was an architect and real estate investor who had assumed control of his wife's family's sugar interests after his father-in-law, Marcelo Cantera, retired. Señor Cantera had come to Cuba from Spain and had made a fortune investing in a sugar mill and refinery during the Depression of the 1930s. Or, there was Olguita's family. Her father, Segundo Casteleiro, was one of Cuba's most prominent merchants, best known for the Lonja del Comercio wholesale food business and the Casteleiro & Visozo office equipment company. The businesses had been good to Señor Casteleiro. His clan was reputed to be one of the dozen wealthiest families in Cuba. A position could certainly be found within the Casteleiro enterprises.

But Roberto would have none of it. A year of working as an assistant to his father had taught him one thing: He was not cut out to be the boss' son—or son-in-law. He wanted a job where his judgment would be questioned. He wanted to compete with his peers. He wanted success untainted by suspicion of nepotism. "I was a freshly graduated chemical engineer, and everyone was telling me how great I was," Goizueta would recall later. "It was obvious to me that, no matter what I did, everyone would say it was great because I was the owner's son. I knew I would always be the owner's son. It got to the point where I didn't know whether I was in fact good or I wasn't." He wanted out, and he wanted up. And if he could find a position that would provide both, he would take it.

Goizueta answered the ad. Driven by the family's chauffeur to Havana's business district down busy Calzada Street, he still wondered about the identity of the company looking to employ a bilingual chemical engineer. It could easily be Procter & Gamble, which produced Camay soap at a Havana factory. Or one of the American tire companies, B.F. Goodrich or Goodyear Tire & Rubber; each had sizable Cuban production operations. General Electric and Westinghouse both had Cuban plants, too. Any of those could use the services of a talented chemical engineer.

When he arrived for the interview, the hiring company was not a familiar name. But if Cia Embotelladora was not known in Cuba, its product most certainly was. Embotelladora's parent company was a household name to every office worker, peasant, and businessman who walked, bicycled, or drove down the crowded streets of Cuba's business district, or through the rich hills of Cuba's sugar, tobacco, and pineapple plantations. Embotelladora was owned by The Coca-Cola Company, whose 6½-ounce "Coca" bottle accounted for nearly half of the country's soft drink consumption. The red disk advertisement proclaiming "Disfruta Coca-Cola"—Enjoy Coca-Cola—was a familiar icon throughout the island country of 6.5 million people. The soft drink was even served at the exclusive Havana Yacht Club, where the Goizueta and Casteleiro families were members. In fact, as a young girl, Olguita had enjoyed a daily breakfast of buttered toast and "Coca," a habit she dropped before marrying Roberto.

The job at Coke interested Goizueta, despite certain drawbacks. Working for his father, he was earning twice what Coke was offering, so he would have to take a pay cut, and there would be lots of travel. The salary was $500 a month, eventually. For the six-month probation period, during which his first child was expected, Goizueta would earn only half that amount. But the job fit well with his education—very well, from the Coke manager's point of view. Many young Cuban aristocrats went to school in the United States, but few could be more qualified than a chemical engineer from Yale. With such a pedigree, the reserved and confident Goizueta seemed the perfect person to join the quality control section of Coke's Cuban operations, with oversight for production processes in Cuba's three company-run Coke plants.

There was just one hitch. At the command of his father, he could not work on Saturdays. When Roberto had told his father he wanted to work on his own, Crispulo withheld his objections and even encouraged Roberto to make the move. Yet he could not do without his son completely, so Crispulo extracted a compromise: "I want you to work with me on Saturdays, so you can keep in touch with the family business." Crispulo figured the "experiment" might last a year—two at most—and it made sense for Roberto to keep current to ease his expected return. Roberto had two younger sisters, Olivia and Vivien, but in Cuba in the early 1950s, there was no chance that one of the girls would someday run the business.

All things considered, Crispulo had responded remarkably well to Roberto's decision to leave the family business. In most Cuban families, such an abandonment would be considered a grave insult and would risk opening an almost unbreachable chasm between the generations. Indeed, Roberto knew most of his friends would find his decision crazy. Many of them would kill to have the opportunities he had, to step into a family enterprise that guaranteed a steady income, and a fortune over time. But Goizueta was willing to walk away from it all with his move to Coke.

As he discussed the job opening with the Coca-Cola manager, Goizueta explained the dilemma presented by his father's request that he continue spending time working for the family company. "I'll work Sundays for The Coca-Cola Company if you want me to," Goizueta said. "But Saturdays I cannot." With a handshake, the deal was done. Goizueta had a job. His starting date: July 4, 1954. Goizueta was struck by the irony. Independence Day in the country of his new employer would be the start of his private experiment in autonomy. He liked the omen.

BREAKING AWAY FROM HIS FATHER WAS THE FIRST BOLD ASSERTION of independence in the life of Roberto C. Goizueta. From the time he was born in his father's mansion to the day he announced he would leave, Goizueta had led an exemplary if unremarkable life of diligence and conformity. From his classmates in Cuba to his classmates at Yale, no one who came across him in those formative years predicted the kind of independence that Goizueta demonstrated by turning away from his father's business and setting out on his own. None saw him as the sort who would one day lead one of the world's great corporations, and become one of the century's most effective chief executives.

At this early stage in his life, with this major step, Goizueta demonstrated an independence of mind and an indifference to the constraints of custom that would mark him as a leader throughout his life. There were no corner lemonade stands or newspaper routes in Roberto's youth to mark him early on as a protocapitalist. His privileged upbringing would have made such undertakings unseemly. But his march to independence was marked with traits that characterized him throughout his life: the knack for quiet leadership that won him Belen Academy's top honor, the diligent work ethic that got him through Yale, the devotion that bound him to Olguita at such an early age and, frankly, the touch of luck that led him to choose a job at Coca-Cola that was a lifeline when Castro's revolution ripped the future out of the hands of so many of his peers in Havana. These characteristics, alone and in combination, would serve Roberto Goizueta as he climbed to the top of Coke, and then took his company's performance to the top of the charts.

After he moved to Atlanta, rose through Coke's ranks, and ultimately vied for the top job, Goizueta's Cuban upbringing became a useful tool that helped improve the trajectory of his career path. His Cuban roots had an exotic appeal to the old-line Southerners running the company as they began focusing on the need to internationalize Coke's management to match the global growth of the business. And his aristocratic breeding gave him an aura that very early on served as a passport into Coke's upper echelon of managers, especially Robert W. Woodruff, the longtime Coca-Cola chieftain who liked to surround himself with people of high social and political standing. Woodruff populated his social life with people as diverse as the golfer Bobby Jones and U.S. president Dwight D. Eisenhower. The more curious their background the better.

Goizueta apparently recognized the value of his Cuban roots early on. He did have an impressive background that would have drawn admiration and attention in its own right. But he also could not resist embroidering the story of his background with details that stretched and sometimes even broke the bounds of credulity. He exaggerated his family's economic standing, underplayed his exposure to the English language, and even overstated his success at Yale. He built a mythology about his early years that helped persuade Woodruff and Coke chief executive Paul Austin that Goizueta was a man of great promise almost from the day he arrived in the United States in the fall of 1960.

He hardly needed to overplay his own history, or that of his family, as independent, driven, and successful people. In striking out alone to start his career at Coke in 1954, Goizueta actually was following in the steps of his own grandparents, who had left Spain during the great migration of the late 1800s that helped settle Cuba as a Spanish colony. Both sets of Goizueta's grandparents were immigrants from Spain. As was the case with most Cubans, the Spanish heritage exerted a dominant influence on Goizueta's young life. His family were Basques, a fiercely independent and reserved ethnic group from the northeastern part of Spain. The Basques are light-skinned—a proof that their ancient ancestors steadfastly resisted commingling with any foreign interlopers, especially the Moors who infiltrated the family trees of many southern Spanish regions. "A foreign land is a land of wolves" is but one of many proverbs that Basques use to reflect, and to shape, their worldview—an admonition Goizueta steadfastly ignored later in his career as he expanded Coke's reach around the globe.

In a book about Basque culture published during Roberto Goizueta's childhood, the English writer Rodney Gallop described "some impressions of the Basque character: loyalty and rectitude; dignity and reserve; independence and a strong sense of race and racial superiority; a serious outlook tempered by a marked sense of humor and capacity for enjoyment; deep religious feeling; and a cult of tradition amounting almost to ancestor worship." These were among the complex and sometimes conflicting cultural influences that washed over Roberto Goizueta as he was raised, among many other Basque descendants, in the most exclusive neighborhood of Cuba's capital city. The characteristics could easily be a profile of Roberto Goizueta, who mixed a strong sense of decorum with a wry sense of humor, whose strong self-confidence sometimes gave way to an attitude of superiority, and whose attachment to his grandfather's aphorisms characterized both his conversations and his management methods throughout his life and career.

The Basque influence surrounded Goizueta as he was raised in the posh Vedado section of Havana, an enclave of mansions and Old World money that dominated the city's business and social fabric. Born on November 18, 1931 in his father's house, Goizueta grew up as a toddler in the baroque mansion his father had built in the hilly Vedado neighborhood that overlooked Havana harbor. As the highlight of the mansion's sumptuous decor, his father commissioned a Spanish touch—a two-story stain-glass depiction of Don Quixote jousting with a windmill. The home was so impressive that the Castro government later converted it into the Cuban National Academy of Sciences, making it one of the few residential buildings that remains in virtually prerevolution condition.

Physically surrounded by his Basque heritage, the young Roberto was greatly influenced by his maternal grandfather Marcelo Cantera's recollections of Spain and his own distinctively Spanish outlook on life. While Goizueta was young, his father was frequently away on business, traveling the country looking after the family's holdings. His grandfather stood in as a welcome surrogate, holding court in an office just off the family living room, reciting verses he had penned, and imbuing Roberto with a sense of his family's ethnic heritage. The aphorisms delivered by his grandfather from a study in the Goizueta's home would serve Roberto well for decades to come. "He'd rather be the head of the mouse than the tail of the lion," Señor Cantera would say, explaining the tendency of ambitious Cubans to go into business for themselves. He counseled discretion by saying, "The fish only gets hooked when he opens his mouth." Another proverb became a guiding light that would help Roberto take confidence in his decisions to make abrupt changes in Coke's strategic direction: "The quality of one's compromises is more important than the correctness of one's positions." And one of Roberto's favorites, "If my grandmother had wheels, she would be a bicycle," served him for years as a cutting rejoinder whenever someone posed a question he considered unanswerable, or one based on improbable assumptions.

Roberto admired his grandfather's business acumen. As a young Spanish immigrant, Marcelo Cantera began building his fortune by trading typewriters and air conditioners. Realizing that Cuba's sugar mills spent vast sums on bags for sugar, he bought acreage and planted crops used in fabricating the bags. Hardworking and thrifty, Señor Cantera impressed on the young Roberto the importance of cash and an abhorrence of debt. He saved diligently during the early years of his life in Cuba, so when the Depression hit Cuba in the 1930s, Marcelo Cantera had the resources to create the family enterprise by buying out struggling sugar mill investors. During the Depression, "he was able to buy a sugar mill and refinery for peanuts," Goizueta would later boast.

The boast tended to overstate Señor Cantera's investment in the sugar business. The connotation of outright ownership exaggerated the nature of the stake held by his grandfather and managed later by his father. The holding company listed as Roberto's place of future employment in his Yale yearbook was called Compania Industrial del Tropico S.A. Its lone mill holding was San Augustin, a small mill near the town of Zulueta, outside of Havana. The owners of record of the San Augustin mill actually were Elier and Alfredo Rodriguez, prominent Cuban businessmen. Señor Cantera owned a minority interest in the San Augustin mill and is not known to have had other mill holdings. The mill was hardly a titan of the Cuban sugar industry. In its last year of operation before the Castro revolution, the San Augustin mill produced only 30,000 tons of raw sugar. The country's largest mills, in towns such as Caracas and Placetas, produced as many as 350,000 tons a year. Still, even a small sugar mill was a substantial, capital-intensive enterprise. A minority stake could be worth millions.

Whatever the precise nature of the clan's sugar holdings, there is no doubt that the Goizueta family were bona fide members of upper-class Havana society. Goizueta's parents belonged to the Havana Yacht Club and the exclusive Havana Country Club. It is not known whether they joined the other two of Havana's "Big Four" clubs, the posh, newly con-structed Biltmore Country Club, where Havana's old money families did their best to mix with the nouveau riche without discomfort, and the Havana Tennis Club, which a few middle-class Cubans were even allowed to join. The Goizuetas were not regulars in the active party cir-cuit of high-society Havana, but they were known to appear at the major annual social events, such as the annual yacht club ball. Crispulo Goizueta was listed as an architect and property owner in the Registro Social de La Habana, the who's who of Havana high society.

A GREGARIOUS YET PURPOSEFUL MAN, CRISPULO GOIZUETA SEEMED to care little about club memberships, the Social Register, and other inconsequential measures of social standing. He had one indicator of consequence: an education at the right school. And for his only son, there was only one choice, Colegio de Belen, the academy of Cuba's upper class. Many of Cuba's political, business, and military leaders were schooled at Belen, a Jesuit-run school on a large tract of land in the heart of the residential Bethlehem Heights district of Havana. More than any single aspect of his upbringing, Goizueta's education at Belen inculcated him with a discipline and sense of status that would stay with him throughout his life. At Belen, Goizueta was com-peting with his country's best young men, and his success at the school filled him with an unshakable self-confidence that sometimes bordered on arrogance.

The Belen Academy was a veritable fortress of wealth and power for the aristocratic class of prerevolutionary Cuba. Built in 1926 to re-place the original school founded in the late 1800s, Belen Academy had a flat, four-story entrance building a block long. Behind it were two open courtyards separated by more classroom space, which in turn opened onto a large semicircular courtyard from which class-rooms and dormitory buildings emanated like rays of the sun. The school was attended by 1,000 of Cuba's most promising young men, 350 of whom were boarders from outlying provinces.

Roberto Goizueta was enrolled in Belen Academy as a first grader, and would stay there through high school. As early as the third grade, he was recognized as one of the school's outstanding students and ranked among the top five in his class in grammar, mathematics, geography, and English. People who knew the young Goizueta described him as a kind of man-child—always serious and mannered, well-dressed, very studious, and quiet. Much of that demeanor was no doubt a result of Belen's regimented approach to education and social training. Priests at the academy sought to mix discipline with an atmosphere of academic freedom as they schooled and polished the young men who were destined to lead their country. The classic course of study included romance languages, an emphasis on Spanish history, and plenty of Roman Catholic indoctrination. The Jesuit hierarchy in Cuba at the time was made up of politically conservative priests who had strong emotional and career ties to Spain. Many of them had come to Cuba after cheering Generalissimo Francisco Franco's fascist victory in the Spanish Civil War of 1939.

All students were not created equal at Belen; there were two separate and segregated classes. One consisted of the day students, like Goizueta, who were almost uniformly from Havana's older, monied families, some nouveau riche, and the political elite. As a third-generation Cuban, Roberto Goizueta was looked on as the progeny of one of the country's more established families. The second group of students—the boarders—were typically from nouveau riche families living in outlying provinces, and were viewed as a lower social group by both the teachers and the day students. The boarders attended a separate Mass every morning, before the day students arrived, took many of their classes separately, and ate lunch in a cafeteria while most of the day students went home.

Goizueta's experience as the scion of an established Havana family differed markedly from that of Belen Academy's other best-known graduate, Fidel Castro. Although they attended Belen at the same time, Castro was four years older than Goizueta and the two never met, but the impact that the experience had on the two men speaks to the important role that social and economic class had on the grooming of two different but very talented students. Castro was an exceptional athlete and a brilliant, if sometimes indifferent, academic. Castro's athletic exploits and his oratorical skill created a sensation. In fact, an article in *Diario de La Marina* headlined Castro's athletic triumphs at Belen and quoted the future revolutionary speaking favorably about fascism.

Castro would not begin espousing radical political views until after he matriculated at the University of Havana and became influenced by some of that school's liberal faculty. Even so, Belen gave him his first exposure to the uglier side of class warfare. Castro came from Oriente, a province of Cuba considered inferior by inhabitants of virtually every other region. And Belen's rigid breakdown between boarders and day students reinforced that class distinction. Still, even though the experience at Belen sensitized Castro to the demoralizing influence of class snobbery, it apparently did not embitter him to the school itself. El Presidente returned to Belen in 1997 for a ceremony enshrining his old dormitory room as a national landmark.

DURING SCHOOL MONTHS, CONCERNS OF CLASS AND SOCIAL STANDING were of no concern to young Roberto. His day was one of regimentation from dawn to dusk. Belen's private bus arrived each school day promptly at 7:30 A.M., and class began at 8:30. He rode home for lunch, returned to school, and got back home late in the afternoon. The school uniform never varied: shirts with half-inch black-and-white stripes, a black knit tie, and chino pants. Pedro Menocal, grandson of a Cuban president, remembers riding the bus each morning as it approached the Goizueta family home—a fence-enclosed, colorfully ornamented rococo house with a courtly garden on a lot 175 feet long by 100 feet wide. As Roberto mounted the bus, his slicked-down hair smelled of violet water and alcohol. "He was always clean, always pressed, very quiet and friendly, but not a mama's boy," says Menocal. Like almost every boy at the school, Roberto often risked punishment from the strict Jesuit priests by stealing out of sight and sneaking a cigarette—the prelude to a lifelong habit of chain smoking.

The headmaster of Belen Academy, Father Armando Llorente, remembers Roberto as a diligent and successful student, especially in the sciences. "He was always serious, but also very charming," Llorente recalls. But in some areas, Goizueta was less than a standout. His grammar was perfect, but his writing was not inspired. "He was just too cautious," Llorente says. Throughout his life, Goizueta took great pride in writing his own major speeches, and was known for meticulous precision in his use of language. But his caution both in writing and delivery made him a less-than-impressive speaker, and he was foreshadowed throughout most of his career by other more gifted communicators at Coke.

Goizueta liked to portray himself as totally ignorant of the English language before he went to preparatory school in the United States. His standard story was that he virtually knew no English before moving to Connecticut for a year of preparatory school after Belen, and that he learned the language by watching Hollywood movies. That does not quite square with the facts. Goizueta studied English at Belen, albeit with primary emphasis on grammar and the written language, not speaking. He was listed as an outstanding English student in his Belen yearbooks, and at summer camps he attended in the United States, he was exposed to the more colloquial use of the language. "He came as a boy to summer camps organized by the Jesuits in the United States. I think he spoke English well," says Llorente.

Like most of the Belen boys, Roberto played team sports like soccer, basketball, and baseball. He was by no means a gifted athlete. Basketball was his best sport, a fact throatily applauded by his dad. Father Llorente remembers Crispulo Goizueta attending almost every one of Roberto's basketball games, and making his presence known. "He was very fanatic, shouting all the time, telling Roberto what to do," Llorente recalls. "It embarrassed Roberto." Still, the priest observed that the father and son had an easy relationship and were quite comfortable in each other's company.

Some of their best father-and-son moments may have been spent at the dog kennel Crispulo Goizueta operated on the outskirts of Havana. In fact, watching his father raise and sell dogs may have been the young Roberto's first real exposure to the marketplace at work. Universally among Cuban aristocrats, Crispulo was known for his boxers and was considered the country's best breeder of that strain of dog. Family friends recall Roberto watching attentively as his father tended to the kennel's fifteen to twenty caramel-colored dogs. Gustavo G. Godoy, today a popular radio personality among Cubans in Miami, recalls buying a boxer on Crispulo's advice after his Havana home was broken into in the mid-1950s. "His face glowed when his dogs were around him," Godoy says. The lesson for young Roberto was clear. His father succeeded with his dogs because he loved the work and loved the product of his labor. Although dogs may have seemed a frivolous pursuit to the uninformed, Crispulo Goizueta took great pride in his work, and did not rest until he was considered the very best at what he did.

Still a dedicated boxer owner today, Godoy was disappointed that Roberto adulterated his father's hobby by raising and showing Pembroke Welsh corgis—hardly the macho and rugged breed favored by his dad. One of Goizueta's dogs, Fizz, won best of breed at the renowned Westminster Kennel Club competition in 1996. "It's just the antithesis of a boxer," says Godoy, laughing. "I was very disappointed."

IF BELEN ACADEMY WAS GOOD FOR EXPOSING ITS STUDENTS TO AN intense education and spirited athletics, it also made a point of introducing the young boys to girls from the "right kind" of families. Such girls were known to attend Havana's two most prominent convent schools, Convent of the Sacred Heart and the Ursuline Sisters Academy. A young debutante, Olga Casteleiro, attended Sacred Heart. As part of a well-orchestrated courtship ritual of the Cuban upper class, Olga mixed socially with the young Roberto at school-sponsored functions and in activities of their social circle at the country club and yacht club.

Olga's family was very gregarious, even boisterous—especially the cousins on her mother's side. At the family's recreational farm outside Havana, it was not unusual for prominent writers and businesspeople to mingle with Olga and her family. Still, says a friend from one of Cuba's wealthiest families, exposure to cultured and serious people did not seem to impress Olga and her cousins. "They were more interested in fashion shows, the league against cancer, and charity balls at the country club," says the family friend.

And increasingly, the young Olguita was interested in Roberto. Despite her lighthearted upbringing, those who knew Olguita over the years say she was serious and goal-oriented and viewed herself as a partner in her husband's career. She also was extremely private and unassuming, characteristics that matched her well with Roberto from the start. "Very unusual for a Cuban, Roberto was always rather closed-mouthed," says the family friend. "We're always talking about what we know and what we don't know. The fact that he was more serious than the norm in Havana society made him attractive to her." Olga's suspicions of Roberto's strong character were confirmed when Roberto was named Brigadier of Belen Academy during his senior year—the school's highest honor recognizing achievement in academics, leadership, and even sports. Before they both left Cuba in 1948 for preparatory school in the United States, there was an understanding between themselves and among their families that Olga and Roberto would be married.

ROBERTO EXPECTED TO ATTEND ONE OF THE BEST AMERICAN UNIversities. It was almost a birthright of bright students of his social class. His father had attended the University of Pennsylvania, and Roberto hoped also to attend an Ivy League school, or one of similar caliber. Despite his strong science background and outstanding performance at Belen, he felt he might not get into the best U.S. colleges. "I didn't know enough English to get into college in the United States," Goizueta would say. And if he did get in, he figured he might fail. Despite the exposure to English at Belen and during summer camp, Goizueta and his parents believed he could not succeed at college without a year of English preparation.

The preparatory school they chose was Cheshire Academy, about a half-hour north of New Haven, Connecticut, and a world away from Belen. Among the East Coast literati, Cheshire was considered a second-tier prep school, a step below the truly elite schools such as Andover Academy and Deerfield Academy. The students were bright, the teachers were well trained, and the preparation was adequate, but Cheshire simply did not have a strong brand name—a concept perhaps more understandable to Goizueta as a career marketer of soda pop than as an 18-year-old preppie, getting ready to go to college. Along with its indifferent academic status, Cheshire had a poor reputation in sports. That circumstance was in no way helped when the soccer coach learned that the young Cuban on whom he had pinned his hopes could barely boot the ball. "We thought of Cheshire as being down on their luck," says Guido Calabresi, a product of Hopkins Academy who would become Goizueta's freshman roommate at Yale, dean of Yale's law school, and, today, a member of the U.S. Court of Appeals. "Cheshire had to make do by taking a large contingent of foreign students."

Whatever its shortcomings, Cheshire Academy did offer the one thing that Roberto Goizueta desperately needed: a movie theater. Belen had given Goizueta a bookish understanding of English, but he felt uncomfortable speaking aloud, and wanted to master colloquial speech before going on to college. To familiarize himself with English, Goizueta spent countless hours at the Cheshire Cinema, a single-screen movie house that had been in business since before the talkies came to town. He watched reel after reel of American movies, memorizing the dialogue, intonation, and phrasing. As the Cheshire Cinema screened Marlene Dietrich in *A Foreign Affair*, Laurence Olivier's *Hamlet*, Erroll Flynn in *Adventures of Don Juan*, and Judy Garland's *In the Good Old Summertime*, Goizueta would be in the theater, mimicking the actors on the silver screen. Adopting an all-American first name, he asked the students and teachers at Cheshire to call him "Bob" instead of Roberto. And while studying in his room at night, Goizueta spent hours with his dictionary, dutifully deciphering the works of T. S. Eliot and William Shakespeare.

The effort paid off. Goizueta graduated as valedictorian of his Cheshire class. For his success at Belen, the school had awarded him an ostentatious medal on a silk ribbon. At Cheshire, he received a more utilitarian and entirely appropriate gift, an English dictionary. It was one of his greatest treasures, and one of the items he most regretted leaving behind when he fled Cuba in 1960 after Castro's revolution. The more lasting result of his Cheshire preparatory work was the acceptance letters he received from some of the cream of American academia: Massachusetts Institute of Technology, University of Pennsylvania, California Institute of Technology, Princeton University, and Yale University. He chose Yale. He knew New Haven well because of its proximity to Cheshire and was impressed by the school's strength in his chosen field of chemical engineering.

For Goizueta, Yale proved to be a first-time experience of a different sort. It marked the only time in his academic career that he did not finish at the top of his class. But not for lack of trying. With his roommate Dick Cook, he routinely trudged to the chemistry lab to study. "Those guys invented the term *grunts*," recalls Fred Graham, a fellow member of Yale's Saybrook College. Cook's academic counselor transferred him into Goizueta's room after he nearly flunked out in his freshman year. Goizueta was chosen as a peer who would force Cook to study and whose work ethic might prove inspiring.

As Cook got to know his new roommate, he was amazed by Goizueta's ability to lock himself in his room for five hours at a stretch, ignore the water fights and record players resonating through the hallways, and never leave his room until the studying was done. "He had learned to do that at the Jesuit school he attended," Cook recalled years later. "I'm certain that ability to concentrate, and to work at a high level of concentration for extended periods of time, served him well at Coke." Cook was most impressed during their junior year, when Goizueta registered for a course in metaphysics to fulfill an elective requirement. Cook and most of the chemical engineering students were taking a far simpler metallurgy class. The move proved to Cook that Goizueta had interests far beyond the narrow disciplines of engineering, and that he would not waste his time on a course that most of his peers enjoyed as a free pass en route to graduation.

Despite his legendary effort, grades did not come easily for Goizueta at Yale. "He was certainly in the top quarter of my class, but not a top student," says Raymond W. Southworth, who taught Goizueta's Introduction to Chemical Engineering course. "I would not have expected him to become chief executive of The Coca-Cola Company." Another professor in the five-person chemical engineering department at the time, Randolph H. Bretton, does not remember Goizueta at all. Goizueta earned academic honors only in his junior year, when he ranked in the top 15 percent of his class. Newspaper and magazine profiles over the years consistently claimed Goizueta finished tenth in his class at Yale, but the university's "class book" for his graduation year does not note any academic honor. The repetition of this false "fact" over the years helped build Goizueta's image as an overachieving man of purpose.

There were plenty of big names on Yale's campus, some of them Goizueta's classmates. William F. Buckley, Jr., whose antiliberal screed *Man and God at Yale* was published during Goizueta's sophomore year, still lurked on campus as a teaching graduate student. "Individualism is dying at Yale, and without a fight," was one of Buckley's few cogent complaints. Connected politicos included Victor Batista, nephew of Cuban President Fulgencio Batista, and

John Bush, son of a Congressman and brother to a future president, George Bush. Timber scion Fred T. Weyerhauser was in Goizueta's class, along with Richard Frankie, the future chairman of the investment firm John Nuveen & Co. National political figures like President Dwight Eisenhower and democratic challenger Adlai Stevenson both spoke on campus, and exiled Russian revolutionary leader Alexander Kerinsky lectured about the rise of the Soviet Union.

Goizueta did not get caught up in the political tempests, the social climbing, or the issues of the day. Indeed, from this early age he proved to be individualistic, a person who pursued his own agenda and his own style both in social and academic pursuits—all habits he exhibited throughout his later career. This was unusual given the highly conformist atmosphere at Yale of the mid-1950s, a bastion of conformity from the sportcoats and ties that were prescribed dress to the ritualized social interaction on campus dominated by the clubs and fraternities that had influenced Yale life for decades. Goizueta stood out as an exception to the rule. "He was his own person at a time when kids were trying so hard to look a certain way, to be preppy, to conform," says Calabresi, his freshman roommate. Committed as he was to Olguita, Goizueta never dated another girl. He saw Olga at least every other weekend, either traveling to New York to visit her at Duchesne School, or bringing her to New Haven for a date on campus. Goizueta rarely attended campus parties. He did not join a social fraternity and was not invited to join any of the university's prestigious and very cliquish clubs.

Though serious and focused, Goizueta was not without personality at Yale. He, Cook, and a third roommate, a husky Pennsylvanian named Paul Oshirak, relaxed in their room by singing along with the 45-rpm records of Broadway shows like *Kiss Me Kate* and *Oklahoma.* Oshirak nicknamed Goizueta "Deano," thinking he looked like the crooner Dean Martin, and Goizueta responded by christening Oshirak "Pablo" and Cook "Coo Coo." They smoked cigarettes together, and occasionally rode bicycles down to the beach outside of New Haven. Cook even was forced to emancipate Goizueta from a fistfight one night, as the two returned from a fraternity party at which they had had a few Scotch whiskeys too many. Goizueta shared all his college experiences with his father in almost daily telephone calls back home—a ritual Goizueta continued, time permitting, throughout his adult life. In moments of crisis, especially during the public outcry after the launch of New Coke in 1985, Crispulo Goizueta would serve as Goizueta's sounding board for major decisions, someone who could express unvarnished opinions with no hidden agenda.

The elder Goizueta paid close attention to those phone calls. He startled Dick Cook at graduation in 1953 by richly thanking him for helping Roberto on the occasion of the fisticuffs after the drinking party. Still, for all their closeness as roommates and study partners, Cook and Goizueta spoke just once in 45 years after college, and never saw one another again. Of his college friends, Goizueta kept in sporadic contact only with Calabresi, and he never returned to Yale for a reunion. He later endowed an academic chair for multidisciplinary study of business and the humanities at Yale, but with his college career as with other chapters of his life, Goizueta preferred to bring down the curtain and move on.

WITH YALE BEHIND HIM, GOIZUETA WASTED NO TIME STARTING HIS career and his adult life. Moving back to Havana, the job at the family company was in hand. A more pressing matter was his impending marriage to Olguita. The young couple had told Father Llorente of their plans to marry in June of 1953. The priest knew Olga, for her social standing, for her charitable work with the poor and at medical clinics, and as a teacher of religion while she studied at Sacred Heart. Olga had always struck Llorente as "shy, elegant, and feminine. Also, she was more religious than Roberto." Llorente was thrilled when he heard the news. "I said, 'Excellent marriage,'" he recalls.

On June 14, 1953, just a few weeks after Goizueta's graduation from Yale, the young couple married in a festive ceremony at Havana's most elegant church, the Church of the Sacred Heart, which was designed after the cathedral at Lyon, France. It was one of the social events of the year in Havana, important enough that the newspaper *Diario de La Marina* listed 87 of the people in attendance by name, and called the celebration "one of the most brilliant of recent times." Olguita chose Roberto's sister Vivien as her maid of honor, and she and Roberto each were accompanied by 12 attendants. The music included "Ave Maria" and Grieg's "I Love Thee," a standard at Havana weddings of the time. And the newspaper noted, incorrectly, that Goizueta had graduated Yale "in chemical engineering with the highest honors and distinctions granted at the famous North American university." Even at that early stage, the mythmaking had begun.

LIFE HAD COMPLETELY CHANGED FOR THE YOUNG COUPLE BY THE time they celebrated their first anniversary. Olga was pregnant, and Roberto was about to leave his father's business and take the new job at Coke. But before Goizueta began work, his father had one last request. He wanted Roberto to buy shares of stock in Coca-Cola. "You shouldn't work for someone else, you should work for yourself," his father said. He suggested that Roberto should buy 100 shares of Coca-Cola, and lent him the $8,000 he would need for the purchase. The shares were placed in a custodial account in New York, where they remained until his death.

The strangeness of his new position confronted Goizueta even before he started work. The day he walked into the Coca-Cola offices to apply for the job, he had run into an old friend from Belen Academy, Miguel Macias, and seemed to feel uncomfortable telling his friend he was applying for a job. Indeed, Goizueta felt his friends all thought him crazy, and many of them told him so, for leaving the family business. But within weeks, Macias and Goizueta were working together, rushing to open Coke's new bottling plant in Camaguey, an industrial town about 350 miles northeast of Havana.

With the plant's inauguration scheduled for noon the next day, and corporate brass from Atlanta expected to fly in, Macias and Goizueta rushed to get the production line ready to roll. Goizueta supervised the final stages of preproduction while Macias oversaw installation of the new bottling conveyors. But the line kept breaking down. The two young managers worked all night, taking turns catching what sleep they could on sacks of petrified sugar waiting to be dissolved once the line was up and running. The line opened on time. To Macias, the experience showed him something about Goizueta's determination to get the job done, no matter what kind of effort it took, and an underlying humility that a rising young executive like Goizueta would work so hard with shirtsleeves rolled up deep into the night to do it. "Whenever I think of that experience, I am assured that the man who felt comfortable sleeping on sugar bags is also comfortable in any business environment, from the grass roots to chairman of the board," Macias said in later years. By any measure, Macias had a successful career at Coke, transferring first to Venezuela after he left Cuba and closing out his career as a vice president in the Australasian division, even though he did not keep pace with his compatriot from Havana.

Early in 1955, Goizueta took his first trip to Atlanta—his first exposure to company headquarters and to the heights of Coke's corporate power. The occasion was an educational program Coke hosted for production employees, but it also provided Goizueta a glimpse of the culture shock he would feel years later when he moved his family to the fast-growing capital city of the New South. Riding in from the airport, he and Olga were struck by the slow, strange accent of the taxi driver. "How far to downtown?" Roberto asked. "Teeyen mayules," came the response. "Geez," Goizueta said in Spanish to his wife. "I wonder what he said." Atlanta struck the Goizuetas as a sleepy small town in contrast to the bustle and ambition of downtown Havana.

While he aspired to great things in his career and put in the hours and effort to make his mark, Goizueta did not skip the mundane details of his work. He was making progress, his domain spreading from one plant to all of Coke's five plants in the country, yet his job throughout his time in Cuba remained inescapably technical. When he presented his first professional paper as a Coca-Cola quality control expert in 1957, Goizueta deliberately strove to go beyond the narrow confines of the topic of his research and to demonstrate the broad thinking and reverence for the Coke heritage that would typify his communications throughout his career. The subject of his study: the battle to eradicate rusty rings from the necks of glass Coke bottles produced at the new Camaguey plant. "It would certainly be blameworthy if due to a faulty washing operation, salt deposits dim the many hours of labor that our ancestors devoted to produce and design such a unique bottle as ours," he wrote. And later, "What would happen if a person asks for a Coca-Cola after reading in one of our posters that Coca-Cola is pure and wholesome, and finds out that the bottle he is given is dirty if only on the outside? That consumer will certainly doubt that the contents of the bottle are pure." Goizueta already had developed a reverence for the product Coca-Cola that would drive him all his life, and he developed a method of removing the spots with an agent derived from, of all things, cane sugar.

BEFORE LONG, RUSTY RINGS WOULD BE THE LAST THING ON Goizueta's mind. In their place, Fidel Castro stepped to center stage.

Days after Goizueta delivered his paper in May 1957, Castro's troops staged their first truly successful guerilla raid from Cuba's Sierra Maestre mountains. The battle of El Uvero became the first step in Castro's long but unyielding march toward the triumphant entry of Castro's troops into Havana on January 1, 1959. Goizueta may in fact have been suspicous of Castro almost from the start, as he claimed in press interviews. "It was obvious to us that Castro was communist, though not to *The New York Times*," Goizueta later claimed. If he really saw Castro that way from the start, he had astounding foresight. Interviews with dozens of Cubans with roots in Havana society indicate that they, like most of their countryfolk, were initially hopeful that Castro could reform the corruption of the Batista regime, reduce state-sponsored violence, and bring economic power to the masses.

The first thing Castro brought Goizueta was trouble. The day after Castro stormed Havana, on January 2, 1959, Olga went into labor with the couple's third child, but the Goizuetas could not rush to the hospital. Castro had forbidden the use of private cars on Havana's streets. In the chaos of the Cuban revolution, the nervous young couple waited several hours for an ambulance. While being driven to the hospital, they passed checkpoints and jeeps loaded with the menacing, bearded guerillas that enforced a capricious and sometimes vicious form of martial law on the streets of Havana.

By the time the baby Javier celebrated his first birthday, the mood in the Goizueta family's exclusive neighborhood was one of fear and apprehension. Armed guards randomly searched the houses near the Biltmore Country Club. Safety deposit boxes were confiscated. "They would decide they were going to take the first, fifth and seventh houses and search them. If you were in two, four and six, you were lucky," Goizueta recalled. "It was just harassment."

At work, there was the constant threat that government troops might take control of a Coca-Cola plant, as retribution against bribes purportedly paid to the Batista regime—a technique Castro was just beginning to employ throughout industry. Goizueta did his best to hold his own against the repeated and unpredictable harassment. His first minor victory over the Castro regime came when he successfully resisted the new Cuban government's insistence that Coke use cooked sugar—rather than the caramel called for in the Coca-Cola recipe—to give Cuba's Coke its brown color. To persuade them sugar would not work, Goizueta mixed one batch with sugar and let them taste the awful result. As another measure of control, Castro's gendarmes checked his brief case one night, to make certain he was not secreting any important corporate documents.

Slowly, deliberately, almost imperceptibly, Goizueta began to make his move. In April of 1960, when Javier was just four months old, he shipped the baby and his siblings Robby and Olga, to live with Olguita's parents, who had already left Havana for Miami. It was still legal to leave the country, but Castro was already limiting how much money Cubans could take with them, in an effort to prevent them from fleeing. Work compelled Goizueta to stay in Cuba, but it was best for the children to leave. He and Olguita could move quickly that way when his work was done and the time was right. "We felt if we had to leave Cuba in a hurry, my wife and I could manage," he later said.

Early in the summer of 1960, Goizueta visited Atlanta, and learned from Coke's political intelligence staff that the situation in Cuba looked serious, and that the plants could be seized by Castro at any time. It was hardly a remarkable revelation, given the steep escalation of hostilities between Castro and the U.S. government during the early summer of 1960. On June 29, Castro seized a U.S. oil refinery after it refused to refine oil from the Soviet Union, and declared he would confiscate all U.S. property "down to the nails in their shoes" if the U.S. Congress reduced the sugar quota. Less than a week later, Congress acted, and President Eisenhower suspended all imports of Cuban sugar. In late August, the U.S. accused Castro of training guerillas to spread communist revolution throughout Latin America, and Castro in a September United Nations speech claimed the U.S. boycott was punishment for his land reforms and nationalization measures against U.S. monopolies.

For Roberto and Olguita, the world had turned inside out in the 22 months since Cuba had cheered Castro's triumphant march into Havana on New Year's Day in 1959. Not only had Castro turned their neighborhood into an armed camp, but many of their friends had already fled the country. The bulk of the early exodus from Cuba came from among their social peers, the upper-class Cubans, and the second wave that followed during the summer of 1960 included their professional cohorts—engineers and other career people whom Castro seemed most likely to detain if he decided to restrict export visas from Cuba.

The days of relatively minor annoyance were long gone now, and Goizueta and the rest of Coke's managers in Cuba worked feverishly to accomplish what they could before the inevitable seizure occurred. Goizueta's penchant for disciplined, detailed work and long-range thinking served him well. Time was of the essence and there was no opportunity to recover any mistakes. The syrup manufacturing laboratory at the Havana plant, built in 1957, was the main technical headquarters for Coke's operations throughout the Caribbean, and Goizueta needed to effect a transition to another headquarters location, in the Bahamas, before Castro ultimately clamped down.

There was one more key strategic task he had to complete before he could leave: the rollout of the new lemon-lime soft drink Sprite throughout the Caribbean. It was Goizueta's job to make certain Havana produced enough syrup to meet Caribbean demand for the new colorless soda. He began the project in June, and finally finished it in early October. Finally, Roberto and Olguita were ready to take their own "vacation."

No one ever said they were leaving for good, but few who left the country after Castro's revolution ever came back. Many secreted out money, but some left with nothing. Roberto confided his plans to no one, but did make a broad hint to Macias when they saw each other one day in Havana. "I am going to go on vacation," Goizueta told Macias, and his friend immediately knew what he meant.

On the last day, Roberto and Olga packed weekend bags, and put only $200 in their pocketbooks. They did not take any photographs or wedding presents, not even Goizueta's Yale diploma or the dictionary that was his trophy as valedictorian at Cheshire Academy. They left their Cuban nursemaid behind. As he left his house for the last time, Goizueta was filled with a sense of disbelief. He still hoped Castro would somehow fall from power, and Cuba would return to a capitalist economy. "It was always in the back of everyone's mind that this couldn't happen 90 miles outside the U.S.," he said.

At the airport, Goizueta furiously worked to memorize whatever he could from Coke's records of its operations in Cuba. He feared they would be confiscated, and he might be arrested, if he tried to take them out of the country. Together Roberto and Olga climbed up the steps to the airplane, and left Cuba for good.

2

Flight to the Top

Arriving at the Miami airport, Roberto and Olguita Goizueta looked every part the Cuban touristas visiting family or friends in the United States. They dressed formally and traveled light, toting only enough baggage for a two-week vacation and no obviously valuable possessions. The Goizuetas had not told their servants that they would never return from their "vacation." But the domestic help almost certainly knew. They, too, had seen the neighbors evacuate over the last several months.

The Goizuetas did not know it at the time, but the exit gate in Cuba literally was shutting behind them. On October 25, in retaliation for a U.S. trade embargo declared just five days earlier, Castro nationalized the Coca-Cola's assets in Cuba and those of 166 other U.S.-owned enterprises. On October 31, Castro banned emigration by engineers and all executives of recently nationalized U.S.-owned firms. Had Goizueta delayed just a few days, the young couple might never have escaped.

When he and Olguita crossed those 90 miles and landed at the Miami Airport, Goizueta was anxious to reunite with his children, his parents and his in-laws. He had not seen them since early summer, when he and Olguita had visited Miami en route to Goizueta's visit to Coke headquarters in Atlanta. But first, Roberto C. Goizueta played the part of the good Coca-Cola man. On a notebook pulled from his travel bag, he prepared from memory an inventory of every piece of plant and equipment that Coke owned in Cuba. In his seven years with the company, Coke had invested millions building two new plants, and dramatically refurbished the Havana plant, as part of a construction binge Goizueta helped oversee.

Goizueta believed the inventory was essential, because it was likely Castro's cronies would damage or destroy much of Coke's investment, whether in acts of retribution against the most high-profile of American companies or simply out of ignorance of how to run a modern bottling plant. Prevented by Castro's guards from carrying an inventory out of his office with him, Goizueta worked solely from memory. Goizueta believed his jotted-down recollection of Coke's assets would have to serve as proof of the company's claims on whatever government booted Castro from power. "I kept records of where all our equipment was for the day when we returned," Goizueta recalled.

Goizueta did not know it at the time, but several of his peers had the same thoughts, and had already carried detailed blueprints, photographs and records with them on business trips to Atlanta. The Coke team evaluated the company's lost assets at $17.6 million, more than five percent of the total U.S. assets seized. Castro's total seizures ultimately were valued at $250 million by General Electric, Westinghouse, Continental Can Corp., Sears, Roebuck & Co. and more than 150 other companies.

In his heart, Goizueta knew he would not return to Cuba as long as Castro retained power. Sitting at the Miami airport, methodically writing down the equipment inventory—purchase date, cost, replacement value, location—was perhaps Goizueta's way of dealing with the turmoil of the deeply uprooting experience he was living. Years later, he would still have trouble describing the emotional wrenching he was going through at the time. "Unless you lived through it, you can't understand," he would say, cutting off any further discussion. He and Olguita had grown up as bright flowers of modern-day Cuba: educated at the best schools, taking college in the U.S., belonging to the best clubs, and relaxing on family country estates. They had great plans for their life together in Cuba. Suddenly, everything had changed.

Before Castro rudely intervened, Goizueta had even dared dream of one day becoming a Coca-Cola bottler, using his father's capital to buy the Cuban bottling operation from the parent company. Crispulo Goizueta had even held some very preliminary conversations with Coke's corporate office in an effort to lay the groundwork for an eventual buyout. No deal was assured, and other Cubans had made similar inquiries, but at least Goizueta's father had made his interest known. Despite the education he and Olguita had received in the United States, and the business trips they had taken to Atlanta, Goizueta had always envisioned his life as a Cuban, living on Cuban soil, in the country his grandfather had first claimed as his own.

THAT DREAM WAS GONE. AND BRIEFLY AT LEAST, GOIZUETA FACED a shocking comedown from the cloistered life of upper-class Havana. For the first time in his life, Goizueta was a salaryman with no other ready means of financial independence. The fall could have been worse, as it was for many of his peers who had nothing immediate to turn to when they fled Cuba. Goizueta at least had his job at Coke. The same job his friends had ridiculed him for taking, overnight had become his most valuable possession.

His $18,000 salary could pay only for a one-bedroom apartment on the Venetian Causeway, in a weary neighborhood in Miami where many refugee families first settled after fleeing Castro. He was pleased to learn that as a nonresident and noncitizen, he would not yet be required to pay income taxes, so the salary would stretch even further. Goizueta never considered selling his Coke stock. The apartment was less than modest, with a sheet hung across it to separate the area where he and Olguita slept from the three children and a Spanish nursemaid. As he walked the streets of Miami in the days after his flight from Cuba, the only vestige of his aristocratic upbringing Goizueta was able to maintain was his impeccable dress. People who saw him in Miami in late 1960 say he wore his typical formal clothes, as carefully pressed and stylishly appointed as if he were on his way to the country club in Havana.

Despite his sudden change in circumstances, Goizueta was not about to let his forced relocation to the United States derail the Coca-Cola career he had built since 1954. The depths of his personal allegiance to The Coca-Cola Company can probably be traced to the fact that his single most valuable asset when he arrived in the United States was his job at Coca-Cola. The job provided him financial security, and a small sense that not everything in his life had been stripped away from him by Castro. The ambition that had led him to leave his father's business he now channeled fully into his career, as if he understood almost intuitively that his job now was his only means of returning his life to some sort of normalcy, and some level of social standing.

Already, he had met several of Coke's top executives, and seemed to feel he could see himself circulating as a peer among them. Goizueta had visited with Paul Austin, then the chairman of Coca-Cola Export Co. and on a trajectory to become chairman of the parent company by 1967, when Austin visited pre-Castro Cuba to open the new Havana bottling plant. And at a dinner in Atlanta in 1958, at a technical conference for Coke's foreign bottlers, Goizueta had met the legendary Robert W. Woodruff.

There was not a Coke person alive for whom the first encounter with The Boss was not a cherished and noted memory. His name was as intertwined with the lore of Coca-Cola as the world's most famous soft drink is intermixed with the notion of Americana. At the time Goizueta was rising through the ranks, there were four key figures in the history of The Coca-Cola Company: John Smith "Doc" Pemberton, Frank Robinson, Asa Candler, and Robert W. Woodruff. Doc Pemberton was a pharmacist who tinkered with patent medicines, and one day in 1886, in the basement of his house in downtown Atlanta, he used a wooden oar in a brass kettle to stir up a strange new brew of caramel, coca leaf, vanilla, lime juice, and five other ingredients. He flavored it with a mix of exotic oils that he later dubbed "Merchandise 7X," then sent the syrup to Jacobs Pharmacy, where a colleague added water and carbonation, and created the world's first taste test of what would one day be called Coca-Cola.

An entrepeneur named Frank Robinson invested with Pemberton, named the drink, designed the distinctive Coca-Cola script, and traveled around Atlanta peddling the syrup as a new fountain drink for drugstores. After a dispute about who really owned the rights to Coca-Cola, Robinson ultimately sold all the assets to Asa Candler.

The son of a prominent Atlanta merchant, Candler had the business sense and the financial means to gradually expand Coca-Cola into a regional success, and ultimately built it into the first soft drink refreshment sold nationwide and overseas.

Then came Woodruff, the man who transformed Coca-Cola from a refreshment into a phenomenon. His father, Ernest Woodruff, had bought the company for $25 million in 1919 from Candler. But by 1923, Coca-Cola was struggling. Syrup sales were down, and the price of Coke's by-then publicly traded stock was tumbling. Robert Woodruff was a 33-year-old automotive executive when his father persuaded him to take over as president of the struggling company, and save it from disaster. Four years later, Woodruff had paid off more than $32 million in debt and preferred stock, engineered a two-for-one stock split, and had begun paying a $5-per-share dividend on Coke's shares. Having taken the company to fiscal soundness, he set his eyes on domination of the domestic soft drink market and expansion worldwide.

Woodruff formed the Coca-Cola Export Corp., a subsidiary company charged with managing Coke's international growth. During World War II, he changed the company forever by exporting Coke to Europe, the Middle East, and Asia by offering U.S. service personnel, a 6½-ounce Coca-Cola for the same price they could buy it at home. He benefited from Supreme Commander Dwight David Eisenhower's demand that the U.S. government build bottling plants around the world and turn them over to Coke, for the sake of military morale. In the United States, Woodruff encouraged bottlers to invest in their operations and pushed for production and marketing standards that gave Coca-Cola uniformity worldwide. Woodruff revolutionized Coke's marketing operations by hiring artist Norman Rockwell, cowriting the memorable phrase "The Pause That Refreshes," and inspiring an advertising artist to overhaul the image of Santa Claus by giving him a broad smile and a Coca-Cola-red suit. Grudgingly, Woodruff allowed Coke's chemists to begin experimenting with new soft-drink flavors to complement Coca-Cola, and Fanta and other flavors were born.

Woodruff retired as an officer of Coca-Cola in 1955, a year after Goizueta was hired in Cuba. He was not listed among the executive officers at Coke, but there was no doubt that, even in his late 80s, he still deserved to be called Boss. His name was revered inside Coke almost as much as the secret formula. He remained chairman of the finance committee of the board of directors, and controlled a majority of the directors' votes. He steadfastly refused to allow the company's two top officers to sit on the finance committee, thereby guaranteeing his uncontested control over Coke's purse strings. Years after his official retirement, Woodruff still routinely exercised his power by refusing to allow the company to borrow money, resisting construction of a corporate headquarters building, and arguing against diversification through acquisitions.

FOR GOIZUETA, THE PERSONAL SHOCK OF HIS FORCED DEPARTURE from his native country had an upside that at first was difficult to recognize, but became more apparent to him as he settled into his new job and his new country. Goizueta began to see that Castro had provided him with an unanticipated, career-changing opportunity. Instead of working for Coke's Cuban bottling operation, he was suddenly working directly for the home office, in Coke's home country. While in Cuba, he had pretty much limited his ambitions to accomplishments on the island. He might have been satisfied becoming Coke's Cuban bottler, perhaps using that business to build a larger operation just as his father and grandfather had assembled their own conglomerates. But cast adrift from his homeland, Goizueta also was untethered from a world of smaller ambitions. "Roberto contributed more to his life and to the company after Cuba than he ever would have had he remained in Cuba," observed Macias, the boyhood friend with whom Goizueta had renewed a relationship after their chance encounter when Goizueta came to Coke for his job interview. Goizueta's immediate task was to relocate his work, and make himself invaluable to the home office. He was hardly the only displaced Cuban, and, competitive as ever, he pushed to make certain he became the leader of the class of refugees. And he was fortunate, because the rest of Coke's Caribbean operations still needed the technical expertise that Cuba had provided.

He set up shop in an office in a hotel near the Miami airport, and hired a secretary to manage it while he traveled throughout the region. Immediately after he landed in Miami, the company had offered

Goizueta a transfer to Atlanta by 1963, but that fell through. Instead, he wound up based in Nassau, the Bahamas, commuting to work from Miami. As a consolation, he at least was awarded his first corporate title at The Coca-Cola Company: staff assistant to the senior vice president for Latin America. He was responsible for coordinating technical operations not just in soft drinks, but in Coke's citrus, coffee, and tea operations throughout the region.

The buttoned-down Goizueta found himself working for Bob Broadwater, a freewheeling executive in charge of Coke's technical operations in Latin America, renowned inside the company for everything from misappropriating a truckload of 7-Up so Coke's chemists could break down the formula to planting coca seeds and cuszo leaf in Hawaii without U.S. Department of Agriculture approval. Broadwater, a survivor of the Bataan death march as a prisoner during World War II, took Goizueta along on three-week jaunts through Latin America, focusing attention on the Venezuelan market where Goizueta would become acquainted with Gustavo Cisneros, a scion of one of Venezuela's wealthiest families. By 1997, the relationship would pay off when Cisneros helped turn his company, then PepsiCo's most successful international bottling operation, over to Goizueta in one of the last great competitive coups of his career. The travel was difficult on Goizueta's family, especially when Goizueta's parents and two sisters moved to Mexico just before Goizueta assumed his new post.

As Goizueta became known in the Miami expatriate community and among other American businesses, job offers started coming his way. His strong education, technical expertise, bilingual abilities, and character attracted several offers that topped his Coca-Cola salary and promised an immediate improvement in the Goizueta family's strapped financial situation. But Goizueta would not even entertain the offers. Once, when he received an offer for a job that would double his $18,000 salary, Olguita begged him to pursue it. "Why don't you at least talk to them?" she pleaded.

"Are you kidding?" Goizueta answered. "I love working at Coca-Cola so much I'd do it for free if I had to." The matter was settled, and he never considered working at another company again.

IN SHORT ORDER, HIS LOYALTY PAID OFF. IN EARLY 1964, THE TELEX machine at the Nassau office clattered a most welcome message. Coke president Paul Austin cabled a demand for Goizueta to appear for work in Atlanta, on "special assignment" to the technical department. A Harvard-educated lawyer who had set precedent by never working at Coke's corporate headquarters until he became president in 1962 at age 47, Austin was intent on bringing a new level of planning and order to Coke's decision-making processes. Woodruff in his decades at the helm had grown The Coca-Cola Company beyond anyone's reasonable expectation, and planted the corporate flag in countries around the globe. But the company under Woodruff was unwieldy, and important decisions were made capriciously, with very little centralized planning. Moreover, Woodruff's financial conservatism, born of his experience wrenching Coke from the brink of insolvency in the 1920s, meant that the company was missing opportunities that a more risk-tolerant executive might capture. Austin was certain he was such a man.

Born the son of a textile executive in the mill town of La Grange, Georgia, Austin had spent most of his boyhood years in New York, earned undergraduate and law degrees at Harvard, rowed for the United States at the Berlin Olympics of 1936, and was lieutenant commander of a submarine squadron in the Pacific during World War II. He joined Coca-Cola's legal department in 1949, after briefly practicing law in New York, and in 1950 moved to Chicago where he met Jeanne Weed, a secretary in the Chicago office who became his wife. In 1951, he was transferred to the New York-based Coca-Cola Export Corp., and by 1954 transferred to Johannesburg, South Africa, to run Coke's operations on the continent. While there, he became polo-playing friends with a businessman named Ian Wilson, an encounter Goizueta would rue more than two decades later when Wilson became one of his chief rivals for Coca-Cola's top job.

While in South Africa, Austin helped push through the development of Fanta Orange, the company's first non-Coke product, by arguing that he could make a market for the drink on the African continent. In 1959, Austin became president of Coca-Cola Export, and two years later became the company's first executive vice president who had never worked in Atlanta. When he became president in 1962, Austin immediately impressed Coke's rank and file by visiting 1,000 bottlers and riding along on delivery trucks. His drive and vision for the company was so widely heralded that it seemed just a matter of time before he would capture Coke's top job. He proved conventional wisdom right by becoming chief executive in 1966, then adding the chairman's title in 1970.

As one of his first orders of business as Coke's new president, Austin wanted to modernize Coke's management systems. He knew intuitively that he would need an outsider to do it, that someone from inside Coke's headquarters hierarchy would politicize and ultimately doom the effort. He made the initial assignment simple enough, a project to overhaul Coke's technical division, so that engineering and research practices employed at headquarters could be standardized, exported, and used as benchmarks for Coca-Cola's global system. But Austin had a much broader vision for the job. Ultimately, he hoped to use an analytically based redesign of the corporation's management methods to enhance informed decision making, set standards of management, and export know-how to Coke's far-flung operations.

Goizueta fit Austin's bill. He was an outsider, and his academic training as a chemical engineer gave him the intellectual discipline to break down Coke's management systems, analyze what worked and what did not, and reassemble them into a more productive structure. Austin had learned of Goizueta while he was president of Coca-Cola Export Corp. Broadwater had recommended him, as did Cliff Shillinglaw, the head of Coke's technical operations, who would oversee Goizueta's day-to-day work in the new assignment. A career-long laboratory man with an intense loyalty to his staff and a reputation for secrecy and even arrogance among those who worked outside his department, Shillinglaw was a tough but caring boss who seemed to take on the promotion of Goizueta as a personal crusade. Despite the technocratic sound of his title, Shillinglaw at the time Goizueta came to work for him was evolving into one of Austin's favorite blue-sky thinkers, and an expert on redesigning Coke's management. Like his young protégé, Shillinglaw was a man whose intellectual breadth transcended his technical training.

The Harvard-educated Austin no doubt respected Goizueta's academic credentials, even if his pedigree was from Yale, and his background as a Cuban fit Austin's plan to internationalize Coke's management ranks to more closely mirror the company's global profile. In Coke's image-conscious executive suite, Goizueta's reputation for genteel manners and strong technical command of his work promised that he would fare well. Goizueta soon earned recognition as leader of "the Cuban mafia" of expatriates like Macias, who took on the tough task of building the Venezuelan market, and Juan Dias, who ultimately became chief financial officer in Mexico. Goizueta was the only one of the group to win a posting to Atlanta, becoming the first immigrant to work at the headquarters building.

As HE BEGAN TO ACCLIMATE TO HIS NEW JOB AT THE COMPANY, Goizueta also was forced to adjust to Atlanta itself. The Atlanta that the Goizueta family suddenly found home was no more multicultural in mindset than Coke's executive suite was in fact. The city in 1964 was caught in a crisis of conscience after native son Martin Luther King, Jr., won the Nobel Peace Prize, and the city's business elite nearly boycotted a dinner honoring King. Only after Woodruff and Austin personally intervened, called the business leaders to a meeting at the all-white Piedmont Driving Club and hectored them into filling the Dinkler Plaza Hotel, did the corporate establishment grudgingly get behind the King dinner. Many Atlantans remember it as the beginning of the city's self-proclaimed reputation as "the city too busy to hate."

Goizueta had hoped to assimilate himself into a Latin American expatriate community, for his own comfort and for the benefit of his children. But he soon discovered that only a few dozen families in his social class were Spanish speakers. Walking down Peachtree Street, Goizueta was painfully aware of people staring at him when they heard his deep Cuban accent. "In 1964, a person not born in Atlanta who came to live here was a curiosity, perhaps to be looked at maybe with distrust," he would recall.

When his children enrolled at a private school, the other students ridiculed their accents. His son, Robby, took refuge in the fact that his facility with numbers was far ahead of his peers, and over time the children were accepted and occasionally were treated as celebrated novelties by the provincial Atlanta families. Goizueta never quite forgave his adoptive home city for its cultural backwardness. Years later, when a business colleague told him that Atlanta was about to become "the next great international city," Goizueta replied sharply, "Before we say we're the next great international city, we have to be the next international city."

Still, Goizueta felt certain he was in Atlanta to stay and decided to purchase a modest four-bedroom house on Jettridge Avenue, and to do that, he would need to borrow money. As a favor to Goizueta and another young transferee, Bob Broadwater brought the pair to Trust Co. Bank, to meet with a banker who handled personal finances for many of Coke's promising young managers. Pulling aside the banker, Brad Currey, Broadwater said that one of the two new recruits was an expert in protein technology. "But that other guy Goizueta, he'll go right to the top," Broadwater predicted. It was the only time in Currey's experience that anyone at Coke ever made such a statement. For Goizueta, the experience with Trust Co. Bank was unique, too, but for a different reason. When he signed the mortgage for his home, which had a market value of approximately $100,000 at the time of the purchase, it was the first time in his life he had ever borrowed money.

Even inside Coke, anyone outside of Austin or Shillinglaw would have questioned Broadwater's sanity to hear him make such a definitive pronouncement about Goizueta. To most, the dark-haired Cuban was a successful but not astounding young executive. At age 33, a job as middle manager in the technical department of Coke's Latin American division was a good start, but hardly the sort of career that would typically have a seasoned veteran like Broadwater boasting to outsiders about Goizueta's prospects. Aside from the trauma of his flight from Cuba, there was little to distinguish Goizueta from many other successful people his age.

What Broadwater and only a few others knew was the nature of the assignment Austin had in mind for Goizueta, and the importance Austin placed on selecting Goizueta for the job. For Goizueta, Austin's special assignment was a watershed. It brought him into headquarters and exposed him almost daily to Austin and others at the highest levels of the corporation. It broadened his knowledge of the corporation far outside the technical division in Latin America and the Caribbean that had occupied him in Cuba and Miami. Now Austin was asking him to solve companywide problems, starting in the engineering division. Over time, Austin would upgrade the assignment, asking Goizueta to assess, redesign, and implement new systems for capital allocation, research and development, salaries, and even the chief executive's decision making.

To most people at Coke, where marketing was king and people were judged by case sales and jazzy marketing programs, the assignment would have seemed anything but sexy. Redesigning the inner workings of the corporation offered little of the exotic sales meetings or back-slapping with bottlers that many of his peers engaged in. But nothing could have suited Goizueta better than the assignment to investigate how the company functioned, or failed to work, how important decisions could best be made, when committees worked and when a lone executive had to make the call. It enabled him to combine the critical judgment of his engineering background with a budding interest in corporate governance. For the first time, Goizueta began thinking about and experimenting with management issues that would be important to him and the company throughout his career.

Goizueta never spoke publicly about this important phase of his career, and no details of the special assignments from Austin ever have been published before now. But knowing about this period is essential to understanding the chief executive that Goizueta later became. In the Austin assignment, Goizueta would focus on the need for interdisciplinary work groups, collaborative decision making, results-driven pay systems, accountability, focus, and planning—all issues that would echo in the manifesto for corporate governance that he would draw up after winning the battle to become Coke's chairman and chief executive in 1980. The management methods for which Goizueta years later would win renown began to take shape in the years he spent inside the belly of Coca-Cola, helping Paul Austin figure out how best to run the company.

To help Goizueta with the assignment, Austin hired Chaplin Tyler, a retired DuPont executive with academic training, like Goizueta, in chemical engineering. An author of several important articles about management structures and compensation systems, Tyler was a veteran of corporate infighting at DuPont with the street smarts to help Goizueta make certain that their recommendations would become actions. Their partnership started off with a memorable first business trip. En route to view some orange groves outside Orlando, Goizueta came down with chicken pox, had to return abruptly to Atlanta, and was hospitalized for several days. Just as he had felt immensely thankful to Dick Cook in college for extricating him from a drunken fight, Goizueta immediately felt a kinship with Tyler for tending to him when he became ill. In a letter to Tyler nearly 35 years later, Goizueta recalled the incident.

Right from the start, Tyler understood that his assignment transcended the specific tasks that Austin had outlined when hiring him. In one of Tyler's first days on the job, Shillinglaw entered Tyler's office and shut the door. "I can't reduce this to writing, but I have a standing assignment for you," he said, immediately riveting Tyler's attention on his next words. "You'll be traveling with Roberto and you'll be talking with him continuously. I'd like you to keep in mind how he performs. All we know is he's destined to be something big." For the second time in just a few weeks, a veteran Coca-Cola insider was telling someone from the outside that Roberto Goizueta had remarkable prospects.

Tyler's first impression of Goizueta was that he dressed the part of Coke's future chief executive even though he still was a very junior middle manager. With impeccably tailored dark suits and carefully groomed hair, he had a seriousness and thoughtfulness that impressed everyone who dealt with him. Goizueta seemed confident working among Coke's top executives, including Austin himself, and an air of nobility came naturally to him. During one early meeting, Tyler could not resist complimenting a particularly attractive pair of Goizueta's shoes. "I thought I had some money, but those are really nice shoes," Tyler said.

"They're just ordinary Guccis," Goizueta responded matter-of-factly, apparently unaware that to most young middle managers, a pair of Gucci loafers would be anything but ordinary.

As they focused on Austin's first assignment, the reorganization of Coke's technical operations, Goizueta and Tyler found a great disparity from one division to the next and between geographic regions, with little coordination or guidance from corporate headquarters. If Austin proceeded with his plans to diversify Coca-Cola away from just soft drinks, the problem would only get worse. Goizueta proposed a simple solution: Create a small core of engineering expertise in Atlanta that would provide leadership for the divisions and subsidiaries. He called it "a centralized, decentralized organization" that would serve as a kind of "engineer bank" for the rest of the company. If a division or some outpost needed engineering expertise, Atlanta would transfer an engineer to the site on a project basis. The team of roving engineers would find local solutions to problems, using the standards set in Atlanta. Goizueta would apply the technique in a subsequent assignment from Austin to redesign Coke's research and development department. The approach of centralized, decentralized decision making—giving people in the field responsibility for decisions as long as they remained within limits set by headquarters—would become a hallmark of Goizueta's approach to broader management and strategic challenges as chief executive of the company.

THE EARLY SUCCESS WITH COKE'S CORPORATE ENGINEERING DEpartment won Goizueta a promotion to vice president of technical research and development in 1966, at age 35 the youngest vice president in the company's history. Along with the job came his first salary increase, from $18,000 to $25,000 a year. Despite his willingness to spend money on clothing, Goizueta had earned a reputation for treating pennies as if they were diamonds in other aspects of his life. Shillinglaw in a note told Goizueta he had decided to push ahead with the pay increase "at the risk of doing violence to your well-crafted budget." One of Goizueta's first tasks in his new job was arranging for the transfer to Atlanta of Roy Stout, an expert in forecasting the orange crop for Coca-Cola's Minute Maid division. Stout ultimately would become Coke's key market research expert during the early years of the Goizueta regime.

Goizueta was settling in to Atlanta, and he felt it was time to become an American citizen. He had officially become a U.S. resident in 1962 by traveling to Toronto and applying to return to Miami as a U.S. resident. Around the same time, Olguita and the children had traveled with him out of the country, to his Nassau office, for the same purpose. In late 1966, the requisite five years of residency had passed, making the Goizueta family eligible for citizenship. But Roberto had traveled so much that he could not meet the 2.5-year minimum requirement for total days actually spent on U.S. soil. He would have to wait until the summer of 1969 to take the oath of citizenship. Even in this important act, Goizueta proved politically astute. As his citizenship sponsor, he chose Joseph W. Jones, personal secretary of Robert Woodruff.

Citizenship carried great importance to Goizueta. Looking up at the flag in the Atlanta federal building on a hot summer day, he contemplated the two things he still had that Castro could not take from him: his education and his job. And he thought, he recalled years later, about the opportunity that life in America had opened up for him. "The first obligation implied in opportunity is that you must seize it," he told a group of immigrants at a citizenship ceremony at Monticello in the summer of 1995. "You must reach out to the opportunity, take it in your hands, and mold it into a work that brings value to your society." The rights and obligations of U.S. citizenship were one of the few subjects about which Goizueta would become emotional, even in front of strangers, years after he swore allegiance over the bible Joe Jones held for him in 1969.

Goizueta knew that the flip side of seizing opportunity is avoiding dead ends. And shortly after becoming a citizen, he was weighing an invitation to take a year away from Atlanta to earn an MBA degree at Massachusetts Institute of Technology (MIT) or take a 13-week management course at Harvard. Charles Adams, head of Coke's public affairs and external relations, had recommended Goizueta for the courses, and Goizueta's direct boss, Shillinglaw, assuming the nomination would not have been made without Austin's approval, urged Goizueta to enroll at Harvard. It was the politic thing to do, he explained. But when Goizueta consulted with Tyler, the consultant told him he would be crazy to abandon what he was doing at Coke. Confused and uncertain, Goizueta approached Austin directly. To his surprise, Austin ordered him not to enroll at MIT, and told him that even the Harvard course might be a mistake. "Your contact with me and with other members of top management is extremely valuable," said Austin, now just weeks away from becoming chairman and chief executive. "It's a benefit you wouldn't be able to obtain at any university." Relieved, Goizueta decided to skip both Harvard and MIT, and stay on the job at Coke.

Not long after the decision to stay put in Atlanta, Goizueta changed offices and found himself for the first time on the fourth floor of The

Coca-Cola Company's four-story red brick building at the corner of Plum Street and North Avenue in Atlanta. Walking the black linoleum floor in the hallways of the building, Goizueta suddenly found his assignments bringing him in regular contact with Woodruff. Chap Tyler believed Woodruff was fascinated by the story of the vast wealth Goizueta had left behind when he fled Cuba. "Woodruff would look on Roberto with almost a sense of deference, and he would be flattered when Roberto would ask him for counsel," Tyler recalled years later.

PERHAPS HIS LIFE WAS PROGRESSING TOO SMOOTHLY, BECAUSE OUT of nowhere, fate shook Goizueta with the only personal crisis of his life that rivaled that of his flight from Cuba. In late November 1970, his four-year-old son Carlos was diagnosed with leukemia. Despite his rigorous work and travel schedule, Goizueta still was a doting father, often dragging Chap Tyler to attend his son Javier's basketball games or inviting him to dinner with his family. As his youngest child and only American-born son, Carlos had always been special to Roberto and Olguita Goizueta. But less than a month after Goizueta first told colleagues of his son's illness, the child was gone. Sitting down two days before Christmas in 1970, Goizueta eloquently expressed his grief in a letter to Tyler:

> *Dear Chaplin:*
>
> *I'm at a loss for words in writing these lines, for the moment is so terrible. But I want to let you know how deeply Olguita and I appreciate the kind letter you wrote us. I know that in the wonderful and rich memories we have of Carlos and in the comfort we receive from friends, close friends, like you, we will find the strength that these moments and the weeks ahead demand of us. To become stronger and better human beings will be the greatest testimonial we can give Carlos.*
>
> > *Warmest personal regards,*
> > *Sincerely,*
> > *Roberto*

Years later, Goizueta would give further testimony to Carlos' short life with a sizable contribution to fund leukemia research at Emory University.

HARD AS THE LOSS OF HIS SON CARLOS WAS, GOIZUETA FOUND IT natural to lose himself back in his work, and a brutal internal battle over control of the company's purse strings. Impressed by Goizueta's work on corporate engineering, Austin had asked him to redesign Coke's capital allocation process. This was a dramatic increase in responsibility, but also an invitation to a battle royal. For years since his official retirement, Woodruff had controlled The Coca-Cola Company by virtue of his seat as chairman of the board's finance committee. His in-house factotum, chief financial officer Fil Eisenberg, jealously guarded the money, and exercised Woodruff's will by approving or rejecting spending plans. Austin resented Eisenberg, and pleaded unsuccessfully with Woodruff several times for permission to fire him. He responded bitterly when Eisenberg in 1963 rejected Austin's plan to acquire the Frito-Lay snack food company, only to see PepsiCo snap it up.

At face value, Goizueta's proposal for capital spending seemed reasonable enough. He suggested creating a five-person committee that would make decisions according to strict guidelines approved by the chairman. But this plan immediately ran afoul of Eisenberg and Woodruff. When Eisenberg complained about the proposal and publicly belittled the consultant Tyler in front of Goizueta and other subordinates, Goizueta kept silent. Face-to-face confrontation was not his strong suit. But then Goizueta went to work, encircling Eisenberg with people who agreed to his plan by appealing directly to Austin and the executives in charge of marketing, engineering, and manufacturing who would stand to become part of the capital allocation committee. Ultimately, Eisenberg backed down, and Austin formed a new committee to consider requests for capital investments. The political tactic of isolating an opponent and making him look like an obstructionist, going over his head when necessary, became a signature Goizueta gambit.

Austin ordered up the most important assignment of the by-now long running management redesign. For more than a year, Goizueta and Tyler had lobbied Austin to apply the techniques of systematic improvement to the chief executive's office itself. Austin seemed to recognize that the variety of demands on his time and complexity of issues made it nearly impossible for the CEO to reach well-informed decisions. The problem would only get worse with Austin moving rapidly toward a diversification strategy. Goizueta again suggested the creation of a five-person management committee, with representatives of each of the company's major divisions and the chief executive officer. The CEO still would have the final call on all major policy questions, but would benefit from a standardized system of advice and consultation.

The last assignment focused on bringing an incentive-based reward system into a more carefully calibrated overall salary structure. The project, which focused Goizueta's attention for the first time squarely on the impact of compensation as an incentive to sound decision making by managers, also brought to an end the series of special assignments under Austin. During nearly a decade of work at the highest level of the company, Goizueta had transformed himself from a relatively unknown middle manager into one of a handful of shining stars at the company. He had promoted and successfully encouraged Austin to adopt new systems and techniques designed to transform analytical decision making into a corporate ethos. Austin would not always employ the systems Goizueta promoted. In fact, he quickly abandoned the management committee of the chief executive's office when it interfered with his ability to operate by gut instinct as he diversified Coke during the early 1970s. But the years of developing solutions to some of Coke's core issues would serve Goizueta years later, when he was in a position to implement them himself.

THE CAREER PATHS OF SUPERACHIEVERS OFTEN ARE MARKED, AT KEY points, by black flags denoting death or disaster that, unfortunate as the circumstances may be, create opportunities. Goizueta was no exception. On February 1974, disaster opened its creaky door for Goizueta. Cliff Shillinglaw suffered a massive heart attack in London, on the tail end of a routine milk run through the Old World and beyond collecting the most coveted ingredients for Coke's secret formula.

He fell ill at Claridge's Hotel, where he always stayed when traveling on Coke's business, and was taken by ambulance to the Middlesex Hospital. Goizueta was the first corporate person notified of Shillinglaw's severe illness, and he jumped into a flurry of action that catapulted him into the center of the crisis, and into Coke's top echelon for good.

Goizueta tracked down Broadwater in Moscow, and insisted that he fly directly to London, to transport some confidential materials that Shillinglaw had been ferrying back to Atlanta. He also immediately sent Klaus Putter, head of Coke's European operations, to debrief Shillinglaw on his visit to India. Even as he was sending these executives to descend on the stricken Shillinglaw, Goizueta phoned Ichauway Plantation and reported to Woodruff's personal secretary, Joe Jones, that Shillinglaw was "in a state of semistupor due to a lack of blood flowing to the brain."

Broadwater's assignment was the most sensitive of the lot. As late as the early 1970s, the production of the world's most popular soft drink still relied on collecting a few exotic key ingredients by unusual means in remote outposts, assembling them at only a few mixing plants in the world, then concocting the syrup brew with the hand of the only two people in the world who knew Coke's secret formula. Shillinglaw had traveled to India to visit Coke's supplier of cassia leaves (a middleman who secreted them out of China) and was en route to Atlanta via Coke's London technical office, where he had stopped to mix a new batch of Coke's secret formula to supply the company's European operations. With Shillinglaw fighting for his life in a London hospital, now it was Broadwater's job to take the blades the size of rubber leaves and somehow sneak them into the United States without attracting the attention of customs inspectors enforcing rules against individuals importing agricultural specimens. Under orders from Goizueta to get the cassia leaves back to Atlanta, Broadwater made the best of his circumstances and folded the leaves into a fur hat he had bought as a souvenir of his Russia trip. "I was afraid I'd get caught," the normally macho Broadwater admitted.

While a flurry of activity surrounded the near-comatose Shillinglaw in his hospital bed in London, Goizueta took part in a quiet, secret, and solemn ceremony back at the corporate headquarters in Atlanta.

The secret formula for Coca-Cola, Merchandise 7X, is kept in a bank vault at Trust Co. of Georgia (now SunTrust Banks). But it is never touched there. Instead, the formula is passed by word of mouth, almost as if it were the ritualistic cant of a secret fraternal order.

The Coca-Cola Company's bylaws dictate that only two Coke executives may know the formula at any given time. By tradition, the company's two top technical officials are designated keepers of the formula. On May 7, 1966, Shillinglaw had learned the formula from Orville May, who himself had received it in December 1948. Now it was Goizueta's turn. With Shillinglaw incapacitated in London, Paul Austin hurriedly ordered May to perform the verbal rite, preempting the board's vote by nearly a month. For good measure, he promoted Goizueta to the position of senior vice president of Coke's technical division. Jones relayed the important news to Woodruff at Ichauway: "Roberto is now our full-fledged Number 2 man in this area."

After May taught Goizueta how to mix the secret formula at Coke's Atlanta technical laboratory and revealed the names of secret contacts and sources for the most sensitive ingredients, the pair flew to London, visited Shillinglaw briefly, then mixed Merchandise 7X. Goizueta would later indicate to associates that he saw the hallowed recipe as little more than another chemical equation, one that might be improved under certain circumstances. In later interviews, he would sometimes claim not to know the formula at all. Even so, he clearly understood the political import of his new status. The day after he learned the formula, Goizueta dictated a letter of thanks to Woodruff—the first epistle of dozens he would send to the Coke chieftain over the next twenty years. Expressing his "deep appreciation" for the honor of his promotion and his induction into the secret order of Merchandise 7X, Goizueta concluded by promising to "conduct myself in a way which will be worthy of Dr. Shillinglaw's recommendation and of the trust you have placed in me for which I will always be grateful."

By year's end, Goizueta was again writing Woodruff a personal note, mixing unctuousness and braggadocio in a manner that would come to characterize his correspondence with The Boss over the years. "I believe I am most fortunate in that these challenging years find me at an age in which my physical energies, God willing, can prove equal to the task ahead," he told Woodruff, drawing an unspoken comparison with Shillinglaw's physical decline. And he concluded, "I consider my biggest task not to get ahead of others but to surpass myself, and to make the ideal in my mind become a reality in my everyday life of work for the Company." While Woodruff was notoriously susceptible to flattery, and every one of Goizueta's peers played up to that weakness, none of them matched the frequency and enthusiasm with which the fast-rising Goizueta penned his notes over the years.

Shillinglaw never fully recovered from his heart attack. By the time he was strong enough to return to Atlanta a few weeks after the coronary, Shillinglaw was shocked to discover that Goizueta had physically moved into his office. Shillinglaw told colleagues he was upset with Goizueta's unseemly impatience, but still admitted he could not think of anyone better for the job. The man who had brought Goizueta to Atlanta spent the remainder of his career developing white papers for Austin, and was never again a significant factor in Coke's technical department, or in the executive suite. On his retirement in 1978, a nostalgic and somewhat disconsolate Shillinglaw posted to Woodruff a valedictory letter. "I confess to some sadness that it seems my official career will end on something of a downbeat. But the majority of time, things have been good, much of it thrilling," he wrote.

GOIZUETA'S CAREER WAS ON THE OPPOSITE VECTOR, STRAIGHT UPward, with plenty of thrills in store for himself and for the company to which he had irrevocably dedicated his career and life. With his move into Shillinglaw's office and job, Goizueta drew ever closer to Woodruff's orbit, and sought every possible opportunity for interaction. For the first time, he became a regular at the daily lunches Woodruff held in his office—a sign of approbation coveted by everyone with a hope of being among the parties of five or six who broke bread with the old man. Courtly as ever, Goizueta referred to Woodruff always as "Mr. Woodruff," while virtually every other living human at headquarters called him simply "The Boss."

On a day-to-day basis, Paul Austin was Goizueta's immediate superior, and Goizueta like everyone else at the upper reaches of the company was faced with the difficult task of negotiating the increasingly turbulent personal relationship between Austin and Woodruff. At first, Woodruff liked Austin's style and desire to strengthen Coke's international business, and accepted his plans to diversify into allied industries. As early as 1967, Austin had paid $30 million of Coke stock to acquire Duncan Foods, launching Coke's food division. In 1971, he approved the "I'd Like to Teach the World to Sing" ad, featuring a multi-ethnic group of young people singing on a mountaintop, even though he personally did not like the ad. Recognizing that the future of the company lay in its international growth, Austin folded Coca-Cola Export Corp. in 1972 and internationalized Coke's headquarters overnight by bringing Export's key executives to Atlanta.

He split the company into three operating groups: (1) the Americas, under an Omaha native named Donald R. Keough; (2) Europe and Africa, under German native Claus M. Halle; and (3) the Far East and Pacific, under his friend Ian Wilson. The betting began almost immediately that one of the three would likely succeed Austin as Coke's next chief executive. Goizueta's name was not yet in the mix.

The troubles between Woodruff and Austin began in the mid-1970s as Austin became increasingly intoxicated with acquisitions, deals that always came at too high a price for Woodruff's liking. And he allowed Coke's core domestic business to languish while he focused attention almost exclusively on international expansion. Ignoring Woodruff's misgivings, Austin in the 1970s purchased the AquaChem water purification business and a shrimp farming operation in Mexico. He bought the Taylor Wine Company, believing that Coke's expertise in carbonated beverages could be applied to alcoholic drinks. One of his more dramatic overtures has remained secret until now. Twice in the 1970s, Austin made serious efforts to acquire American Express, the financial services company. The proposed deal fell apart both times over valuation of the company's insurance assets and Woodruff's skepticism of such an unorthodox acquisition. Rumors, at the time, that Coke was considering AmEx Chairman James R. Robinson III, a Coke board member, as a possible successor to Austin can perhaps be traced to the secret AmEx bid.

As the war of wills between Austin and Woodruff escalated, Goizueta and other top Coke executives recognized that a single misstep could alienate one or the other of Coke's titans with dire consequences. Goizueta was first confronted directly with the dangers just as he was taking control of the technical department in 1974. Austin at the time was waging a bitter campaign to oust Charles Duncan, Jr., who had joined Coke with the Duncan Foods acquisition. Duncan quickly became a Woodruff favorite, a daily lunch partner, and Woodruff's candidate to succeed Austin.

There was intense pressure to choose sides—to back Austin or Woodruff in the battle over Duncan. Alone among Coke's top executives, Goizueta somehow found a way to stay neutral. "Goizueta was the most astute politician of all of us. He avoided taking sides and was very clever about it," recalled Broadwater. Duncan, whom Coke made blindingly wealthy by buying his family's company, in 1974 quit in disgust rather than put up with Austin's harassment.

In Duncan's place, Austin assigned J. Lucian Smith to the hot-seat presidency of The Coca-Cola Company, a man only three years Austin's junior and hence not a challenger for his job. It was clear that Woodruff and Austin, instead of focusing on Smith as a potential leader, were sizing up the next tier: the three group presidents—Keough, Wilson, and Halle—and from Woodruff's perspective at least, Goizueta. The race for succession was wide open, and Goizueta immediately increased his courtship of Woodruff. One colleague from the time recalls Goizueta arriving early to work each day, circulating through the offices of Austin, Smith, and other top executives to pick up news and gossip, then visiting Woodruff's office to deliver the dispatches himself.

When Woodruff was not wintering on his 30,000-acre Ichauway Plantation, in his waning years he spent most of his time at his mansion on Atlanta's Tuxedo Road, a home built in an updated Georgian style that local real estate wags called "Rococacola." While others among his peers dismissively called visits to Woodruff's house "the duty," Goizueta seemed to relish them. He made a Tuxedo Road stop a daily ritual of his drive home, hardly a big inconvenience since it was not more than a mile away from Goizueta's house on Jettridge Drive. Unlike his rivals for the top job, who were on the road more than half the year, Goizueta's work at this stage kept him in Atlanta, where he could lobby Woodruff and play a sharp inside game at the corporate tower.

The lengthy bull sessions at Woodruff's home, relaxing with a cigarette and vodka-and-tonic while talking Coke with his mentor, reminded Goizueta of the long afternoons at his grandfather's knee back in Havana. Sitting close enough to Woodruff so the enfeebled old man could grasp an arm or touch a shoulder to make a point, "I viewed him almost as my grandfather, and some people have said that he looked on me as a son," Goizueta unabashedly recalled. In 1978, when Woodruff asked Goizueta to provide him a signed photograph to hang on the wall at Tuxedo Road, Goizueta was thrilled, and inscribed a note expressing his pride in taking a place in Woodruff's "rogues gallery at home."

But history had showed that simply being kind and caring toward Woodruff was no guarantee of success. The Boss had a way of taking a shine to, then quickly discarding, his favorites over the years. To win Woodruff permanently, Goizueta knew, he would have to continually impress the old man with energy, good humor, and creative ideas. Goizueta seemed intuitively to understand that he would need to break the constraints of his narrow role as the company's chief technical officer. He had to prove himself a worldly and broadly focused executive, at ease in any forum and engaging in virtually any topic relevant to The Coca-Cola Company.

Previously, when asked to speak to groups of engineers or other technicians befitting his job at Coke, Goizueta followed form and gave the groups exactly what they expected. His number-crunching reviews covered everything from bottling efficiencies to the benefits of saccharin as a sugar substitute. By 1978, though, at the same time that Woodruff was hanging his photograph at Tuxedo Road, Goizueta moved decisively to prove that he was no narrow technocrat. He astounded a group of chemical engineers with an expansive talk about the cornucopia of opportunity Coke offered the world: everything from glass factories in Africa to water purification in Egypt to "relaxing world tensions" by offering a moment of refreshment in Coke's 6½-ounce bottles. To explain the Coke approach, he quoted political philosopher Edmund Burke: "I aim to serve your interests, not your desires." And Goizueta made certain that Woodruff appreciated his erudition. He sent the old man a copy of his speech.

Goizueta also sent Woodruff copies of uplifting or humorous poems. He sent flowers on Woodruff's birthday and anniversary with the company. When he asked Woodruff for permission to see the Kentucky Derby from The Boss' traditional box at the Colonel Matt

J. Winn Room, Goizueta made a point of inviting a Woodruff crony, Boisfeuillet Jones, to join him, Olguita, and other guests for the race. On a visit to England to speak to a technology conference outside of London, Goizueta penned a postcard, noting that he was staying "in Sir Winston's Room. Churchill used to spend weekends here during the war. I'm bathing in the largest bathtub I have ever seen." Goizueta probably did not realize that Woodruff had embarrassed himself during World War II when Churchill failed to accept a case of Coca-Cola and box of La Corona cigars delivered to Churchill's bunker in London.

AS GOIZUETA INSINUATED HIMSELF EVER MORE STEADILY INTO Woodruff's circle, a rival in the form of Ian Wilson was working the same magic on Austin. The two men had remained close since Austin hired Wilson, the son of a South African aristocrat whom he had met while playing polo in Johannesburg. Starting as an accountant in Johannesburg, Wilson quickly rose to head up Coke's sizable operation in the richest country in sub-Saharan Africa. Brought to North America by Austin, Wilson resuscitated Coke's ailing Canadian operation. Then Austin assigned Wilson to head up Coke's push in the Far East—a perfect posting for a successor-in-waiting. The region featured some of Coke's fastest developing markets, with Japan itself vying against the United States as the company's single largest contributor to corporate profits. Hard driving and competitive, an unforgiving taskmaster to people who worked for him but charming and witty when it served him, Wilson had the international experience and the soft-drink know-how that would make him a serious rival to Goizueta.

Unknown to the public at the time, a struggle, literally to the death, was building at Coke's headquarters over the succession issue. Besides acting erratically and drinking heavily, Austin was showing signs of undiagnosed Alzheimer's disease, which quickly was leading to dementia. Woodruff, meanwhile, entered Emory University Hospital, in July 1979, with dementia compounded by pneumonia. Wordlessly marking the solemnity of the occasion, Woodruff's brother George donated to Emory the entire $100 million in Coke stock held by a trust in the brothers' parents' names. The staff at Ichauway was told that Woodruff would not live to see another winter on the plantation.

But when Austin abruptly fired Luke Smith a month after Woodruff entered the hospital, The Boss rallied and recovered. At the November board meeting, Austin proposed promoting six top executives to vice chairman, creating a wide-open field of competitors for the top job. He stole the idea from his work on the General Electric board, where a similar runoff would lead to the accession of a virtual unknown, Jack Welch, to the chairmanship. In the years to come, Welch and Goizueta would become deans of the American corporate establishment, held up by the press and Wall Street as among the most successful and admired executives in the history of American business.

With Woodruff passively looking on in the Coke boardroom in November of 1979, the board elevated Ian R. Wilson, 50; Donald R. Keough, 53; Claus M. Halle, 52; foods division head Ira C. (Ike) Herbert, 52; corporate marketing chief Albert E. Killeen, 67; and Roberto C. Goizueta, 47, to the company's new "office of the chairman." Another member of the office, financial officer John K. Collings, Jr., 51, completed the group, referred to inside Coke by the sobriquet "the Seven Dwarfs" or, more frequently, "the vice squad." Austin, meanwhile, won the board's approval to stay at work through March 1981, a year past his mandatory retirement age, and enough time to sort out the mess he had created.

The press and Wall Street analysts immediately tagged Keough as the heir apparent. As head of coke's U.S. operations, the affable but hard-nosed midwesterner was best known to them. He had won the loyalty of bottlers in 1978 by forging a compromise on Coke's controversial demand to be released from the original 1929 contracts that had fixed the price bottlers paid for Coke syrup "in perpetuity." But Keough was no shoo-in. With domestic profits flat and the company losing its market-share dominance to Pepsi for the first time, several board members held Keough responsible for Coke's sagging stock price. Keough's vulnerability was obvious when an attempt to rally bottlers in San Francisco failed to quiet concerns of some of the company's largest bottlers that the company was not doing enough to promote domestic sales and thwart an upsurge in Pepsi's supermarket sales. "No one at the company will argue that we have not performed as well as we should have," the normally circumspect John T. Lupton, the nation's largest bottler and a Coke board member, complained publicly, just weeks after the rally.

Still, Austin recognized Keough's gifts as a motivator and deal maker. Despite his admiration for Wilson, he first approached Keough and gave him a shot at the job. Calling Keough into his office, Austin told the avuncular head of Coke's Americas group that he was prepared to nominate him as the next president of Coca-Cola. Wary of suffering Luke Smith's fate, Keough demurred. "I'm not interested in the presidency, Paul," Keough said. "I want your job." Austin abruptly dismissed Keough from his office and from his succession planning. Afterward, Keough recognized his mistake, but by then it was too late.

Poor operating results also tarnished the standing of Halle and Herbert. Collings seemed too narrow. Killeen was too old. But because of his ongoing success in building Coke's new wine business, Killeen had sway with Austin and the board. And Killeen was backing Wilson. The world at large did not know it—indeed, inside Fortress Coke it was not yet understood—but in Austin's mind, the race was now narrowed to just two men: Goizueta and Wilson.

The members of the vice squad could see where events were leading, so they spent their time forming alliances, hoping to set themselves up for the post-Austin era. It was a time of great tension and shifting loyalties. In a whispered conversation in Coke's executive suite one day, Keough shared his thoughts with Wilson, "I'll never work for the Cuban. What about you?" Wilson agreed, and the two men parted.

Goizueta played politics by withholding support for projects that would not further his cause. Coke chief financial officer John Collings was trying to revamp the company's financial planning operations and was following the pattern Goizueta had set with his redesign of the corporate engineering and R&D operations. He stopped short of creating a "bank" of planners, as Goizueta had done with engineers while working on special assignment, but he wanted to pull financial planners together from around the world and have them coordinate their work. To win approval for the plan, Collings knew he would need Goizueta's support.

He would not get it. When Collings approached Goizueta with the plan and told him he needed backing to make it fly with Austin, Goizueta would not go along. "It's not time," he said. "It's not time."

Goizueta's refusal to support the proposal flabbergasted Collings and killed the plan. But shortly after Goizueta took charge, in the summer of 1981, he would launch the first-ever meeting of financial planners. To one of Collings' former staffers who had lobbied for Goizueta's support, it seemed obvious why he held back. "He did not want us to change the company. He wanted to change the company," the former executive said. "Roberto was political from day one."

GOIZUETA KEPT HIS OWN COUNSEL AND CONTINUED TO FOCUS INtensely on his own prospects and what he could do to improve them. The inside game had worked for him to this point. Coke's new $120 million office complex, dressed up with more than $6 million in furnishings selected by Austin's wife, opened at almost the same time that Austin launched the horse race, and Coke insiders remarked with import that Goizueta's clout could be measured by the presence of a brand new technical building standing in the shadow of the twenty-six-story office tower. Goizueta helped ease Woodruff's grudging acceptance of the new building by ordering a construction crew to raise the toilet in Woodruff's office by one inch so it would precisely match the height of Woodruff's porcelain throne in the old Plum Street building.

With the stakes now sky-high, Goizueta grew frustrated by the limitations of his domain. He successfully persuaded Woodruff to replace half the sugar in Coke with high-fructose corn syrup, saving the company $100 million a year. But that was a relatively technical accomplishment that seemed to underline the narrowness of his job. When Goizueta became a vice chairman, he got his first operations job, head of the AquaChem water treatment operation. But he got nothing but yawns when he took directors and executives to observe the construction of water boilers at AquaChem plants. The experience left a lasting impression that he would apply as chairman of the company. "The worst waste of time for a company is to try to do well in something which we have no business doing," Goizueta concluded.

Goizueta knew he had one, and only one, opportunity to truly shine: the introduction of a new diet version of Coca-Cola. As head of technical operations, he had spearheaded the laboratory work since 1975, when he launched an ultra-secret effort he dubbed "Project Triangle." In research conducted by a little-known marketing man named Sergio Zyman and Coke's research director Roy Stout, the prototype product labeled "Diet Coke" had trounced both Diet Pepsi and Coke's own diet drink, Tab. Partnering with Keough, who would oversee the marketing of the new drink, Goizueta was ready for launch.

But in April of 1980, Austin abruptly killed the project and refused even to tell the board he had considered it.

Austin's retreat mortified Goizueta. Austin may have lacked the energy to launch a new drink. And he might have had sound misgivings about Diet Coke's likely cannibalization of Tab. But to Goizueta, Al Killeen's fingerprints were all over Austin's sudden about-face. Killeen, an outspoken Wilson ally, had pointedly warned Austin, and anybody else who would listen, that the company faced lawsuits from bottlers if it put the "Coke" name on any product except the original soft drink. Goizueta had a career-long distrust of legalistic excuses for abandoning sound strategies, and suspected that office politics were at least partly responsible for Killeen's legal misgivings.

With a new Diet Coke dead, the game appeared to be turning Wilson's way. The Asian market, particularly in Japan, was on a roll. Wilson had developed a reputation as an extremely demanding manager prone to exaggerate his successes and minimize his failings, but he felt certain the numbers in Japan would speak for themselves. Wilson also began cultivating Woodruff. Unlike Goizueta, whom Woodruff seemed to consider as anything but a sportsman, Wilson fit easily into Woodruff's hunting and shooting set. Almost as soon as Wilson began work in Atlanta, Woodruff had nominated him to become a member of the prestigious Peachtree Golf Club. Even after twenty-five years in Atlanta, Woodruff had not afforded his Cuban-born protégé the same honor.

Woodruff also invited Wilson to Ichauway, and gave the South African reason to believe he might be able to grab the brass ring at Coke. In mid-December 1979, Woodruff had asked Wilson to visit for a week of shooting along with Coke's newest board member, James B. Williams, a rising-star at Trust Co. Bank. After watching the two men shoot skeet on a beautiful December day, Woodruff sat at the round table in Ichauway's gun room and informed the pair why he had brought them there together. "I want you to take over my company," Woodruff told Wilson. "But don't say anything to Austin, because I will organize this."

Turning to Williams, Woodruff added, for good measure, "I want you to run my bank."

Both men effusively thanked Woodruff for the honor he seemed prepared to bestow on them. Williams gushed in a thank-you note, "Your interest in me, your splendid example and your words of encouragement have really been an inspiration to me and have in fact changed the direction of my career."

Wilson was more focused on the possibilities of his newfound relationship with Williams. "It was an added pleasure being there with Jim Williams. With his election to our Board, our paths will cross more frequently," Wilson wrote, hopefully. "I truly enjoyed getting to know him—he is a fine person and a very polished businessman." And, Wilson did not yet know enough to add, Williams is one hell of a hard-ball politico. Swords, not paths, were about to cross between himself and Williams. Loyal to his native Atlanta and influenced by Joe Jones and others who wanted to see Coke run by an executive with Atlanta roots, Williams would quickly turn on the foreign-born Wilson and, ironically, choose the Havana-born Goizueta.

To Wilson, it seemed he had won the duel with Goizueta. Austin had already told him in late 1979 that he planned to nominate him as chief executive, and the pair had even celebrated at a festive dinner with their wives. Secure in the comfort that he was about to become the next chief executive of The Coca-Cola Company, Austin embarked on a two-month business trip to Asia, a sort of farewell tour of the domain.

It was the mistake of Wilson's career. Back in Atlanta, Coke's old guard was moving against Wilson. After Austin formally nominated Wilson for the job, board members quickly barnstormed Woodruff with complaints about Wilson's abrasive style. Williams persuaded Goizueta and longtime Woodruff crony John Sibley to march with him into Woodruff's office and argue against Wilson's nomination. They raised concerns about a possible boycott against Coke if a white South African were nominated to run the company. After the anti-Wilson jawboning session, the normally discreet Goizueta blurted out his troubles in a chance encounter with his old mentor, Bob Broadwater. "We almost had a disaster here. We almost had Wilson as president," the rattled Goizueta reported.

Wilson should have seen it coming. In his last appearance before the board as a contender for the top office, in late January 1980, Wilson had proudly reported that Japan's net income was, for the first time, about to top the contribution from the United States. Wilson expected a cheer, but to his astonishment, the directors greeted the announcement in silence. To the Atlanta-centric board, this was only a grim reminder of how poorly the U.S. operation was doing under Austin's leadership. And Wilson, with his internationalist viewpoint, South African accent, and close ties to Austin, seemed part of the problem, not a cure.

Keough was onto the news well ahead of Wilson. He had never taken Wilson seriously as a rival, and by early 1980 felt certain the contest had boiled down to himself and Goizueta. On February 14, 1980, Canadian liquor tycoon Edgar Bronfman threw a birthday party for Austin in New York. Afterward, Goizueta and Keough took their wives to the St. Regis Hotel for drinks. Working for "the Cuban," it turned out, did not look so bad after all. "Listen," Keough said. "It looks like it's either you or me for this thing. One of us is going to be chairman, and one of us is going to be president. Let's agree that whoever it is, he picks the other guy as his number two." Still uncertain whether Woodruff ultimately would come around, Goizueta readily agreed to the deal.

By late May, Woodruff finally saw Goizueta as his only choice. He summoned Austin from a trip to New York, and told him Goizueta was the man. Austin could see that the fight was over. Despite Woodruff's age and physical decline, The Boss still controlled a majority of the board. There was nothing Austin could do to save Wilson.

Austin called Goizueta to his office. "I have just recommended to Mr. Woodruff that you become my successor and that you be elected president, but Mr. Woodruff wants to talk to you personally," Austin said.

Without another word, Goizueta nervously walked to Woodruff's office, interrupting his lunch. "How would you like to run my company?" Woodruff asked.

"That would be an honor, and I would do my very best," Goizueta responded, his voice not betraying the nervous shaking in his legs. "But may I have one request?" he asked.

"You can ask me anything you want, but that doesn't mean you're going to get it," Woodruff joked, gently reminding Goizueta that there was still but one Boss at Coke.

Goizueta allowed that he would like to see Keough remain his "right-hand man."

"Well, you can do that. But you have my blessing in anything you do," Woodruff told him. "Good-bye. I'm going to take a nap."

It was all over but the voting, but if Goizueta expected a triumphant march to the presidency, he was disappointed. On May 30, 1980, Austin called directors to a special meeting in Coke's new pecan-paneled boardroom. When they arrived, those few who did not know the agenda discovered that it was time to name a new president.

Austin grew preoccupied during lunch before the meeting started. Rising to leave the room, he whispered in Woodruff's ear, "Boss, I've got to go do some work now."

The board nominated and elected Goizueta without discussion. Several directors said afterward they felt railroaded by the whole exercise.

When Goizueta entered the room as the company's new president and heir apparent to the chairman's office, the directors broke tradition. Stunned that Coke's long succession battle had come to such an abrupt end, they forgot to rise in spontaneous applause for their new leader. In the quiet boardroom, Goizueta stopped by each director's chair, shook hands, and shared a few words of congratulations.

Goizueta's grasp was soft, as always, in the manner of the Cuban aristocracy. The directors did not realize it yet, but they had just shaken hands with the man who would change Coke's destiny for good.

3

"The Spanish Inquisition"

As he sat in the president's office for the first time, early in the morning of June 2, 1980, Roberto Goizueta took advantage of the quiet moment to mark the occasion with a one-paragraph note to his benefactor, Robert W. Woodruff. "I would be remiss if I did not begin my first day as President of our great Company with a word of deep appreciation to you," he wrote, typing the letter without assistance of a secretary. "You have honored me beyond all expectations. I will let my performance on the job speak for itself. I pledge to you my total commitment to honor you, and those who made me their choice for the job, by moving our Company ahead to even higher levels of growth and achievement."

Goizueta was fortunate to have one sparkling instant to savor his accomplishment. In the twenty-six years almost to the day since he had first answered that help-wanted ad in the Havana newspaper, he had overcome long odds, bested Wilson and other worthy rivals, and now was second-in-command of one of the world's great enterprises and the only company (besides his father's) that he had ever worked for. He had played an insider's game at a company obsessed with outside appearances, and won. Without ever selling a case of soda pop or approving an ad, he had laid claim to one of the most coveted jobs in the world—second-in-command and heir apparent at The Coca-Cola Company.

But Goizueta's peace was quickly shattered. As they absorbed the news of his anointment, Coke's contentious bottlers mounted a rump effort to derail Goizueta's climb to the corner office, and put Don Keough on top at Coke. Even Woodruff would stand in his way. Upon receiving Goizueta's thank-you note, Woodruff had an assistant photocopy it, and placed the original in a scrapbook of important memorabilia. He was quite happy to see the Cuban sitting in the president's chair. But if Goizueta assumed, as he seemed to, that The Boss was ready to promote him automatically to the chairman's slot, he was gravely mistaken.

The Boss was not done meddling. After his bitter experience with Austin, he was leery of letting one executive consolidate enough power to countermand him as the ultimate authority at The Coca-Cola Company. Goizueta could have the titles he would need to keep the company running—president and chief executive officer—but Woodruff wanted to keep running the board. And after half a century of successful boardroom politics at Coke, Woodruff intuitively saw he would lose control of Coke's affairs if he let his protégé claim the chairman's slot. If Goizueta ran the board meetings, he would be positioned to dictate to Woodruff's prized Finance Committee. Woodruff knew that if he lost his hold on Coke's purse strings, his control of the company would end.

Physically weak and mentally depleted, the 90-year-old Woodruff still was sharp enough not to repeat an earlier mistake he had made. In the mid-1960s, he had let Austin consolidate too much power, because the strong young Harvard Law School graduate and Coca-Cola Export Company star had seemed such a promising leader. Woodruff regarded Goizueta even more highly than he had Austin, but there was no telling where the 49-year-old Cuban would take Woodruff's company if given unfettered reign. Woodruff wanted a new chairman. And he decided to take the same course he had in other decades, when he chose warmed-over Coke executives to sit as his proxy in the chairman's slot. Luke Smith, who had worked as a consultant since Austin fired him in 1978, was Woodruff's candidate. Almost as soon as he had tucked away Goizueta's thank-you note in the scrapbook, The Boss began quietly promoting Smith for chairman among his cronies on the board.

If Woodruff could conduct the matter just right, Smith might have a chance. Following the May 31 board meeting, directors were shellshocked over the perfunctory and preordained process by which Goizueta was named as Coke's president and heir apparent. Two board members, driving home together from the meeting, discovered that neither had been warned that they would name a new president at the meeting. "I wish I knew what is going on," director George Craft told *The Wall Street Journal.* With his close ties to the Atlanta contingent on the board, Woodruff calculated that he might channel the directors' sense of dismay into a vote for a nonexecutive chairman who could be used as a counterweight to Goizueta.

Woodruff was not the only one who had problems with Goizueta. The bottlers wanted his head. The attempt to generate warm feelings at the Great Get Together rally in San Francisco the prior summer had washed away quickly, and resentments stemming from the contract amendment and Coke's poor domestic performance bubbled to the surface again. John T. Lupton, the system's biggest bottler and the only one with a seat on Coke's board, began lobbying immediately for an alternative to Goizueta. His choice for chairman: Charles W. Duncan Jr., whom Austin had ousted and who had become Secretary of Energy in the Carter Administration. Lupton at least had a passing acquaintance with Goizueta, unlike virtually everyone else among Coke's more than 500 bottlers nationwide, next to none of whom actually had met the man.

Goizueta's rise shocked the bottlers, in part because they had convinced themselves almost from the start that Keough was a shoo-in for the job. The stocky midwestern back slapper seemed the perfect antidote to Austin's aloof internationalism. He was a back-to-the-basics manager who understood their business and would refocus attention on the U.S. market, where, in their view, Coke belonged. Many of the bottlers had not updated their views of the succession battle since early press reports had simplistically and wrongly guessed that Keough would get the job. Nothing the bottlers had heard from Coke's new corporate tower—in this time of strained relations, they did not hear much at all—had led them to think otherwise.

The bottlers nevertheless sensed the succession game was still afoot, and they were right. Goizueta, after all, had only been *named* president. Austin still held the CEO slot and the chairmanship. It was not inconceivable, they figured, for Keough to leapfrog Goizueta, and set their world right. The bottlers moved quickly. Immediately after the announcement of Goizueta's promotion, bottlers from Iowa, Texas, Florida, Alabama, and other states called or wrote Woodruff and pleaded with him to intervene and promote Keough. Goizueta, with his foreign name and Cuban birthright, sounded to them like another Austin, only worse. Austin, at least, had Georgia roots before Harvard scrambled his brain.

Keough believed to his bones that the game was up. The day of the board's vote, he had swallowed his disappointment and phoned Goizueta with congratulations. Goizueta's response: "We've got a lot of work to do." To Keough, it was a tacit confirmation that Goizueta planned to stick by his commitment to make him Coke's number two man. Even so, Keough did nothing to stop the bottlers' rump effort to topple Goizueta. He breezily granted approval when bottlers sought his OK before contacting Woodruff. Keough asked only that they say he had not instigated the nomination drive.

Bobby Wilkinson, a bottler from Huntsville, Alabama, took the most jingoistic stance against Goizueta, whom he had never met. "This is an American company manufacturing an American product in an American way," he wrote in a letter requesting that Woodruff make Keough Coke's next chief executive. Coke needs Don Keough, Wilkinson concluded, "a dynamic American salesman . . . to lead your renowned Company to even further magnificent success."

While a renewed power skirmish was carried on around him, Goizueta conducted himself in the only way that made sense—as if the board's designation of him as president meant that he ultimately would succeed Austin. Despite Woodruff's ongoing backroom dealing, Goizueta had reason for confidence. Unlike Austin, he had never fought with the old man. And the years of doting on him, in the end, seemed destined to pay off.

At least one potential rival, Ian Wilson, was completely done for. A few days after the board meeting, NBC-TV news got wind of a grand jury investigation into allegations that Wilson had attempted to bribe an immigration official in an abortive effort to obtain U.S. citizenship, which he desperately needed during the succession battle, when he feared his credentials as a South African citizen could turn the contest against him. When it was time for the world to find out about Wilson's immigration troubles, Goizueta did nothing to soften the blow. As head of Coke's public relations effort, Goizueta played an active role in defending Coke's image around the world. But when reporters called about the Wilson allegations on June 9, Coke's vaunted public relations machine went almost mute. "Since this Washington matter is before a grand jury, we feel like we shouldn't comment on it," was the concise statement. Wilson never was charged in the incident, but his already debilitated Coke career was over. Goizueta was less-than generous in his postmortem of Wilson. When asked later whether Wilson had been his chief rival for the top job, Goizueta bitingly dismissed his erstwhile rival. It was Keough, not Wilson, whom he had worried about, Goizueta said.

FOR THE FIRST TIME IN HIS LIFE, GOIZUETA WAS A FIGURE OF PUBLIC interest, and the normally reserved and discreet Coca-Cola aristocrat seemed to relish the attention. In press interviews in the days after his election, dressed neatly as always but unusually expansive with reporters, Goizueta showed self-confidence bordering on arrogance when he described his management philosophies. He displayed a penchant that popped up often through the years: He recounted history in a way that fit his current business agenda. And he set out a series of goals, some of which he would never reach. Carried away by exuberance of the moment, he broke one of his most basic tenets by making forecasts he could not fulfill.

His first objective in the interviews was to portray himself as full of vigor and bright ideas, and totally comfortable at the helm of Coke. Consciously hewing to Woodruff's belief that successful people need a sense of humor, especially regarding themselves, Goizueta told jokes at his own expense while, nevertheless, making a point about his company or himself. He showed reporters lead coasters he had mistakenly purchased from a con artist in Mexico, who had persuaded them they were made of silver, underlining a message that appearances can be deceiving. He pointed to a sign on his desk that read, "Plan is a four-letter word," a strange choice of furnishings for a man who placed such high emphasis on careful and accurate planning. He even joked that his area of oversight—Coke's administrative, legal, and technical divisions, management training and AquaChem—was "the smallest profit center in the company."

Despite the efforts at self-effacing humor, Goizueta's ego still showed through. He bristled at notions that he was a rushed, compromise choice, railroaded through the board as part of Woodruff's effort to undermine Austin. He rejected any suggestion that he was appointed to the job as Woodruff's toady, to do The Boss' bidding. "I've always taken a great deal of pride in being my own man," Goizueta declared. "I've gotten to this position by being my own man. And I expect to be my own man from now on."

The fresh-faced Cuban executive declared that his managerial approach would be to "be in the midst of a crowd, but to have the independence of solitude." He'd get along fine with Austin, he declared, because his training as a chemical engineer and Austin's legal background were complimentary. And, characteristically circling his hand in the air to delineate his objectives one by one, he explained that he intended to go beyond his technical origins to focus on four key areas: "Financing, technical, marketing, and team spirit."

When explaining his background to the curious reporters, Goizueta explained that he left his father's business in Cuba because he was disenchanted with stringent government regulations. It was the first and perhaps the only time he publicly placed that interpretation on the monumental decision to move out on his own. But the statement fit the antigovernment mood that later that year would sweep Ronald Reagan into the presidency. And it very conveniently provided Goizueta an opportunity to indirectly take a lick at the regulators whom Coke recently had trounced in two crucial bureaucratic battles: the Federal Trade Commission's futile effort to declare Coke's exclusive bottling territories a violation of antitrust laws, and the Food and Drug Administration's reluctant approval of saccharine as a safe substitute for sugar.

Goizueta spoke out about heightened political tensions around the globe. He cited "the strong trend of nationalism sweeping the world" as a threat to his company's growth, unless Coke became part of the economic fabric of the countries where it did business. "Why shouldn't each country have its own national aspirations?" he asked. "I think they should. But I also think that we can support them and their local economies better than any of our competitors."

Still, in striving to appear thoroughly prepared and widely familiar with Coke's various business objectives, Goizueta uncharacteristically overreached when stating his long-term objectives. Foreshadowing years of frustratingly unrealistic optimism about Coke's foods business, Goizueta related a desire to "clone the foods division around the world." He expressed particular pride in his role in developing Minute Maid lemonade crystals, describing them as "a real breakthrough." Perhaps that was so. But the consequence of such a highly technical development was lost on a public looking for a broader gauge of leadership from Coke's new chief-in-waiting, especially one who had seemed such a noncontender just days earlier.

He dramatically underestimated Coke's future capital needs, perhaps betraying his weak background in corporate finance. Goizueta declared Coke would not need to borrow any more than the $100 million note offering that was announced just three days before his election as president—Coke's first debt offering since Woodruff had paid off the company's bills and avoided bankruptcy before the Great Depression. When Austin first proposed the offering, Woodruff had declared angrily, "You must be broke. You have to borrow money." But Goizueta and Jack Stahl, a bright young financial analyst in Coke's treasury department, helped persuade Woodruff that Coke needed the funds to avert a cash shortfall threatened by Austin's spending $126 million to build and furnish Coke's new headquarters tower, $65 million to purchase the Atlanta Coca-Cola Bottling Co., $15 million to acquire nearly 10 percent of Coke's New York bottler, and substantial outlays for Coke's money-guzzling wine business. Goizueta's "no new borrowings" pledge would barely last through summer.

Goizueta's greatest early faux pas came when he declared a long-term objective of building domestic earnings to the point that they equaled Coke's returns from its overseas operations. It was his first public break with Austin's legacy of expansive international growth. Coke had huge growth prospects overseas. Japan's soft drinks operation, alone, had topped Coke's domestic results in 1979 for the first time ever—as Wilson had announced in his disastrous final presentation to the board. In the hotly competitive U.S. market, Coke was losing, not gaining, share, and Pepsi-Cola was picking up most of what Coke lost. Domestic profits were under assault. Add it up, and the domestic parity with Coke's international results was a risky and virtually unattainable goal. If Goizueta were serious, he would have to do something dramatic, and probably very costly.

There, however, was a clear political payoff to declaring a drive for domestic parity. Predicting a 50/50 split appealed to Coca-Cola's disgruntled domestic bottlers. Not by accident, that was the very group

Goizueta needed if he wanted to prevail ultimately in the struggle to become Coke's new chairman. Conveniently ignoring lingering hard feelings from Coke's effort to force a new contract on the bottlers, Goizueta blamed inflation and an incipient recession as the chief source of bottlers' woes. "The future of the bottlers and the future of the company are inexorably tied to each other," he declared, promising management cooperation and financial backing. His efforts on behalf of bottlers "are not just because I'm a nice guy, but because it makes good business sense."

GOIZUETA KNEW HE HAD TO PLEASE THE BOTTLERS, ABOVE ALL OTH-ers, if he hoped to reach Coke's very top rung. It was the bottlers who were shouting in Woodruff's ears with their complaints about the business, their advocacy for Keough, their unfamiliarity with Coke's new Cuban-born president. Even the few bottlers who spoke in favor of Goizueta's promotion did not do him much good. "I'm tickled to death that they finally named somebody president," said bottler Sam Woodson of Fort Worth, Texas. "As far as I am concerned, they could have named anybody president just so somebody was it. You can't have five or six guys wandering around in the Atlanta office wondering which one of them is really in charge." It was hardly a ringing endorsement.

The best way to woo the bottlers, Goizueta figured, was to give them a big bear hug and invite them onto his team. He set out to do just that by inviting Coke's top bottlers to a day-long Atlanta meeting. In a deft political move, he employed Keough to do much of the heavy lifting, using the day's agenda to make it clear who was boss, and who was number two. On July 10, 1980, Goizueta hosted, at Coca-Cola headquarters, a daylong meeting of fifteen of Coke's top domestic bottlers. He chose the list well: Several of the invitees in letters to Woodruff after Goizueta's promotion, had urged that Keough become Coke's next chief executive.

For several of them, Goizueta's opening remarks offered a first encounter with Coke's new chief. The bottlers spent the rest of the day with far more familiar countenances: Keough and Coke-USA president Brian Dyson, who had hosted the Great Get Together in San Francisco a year earlier. Keough and Dyson laid out the broad strokes of Goizueta's plan. The two had starred in a campy in-house movie depicting top Coca-Cola officers gunning down the "Big Blue Gang" from Pepsi and were good with rev-'em-up rhetoric at bottlers' rallies. But these bottlers had not come for a pep talk; they wanted to talk turkey. Keough delivered, apologizing that in the past Coke executives had given the impression that "they were in one continuous meeting that cannot be interrupted by anyone, particularly a bottler or customer." He promised that Coke, under Roberto Goizueta, would do much better.

Dyson claimed that he expected improved results from a decision, made earlier in the year, to deploy in the field more of Coke's corporate ground troops. Goizueta viewed information from the field as a key ingredient of competitive intelligence, and he intended to use the field agents to increase both information flow and Coke's response to bottlers' needs. Dyson also promised to increase Coke's financial support for bottlers' advertising, an initiative first launched in 1989 to assuage the bottlers' outrage after the contract dispute.

Goizueta batted cleanup, hosting dinner at one of Atlanta's most exclusive private facilities, the Capital City Club downtown. To avoid dinging anyone's ego with the seating arrangement, Goizueta prescribed that the bottlers pick their seating assignments by lot from tags placed in a silver bowl. This tickled Crawford Rainwater, a bottler from Pensacola, Florida, who drew the seat next to Goizueta. Over a dinner of Georgia crabmeat and beef florentine, washed down by fine wine from Coke-owned Sterling Vineyards in California's Napa Valley, Goizueta gave the elite bottlers a first glimpse of his management style, the mixture of cheerleader and task master, detail maven and grand visionary, that would characterize Goizueta's approach throughout his chairmanship.

The approach, Goizueta explained, would be one of shared responsibility and shared opportunity. Both sides, the Atlanta crowd and the bottlers, would have to work hard to improve their relationship and their businesses. He promised a more aggressive, focused, and responsive approach from Atlanta, but demanded that the bottlers get tougher, leaner, and more competitive. "If your sales decline for a single week, we want to know why," he said.

Then Goizueta unloaded his most dramatic and far reaching news. It was time to "refranchise" the Coca-Cola bottling system, he said. The parent company intended to weed out weak bottlers. The purchase of Coke's Atlanta bottler and investment in Coke's New York bottler were just the start of a broader program of investment. Third-generation

Coke bottlers looking for an exit strategy would find a ready buyer in Corporate Coke. The parent company intended to refurbish weak franchises and put them back out for sale to the stronger members of the Coca-Cola system. Those strong bottlers could do a more aggressive job of selling Coca-Cola and the company's other soft drinks. The value of every franchise would climb if fewer weak bottlers were for sale and the system over all got stronger.

The meeting had its intended effect. It introduced Goizueta and showed him fully in charge. Charlie Millard, the longtime New York bottler who had just sold part of his business to Goizueta, wrote a letter praising the meeting. "The bottler meeting was a most auspicious start to your presidency," Millard wrote. "You would have been proud—to hear Don and Brian position the company under your leadership. . . . The meeting and dinner with you was an outstanding ending to a memorable day." Politically, Goizueta's tactic had worked. By having Keough and Dyson present his bottlers' strategy, he had presented himself to the group as their clear boss, taking the teeth out of any potential Keough rivalry.

To add a personal touch to the relationship, Goizueta sent porcelain boxes from Tiffany's to the wives of the bottler attendees at the all-male meeting. In a note to Woodruff, he boasted about the meeting's success, dropped the names of some of Woodruff's longtime bottler friends who had attended, and explained his decision to send the porcelain gifts. "It never does any harm to get on the good side of the wives of our main bottlers," Goizueta wrote, adding a sexist twist to one of Woodruff's most frequent bromides about the need to maintain strong ties to bottlers.

Woodruff again had become Goizueta's favorite pen pal. In one note to Woodruff, he attached a copy of an industry trade publication that spoke favorably of Goizueta's financial acumen. "They now have me pegged as a 'very, very strong financial manager,'" he boasted. Goizueta failed to mention to Woodruff that the *Leisure Beverage Insider* story he stapled to his note included a current assessment of Coke's ongoing executive-office shuffle. It predicted that Keough ultimately would end up in Coke's top spot: "Maybe now, say Big Coke observers, it is more likely than ever before."

While Goizueta played the inside game, his friends at Trust Co. used high-level boardroom politics to warn Woodruff not to meddle with Coke's destiny. In the ether of Atlanta's top companies in the early 1980s, two boardrooms stood as first among equals: those of The Coca-Cola Company and Trust Co. of Georgia, home to Coke's secret formula and bastion of old-money Atlanta. To hold a seat on both boards was the ultimate in corporate cachet. At the time Goizueta was named Coke's president, Austin was the only Coke executive among the nine Coke board members who also served on Trust Co.'s fifteen-person board. Two of Goizueta's biggest supporters outside the company, Trust Co.'s Jimmy Williams and his fellow bank board member John Sibley, lobbied to get Goizueta onto the Trust Co. board. Woodruff heard the news just a few days before Goizueta hosted the bottlers' meeting and recognized it as a strong statement by Williams and Sibley that it was time to conclude Coke's long-running succession drama.

Woodruff was boxed in. In just more than a month's time, Goizueta had laid down a marker with his expansive strategic comments to the press, raising the level of the company's potential embarrassment if Goizueta did not end up with the top job. He had headed off the incipient bottler uprising with the Atlanta meeting, and knocked Keough out of contention in the process. And Goizueta had secured a signal of support from one of Atlanta's most important companies—the sort of testimony that resonated with the tradition-bound Woodruff.

Then on July 19, in a fortuitous if sad occurrence, Luke Smith died of a heart attack. Woodruff already was backing away from his temptation to scramble the succession picture again, but Smith's death settled the matter. His first choice for the chairman's job was gone. As had happened with Shillinglaw six years earlier, a black flag once again waved Goizueta forward at a crucial point in his career. On August 6, the white smoke puffed above Coke's North Avenue tower. The Coca-Cola board had at last elected Roberto C. Goizueta chairman and chief executive officer, effective March 1, 1981.

At once, Don Keough became one of the hottest names in corporate America. Headhunters and colleagues from around the country called to inform him of opportunities to take charge at companies across the country. Keough again talked with Goizueta, who reconfirmed his intention to keep Keough as his number two man and treat him as a partner. As evidence of good faith, Goizueta even promised to keep his hands off Coke's marketing—one of the company's core strategic assets, and one that was at once both Goizueta's most glaring weakness and Keough's biggest strength.

Keough was a born salesman. The son of a Sioux City, Iowa, cattle-man, his Irish-American mother sent him to Catholic schools and in-stilled in him the importance of a good education. After a brief stint in a Navy medical unit, he attended Creighton University, where he was an award-winning debater, studied marketing, and met his wife Marilyn (Mickie) Mulhall. While working at Omaha's start-up televi-sion station, WOW-TV, Keough befriended the young Johnny Carson and met another on-the-rise Omaha boy, an investment broker named Warren Buffett. The unassuming Omaha investor was just converting a company called Berkshire Hathaway into a sort of closed-end invest-ment fund, and invited Keough to invest. "Don, you've got a wonder-ful group of children. Have you given any thought to how you're going to get the kids through college?" Buffett asked. Keough decided not to invest with Buffett.

Attracted to the business side of television, Keough migrated to-ward the advertising department, and soon left WOW-TV to take an advertising job at Paxton and Gallagher, maker of Butter-Nut Coffee. He came to Coke through a succession of acquisitions: the Swanson family bought Paxton and Gallagher and sold the renamed Swanson Foods to Duncan Coffee Company, which in turn was purchased by The Coca-Cola Company. Keough worked eleven years for Coke's foods unit in Houston, and his reputation as a winning salesman and demanding manager won him a posting to Atlanta as executive vice president of Coke-USA in 1973. Austin named him president of the division a year later. By 1978, Keough had marched his way into the Seven Dwarfs' contest.

But it was the middle of 1980 now, and Coke's succession show-down was done. Keough had lost. He would not become Coca-Cola's chairman or chief executive officer. He consulted with his wife Mickie and with a few bottlers and other close allies in the Coke sys-tem. Then, in an emotional off-the-cuff talk to a group of Coke's top twenty-five bottlers, called the President's Council, Keough spoke about the anguish of coming so close to Coke's top job, then seeing it grabbed away. "At times it's been difficult for me," Keough said. "The phone has been ringing off the hook with these search people asking me if I am interested in a new job," Keough told the group of bottlers, who sucked the air from the room in a collective deep breath. "The answer to them has been, "No." I can't think of a job I'd rather have than the one I have now at The Coca-Cola Company."

The bottlers greeted the news for a moment with a hush, then loud applause. Keough launched into a brief ode to the Coca-Cola family, the power of the trademark, and the importance of Coke's bottlers. The bottlers had come to expect that from Keough, but they had not expected to hear him be so frank about his sense of loss from placing second in one of the most brutal and public executive horse races in American corporate history. "It was the damnedest letting hair down that I've ever heard from a man," remarked Crawford Johnson III, one of the bottlers present.

FOR GOIZUETA, THE SAME OLD QUESTIONS ABOUT HIS PREPAREDNESS for Coke's top slot cropped up again. This time he had less patience with the line of inquiry. "It is the curse of the engineer that the fellow who drives the locomotive and the fellow who designs it are both called engineers," Goizueta declared.

Now it was time to start acting like the chairman of the board of The Coca-Cola Company. It was time for Goizueta to truly put his mark on the company, setting his own agenda, and steering his company on the course he chose. From the start, it was clear he could do so without interference from his predecessor. Austin, already hobbled by the still-undiagnosed Alzheimer's disease that many of his colleagues had attributed to heavy drinking, announced he would quit Coke's board after his March 1 retirement. For Goizueta, that meant he would not have to worry about the problem of second-guessing by Austin.

He still had to reckon with Woodruff, however. On a personal level, Goizueta sought Woodruff's counsel, just as he had once conferred with his grandfather and still routinely sought his father's opinion on major decisions. Goizueta's attachment to Woodruff grew out of the traditional Basque respect for elders. But it also arose from his feeling of obligation to the man who had selected him, as far back as 1974, as a young man of promise. There was little left to gain from Woodruff other than continuing good will, but Goizueta sent him thoughtful notes when he traveled, remembered his birthdays and employment anniversaries, and visited the Tuxedo Road mansion often when the old man was in town.

Whatever his feelings of loyalty and respect toward Woodruff, Goizueta was not about to let him interfere with his agenda for rejuvenating The Coca-Cola Company. He wanted Woodruff's approval, and recognized the power that backing from The Boss still held among the more senior members of the board of directors. But Goizueta also wanted to make certain that Woodruff could never block his program as he had done to Austin.

AT HIS FIRST BOARD MEETING AS CHAIRMAN-ELECT, IN EARLY SEP-tember, Goizueta made a number of moves designed to expand his authority on the board and eliminate other threats to his power. The Coke board reflected the cronyism and almost Victorian sensibilities of the Woodruff era and was a far cry from the modern notions of corporate governance Goizueta had devoted himself to since his days working on special assignment for Paul Austin. As with everything else he did at Coke, Goizueta wanted to make the company's board a thoroughly modern, competitive, and dynamic appendage capable of helping him exercise his will over the company and its prospects for success. This would mean replacing personnel, revamping bylaws, and, significantly, modernizing the way Coke's board handled the company's money.

Goizueta moved early to chop out the dead wood, imposing a series of bylaw changes prohibiting renomination of board members after their seventy-first birthday, an edict designed to flush Woodruff and his cronies off the board at the end of the three-year terms Goizueta instituted in place of open-ended service. Besides bringing new blood onto the board, the moves would prevent Coke's having a board perhaps too old and out of touch with the business to properly understand the complexities of the modern-day Coca-Cola Company. Less noticed at the time was a provision Goizueta inserted into the bylaw changes that prohibited the president and chief executive of the company from sitting on the board of directors after their retirement, regardless of the circumstances. For Austin, that would have eliminated the uncomfortable situation of having Luke Smith remain on the board even after Austin had fired him. For Goizueta, it meant that Keough, or whomever else filled the presidential slot, would never be a threat to his authority by staying on the board if he retired ahead of Goizueta, as he was expected to.

Rejuvenating the board's composition would pay off in the long term. But Goizueta also needed immediate and dramatic change. If Woodruff and everyone else on the board did not understand already that Goizueta was fully in charge, nothing would demonstrate it to them more clearly than seizing control of Coke's purse strings. That meant snatching the purse power from the finance committee, the vehicle Woodruff had used as a nettle, a governor, or a bludgeon, depending on the circumstances, throughout Austin's reign. Goizueta wanted control of Coke's capital. He needed to reduce the finance committee's role as a roadblock to progress. He could not abide the committee's blocking efforts to add debt to Coke's balance sheet. And he did not want it to block a plan he was developing to reduce Coke's imprudently high dividend payments to shareholders.

Again, Coke's new boss wasted no time. Without warning Woodruff in advance, Goizueta, at his first board meeting as chairman-elect, proposed adding to the board's finance committee the company's two top executive officers—himself and Austin (at least until Keough moved in after Austin's retirement). Woodruff missed the September board meeting, and he howled when he heard ten days later that Goizueta had outflanked him. "Not until today did Mr. Woodruff learn about the action taken," Woodruff's assistant Joseph W. Jones wrote to Garth Hamby, corporate secretary. "This is contrary to his concept of the function of the finance committee." But it was too late. The rules were changed for good, and by the spring of 1981, Woodruff would drop off the finance committee.

Just because the old man suddenly had lost the trappings of power did not mean Goizueta considered Woodruff powerless. On this point, even Goizueta's wife reminded him that Woodruff had demonstrated time and again an ability to rise up after hearing one would-be successor or another read his last rites. Olguita did not want to see Roberto mistakenly underestimate The Boss. Without the finance committee at his disposal, Woodruff lacked an obvious platform for a comeback, and he seemed physically incapable of mounting a challenge. But with his coterie still dominating the board and his track record of resiliency, Woodruff did not need structure to exercise power. He remained a potentially destructive force if not handled right.

Goizueta decided he would still seek Woodruff's counsel on big issues and would try to persuade him to endorse his major moves whenever possible. And he chose an eye popper for his first challenge. To execute his program of resuscitating Coke's weaker bottlers, Goizueta discovered he would need $200 million just for starters. The borrowing came on the heels of Austin's $100 million bond issue. And it countermanded Goizueta's own declaration that Coke would not need to go to the credit markets any time soon, so it was a risky move not just regarding Woodruff, but for Wall Street's purposes, too.

The Wall Street analysts could be brought into line. In Austin's last few years, as Coke's results declined, CFO Fil Eisenberg had virtually cut off communication with Wall Street. But Goizueta had reversed Austin's standoffish policy and embraced analysts, inviting them down to Atlanta, and meeting with them in small groups or individually in New York. Bringing Woodruff into the age of modern corporate finance would be another matter, but Goizueta already knew the drill well. As he would do as long as The Boss was engaged with the business, Goizueta began carefully and deliberately selling Woodruff on the notion of increasing Coke's debt during his frequent Tuxedo Road visits.

It helped that Goizueta had a specific need for the money. Already in the midst of being engaged in transactions to strengthen Coke's Detroit and Baltimore bottlers, Goizueta learned that The Coca-Cola Bottling Company of New York was again in play, with an asking price that topped $200 million. Trade rumors had it that Procter & Gamble wanted the bottler, to help lead its aggressive push into the soft-drink business following its mid-1980 acquisition of Crush International. Or perhaps Seven-Up, rumored to be considering a cola entry, might make an offer. Goizueta worried most about another, more likely scenario. A financial buyer could acquire the New York bottler and milk it dry, killing Coke's prospects in the vital New York market. "We can't let that happen," he told Keough.

Goizueta wanted to buy the New York bottler, and then, as quickly as possible, flip the company to a buyout group composed of friendly investors and Coke-New York's current management. But the deal would not fly with Coke's board unless Woodruff agreed to back any borrowing that might be necessary. For Goizueta, that meant approaching Woodruff about borrowing money for the second time in less than a year. He did his best to make Woodruff believe that the strategy was merely a modern adaptation of a Woodruff tactic from long ago. "Mr. Woodruff, you invented debt," he told the old man during a lengthy Tuxedo Road conversation, reminding Woodruff of a recapitalization move back when he ran the company. "Remember, you invented preferred stock. You called it Class A, but it was preferred stock." If Woodruff had used a form of debt known as preferred stock, Goizueta argued, there was no reason to withhold approval from a different, and cheaper, debt, thanks to Coke's triple-A credit rating. Woodruff ultimately backed the borrowing. In November, Goizueta inked the Coke-New York purchase for $215.8 million, his first major capital outlay.

THE FLURRY OF ACTIVITY WITH BOTTLER BUYOUTS AND BOARD-room maneuvering did not mean Goizueta was ignoring the nuts and bolts of the company. As soon as he became president, Goizueta began a detailed study of every aspect of Coke's business. Although proud of and confident in his abilities, Goizueta had enough self-confidence to admit his limitations. He even exposed his lack of knowledge to subordinates by asking dozens of questions ranging from simple queries about market size to complex calculations of rates of return and the present value of invested capital.

During the summer and early fall of 1980, Goizueta roamed Coke's North Avenue tower peppering executives with questions. Goizueta was not a marketing man, and he spared Keough a detailed grilling about the state of Coke's marketing initiatives. But everyone else was fair game. Goizueta felt he knew Latin America well and was inclined to trust his instincts in that region. But he needed to learn about Europe, Africa, and the Far East and leaned heavily on the regional presidents of those regions.

He placed special emphasis on learning Coke's financial intricacies. Given his lack of sophistication with corporate finance, Goizueta was blessed that Austin and Woodruff had left him a fairly uncomplicated balance sheet—with only $31 million in long-term debt at the end of 1979, before the $100 million bond issue needed to fund the construction of Coke's tower. But Goizueta knew Coke's numbers well enough to recognize that he needed to unlock the power of Coke's assets by leveraging the balance sheet. In the merger-crazed early 1980s, it was not beyond reason that Coke's unleveraged financial status might attract a hostile takeover effort. The large blocks of stock in friendly hands at Trust Co. and Emory University would make a hostile bid an extreme longshot, but in the day of the junk bond, it seemed nothing was impossible.

As he began building his financial plan, Goizueta engaged in an unusual dialectic with Sam Ayoub, the number two officer in the finance department. An Egyptian-born former currency trader, who had helped emperor Heile Selasi launch Ethiopian Airlines, Ayoub was confident, opinionated, and more than competent. John Collings, the chief financial officer, was not a natural tutor. As one of Goizueta's key executives during the transition, he was absorbed with other matters. Instead, Goizueta ate up Ayoub's time peppering him with questions about currency conversions, debt coupons, country-by-country profit forecasts, and even more basic matters. "He'd start asking questions and more questions, sometimes fifteen or twenty times a day," Ayoub recalled.

At one point, Ayoub grew impatient with Goizueta and argued loudly with him about a financial idea Goizueta was mulling. Goizueta excused himself from Ayoub's office and returned to his own. A few minutes later, he summoned Ayoub. "I don't want you to be a yes man," Goizueta began. "I don't object that you fight with me. I don't object that you shout at me, but always with the door closed. You and me alone."

Ayoub got off easily. In his case, at least, Goizueta was benign and collegial in manner and seemed to have no particular agenda at work, other than making certain he understood Coke's finances before he began turning them inside out. But as he poked around Coke's executive offices, turning over whatever rocks caught his eye, Goizueta began zeroing in on the areas where he saw weaknesses, especially the non-soft-drink businesses and certain regions of the globe where Coke was underachieving.

IT WAS ALL A BUILDUP TO THE BATTERY OF POINTED, PROVOCATIVE, and sometimes even malicious questions that rained down on Coke's top worldwide executives during a reign of interlocutory terror that became known as "The Spanish Inquisition." To those who had only heard about, but not yet witnessed, the impatient and sometimes even abusive side of Goizueta, the experience was shocking. It was not easy on anyone involved. But to some who endured the trial, it also was the first concrete sign that Coke's new chief was planning to put a strong personal stamp on affairs at his company. Financial results would count above all else. And people would be held responsible, for good or ill, for whatever happened on their watch.

The Spanish Inquisition started innocently enough. Under Austin, Coke executives from around the world were accustomed to flying into Atlanta each fall for a two-week business review and planning session. There, they discussed their five-year plans, and were handed a list of objectives that corporate managers had drawn up as their next year's budget. In the midst of Austin's global expansion program, much of the time was spent discussing opportunities to open new markets on different continents worldwide. The budget meetings were full of cheerleading sessions, wish lists and hopeful promises, but there was little hard-nosed planning and almost no accountability.

Goizueta would have none of it. Five-year plans, he felt, were a waste of time. No one could predict with any accuracy what the world would look like in five years. He wanted three-year plans, and he told the executives he would hold them accountable for meeting their three-year targets. He demanded that executives file their plans well in advance of the sessions, so he, Keough and Collings could dissect them and look for any weaknesses. Instead of waiting passively for headquarters to dictate the year's goals, each division chief now had to present a brief of his plans, and be ready to defend it. "I want you to tell me what you need to do to expand your business, what kind of capital you need to do it, and what kind of net return you're going to get," Goizueta demanded of the division heads. Turning to Keough and Collings, he reminded them that the new Coke triumvirate had their own job: to do their homework, and challenge every assumption. At the end of the day, the data would determine the few budgets that Goizueta approved, or the majority that needed a rewrite. "Facts are facts," he wrote, again and again, at the top of the budget plans, sending most of Coca-Cola's seventeen division executives back to work revising their plans.

For just about everyone involved in the budgeting process, the change from the Austin days was shockingly abrupt, and even painful. Goizueta wanted it that way. The hidden agenda, he told Keough, was to see how his executive team performed under pressure. He wanted budget season to be an adversarial process. "You saw what kind of intestinal courage they had. You saw whether they were technical or strategic, and who were the kind of people you wanted to move to better positions," Keough recalled.

As one shaken manager left the room after one session, Goizueta turned to Keough and remarked that budgeting was no longer a perfunctory exercise. "People have got to believe they are living or dying by these numbers," he said.

"Yes," Keough agreed, "We've got some toilet training to do."

IN SOME WAYS, THE INQUISITION WAS AS DIFFICULT ON GOIZUETA as it was on his underlings. As he pierced and probed, he found that the financial affairs at Coca-Cola in many ways were even weaker than he had feared. For years, no one had really focused on the cost of capital or the economic return on Coke's investments. Because Woodruff would not let Austin borrow money, Austin had responded by fueling his acquisition binge with Coca-Cola stock. But that capital actually cost more, about 16 percent per year, than even short-term bank borrowings would have cost Coke in late 1980. All the businesses except soft drinks—the wineries, the water purification, the plastics, even the foods—were generating less than 10 percent. "We're liquidating our business, borrowing money at 16 [percent] and investing it at 8 [percent]. You can't do that forever," Goizueta exclaimed.

The horrors Goizueta discovered during the Spanish Inquisition were not limited to Coke's financial mismanagement. Strategically, the company was adrift as well. As he broke down Coke's business into its widespread component parts, Goizueta found there was no coordination, no central planning, no strategic thinking to the company's global ambitions. Decisions under Austin, he believed, were made on a purely situational basis, with no central direction or judgment parameters from headquarters. In Europe alone, Coke was pursuing three totally separate strategies in different countries, pushing packaging innovations in Belgium, line extensions of Sprite and Fanta in Germany, and bottling investment in Spain. There was no cohesion, no effort to take advantage of Coke's huge potential economies of scale. "This company has no sense of direction whatsoever," Goizueta declared at one point. "None."

Goizueta decided that he needed a model by which he and his managers could assess the business. Logical and methodical as ever, he created a matrix that broke down The Coca-Cola Company into component parts. He wrote the company's operations across the top of a sheet of paper: Concentrate, Bottling, Wine, Foods, AquaChem, Plastics. Some of Austin's diversions, like shrimp farming in South America, were such obvious losers that their fundamentals were not worth examining. On the vertical axis, Goizueta listed what he considered the vital financial characteristics of any business: Margins, Rate of Return, Cash-Flow Reliability, and Capital Requirements.

On that basis, Coke's concentrate business—the one on which Woodruff had built his company—proved a big winner. Bottling, a little less so, but still a solid enterprise. Coke's foods business was next down the line, because it ate up huge doses of capital and was vulnerable to weather. The wine, water, and plastics divisions were longshots at best. Goizueta was not comfortable with wine, which required huge inventory costs because the product was not available until years after it was bottled. The capital required for building AquaChem's huge boilers was too much, and the political purpose served by giving Coke a way to offer water-purification technology to host countries, especially the Arab League nations boycotting Coke because it did business in Israel, was not enough to save the business. Plastics just did not fit into Coke's mix.

At the start of the Spanish Inquisition, Goizueta was shocked to learn how little Coke's managers knew about the financial end of the business—ironically enough, a criticism that could have been levied against him just a few months earlier. "None of our operating executives can read a balance sheet," he grumbled. By the time it was finished, he had taken them to school and prepared them for one of the most far-reaching and important strategic imperatives of his tenure. From that point on, Goizueta warned at one of the closing budget sessions, the corporation would charge its operating units a set percentage for the capital they used. Performance, he declared, would be judged on the basis of "economic profit," the unit's operating profit after a deduction for the cost of capital. He had not put a name to it yet, but Goizueta would later refine this notion into a concept that became a trademark of his management approach: economic value added, he called it. Strategic planning would be taken seriously, Goizueta said, and objectives would be met. "Don't even come to us with a project that doesn't yield more money than the cost of money," Goizueta warned, flanked by Keough and chief financial officer John Collings. "You'll get no hearing, much less a 'No.'"

WHEN THE EXECUTIVES LIMPED AWAY FROM THE SPANISH INQUISItion and returned to their posts in Atlanta and around the world, the effect was both immediate and long term. In operating units from Los Angeles to Kuala Lumpur, Coke managers reorganized the way they ran their businesses. They stopped keeping excess inventory of syrup on hand, just in case of an emergency. They quickly switched from stainless steel syrup containers to plastic and cardboard, saving Coke a great deal of money in one blow. They drew up detailed economic models before launching plans for plant expansions or other major investments. "When you start charging people for their cost of capital, all sorts of things happen," a satisfied Goizueta declared.

The change of approach was desperately needed. Profits, which had grown 13 percent a year in the late 1970s had stopped short, and forecasts showed they would be flat—zero gain—for all of 1980. The stock market certainly was aware of the troubles. Coke's shares had fallen 50 percent since their high in the mid-1970s. Performance in the consumer marketplace was not much better. In September, Goizueta had penned a note to Woodruff boasting, "Some very good news!" Coke's market share in the United States was growing faster than Pepsi's. But Goizueta could not bring himself to mention to Woodruff that Pepsi-Cola still topped Coca-Cola in the key category of supermarket sales—another unfortunate legacy of the Austin regime.

To have a lasting impact on the numbers and Coke's corporate culture, Goizueta realized, he needed to completely overhaul the way Coca-Cola did business from the top down. It would take a long and difficult battle to mold Coke into a world-class company at every level of operation in every market around the globe. But his job, as he saw it, was to shrink the time line, to jolt Coke into the future abruptly, to shake up the managers and make them understand. It was time for these people to get on board or get out.

Goizueta hired consulting firms, picked the brains of Collings and Keough at Coke, and conferred with Jimmy Williams and a few other close associates as he tried to devise a plan for jerking his company into overdrive. He did due-diligence work, to see if action in the field confirmed what he was hearing at headquarters. In January of 1981, Goizueta and Williams took a two-week tour of Coke's South American operations, visiting six of the major markets but skipping Venezuela, the only country on the continent where Pepsi held a lead over Coke. The South American jaunt established a precedent for Goizueta of routinely bringing a board member with him when he took lengthy foreign business trips. Goizueta chose Williams for his first major trip, in part because of their close relationship and because he believed Williams could help him to focus on setting an agenda for his reign at Coke.

There were serious security concerns on the South American jaunt. Coke was under fire in Guatemala, where unions blamed the local Coca-Cola bottler when a union official had his throat cut while unloading cases of Coke from a truck. Pro-communist organizations had spread anti-Coke propaganda throughout the region. Recognizing that they might be targets of a terrorist attack, Goizueta and Williams traveled under assumed names and removed the Coca-Cola tags from their luggage. But the ruse did not work. Coke's new top man and the red-haired, blue-eyed Williams could not travel through South America incognito. While checking out of a hotel in Bogota, Columbia, a clerk handing receipts to the two men forgot to play along with the false names and said with a broad smile, "Thank you, Mr. Goizueta." Williams and Goizueta eyed each other, and burst out laughing at the ineptitude of their cloak-and-dagger work.

EVEN BEFORE HE LEFT ON THE SOUTH AMERICAN TRIP, GOIZUETA had decided to take dramatic measures that would make everyone on his senior staff realize they were operating in a new world at The Coca-Cola Company. The Spanish Inquisition had set the right tone, creating a healthy fear and an understanding of the need for change. But without an overarching vision, the revamping would not mean anything. The next step was to establish a vision for the company— guiding principles that would carry Coca-Cola through the decade of the 1980s, and a blueprint for how to implement those principles in Coke's day-to-day operations.

Two measures would set the process in place. First, Goizueta began the task of creating a mission statement for the company. When that was done, he would gather his top management from around the world and make them sign on, face to face, to his program. Booklets of platitudes had a habit of finding their way to bookshelves in managers' offices and staying there, ignored and useless. The follow-up conference would stop that from happening. It would give Goizueta a chance personally to lay down his vision, and the law.

Goizueta wanted the mission statement to combine an overarching vision of The Coca-Cola Company's mission for the next decade with a set of specific strategic steps. Objectives were useless, he knew, with-out a means to get there. And in setting the objectives, he continued the same Socratic method of information gathering that began with questions to Sam Ayoub about finances, continued in force with the Spanish Inquisition, and now would come to a climax as he synthe-sized his vision for the challenge ahead.

He approached anyone he could find who might share knowledge and experience with him. On the trip to South America, he peppered Jimmy Williams with ideas. He constantly floated draft statements to Keough, Collings, and others among his closest associates. His col-leagues marveled at his seriousness and diligence for what they at first assumed was going to be a fairly perfunctory exercise. "I wondered how important it was, whether it was worth all the effort," Keough said. "But as I began to recognize how important it was to him, I real-ized he was up to something big."

In some instances, Goizueta's questions betrayed a surprising lack of sophistication about Coke's operations, and especially about nu-ances of corporate finance, such as the use of debt as a financing tool. Sometimes, his prose was all but unreadable. "I wouldn't have known how to write a chemical engineering report, and he didn't know how to write a financial report," recalled one of the executives who saw an early draft of the mission statement. Occasionally, people who read his rough drafts wondered if the chemical engineer was not just slightly over his head writing a creed in his second language, covering sophis-ticated issues that were fairly new to him, and boiling down a strategic vision into a few typewritten pages.

One of Goizueta's most important exercises as he completed the mis-sion statement and prepared for the management conference that would follow was a dialectic he conducted with management consultant Michael Kami. A Brazilian native and former IBM corporate planner, Kami was an expert in organizational change. By the time he turned to Kami at the beginning of 1981, Goizueta was beyond looking for blue-sky ideas. He had formed his opinions and was on the verge of imple-mentation. He wanted to use Kami to put his ideas to a test, much as he had challenged his managers during the Spanish Inquisition.

In the years he had spent preparing for this moment, as far back as his special assignment days with Chap Tyler, Goizueta had established a set of beliefs about the chief executive's role at a major company. His job, he decided, could be broken down into three major parts. He alone, and no one else, was responsible for "the leadership role" at the company. Only he was responsible for Coca-Cola's financial security. And only he could decide what jobs to delegate and to whom they should be delegated. "In a perfect world, every decision would fall into one of those categories," Goizueta told Kami.

The consultant was impressed. Most new chief executives have strong opinions, but never had he seen one start out with such a theoretical underpinning to his ideas for running the company. "He thought things through completely in his own mind," Kami said. As the roving discussion with Kami led to specifics over the next several weeks, Goizueta laid down several important points. As much as possible, he wanted to stick with Coke's current management. A housecleaning in the executive ranks would only exacerbate the palace intrigue that had gripped Coke in the past two years, and would not solve the problem of a lack of direction from the top. He would focus on global opportunities. "A lot of markets will be opened, and The Coca-Cola Company must be there, ready to move," Goizueta told Kami.

The new Coke chief seemed proud that the management team he was building represented both an ethnic and a generational change from the past. Besides himself, Goizueta was actively promoting his reliance on Egyptian financier Ayoub, the Argentine-born Brian Dyson at Coke-USA, a Mexican marketing whiz named Sergio Zyman, and now the Brazilian Kami. A polyglot sensibility was sweeping into the executive suite of the company once so dominated by old-line Georgia families. "We're a kind of United Nations," he said.

This was a time before people started calling themselves "agents of change." But that's precisely how Goizueta saw himself. "Whatever was done before is not necessarily the right policy. We want to challenge the policy, present alternatives, and do it," Goizueta said. He was serious about delegating decisions to the field, within the parameters of the strategic objectives set at the annual planning sessions. The old "centralized decentralization" concept, which he first employed while redesigning the engineering department in 1965, was making a comeback.

"That won't always come true, but at least it's a nice objective at the outset," Kami replied. The secret, Kami noted, would be to empower people to feel comfortable taking risks. Without a willingness to accept calculated risk, delegation would only lead to a stalemate. Goizueta liked the thought, and asked Kami to speak at the management conference about the power of risk taking as a competitive force.

THE WORK ON THE STRATEGY STATEMENT WAS COMPLETE. BUT before Goizueta could present it at the board's March 4 meeting—his first as Coke's new chairman and chief executive—he happily undertook a rite of passage. At long last, nearly a decade after he became a satellite circling closely around Woodruff, Goizueta finally received an invitation to join The Boss at Ichauway for the last week in February. His mates for the visit were Jimmy Williams and Joe Jones, two of his biggest backers from early on, and Charles Duncan, who was returning to the Coca-Cola board.

If Woodruff had not invited Goizueta earlier because he suspected that the Cuban aristocrat was not a sporting man like Keough, Wilson, and others who had paid visits to Ichauway before him, his instinct proved true. Goizueta appeared at the plantation dressed incongruously, with a yellow ascot around his neck but a brown flannel shirt on his back. He stood in sharp contrast to the suede-elbowed hunting garb that others in the party wore at Ichauway. Goizueta had never shot skeet, much less birds, so he spent his first afternoon shooting at Coke cans lined up on fence posts by Ichuaway's army of African-American caretakers. Williams was encouraged by Goizueta's quick study of the sport. At night in the Ichauway gun room the hunting party drank and talked shop.

At the March 4 board meeting, Goizueta presented a report on Coke's market performance, the financial figures, and the stock price. He related reports from the management consultants he had hired to help him lay out a strategic plan for the company. One of the firms, Arthur D. Little, had recommended that Coke consider a move into either entertainment or pharmaceuticals. A move into either sector would be a dramatic cultural break away from Coke's roots in soft drinks and foods, but it would boost domestic revenues and help Goizueta get to his targeted 50/50 split between domestic and international. A major diversification move would be dramatic, but to Goizueta, the most important point on the agenda was the unveiling of the mission statement for the company. Printed on brown heavyweight paper, it was titled, simply, "Strategy for the 1980s. The Coca-Cola Company."

If the directors or anyone else at Coke took the statement lightly, they made a big mistake—and they did not understand Goizueta. For Coke's new chief, a statement of principles and objectives was a serious undertaking, a compact with the future that he intended to keep. It outlined Goizueta's view of the business, broken down into seven major parts, and hinted at strategic changes he was ready to undertake.

"Our Challenge," the statement opened, will be to enhance and protect the Coca-Cola trademark, giving shareholders an above-average return and entering new businesses only if they can perform at a rate substantially above inflation. "Our Business," he wrote, will continue to concentrate in soft drinks, emphasize leadership in other segments, and most likely expand into "industries in which we are not today." Only market segments with inherent real growth would be attractive. "Our Consumers" will include bottlers and end users worldwide. "Our Shareholders" will want protection and enhancement of their investment. "Our 'Bottom Line'" will focus on reaching goals, effecting real profit growth, and reducing the percent of earnings paid out as stock dividends, leaving more capital to reinvest in the business. "Increasing annual earnings per share and effecting increased return on equity are still the name of the game," he wrote in the statement's seminal sentence.

The final two sections focused on the role that individuals would play in implementing the strategy. "Our People" will have the characteristics of "courage and commitment," and "integrity and fairness," and be focused on the spirit of entrepreneurship. The statement concluded with a broad-based section about "Our Wisdom," an exhortation of guiding principles, a code of conduct that Goizueta believed would make Coke a leading company as it entered the final decade of the twentieth century. As they worked their way into the 1990s, Goizueta wrote, Coke's employees must consider "the long-term consequences of current actions," sacrifice short-term gains when necessary, adapt to changes in consumer tastes and needs, and become a welcome part of every country in which Coke does business. Finally, every Coke employee must exhibit "the capacity to control what is controllable and the wisdom not to bother [with] what is not."

No one on the board mistook the almost ethereal tone of the Strategy Statement as an indication that Goizueta was going to be the kind of big-think CEO who is perhaps more enamored of elaborate management theories than fighting in the marketplace. The Spanish Inquisition had proved Goizueta was prepared to launch the kind of guerrilla warfare needed to take Pepsi by the throat, regain leadership in all market segments, and squeeze the potential out of the farthest reaches of Coke's vast system. Goizueta, the board was learning, was a unique mix of high-minded corporate philosopher and dirt-under-the-fingernails street fighter.

He proved it, once and for all, at a Palm Springs conference of Coke's top managers in April of 1981, less than a month after officially assuming the chairmanship. It is customary at big companies for new executive teams to invite their elite managers for a retreat, to put their stamp on the new era. It is not, however, typical to open the session with a harsh kick in the ass strong enough to shake up even the old-timers waiting to collect their gold watches. But after the Spanish Inquisition, Coke's management corps knew not to expect the predictable from Goizueta. Even so, no one could have anticipated the fusillade that launched the Goizueta era at Coke.

"There are no sacred cows" was the most memorable phrase Goizueta uttered during the five-day conference, but it was hardly the only headline. In his opening remarks, Goizueta announced that a period of rapid change was about to take place at The Coca-Cola Company, and the forty executives in attendance had better be ready. "Those who don't adapt will be left behind or out—no matter what level they are," he warned. As an aide passed out copies of "Strategy for the 1980s," Goizueta warned everyone not to mistake it for a list of platitudes. "Don't take it lightly," he said.

Goizueta paid particular attention to the literal meaning of words, a habit he had adopted as far back as Cheshire Academy, while perfecting English by studying his dictionary and the movies. "I happen not to like the term 'strategic planning,' because it can lead to misinterpretations. To my mind, corporate strategy deals with what we want to be as a company, and planning, and specifically long-range planning, deals with how we become what we want to be," he stated. In case anyone suspected a distinction without a difference, the new chief underscored the point. "This may seem like an exercise in semantic hairsplitting," he said, as if reading the minds of many in attendance, "but it is in fact critical to our collective understanding of our ground rules or operating philosophy for the future." As the Spanish Inquisition had so vividly proven, plans would have dollars-and-cents meaning at Roberto Goizueto's Coca-Cola.

With the audience's attention firmly in his grasp, Goizueta laid waste to Coke's self-image as he listed and then slayed the company's "sacred cows." If Coke's executives wanted to see world-class marketing, they should look at Procter & Gamble, not Coca-Cola, he said. The distribution system needed a facelift. People needed to take bold risks to survive. Concocting soda-pop formulas and processing orange juice did not amount to world-class technical strength. And the culture of complacency must change. "The only company that continues to enjoy success is the company that keeps struggling to achieve it," Goizueta said.

To those who were listening with open minds, Goizueta's concluding passage was filled with portent. "Just to give you an example that there are no sacred cows," he began, "let me assure you that such things as the reformulation of any or all of our products will not stand in the way" of seizing a real or perceived market advantage from a competitor. "The days are gone in which an inflexible adherence to a sacred cow will ever give renewed impetus [to] or breathe life into a competitor," Goizueta swore. In other words, the day of New Coke was not far away.

It was the speech of Goizueta's career. Known even within Coke as a halting and uninspiring speaker, Goizueta had galvanized his executives and catalyzed the Palm Springs conference. The "No Sacred Cows" speech breathed energy into a five-day program that covered topics ranging from the mundane "Enhancing Bottler Performance" to the buzzword of the 1980s, "Adopting Entrepreneurship as a Company Lifestyle." The daylong sessions concluded after dinner, followed by drinks with Keough at the resort bar. Goizueta used the five days to visit, one by one, with every one of his top managers. "Now we've got a compact," he would say, after they told him they agreed with his plans.

The consultants had their say, too. Michael Kami spoke about the need for speed in decision making and implementation, and created one of the conference's key buzz phrases when he advised executives to ask themselves, "How many times have you been turned down?" Until you've proposed an idea that is rejected, Kami counseled, you have not pushed the limits, and have not created change. Peter Drucker, the famed expert on management theory, delivered a talk about "Leadership and the New Management Breed," but for many in the audience the famed guru was a disappointment. It is not surprising that in 1997, Drucker said he could not recall sharing a single word with Goizueta, and did not remember anything he himself had said at the landmark Palm Springs conference. He served Coke well through the Goizueta era, though, as Don Keough's favorite big-think consultant.

At the conclusion of the conference, Kami spent a moment watching Goizueta share quiet words with the managers, one by one, as the session broke up. They looked apprehensive, uncertain about the future. Then it was Kami's turn. Goizueta extended his hand, and congratulated the consultant on his preparation and execution at the conference. "Well," Goizueta said, "we're off to a start."

The start of something the likes of which no one had ever seen before, Palm Springs was a great opening act. But impressive as it was, it was only an overture to the series of wrenching changes Roberto Goizueta held in store for the world of Coca-Cola.

4

A Break from the Past: Diet Coke and Columbia Pictures

The "no sacred cows" speech at Palm Springs was a primal roar from Goizueta, a long-awaited declaration of unrivaled dominance over Coca-Cola and its future. Beginning with Miguel Macias, the boyhood friend with whom he first worked at Coke in Cuba, and ending with Don Keough at the top of Coke's headquarters building in Atlanta, Goizueta had outmaneuvered, outrun, and outlasted every one of his rivals. After twenty-six years of striving, Goizueta had at last reached the peak of The Coca-Cola Company. Now, with the Spanish Inquisition, mission statement, and Palm Springs meeting behind him, it was time to stop jawboning and get to work.

Goizueta knew better than to rest on his laurels. The board of directors, awoken from the drowsy sleep of the Austin era by the succession struggle that played out before their horrified eyes, suddenly was awake and making new demands. The orders were clear: The board told Goizueta he had three years to make a plan, and make it work. If he could not show results by then, he would be out.

Over the next few months, Goizueta would launch a flurry of initiatives designed to set the tone for his reign and set Coke onto a new and more profitable course. He would unload empty and excess baggage accumulated during the Austin years, everything from extraneous businesses like shrimp farming and wine production to uncooperative executives in underperforming regions like Asia, Latin America, and Europe. Declaring that Coke was in effect liquidating its own business by constantly raising its stock dividends, he slowed the growth in dividend payments, took money that otherwise would have gone to shareholders and invested it, primarily in rehabilitating the Coca-Cola bottling system. Two bold experiments, the launch of Diet Coke and the purchase of the Columbia Pictures movie studio, would establish his virtually unlimited tolerance for risk and, over time, his ability to handle both success and failure. As time passed, the burst of activity would stand as evidence that Goizueta was serious at Palm Springs when he put "sacred cows" on his hit list.

To make it all work, Goizueta knew he needed to persuade everyone who worked with him or for him that none of them would succeed unless everyone was wholly committed to the new regime. He had made a point at Palm Springs of securing commitments from each of the forty top Coca-Cola executives who had attended. To spread the word, he videotaped a sanitized version of the "no sacred cows" speech and showed it in mandatory sessions for headquarters employees. Copies of the mission statement became as prolific as the little red book in Mao's China. He showed the videotape to the board of directors and let them know that they were part of the new discipline at Coke, too, by demanding that board committees meet more often and by starting board meetings earlier in the day so he could build a fuller agenda.

Goizueta let everyone know he was serious about rewarding performance, and just as deadly serious about calling for an accounting from those who failed. "Once in a while, to make a point, you have to have a flogging in the town square," he explained, more than once, to groups of managers. "There's more to it than just the pain of the lash, it's the crack of the whip that has a beneficial effect on everyone who hears." The Spanish Inquisition had taught everyone that the annual budget process no longer meant creating five-year wish lists, as was the case in Austin's last years. Within weeks of the Palm Springs meeting, Goizueta's lash was cracking through Coke's corridors with a fury that no one at The Coca-Cola Company could recall ever seeing before. Before the first anniversary of Goizueta's "no sacred cows" speech, at least six of the forty executives in attendance at Palm Springs were forced out of the company or reassigned to dead-end jobs. "Roberto was a tyrant. He fired anybody who disagreed with him," said finance man Sam Ayoub, whom Goizueta frequently consulted.

"Fired" is not precisely the right word. Outright firings were not part of the Coca-Cola culture and never became part of Goizueta's style. There is no evidence that he personally fired anyone, and he rarely ordered subordinates to do so. More typically, he preferred a less direct, but also less humane method. "Coke never fires anyone," Goizueta had explained to the consultant Chaplin Tyler in the early 1970s. "We just ignore the guy. His "In" box remains empty. He isn't invited to conferences. He isn't given assignments, but his check keeps coming. Within three weeks, he walks in and says, 'Boss, I'm a nervous wreck. I quit.'" In the initial housecleaning of his chairmanship, Goizueta relied on Ayoub and others to move underperforming executives out of their jobs, in short order replacing executives in Europe, the Pacific, and Latin America.

Goizueta also made it clear that he had little reverence for the past by the way he treated Austin's legacy. In statements to reporters about his management style, he emphasized that he was "the conductor" of Coke's orchestra, not "a violinist." Some Austin loyalists read the statement as a petty slap at Austin, who favored describing his tension-inducing management style as that of a violinist who makes music by "keeping the strings taut." Later, at a dinner he hosted honoring Keough, Goizueta made a point of recognizing all of Coke's retired leaders in the crowd, but overlooked Jeanne Austin, representing her recently deceased husband. Some in the audience saw it as an intentional slight. Keough attempted to cover the oversight by recognizing Ms. Austin when he took a turn at the podium.

To Goizueta, it was essential that everyone, at every level of the company, understand the magnitude of his break and the literal importance of his mission statement for the 1980s. In the statement, he had warned that, "By and large, industrial markets are not our business." By July, he had sold AquaChem, where he personally had worked but which failed him because it returned only 8 percent on Coke's investment. He booked a $29 million profit and sent a clear message: If Goizueta would unceremoniously unload a business where he personally had worked over the last two years, then he would sell anything that was not contributing.

IT WAS NOT ENOUGH JUST TO TERRIFY COKE'S MANAGERS AND UN-load corporate assets. For a time, a purge can have the exhilarating ef-fect of demonstrating the confidence and vigor of a new leader. But if the bloodletting continued and Coke's bottom line did not improve, Goizueta ran the risk of looking like a power-mad tyrant. To prove that he intended to build the business, too, Goizueta began investing aggressively in the bottling system at the same time he was attacking weakness in the rest of the company.

One of the secrets to Coca-Cola's growth since the late 1800s had been the company's decision to sell bottling rights to independent businesspeople, who themselves would make the heavy capital invest-ment required to bottle and distribute Coca-Cola. The system had served Coke well since Asa Candler created it in 1899 by giving away the rights to two Chattanooga lawyers, allowing them to divide the country into territories, and sign contracts with bottlers who would serve those areas. Coke sold its syrup to the bottlers and bore a major-ity of the cost of advertising and marketing the Coca-Cola brand. By 1981, though, much of the system had broken down, as third-generation bottlers did not invest enough money to keep their systems modern, or financially-driven buyers purchased the rights and milked the companies for their sizable cash flow. Worse still, as the rancorous contract negotiations of the late 1970s had shown, Coke had precious little control over its bottlers and was unable to force them to update their machinery, improve marketing programs, or even support new product introductions.

At the Atlanta meeting of top bottlers in 1980, Goizueta had laid out his strategy to strengthen the system. Now it was time to put that plan to work. "I'm going to insist and insist very strongly that the management of our thirteen divisions around the world give absolutely 100 percent to those bottlers who are willing to put forth the neces-sary efforts to grow their businesses," Goizueta promised. Now he was ready to provide proof. In January 1981, even before he officially took over as chairman, Goizueta invested $200 million in Coke-New York. At the time, Wall Street rumors had it that a mysterious financial buyer was considering making a hostile takeover bid for Coke-New York, with an eye toward milking its sizable cash flow. But the rumors were only half right. The most immediate threat to Coke-New York's management control actually came from inside the Coke system. In late December 1980, Keough got a call from Charles Navarre, a long-time Coke bottler based in New York. Navarre was considering making a takeover bid for Coke-New York, which was vulnerable because Coke-New York's management owned only a minority share of the company's equity.

Keough immediately phoned Millard and told the Coke-New York chief to prepare his defenses. Millard was one of the system's strongest bottlers, and by giving him a heads up, Keough was putting substance behind Goizueta's promise that Coke would stand behind bottlers who were doing a good job. Millard considered mounting a management-led leveraged buyout, but his lawyer, the takeover specialist Joseph Flom, told him he was crazy. "The minute you do that, you've run up a 'For Sale' sign. You're dead meat," Flom warned him. "You've got to get The Coca-Cola Company to come in as big brother in your LBO." Millard asked Keough if Coke would help, and Keough persuaded Goizueta that he needed to help Millard. With Coke's money, an investment by Millard's team, and a financing package led by the Prudential Insurance Co., Millard retained control of his company, and Coke took a minority stake and two seats on the board.

After half a decade of rancor over the bottlers' contract, Big Coke at last had made a positive move in defense of one of its bottlers—even if it did come at the expense of Navarre, himself a Coke bottler. To show that his activist intervention was no fluke, Goizueta helped Coke's successful Indianapolis bottler gain control of the struggling Chicago and Wisconsin franchise. And he bought control of Coke's Fort Worth, Texas, bottler from a group of financial owners, then quickly flipped it to John T. Lupton, the big Chattanooga bottler and Coke board member who only a few months earlier had maneuvered to stop Goizueta from becoming Coke's next new chief executive. By the end of 1981, Goizueta would approve Coke's participation in more than $500 million in bottler transactions, often buying and then quickly selling bottlers, sometimes holding them to upgrade their operations, and sometimes simply working to bring buyer and seller together.

To those who were paying attention, the message was clear. Goizueta had a Darwinian view of Coca-Cola's bottling system. The day was passing when 500-plus independent bottlers carried on the business just as their grandfathers had done alongside a young Robert W. Woodruff.

Financially powerful and managerially competent bottlers would survive. The rest had better cut the best deals they could. Goizueta's comment about helping bottlers who were serious about building their business carried an implicit warning to those who failed to meet his litmus test. Determinist though it was, Goizueta's approach came as good news even to many of the weaker bottlers. Those looking for a viable exit knew they had a buyer in King Coke, and those who thought they had staying power could look for a better relationship with Atlanta.

At THE SAME TIME, AND DESPITE HIS PROMISE TO THE BOTTLERS that he planned to focus on bringing domestic results into parity with international profits, Goizueta knew he needed to shore up international bottling operations. In 1980, a strike against Coke's Mexico bottler had hurt results, despite an aggressive building program in that country. Japan's operating profit fell 10 percent because of poor weather and a weak economy. Runaway inflation in Brazil caused results from that country to erode, despite higher shipments of Coke syrup. It irked Goizueta that Coke had so little control over conditions in any of those countries. Politics, economics, and even weather were an inevitable part of running a global business. But Goizueta could not stomach the fact that The Coca-Cola Company, despite the power of its global brand, had so little say about how its product was bottled, shipped, and marketed around the globe.

That's when John Hunter, whom Goizueta had just put in charge of the Far Eastern region, came to Goizueta with an idea. In the Philippines, Coke had dominated Pepsi since American armed forces popularized the drink during World War II. But Pepsi took a commanding market-share lead in the 1970s when Coke's bottler, the San Miguel Brewery, neglected soft drinks while building its beer business. And the owners, the Soriano family, were so irritated by the poor level of Coke's Pacific region managers that they forbade any Coke people from visiting the bottling plant. By early 1981, Pepsi's sales dominated Coke by a 2-to-1 margin.

Hunter had spoken to the Soriano family and wanted Goizueta to invest $13 million of Coke's money to buy 30 percent of the bottler and, perhaps more important, run the San Miguel bottling operation under a joint operating agreement. At first, Goizueta did not like the proposal. His chief financial officer, John Collings, opposed it, because he could not fathom spending so much money on an economy as weak as the Philippines. Fil Eisenberg, the former CFO who had been Austin's nemesis and now chaired the finance committee, would never approve it. The only finance person favoring the deal was Sam Ayoub, whom Goizueta had assigned as financial overseer of the Pacific region.

As he listened to Hunter and Ayoub argue the case, though, the San Miguel proposal grew on Goizueta. Although the Philippine market was small by most standards, it could still be used to make an important point: Coke would intervene to improve its bottlers, even half way around the globe. It would test Coke's ability to turn around a troubled bottler with only a minority ownership stake. But when Ayoub presented the plan to the board's finance committee, Eisenberg predictably objected with the concurrence of most of Coke's old-line board members. "It sounded like a hell of a lot of money to me," recalled Jimmy Sibley, who in 1980 had taken the board seat long held by his father, Woodruff confidante John Sibley. But Goizueta argued for approval and won the day, sending an important message that he, and not the finance committee, was going to call the shots on Coke's global spending strategy.

There was far more riding on the decision than just the then unheard-of $13 million investment. If the Philippine experiment worked, Goizueta knew he could clone the idea of minority bottler investments in strategic markets around the globe. To gauge the situation, he traveled to the Philippines and the Pacific region with Sibley, finance man Ayoub, and their wives. In Manila, the Coke dignitaries stopped at Malacanang Palace and presented Philippines president Ferdinand Marcos with a finely crafted crystal dish. Taking the dish from Goizueta, Marcos peered into the bottom, looked up, and declared, "I see a great future for The Coca-Cola Company in the Philippines." Marcos had been a fan of the company ever since Coke under Austin invested thousands of dollars in one of his wife Imelda's charities, a move that silenced concerns she had begun expressing about the lack of nutritional value in Coca-Cola.

Goizueta made certain Marcos was right. To oversee the effort to completely rebuild the Philippines operation, he assigned a gung-ho Irishman named E. Neville Isdell. His job: Reverse the market share figures. The 6'5" Isdell invested almost boundless energy into everything from pep rallies at the plants to inspections of the restrooms to cut-throat pricing and aggressive product giveaways. He dressed the-atrically, one day wearing battle fatigues to underscore the war with Pepsi, and a jogging suit for the Philippine launch of Mello Yellow, which Coke was touting as "the world's fastest soft drink." By Novem-ber 1982, Coke had pulled even with Pepsi, and by mid-1983, Coke re-gained its 2-to-1 lead. Goizueta had an answer to his question about Coke's ability to use its minority ownership in a bottler to reverse for-tunes in a market half a world away. And to underscore his promise that initiative would be rewarded, Goizueta brought Hunter and Isdell into his inner circle, and gave them high-profile, fast-track appoint-ments over the next several years.

On April 16, Goizueta had visited China to open a new bottling plant in Beijing, marking the occasion with a telegram to Woodruff. Whatever the ultimate importance of the China market to Coke, the tiny Philippine operation ultimately would achieve equal renown as Goizueta's first move in what would become the "anchor" bottler concept. Over time, Goizueta would build Coke's entire interna-tional bottling effort around the notion of taking minority owner-ship positions in underperforming but high-potential bottlers, then working with local management to improve the bottling and market-ing of its product while at the same time keeping the demand for Coke's own capital outlays as low as possible. By extracting maximum financial results with a minimum cash outlay, the anchor bottler strategy would become a classic example of Goizueta putting the eco-nomic value-added (EVA) concept into action. Ultimately, he re-fined the EVA regimen to the point that he would approve capital outlays for anchor bottler investments only if they promised a 20 per-cent return on Coke's capital.

FOR GOIZUETA, THE PHILIPPINE INITIATIVE PROVIDED WELCOME relief from a threatened boycott by Jesse Jackson, the civil rights leader who in 1980 had begun threatening to lead Chicago-based Op-eration PUSH in a boycott of Coke because of the company's poor record in hiring and promoting minorities. To handle the matter, Goizueta and Keough persuaded William Allison, who had become Coke's first African American board member during Paul Austin's tenure, to return from retirement to negotiate with Jackson. But when Jackson called Allison "a messenger with no power," a boycott looked imminent. Keough hurriedly completed talks with Jackson and on August 10 announced Coke's new $32 million minority initiative at a 90-minute press conference surrounded by Jackson, Southern Christian Leadership Conference chief the Rev. Joseph Lowery, and nearly a dozen African American clergy.

The deal's promise of an innovative venture capital package for minority business people was immediately popular among Jackson's followers, but it invited a hailstorm from many of Coke's bottlers, and from the crusty *Atlanta Journal-Constitution* columnist Lewis Grizzard. "People resent the fact that one man can snap his fingers and a giant company like Coca-Cola will go to its knees," Grizzard wrote. Sensitive to the criticism, Goizueta wrote a two-page letter to Coke's directors, outlining minority initiatives Coke had undertaken before the PUSH threat. To his credit, he made good on the commitments he made to Jackson. By 1983, Coke had its first African American bottler, Bruce Lewellyn of Philadelphia, who invested with other African American businessmen including Coke pitchmeister Bill Cosby. He recruited more minorities and spent slightly more money on advertising targeted to minority customers, employing minority-owned firms to contribute to the work. Allison, a former civil rights activist, had mixed feelings about both his PUSH experience and his prior service on Coke's board in the 1970s. "You end up resenting being used in that sense," he says, "But at the same time, somebody's got to do the job. I just figured, why not me?"

The two early "P" decisions—the Philippines and PUSH—had set an important precedent for Goizueta as Coke's new CEO. The dollar figures were about the same, but he took a direct, personal interest in the Philippines and delegated the entire PUSH matter. Goizueta knew from the start that the Philippines had long-term strategic consequences, while the minority problem would blow over if properly handled. When he first was named president, Goizueta had talked about the delegation decision as one of the chief executive's three primary roles, along with leadership and looking after its finances. The two Ps gave him an opportunity to put meaning behind those words.

As HE HANDLED THE PUSH MATTER, GOIZUETA WAS EXPERIENCING discrimination at a very personal level. Goizueta's closest friends knew that his children sometimes had been ridiculed for their accents and foreign-sounding names in the 1960s after the family first moved to Atlanta. But few were aware that Goizueta continued to be subjected to an irritating form of nuisance discrimination even while he served as chairman of The Coca-Cola Company. Despite personal backing by Robert W. Woodruff, Goizueta had a difficult time obtaining membership in one of Atlanta's most exclusive private clubs, the Peachtree Golf Club on the city's north side.

In early July 1981, a Woodruff associate named Augustus H. Stern nominated Goizueta to become a member. Woodruff seconded the nomination. "I have had a personal acquaintance with Mr. Goizueta for nearly twenty years and, in his position as chairman of the board of directors of The Coca-Cola Company, I have a deep interest in his future success," Woodruff wrote, asking the board to expedite Goizueta's nomination. There was no more certain endorsement in the city of Atlanta than a personal letter carrying Woodruff's signature. And there was not a stronger corporate pedigree than the chairmanship of Coca-Cola. In Woodruff's five decades as head of Coke, he had sparingly doled out his personal support for club memberships, limiting his requests to only the select among Coke's most elite executives, or leaders of closely allied companies like the Trust Co. bank.

Never in Woodruff's decades of membership had the Peachtree Club hesitated when he endorsed a nominee. But when the Cuba-born Goizueta's name came up, it withered on the branches at Peachtree. Finally, in March 1982, nearly a year after his initial letter, Woodruff ran out of patience and penned a second letter. "I hope this board will be able to act favorably on this nomination in the near future," Woodruff concluded in a terse, three-sentence memo that he copied to a handful of personal associates on the board. At last, on June 25, the Peachtree Club's board approved Goizueta's membership. Perhaps the indignity of waiting nearly a year was mollified somewhat for Goizueta by his locker assignment: the one previously held by his erstwhile bitter rival, Ian Wilson. But even as a member, Goizueta still had occasional moments of discomfort. While playing golf with Olguita one day in 1982, Goizueta wore a polo-style shirt with "Drink Coca-Cola" embroidered on the chest. One club member, not recognizing him as a fellow member of Atlanta's corporate nobility, approached Goizueta between holes, and tried to order a Coke from a puzzled Roberto Goizueta.

Goizueta rarely used the Peachtree Golf Club. When he took charge at Coke, he had promised to "keep my head down and concentrate on the followthrough." That he did. From the "Spanish Inquisition" to "no sacred cows" to "whippings in the courtyard" to the Philippines investment, Goizueta made it clear he was intent on making his tenure a landmark in The Coca-Cola Company's 96 year-old timeline. To insiders, his drive and vision were obvious, but outside the company, few had noticed yet. That would change abruptly in the space of a few months in 1982. Less than a year into his new job, Goizueta would unveil two major strategic initiatives that would change the course of the company's future. With the acquisition of the Columbia Pictures movie studio and the introduction of Diet Coke, Goizueta declared that a new Coca-Cola Company was at hand.

THE ROAD LEADING COKE TO HOLLYWOOD STARTED WITH A BLANK map in the fall of 1980. While he was developing the Mission Statement for the 1980s, Goizueta had hired the A.D. Little consulting firm to conduct a study of Coca-Cola's opportunities outside the soft-drink industry. It was a defensive measure. Goizueta had promised bottlers and the board that he would bring Coke's domestic income into par with its international business. There was just one problem: Coke's soft-drink business was not capable of reaching that goal. With the Pepsi Challenge running amok in the marketplace and Coke trailing in supermarket sales for the first time in its history, Goizueta and his team knew the domestic soft-drink business could not grow quickly enough to reach parity with Coke's vast overseas sales. To bring The Coca-Cola Company back into balance, Goizueta would have to take a dramatic and risky step. He would have to make a significant acquisition outside the soft-drink business. The target would have to be large enough to bring Coke's total domestic revenues on par with the international business, and its domestic growth would have to be strong enough to enable Coke's U.S. business to keep pace with its quickly expanding opportunities around the world.

To reach such an aggressive goal, Goizueta turned to outside help. He asked A.D. Little to conduct an exhaustive "business opportunity review." The firm broke down the United States into a variety of demographic groups, parsed the gross domestic product of various business sectors, measured capital spending, and made forecasts in each of several categories. The initial sweep came up with a grab bag of suggestions, everything from temporary help to flavors and fragrances to foods. But by April 1981, Coke and its consulting firm were focused on two areas: entertainment and pharmaceuticals, the only two industries growing fast enough, with high-enough margins, and sizable-enough domestic earnings to satisfy Coke's investment goals.

The search was conducted in such extreme secrecy that the names of targets that Goizueta considered but rejected have never been published. Of seven entertainment companies identified as possible targets, the leading picks were The Walt Disney Co. and Columbia Pictures Industries. Disney in late 1981 was a financially troubled, poorly led concern ineffectually milking its library of classic cartoons and theme parks. Columbia had just emerged from an embezzlement scandal involving a top officer and had paid greenmail to stop a hostile takeover bid by Kirk Kerkorian. In pharmaceuticals, the only significant candidate was Schering-Plough Corp., the New Jersey-based pharmaceutical company.

To assess the options, Goizueta set up a competitive showdown among his top executives, breaking them into two teams, assigning one to entertainment and the other to drugs. The parameters of the decision were clear, he told them while launching the study at a September meeting in a conference room at Coke headquarters. Any deal had to be friendly, not hostile, because a hostile deal would hurt Coke's image with consumers. The target had to have predictable earnings. And it had to be large enough to help Coke approach 50 percent domestic operating income. "You've got to make an acquisition that not only does not dilute our stock, but buys me $50 million of after-tax earnings," Goizueta told the group as he gave them their top-secret assignment. "We don't want anyone big enough to change the character of The Coca-Cola Company, and we don't want someone too small because they wouldn't have an impact."

As the Coke teams began their work, Ike Herbert, the head of the entertainment team, met in Phoenix with Karl Eller, a well-known communications industry entrepreneur. The two had started their careers and friendship working at advertising agencies in Chicago, and Eller now was president of Columbia's radio stations. Over breakfast at the Biltmore Hotel in early October 1981, Herbert mentioned that Coke was looking toward diversification to balance its earnings from soft drinks. Eller responded matter of factly, "You ought to buy into entertainment." The cash flows could be huge, and the investment wasn't necessarily that large.

"I don't think Coke should be in the entertainment business," Herbert said between bites, adding coyly, "You've got to worry about R-rated movies. We've got enough problems." Eller mentioned that Columbia might be for sale if Coke ever got interested, but left the breakfast convinced Coke wasn't a buyer.

Back in Atlanta, two of the three potential targets quickly washed out. Although Disney's earnings were falling and management was weak, the company almost certainly would resist a takeover. With Goizueta unwilling to back a hostile deal, Disney was done. Schering-Plough made no sense because of the huge investments required for research and development. "In drugs, you spend $100 million on research, and you don't know what you've got. At least in the movies, when you spend $100 million you know right away if you've got a hit or not," Goizueta later said. The triage was over; Columbia was the target.

Goizueta told Herbert to call Eller and set up some talks. Phoning Eller, Herbert got to the point. "We just got the results of the study and guess what's on top of the list?" he stated. "Columbia Pictures."

"I'll set up a meeting right away," Eller said, his initial surprise washing into the giddy thought that Columbia might actually wind up in the hands of Coke.

Eller agreed with the site Herbert requested, the 21 Club in New York, for a get-acquainted session between top Coke and Columbia management. During the merger-mad 1980s, the 21 Club was the midtown New York lair for dealmakers on the prowl. The trucks, planes, trains, and other big-boy toys hanging from 21's trademark ceiling are decorated with the corporate logos of some of the Fortune 500 companies controlled by the club's regular clientele. The club was Don Keough's favorite New York watering hole, and its see-and-be-seen main room would serve Coke in many important luncheon meetings during the Goizueta era.

For this highly secretive conclave on the day before Thanksgiving, Keough held court, not in the downstairs bar, but in a quiet upstairs room, in virtual seclusion. Around the table sat the key players in the future of Columbia Industries and Coca-Cola, minus one. Goizueta stayed in Atlanta, intentionally remaining aloof at the initial courting stage. Keough, Ayoub, and Herbert sat with Eller, Columbia president Fay M. Vincent Jr., and Herbert Allen Jr., chairman of Columbia and the lead partner in Allen & Co., owner of a majority of Columbia's stock. The talk went well, with much attention to the word of the 1980s, "synergies." The Coke people thought they could bring new marketing techniques to film distribution, and the Columbia team liked the idea of tapping into Coke's cash hoard to fund film production. Professionals that they were, no one on either side talked money. That would come later. But Allen made it clear that Columbia would not come cheaply. At the end of the lunch, he told Keough that his asking price "will knock your eyes out."

Back in Atlanta, Keough told Goizueta, "We like each other."

A few days later, Goizueta traveled to New York, for a face-to-face meeting with Herbert, Vincent, and Eller. The Columbia executives boasted about the studio's production schedule and its library of 1,800 films. The biggest profit center, and one they would continue growing, was television syndication sales. This startled Goizueta. Although it was good news, it bothered him because the A.D. Little study had completely overlooked television. If A.D. Little had missed that key point, there was no telling what else they overlooked.

There clearly was more due diligence for Goizueta to do, but the most important result of the meeting was that he liked the Columbia people and felt he could do business with them. He was impressed especially by the plain-speaking Herbert Allen Jr., with whom he seemed to form an instant bond. Like Goizueta, Allen was a man of discipline, waking each morning at 5:30 A.M., and finding his bed by 9:30 at night. He shared Goizueta's low-key manner and dry sense of humor, and his belief in speaking to the press only when it served his business purposes. He had a yen for celebrities, routinely rubbing elbows with people like Candace Bergin and Walter Mondale. Allen did not share Goizueta's taste for hard alcohol, limiting himself to some wine at dinner, and would not let anyone smoke in the Allen & Co. offices. Out of respect for his no-smoking policy, Goizueta usually refrained from smoking in Allen's presence.

Just two years out of Williams College in 1964, Allen had joined Allen & Co., an investment firm started by his father and uncle. Charles and Herbert Allen Sr. wanted to spin off their small investment banking operation into a separate company, and Herbert Allen Jr.

volunteered to run it, chipping in with a group of employees and relatives to put up the $1 million purchase price. By 1982, the younger Allen had parlayed the original capital into $35 million in net worth, mostly by investing in about 70 small, high-technology stocks. His original $2.5 million investment in Columbia was unusual both because of its large size, and because it was an established company. If he got what he expected to get from Coke, Allen would make more than $40 million for his firm.

BY THE TIME THE TWO SIDES MET AGAIN, AT COKE'S HEADQUARters on Sunday, January 17, 1982, everyone was packing heat. Coke's financial team under Sam Ayoub had run through all of Columbia's public filings, and felt certain they had a take on the business. Ayoub had overcome initial reservations about the movie business and concluded that Coke could improve Columbia's results by boosting film production and applying Coke's marketing savvy to the movie business.

Allen and Vincent faced off against Goizueta, Keough, and Ayoub, near the foot of the sweeping staircase that dominates the open-air, three-story executive suite at the Coke tower. Except for Goizueta, everyone was dressed casually, with open shirts and sweaters or suitcoats. But Goizueta had on his customary dark suit, and for this occasion, he sported an ascot around his neck.

"I'm a little confused here," Allen said, sizing up Goizueta. "You look like a movie director. I thought you were buying and we were selling."

The comment broke up Goizueta and broke the ice. But it did not make the dealmaking any less onerous for the Coca-Cola crowd. Price was not Goizueta's top concern. He was more concerned with getting Columbia before another bidder emerged. It was rumored that Time Inc. might try to buy the studio. Allen had not confided even with Vincent how much he planned to demand for Columbia, but everyone involved knew the number would be big. Even so, when Allen began the negotiation by asking $85 a share for his company, Goizueta nearly choked. At that price, Columbia would fetch $1 billion, far more than Goizueta ever would pay for the studio. "That's so far off it isn't funny," he said.

Goizueta, Keough, and Ayoub had taken part in more than $1 billion of Coca-Cola bottler transactions, but in those deals, the other side had little negotiating leverage over the company that supplied their main ingredient, Coca-Cola syrup, and in those deals, the three men knew the industry intimately. For the Columbia talks, Goizueta had tried to enforce discipline on his team at the outset. "If any one of us says no, it isn't going to happen," he told Keough and Ayoub.

Allen's huge asking price undercut Goizueta's attempt to keep the price low. In a flash, the Coke executives recognized that they were not in bottling land any more. If they wanted to do a deal, they would have to take a virtually blind leap. Goizueta recessed with Keough and Ayoub, then returned, with Ayoub carrying a series of bid envelopes in his briefcase. Vincent spotted them as Ayoub reached in to make Coke's first bid. "Skip that one, Sam, and go to the second one," he said. The envelope Ayoub opened offered $68 a share for Columbia.

After a perfunctory round of to-and-fro, Goizueta agreed to pay $75 a share for Columbia, or a price tag of $690 million in a combination of cash and Coca-Cola stock. To get the deal, Columbia also forced Goizueta to buy Outlet Co., an owner of television and radio stations, but let Coke out of that commitment when Outlet declared bankruptcy shortly after the deal was struck. For Allen and company, it was an astounding coup. Goizueta had agreed to pay nearly double Columbia's market price, and an eye-popping five times Columbia's book value—the richest price-to-book ratio for any entertainment deal in 1982—for one of Hollywood's weakest studios. Just nine years after buying into Columbia, Allen cleared $40 million, plus $7 million in investment banking fees he charged for arranging the deal, off an initial investment of just $2.5 million. Adding to the booty, he also netted a seat on The Coca-Cola Company board, effective that August.

FOR GOIZUETA, THERE WAS STILL A FINAL DETAIL TO TAKE CARE OF before the deal was complete in his mind. He and Ayoub hopped a Coke jet to southern Georgia to tell Woodruff. Goizueta knew Columbia would add substantially to Coke's debt load. Combined with the borrowing for the Coke-New York investment, it would bring Coke's total debt to $460 million by the end of 1982, or 16 percent of capital.

Woodruff had come to the point that, even if he was not quite comfortable seeing Coke take on debt, he understood that he could not do anything to stop it. When Goizueta laid out the deal to him, though,

Woodruff had another concern. If his company was changing, his influence must be falling, too. "What happens to me?" the enfeebled old man asked Goizueta.

Goizueta explained that he purposefully had structured the cash-and-stock deal so Woodruff would remain Coke's largest shareholder. "You're still The Boss, and instead of being the boss of The Coca-Cola Company, you're now the boss of Coca-Cola and Columbia," Goizueta explained.

Then he told Woodruff the most important reason he had come to Ichauway. The Columbia deal was such a far-out step, he knew, that he needed Woodruff's backing to ensure board approval. "Mr. Woodruff, we want you to come and attend the board meeting and approve this deal," he said.

When Goizueta announced the deal the next day, Coke's stock took a hit, losing 10 percent of its market value over the next few days. Analysts hammered Goizueta for overpaying for Columbia, and for surprising Wall Street. This angered Goizueta because he felt he had given everyone fair warning with his Mission Statement for the 1980s. Despite the bad press on the deal, Woodruff attended Coke's April board meeting and dutifully backed Goizueta. It was his last official act in the last board meeting ever attended by The Coca-Cola Company's legendary Boss.

THE FIRST FILM COLUMBIA RELEASED UNDER COKE'S TUTELAGE, the comic-book-inspired musical *Annie*, was a bust, and invited further catcalls from Wall Street. But Columbia's two holiday releases, *Tootsie* and *Ghandi*, both were critical and commercial hits. Goizueta was starting to enjoy the role of movie mogul. He built a screening room at Coke headquarters, where top executives and their spouses would gather on weekends to watch the latest releases.

Flush with the excitement of the deal, Goizueta and his colleagues went Hollywood, if only briefly. Keough subscribed to *Variety*, the movie industry newspaper, and was shocked when one of his first copies contained a front-page story proclaiming that Columbia Pictures had signed a huge, six-picture deal. Goizueta had promised Allen and Vincent that Coke would not meddle in the movie business, but the story still surprised Keough enough that he called Vincent. "What's this all about, Fay?" he asked.

"There's no truth to it at all," Vincent said. When no movie deal of any size emerged, Keough stopped reading the Hollywood papers.

Goizueta and Keough made a tradition out of traveling to Hollywood with their wives, Olguita and Mickie, for the Academy Awards. They stayed at the Bellaire Hotel, and lounged around the pool. During a lunch at the Bellaire while in Hollywood the first time, with *Gandhi* poised to clean up at the awards, the duo learned that Coke's stock had hit an all-time high of $50. "We're real movie moguls," Goizueta said, laughing.

By the end of Coke's first full year in the movie business, Goizueta had plenty of reason to grin. Vincent delivered to him a deal arranged before the buyout, a joint production agreement between Columbia, cable programmer Home Box Office, and the CBS television network. The resulting entity, Tri-Star Pictures, would help enable Columbia to produce movies off of its own balance sheet, with HBO and CBS footing a substantial share of the cost. By the end of 1983, Coke's first full year running the studio, Columbia posted a $90 million profit—50 percent higher than Goizueta had predicted after announcing the acquisition. Criticism of the Columbia deal by Wall Street and the press had always gotten under Goizueta's thin skin, and now he could not resist a moment of gloating. "The next three years are going to be the 'I told you so' years," Coke's CEO boasted. "Some of these critics are going to eat their words."

THERE IS LITTLE DOUBT THAT ONE OF THE FACTORS FUELING Goizueta's immense confidence was the remarkable success of the initiative launched just after he jumped into the Columbia deal: Diet Coke. A diet version of Coca-Cola had been a Goizueta dream since the mid-1970s, when the technical department was hard at work developing a product. Paul Austin's last-minute cancellation of the end project, especially coming at the end of the succession horse race, was perhaps the biggest setback at that point in Goizueta's career.

Diet Coke would not launch until the fall of 1982, eight months after Coke got into the movie business, but it was an active and central project on Goizueta's agenda from the moment he rose to the presidency on May 30, 1980. Three days after Goizueta's promotion, on June 2, a marketing manager named Sergio Zyman typed out a memo to Coke-USA chief Brian Dyson. Officially, it was a recap of the marketing group's work leading up to Austin's cancellation of the project. In reality, it was a manifesto for resuscitating Diet Coke.

Zyman identified three major objectives: capitalizing on the trademark with the first line extension of the Coca-Cola brand, improving bottler relationships with a burst of creative new products and marketing that would boost their bottom lines, and dominating Diet Pepsi in the diet cola segment. Because Pepsi already had Diet Pepsi on the market, there was no new product that it could introduce to counter the launch of Diet Coke. With the hype that would naturally follow Diet Coke's introduction, the new soft drink would grab huge market share. "This could be the silver bullet," Zyman wrote.

Hyperbolic, hyperaggresive statements were typical of Zyman. Born in Mexico, Zyman had joined Coke in the mid-1970s, after a stint with Pepsi-Cola. While at Pepsi, he had developed a reputation as a flamboyant marketer and sometimes abusive taskmaster, a quality that earned him the sobriquet "the Ayacola." He did not like the nickname, which of course meant he would never shake it. Zyman also developed a grudge match with Pepsi's Roger Enrico, who accused Zyman of underhanded political tactics while at Pepsi. When he first arrived at Coke, Zyman crossed swords with one of Coke's top marketing executives, Marvin Griffin, who refused to work with the abrasive young manager and persuaded his bosses to send Zyman to Harvard University for a six-week management training program. But as planning for a new diet Coca-Cola gained momentum, with Paul Austin's encouragement, in early 1980, Keough ordered Zyman to abandon Harvard and begin work on the Diet Coke campaign—a change of plans that earned the project its code name—Project Harvard.

Austin's abrupt cancellation of Project Harvard shocked and angered everyone involved with the project. However, with Goizueta, one of Diet Coke's chief backers, rising to the presidency, Zyman knew Diet Coke would again be a top priority. Wearing his ambition on the custom-tailored sleeve of his double-breasted, European-cut suitcoat, Zyman seized on Diet Coke as his opportunity to make an indelible mark at The Coca-Cola Company. This kind of drive and aggression appealed to Goizueta—especially since Zyman's pet project also was one of Goizueta's prizes.

Writing almost as if with Goizueta's own pen, Zyman warned that the Diet Coke push must succeed at all costs. "Perceived failure of our plans will have a disastrous effect on all our publics, including the bottler, the trade, and the investment community. The resulting feeling of frustration can be lethal in terms of its effects on our overall credibility," Zyman wrote in his memo to Dyson. He included in the memo a schedule for market research, development, and advertising that ended with a June 1, 1982, launch date. On August 16, 1980, just a few days after he was named chairman and chief executive of Coca-Cola, Goizueta greenlighted the Diet Coke project, with an original launch budget of $250 million just for research, and held Zyman to his original timetable.

Goizueta always felt Diet Coke would be an easy winner in the marketplace. He had overseen laboratory development of the product, and knew the innovative flavoring of the new soft drink would make Diet Coke's taste far superior to Coke's own Tab or any other diet drink. Results from research by consultants A.D. Little indicated great potential demand. The "Coke" trademark was so powerful that when Coca-Cola research director Roy Stout poured Tab into glasses and called it Diet Coke, consumers preferred the faux Diet Coke over the correctly labeled Tab by a 12 percentage-point margin.

Still, the launch of Diet Coke was fraught with potential pitfalls. There was the risk that Tab and Diet Coke would split the market between them, opening the way for Diet Pepsi to overtake Tab and become the top diet drink. Coke's lawyers objected to the legal risks of applying the Coke trademark to another product, a tired argument that had always seemed narrow and overly cautious to Goizueta. It was possible the bottlers might sue, claiming Coke's use of the name on an allied product violated exclusivity and pricing provisions in their contracts, but Goizueta believed the company had a strong legal defense. Besides, if the product got into the marketplace and proved profitable enough, the bottlers quickly would get out of the courthouse and fall in line, demanding Diet Coke in their markets. A group of bottlers did sue, but Coke ultimately beat them in court.

Of course there would be Woodruff to deal with, too. Unlike the company's lawyers, who were hired to do his bidding, Goizueta did not have the clout or the desire to order Woodruff around. His track record with the old man was perfect. Even on controversial decisions like adding debt or acquiring Columbia, the old man ultimately had come around. This one could be different. Goizueta knew Woodruff's instinctive reaction to the Diet Coke proposal would be to defend his cherished Coke trademark.

It was time to visit Tuxedo Road. Ushered into Woodruff's dining room, Goizueta laid out the case for Diet Coke, based on the unrelenting growth in demand for diet soft drinks. He decided to turn the trademark issue to his advantage, by gussying up Tab, claiming that the diet soft drink was growing so fast that it might one day eclipse Coke's flagship drink. "Mr. Woodruff, slowly but surely your company—The Coca-Cola Company—is becoming The Tab Company," Goizueta warned. In truth, Tab's market-share numbers had not grown since Diet Pepsi was introduced. Diet Pepsi's early strength, much of it at Tab's expense, hardly made Tab look like the juggernaut that Goizueta was describing. Fortunately for Goizueta, Woodruff did not follow the Nielsen numbers the way he once had, so he bought the argument. He urged Goizueta to push on with Diet Coke.

GOIZUETA WHIPPED HIS TROOPS INTO FURIOUS ACTIVITY. WITH HIS emphasis on fast action, it bothered him that the Diet Coke project had slipped behind Zyman's original schedule, meaning the new product would miss the key summer selling season. No further delay would be tolerated. Coke hired a package-design firm, which ultimately took six months and 150 tries before arriving at the red-on-white "Diet Coke" can used for the product launch. As a sign of his confidence in the new product, Goizueta brought Coke's New York bottler into the planning process, designating Charlie Millard's high-profile territory as the launch site.

On April 16, Goizueta headed a high-level planning meeting for the Diet Coke launch. "The three most important objectives," he said in opening the meeting, "are trademark, earnings, and international—not necessarily in that order." Everyone in the room knew that earnings, above all else, always topped Goizueta's list.

Ike Herbert warned about a Pepsi Challenge-style response from Pepsi. "You can kiss the book on it," he said. But Keough countered that the market research indicated that Diet Coke would beat Diet Pepsi, so a Challenge campaign was not an option for Pepsi. This discussion concerned Goizueta, and he ordered research director Roy Stout to conduct a nationwide extended home-use study on the new diet soft drink before the fall introduction. That was in addition to the theoretical tests Stout already was conducting, testing consumers' reaction to the concept of a new diet drink from Coca-Cola without letting them actually taste the product. The meeting ended with a review of the graphics for the Diet Coke can, with all agreeing that the design still was not ready.

Even though the testing for Diet Coke would be one of the most extensive research studies ever conducted by the company, Goizueta would later tell reporters that he was so confident in the drink that he launched it with no test marketing at all. "Market testing is to see whether you are going to succeed or fail. But as far as I was concerned, failure was just not an option with Diet Coke," he would brag to *The New York Times*. Technically, it was true that Coke had not conducted an official study in a geographic area that would serve as a proxy for nationwide results. But given the huge volume of market research conducted under Roy Stout's direction, it was preposterous and misleading to leave an impression that Diet Coke was launched on blind faith.

There certainly was no test marketing needed in New York, where Charlie Millard's troops had effectively primed the market for the Diet Coke launch, leaking information to the press and talking up the new product among Coke-New York's retailers. Advance buzz about Coke's new diet drink was so pervasive that by the time the product actually launched in New York in August 1982, it already had a name recognition on those streets of around 80 percent, without a dollar spent on advertising. The launch celebration before 6,000 people, with the Radio City Music Hall Rockettes literally kicking off the new product, got extensive media coverage. A $150,000 party followed at a pier Coke rented on the Hudson River. Goizueta missed all the excitement, though. He stayed in Atlanta, letting Coke-USA chief Dyson and Keough debut the new product.

In keeping with Goizueta's grand ambitions for Diet Coke, Zyman had turned away from Coke's usual ad agency, McCann-Erickson, and instead hired another arm of the Interpublic Group, SSC&B. He directed the agency to develop ads emphasizing taste, rather than calories, with a theme "Just for the Taste of It." Men were a key target, even though they traditionally were not diet soda drinkers and barely touched Tab. The best of SSC&B's ads also was the most expensive—at $1.5 million for the 30-second spot—making it one of the costliest ever for the soft-drink giant. "Premier" featured celebrities including

Joe Namath, Sally Kellerman, Bob Hope, and Carol Channing arriving in limousines, as if to the premiere of a movie. The images then cut inside Radio City Music Hall, with the Rockettes kicking their tribute to Diet Coke. Herbert thought it was too flashy and overwhelmed the product itself. But the movie theme caught Goizueta at the height of his rapture with Hollywood. The chairman loved it.

He also loved the results. By the end of 1983, Diet Coke was the best-selling diet drink in the United States, and by the next year had climbed to number three in the entire soft-drink market, topping Philip Morris' popular "uncola" drink 7-Up. To make certain that happened, Goizueta had approved launching Diet Coke with one of the most costly advertising expenditures in soft-drink history, a first-year marketing budget of $100 million.

To New York bottler Millard, the spending was out of control, motivated more by the desire of Goizueta and his team to assure themselves Diet Coke would not fail than by the necessity of the competitive marketplace. "It was cover-their-ass insurance," Millard says. The overspending had a bottom-line downside to Millard and the other bottlers: Their contracts required them to nearly match Coke's spending in their local markets, with a 55 percent to 44 percent split between Atlanta and the bottlers. But when Millard complained, Keough defended the spending program and refused to budge.

At Coke's North Avenue tower, the only aftertaste of failure from the Diet Coke launch was the crushing blow it dealt to Coke's venerable diet drink in the hot pink can. The realities of the soft-drink business caught up with Coke's original Tab. Coke's bottlers were willing to put only one diet drink on their canning lines and carry only one on their trucks. Retailers were wary of devoting too much shelf space to two Coca-Cola products in the diet category. And Coke quit supporting Tab with advertising dollars. The company's first diet soft drink was left to die—contrary to what Stout's research had predicted.

To the objective observer, the failure of Stout's research to anticipate Tab's virtual demise should have set off alarm bells. After all, the forecast that he produced—that Tab would not be cannibalized by Diet Coke—happened to fit the outcome Goizueta had needed to help persuade Woodruff and Coke's board that the new diet soft drink was virtually without risk. A scientist by training, Goizueta liked to think of himself as an objective seeker of facts who would never let ambition get in the way of sound decision making. "Keep the scientist's candor," was one of his mottos. In other words, don't screw up good research by skewing it to reach preordained results. But somewhere along the way, the research by Stout and others had failed to identify the virtual death knell that Diet Coke would deal to Tab. It should have been a warning for the next time Goizueta considered a chancy new product launch. But quite clearly, it was not.

EVEN AS THE ROCKETTES WERE KICKING AWAY ON BEHALF OF DIET Coke, Goizueta was making his last break with the Austin era by unloading Coke's wine business after a frustrating three years of trying to make it work. Goizueta's solution to The Wine Spectrum's profit troubles was pure Coke: boost production and profits would surely follow. By 1992, he had nearly tripled production, conducted a costly and unsuccessful coupon campaign, and spent $34 million updating a winery, then the largest-ever Coke investment in a production facility. But Goizueta soon learned that the faster he grew the business, the less he earned, in part because a boost in wine production did not produce higher revenues for several years because wine needs to age.

When a Wine Spectrum executive told the board that the best Coke could hope for from wine was a 12 percent return on capital, Goizueta promptly decided it was time to get out. For Goizueta, it was a simple calculation based on the principle of economic value added. At its current 3 percent return, The Wine Spectrum was not covering Coke's cost of capital. And even its best-case scenario would not bring it close to the 20 percent return Goizueta expected from all business lines. Goizueta was thrilled when the Canadian distillery Joseph E. Seagram & Sons approached him and bought the company for $210 million in August 1983, enabling him to save face by pocketing a tiny profit.

With the sale of The Wine Spectrum, Goizueta had put most of the major planks of the Mission Statement into place. He had spent more than $2 billion shoring up Coke's domestic bottlers and set precedent with the investment in the Philippines. He had bought Columbia and launched Diet Coke. He had unloaded operations that did not add economic value to Coke's business. He was slowly lowering dividend increases, en route to the lowest jump in the company's history, a hike of only two cents per share in 1984.

He was starting to set some financial records, too. Like a proud son, he frequently went out of his way to make certain that Woodruff was made aware of every new success. While on a business trip to Tokyo, Goizueta was pleased to see Coke's stock, which had dropped 25 percent in value during Austin's last two years, set a new record. He cabled Woodruff: "Your leadership from Tuxedo Road paying handsome dividends as our stock price has reached a new high." Since he became chairman, the company's stock had become one of the market's fastest growing issues. He believed net income, which topped $500 million for the first time in 1983, would reach $1 billion by 1990. Success at the top of The Coca-Cola Company had fed Goizueta's ego and seemed to give him a sense of invincibility. "I didn't think it would be so much fun," he told a reporter late in 1984.

On the occasion of Woodruff's ninety-fifth birthday in December 1984, Goizueta sent a note boasting that Coke's share of supermarket sales was growing faster than Pepsi's. The note neglected to make the more important point that "the competitor" still held the overall lead. It was a blemish Goizueta felt certain he could erase. With most everything, even the movie business, moving in his favor, Pepsi-Cola's lead over Coke in supermarkets grew more irksome with each passing day. It was time to do something dramatic. In the late 1970s, Goizueta had launched research into a new formula for the world's most successful soft drink, but Paul Austin had shelved his work. Brimming with confidence, Goizueta was convinced it was time to go back to Coke's laboratory, and launch a new taste attack on Pepsi Cola. In this, as in so much else associated with the launch of New Coke, he was gravely mistaken.

5

"Give Me Back My Coke!"

It was January 2, 1985, and finally the years of planning had come into place. Over the Christmas holidays, Roberto Goizueta assembled the key decision makers, and forced a final call on the question that had kicked around The Coca-Cola Company for years: Should we change the formula?

There was not one good reason to do it. From Roberto Goizueta's perspective, there were many. On the heels of the immensely successful Pepsi Challenge, PepsiCo had signed up the hugely popular singer Michael Jackson and was trouncing Coca-Cola by creating an image of itself as youthful, energetic, and sophisticated. Coca-Cola had lost its lead in supermarket sales in the 1970s, and the gap with Pepsi-Cola was widening. If the trend continued, Pepsi might take the overall sales lead by convincing big fountain customers like McDonald's that consumers would welcome a switch at their stores. Perhaps most importantly, Goizueta had a new formula. He had carefully sponsored Coke's research into a flavor that could beat Pepsi since his days overseeing Coke's technical department, and at last, there was a flavor that beat Pepsi in blind taste tests. Let people know they were drinking a product from Coca-Cola, and the positive results went almost off the charts.

It seemed Roy Stout's market research team had studied the question in almost every conceivable way, and the results were an emphatic "Yes." The marketing studies made a strong case for a launch.

110

Over the Christmas holidays, the team of Don Keough, Brian Dyson, Ike Herbert, and Roberto Goizueta met in the executive suite and agreed unanimously. The time was right to launch a new formula for Coca-Cola. They made an equally important second decision: Pull the original formula off the market. Two sugared versions of Coke would compete with each other, and could hand Pepsi-Cola the overall lead. Besides, the new Coke was such a winner that no one would want the old Coca-Cola in any case.

Self-doubt was not a big part of Goizueta's makeup. As long as he could control the important contingencies, he was among the most confident people on earth. But as the launch of a new Coca-Cola dawned, Goizueta could see his ability to control events diminish as the new flavor—already dubbed "New Coke" inside Coca-Cola—began shifting to the public arena. And for a rare moment, a bit of doubt must have crept into Goizueta's thinking.

On January 2, Goizueta summoned Harold Burson to his office, and made the well-known public relations executive the first person outside of Fortress Coke to know the dramatic news: Goizueta would soon introduce a new formula for Coca-Cola, taking the old recipe off the shelves. Obviously, this called for a major public relations offensive—a press campaign, presentations to Wall Street analysts, announcements to bottlers, and wooing of consumers. The immediate news would get global publicity, and Goizueta wanted to follow that with bottlers' meetings and product rollouts around the world. Goizueta turned to his personal public relations counsel, the chairman of the Burson-Marstellar agency, to guard against any major foul ups.

Then came the question. "Harold, what is my Achilles' heel?" Goizueta asked.

Burson thought hard. Typically, Goizueta had covered the bases in his strategic planning. With his background as a chemist, Goizueta certainly had the technical basis to declare that the new formula was better. Thorough as ever, Goizueta had raised all the key questions, and answered them as best he could. But the best-laid p.r. campaigns often crash for want of anticipating just one key question, and Burson feared that Coke's research efforts had failed to identify that question. "Your greatest vulnerability is in your research," he said.

"What do you mean?" Goizueta responded.

"There's just no way to know whether the public will really accept this," Burson said.

Goizueta thought he knew. Director of research Roy Stout had re-fined a trial test in one market. Goizueta knew he could not afford an error and ordered Stout to roll out the trial to twenty separate markets. In every taste test, purchase study, and focus group, whether in blind tests or labeled, Coke's new formula trounced Pepsi's, and Coke's 99-year-old flavor wound up last. Stout's behavior studies showed peo-ple would buy New Coke, and The Coca-Cola Company could re-capture from Pepsi its unchallenged position atop every category of soft-drink sales.

Burson was seasoned enough to know how consistently numbers lie. The tests sometimes are not set up well, or there is a subconscious bias that sneaks into the phrasing of the questions. The focus groups discern who's sponsoring the research and slant their answers. "What happens if the methodology wasn't good? If he asked the wrong question?" Bur-son asked. "Hire another firm," he advised. "Verify the results."

Goizueta did just that. And the new firm's results came back just as he expected. In head-to-head taste tests, consumers chose the New Coke 53 percent of the time, and picked Pepsi only 47 percent of the time. It was a slightly smaller win than Stout's research had shown, but still a big boost for Coke. For the $46 billion soft-drink market, a six-point difference in market share would be worth $760 million in retail sales, just from the taste alone. Coke's crack marketing effort would only multiply the impact.

The results satisfied Goizueta. The plans for the New Coke launch continued undeterred. If anything, the double check that Burson sug-gested had only increased Goizueta's confidence.

There was just one problem. Burson's misgivings were on target. He had not been able to pinpoint precisely what the oversight was, but a key query had never been posed. As Burson, Goizueta, and the world would soon learn, they had neglected to ask loyal Coke drinkers, "How would you feel if we took your Coke away?" Nowhere in any of Stout's data was there any information forecasting a violent consumer reac-tion if Coke kidnapped the nation's favorite soft drink. It was a glaring oversight, one that changed the history of Coca-Cola, and led to the biggest crisis of Roberto Goizueta's career.

The key question was not in Stout's research, but that does not mean it had never been asked. There was one person at Coke who knew very early just how much damage that question could do: marketing guru Sergio Zyman. More than three years before the launch, a focus group had reacted with verbal violence when Zyman asked how they would feel if The Coca-Cola Company reformulated Coke and pulled the original formula from the shelves. The warning apparently never got to Goizueta, but even if it had, there was plenty of promising research to steamroll the response of a few isolated focus groups. In his whipped-up enthusiasm for the launch of New Coke, Goizueta was determined to take what he would later describe as "the surest step we've ever made."

THE MOVE TO NEW COKE WOULD BE MORE COMPLEX, AND MORE risky, than anything Goizueta had ever done. Woodruff had talked about the need to foresee events "over the next hill," and New Coke was a "just-over-the-next-hill" objective—to use Woodruff's apt phrase—that Goizueta pursued quietly and purposefully from the day he became chairman. At the Palm Springs conference, Goizueta had posted notice, declaring he would consider changing the formula if he thought it would help the company. A little-known financial executive named M. Douglas Ivester was dumbstruck. "They're going to change the formula," he later recalled thinking to himself.

Goizueta the chemist-cum-CEO turned naturally to his laboratories to help Coke regain its domination of Pepsi-Cola in every market segment. All he needed was a new recipe, and he would be ready to go. The laboratory did not disappoint. Just weeks after the Palm Springs meeting, Maurizio Gianturco of the research lab appeared in Goizueta's office with promising news. In lab work conducted alongside the search for Coke's new diet soft drink, Coke's chemists had made a remarkable find. It was a new flavor combination that could be used in The Coca-Cola Company's sugared soda, in other words, in Coca-Cola itself.

A newly created blend of essential oils had a unique "flavor complex," Gianturco told Goizueta, "that would have wider acceptance or wider preference than Coca-Cola now has."

This was more than just a lab report. As a veteran of an abortive Project David effort under Paul Austin, Gianturco knew the import of what he was saying. David was so named because it was the fourth sweetest of five flavors under study at the time—Alpha, Beta, Charlie, David, and Edward. It was sweeter than Pepsi, and had some promise, but Austin had killed it before any significant research was done. The new formula had the sweetness profile of David, but the flavor complex gave it a unique taste that Gianturco expected to match up well against Pepsi. He wanted to pursue this new flavor, and fast. "Just go ahead and proceed," Goizueta ordered him.

At last, Goizueta had before him the goal that Austin could never quite reach. He was confident his technical people could create a new Coca-Cola that would beat Pepsi-Cola in taste tests. He would need a marketing plan ready when the new flavor was ready to pour. But there was a major hitch. With the Pepsi Challenge in full swing, a leak from anywhere that The Coca-Cola Company was considering a new formula for Coke would have disastrous consequences in the marketplace. It would cost Coca-Cola the element of surprise and might prematurely kill the project.

Running traditional market research was too risky. But moving ahead with no data about consumer response would be foolhardy. Goizueta needed some way to get a sense of how consumers might react before he pushed ahead to mount a full-scale research and launch effort. Fortunately, there was a tool at hand. Zyman, in the midst of final plans for the Diet Coke launch in 1981, also was developing a new advertising campaign for the flagship brand. Together with John Bergin, the head of Coke's advertising for the McCann-Erickson advertising agency, Zyman was criss-crossing the country conducting focus-group studies of a proposed new advertising slogan, "Coke Is It."

At Goizueta's request, Zyman asked the moderator of each focus group to pose a hypothetical question that would aid Coke's research. Zyman meticulously laid out the instructions. "I want you to say, 'The last question on the docket today will be a fake story—that The Coca-Cola Company is about to launch a brand new cola,'" Zyman told the moderators of at least four focus-group sessions in different parts of the country. "As a matter of fact, this new product is already on the shelves in Denver, Colorado. The product is similar to Coca-Cola, and as a matter of fact, it has replaced Coca-Cola. Denver is madly in love with the product. We'd like to get a sense of how you'd react."

The groups went berserk. They responded with passion and abuse that Bergin and Zyman had never seen in their decades of work in marketing. "What do you mean you're taking away my fucking Coca-Cola?" one participant raged. Others were less polite. When the moderators followed up by asking about the possible removal of other products, the focus groups stayed mad. "We don't give a shit about Budweiser or Hershey, but you can't take Coke away," one group member said.

Both the question and the responses shocked Bergin. The question brought to mind a conversation he once had with Goizueta while flying from New York to Atlanta at the height of the Pepsi Challenge in the late 1970s. "I have actually got a formula now for Coca-Cola that does not have one ingredient in it that was in the original formula," Goizueta boasted. At the time, it seemed to Bergin an academic point, an instance of Goizueta quietly touting Coke's research labs. At the time at least, it did not seem to be a statement of intent that Goizueta might actually do something with his new recipe.

When Zyman posed the hypothetical question to the focus groups, Bergin perceived that the new formula was very much alive in Goizueta's mind. Goizueta needed to know what Bergin had just witnessed. Coke was facing a disaster if he moved ahead with a new formula and took the original flavor off the shelves. Flying back to Atlanta on Coke's Gulfstream III, Bergin said to Zyman, "I don't know what you're up to, but you saw the same thing I saw today. You've got to go back and make sure that Roberto knows and everybody knows what those people said."

Zyman brushed off Bergin's demand and quickly changed the subject. On the verge of the supremely successful Diet Coke launch, the confident and ambitious Zyman was not easily dissuaded from a challenge. And like most of the people involved at the start of the New Coke launch, Zyman had his eyes on another major career feat—perhaps the biggest of his tenure. Everyone at the top levels of Coca-Cola knew Goizueta's enchantment with the new formula, and his frustration with Coca-Cola's market share. Goizueta was not going to unload this project because of a few focus groups. Besides, there was no rush to raise caution flags now. If people hated the idea of a New Coke as much as these focus groups indicated, it would show up in the research after Goizueta greenlighted a more formal market study.

There was plenty of data already in hand to indicate success for a New Coke. In a 1980 test, Stout had shipped two cases of cola—one a reformulated Coke, the other Pepsi-Cola—to two hundred families and interviewed them after they drank all of the product. Half the Coke cases were labeled as New, and half with Coke's traditional label.

Stout found that consumers actually liked the idea of a New Coke. The test families preferred Pepsi to the reformulated Coke labeled as "regular," but they chose the bottles labeled "New Coke" over Pepsi. However, Stout never asked the families how they would respond if Coke's original formula were pulled from the shelves.

IT WAS IMPORTANT THAT ZYMAN NOT DERAIL THE NEW-FORMULA search if he wanted to please his boss, Coke-USA president Brian Dyson. The manor-born Argentinean's motto was "Ready, Fire, Aim," and by 1982 he had sworn he would see Coke reflavor its flagship brand. After he took the Coke-USA job in 1978, following years in Coke's South American operation, Dyson grew almost obsessed with the task of retaking the lead in supermarket sales from Pepsi. Roy Stout's market research indicated that one factor—taste—was uniquely the cause of Coke's market malaise. The trends were clear. Unless Coke acted, Pepsi would overtake Coke in all categories, not just supermarkets. "I'm not going to sit on my ass and watch that," Dyson swore. "To do nothing means that I cannot touch my product even though I know I can make a better product. Eventually, something that doesn't change in the face of change will whither and die. That's the law of nature."

Dyson's emphasis on action and results was music to Goizueta. Despite his courtly manner, Goizueta could be hypercompetitive. He pointedly never drank Pepsi-Cola, not even to taste it, and he preferred to dismissively refer to Pepsi in public as "our competitor" rather than let the name of his rival cross his lips. Like Dyson, he saw the possibility of New Coke as an irresistible attraction, a way to reverse the mismanagement of the 1970s in one blow, to beat Pepsi good. Goizueta liked to use a Spanish aphorism to explain the dichotomy: "Just because a man is courteous, don't think he isn't brave." He surrounded himself with people who wore their aggression far more obviously than he. Don Keough did. In Zyman and Dyson, the courteous part was sometimes optional.

Keough had recruited Dyson to Atlanta in 1978 to head Coke-USA and doggedly persuade reluctant bottlers to sign the new amended contract. Dyson impressed Keough with his persistence, and his flair for negotiating a deal. Some bottlers found Dyson abrasive or arrogant, but Keough learned that he got results. He hosted "The Great Get Together" bottlers' convention in San Francisco in

1978, the first all-bottlers meeting in years, launching the effort to reunify the troops after the bruising battle over Coke's demand to force a new pricing formula onto its bottlers. Dyson's message at the meeting: Time to shake up the market.

Dyson set out to arouse the competitive instinct in the sometimes sleepwalking Coke system with gonzo stunts for bottlers, merchandisers, and sales staff. A triathlete and notorious night creature, he had a flair for the dramatic. Dyson hired retired football star "Mean" Joe Greene, who had starred in a famous commercial launching the "Have a Coke and a Smile!" campaign in 1978, to sledgehammer Pepsi vending machines at bottler meetings. At Pepsi Challenge launch sites, he ordered Coke trucks to encircle the taste booths. He created a video in which a tank rumbled up a hill, spied a Pepsi vending machine, and blew it into dust. Goizueta loved it.

FOR A PROVOCATEUR LIKE DYSON AND A WARRIOR LIKE GOIZUETA, it was easier to talk about changing Coke's taste than trying to fix the other problems plaguing Coke's system and the soft-drink industry in the early 1980s. Despite Goizueta's efforts to "refranchise" the Coke system by brokering the purchase and sale of struggling bottlers, much of the system still was in bad shape. For many bottlers, the new contract giving Coke more control over syrup pricing would hasten their demise. A proliferation of new products, both from competitors and from Coca-Cola itself, strained bottlers by introducing new competition, complicating the bottling and distribution process, and adding to marketing costs. Coke had quadrupled its advertising outlays since the Pepsi Challenge started, and bottlers were contractually obligated to chip in their share. Despite the outlays, though, Coke's market share in all sales channels was still declining.

Some analysts even thought Coke's key customer base was aging as new-age products like bottled teas and juice drinks debuted. *Business Week* magazine ran a cover story about the "graying" of the cola market, and many experts thought the slow growth of the early 1980s was the vanguard of a long-term decline. Goizueta never bought any of it, but everything would look a lot better if he could boost Coke's market-share figures. He would not tolerate the flagship product of The Coca-Cola Company placing second in any category for an indefinite period of time.

Partly because of his training as a chemist, numbers told Goizueta stories, and the research figures that Dyson and Stout placed before him persuaded him that he could solve Coke's market woes by creating a new flavor. Not everyone saw the new formula as the solution to Coke's troubles. As the top Coke man closest to the bottlers, Don Keough felt the impact of the declining fundamentals as much as anyone. But when it came time for him to jump on the New Coke bandwagon, Keough's first instinct was to put on the brakes.

Keough rebuked Dyson and Stout when they first asked for support in their campaign for funds to continue researching a possible new formula. It sounded like insanity, Keough said, almost as bad as changing the American flag. But Goizueta seemed intent on marrying his background in the technical department with his growing belief in his own marketing prowess, and the chief executive seemed convinced that taste was the key issue. Keough fell silent and ultimately backed the switch.

In September 1983, Goizueta at last gave orders to "explore the possibility of a reformulation." His instructions were clear. He wanted Gianturco's chemists to renew efforts in the labs, and just as importantly, Dyson and Stout needed to step up development of a marketing program for a launch. It was time for Zyman to indulge his flair for the cloak and dagger and open a top-secret office on the twenty-fifth floor of the Coca-Cola tower. There he would work without a secretary, shredding virtually everything that came out of his computer printer. And at last, Zyman could anoint the search for a New Coke with its first of several code names: Zeus, Tampa, and Eton among them. At least one of the nicknames, Tampa, was created specifically to be leaked as a diversion, to give competitors the impression that Coke might be considering a new orange-flavored soft drink.

Stout conducted a battery of tests. Results were mixed. But they tended to show that, based on taste alone, a new formula carrying the Coca-Cola brand name could woo a majority of committed Pepsi drinkers. It would alienate only about 5 percent of Coke's most diehard customers. Other tests showed a disturbing trend. While a strong majority of focus group respondents declared that Coke was their favorite drink, they were far more hesitant to say which product they actually drank. Many would not declare, and a number drank Pepsi. It peeved Goizueta to hear the results. "Coca-Cola is part of the landscape," he said. "People like to look at it, but they don't drink it."

GOIZUETA GREW RESTLESS WAITING FOR THE LABS TO PRODUCE A best formula. At one point, he told advertising man Bergin he was tempted to go retro. "I would love to get back to World War II Coca-Cola," Goizueta declared. The war-time Coke had a higher caffeine content and cheaper ingredients. Both could be advantageous, Goizueta explained.

"Why don't you do it?" Bergin asked.

"The thought that 'Here's World War II Coca-Cola' would be a terrible slogan," Goizueta said, and never mentioned the idea again.

In early September 1984, Gianturco at last told Goizueta his chemists had found a new product that would be the winner. Stout was skeptical at first, but when consumer tests came in, he converted overnight. In blind tests, which the original formula lost by as many as 18 percentage points, the new formula beat Pepsi by six to eight points, a huge swing. Among Pepsi loyalists, who typically favored Pepsi 70 percent of the time in blind tests, the new formula scored 50/50. On September 11, Goizueta told Gianturco that he was declaring the newest concentrate the winner, and personally celebrated with the twenty-six technical staffers who had done the lab work.

Now it was time to decide what to do with the new formula. Even though Goizueta went through the motions of consulting with his top officers over the next few weeks, he knew exactly what he wanted to do. In early October, after chief financial officer Sam Ayoub told Goizueta he would retire at year's end, Goizueta called his assistant Doug Ivester to his office. "I've got two things to tell you," Goizueta said. "One, we're making you chief financial officer. Two, we're changing the formula."

It was the first time Goizueta had stated his plans so flatly to someone not directly involved in the research and marketing of the product. Ivester thanked Goizueta for the honor of his new title. But through his mind, one thought was racing: "Great, I've just become chief financial officer of the *Titanic*."

Goizueta led a roving, almost continuous discussion over the next few weeks about the strategy for launching a new formula. The imponderables mounted: Whether to launch at all? Launch as a line extension, or replace the original formula? Perhaps launch without an announcement, and see if people noticed? Dyson and Zyman pushed for a fast launch of the new taste, and Dyson urged Goizueta to place only one Coca-Cola on the market—New Coke—even though the bottling system could handle both formulas if necessary. Keough, who remained somewhat skeptical, insisted that the best product in the world should be called Coca-Cola. There was no sense launching a new product if it was not the world's best. If it was unanimous that the new product was the best, there was no point having a second-best Coke on the market.

For Goizueta, the issue was simple. "I don't want a product that can beat Coca-Cola in blind taste tests," he said. Clearly, the new formula could do that. "And I don't want people comparing Coca-Cola" to another product from The Coca-Cola Company. That would be a self-defeating formula. By the time Goizueta, Keough, Herbert, and Dyson met over the Christmas holidays to give the new formula a final vote, it was almost a formality. The vote was unanimous, and New Coke was on its way to the market.

GOIZUETA FLEW TO ICHAUWAY PLANTATION THE NEXT DAY TO SELL Woodruff on the plan. With prodding, the Boss had approved, adding debt to the balance sheet, launching Diet Coke, even buying Columbia Pictures. But this was different. This was the formula Asa Candler had bought from Doc Pemberton, the one Woodruff's father seized when he bought The Coca-Cola Company, the one Woodruff had built into a global symbol of America.

Woodruff had resisted changing the formula in the past, but Goizueta felt this time might be different. He had worked on The Boss for more than a year, carefully and deliberately explaining the problems and opportunities his company faced, the success of the Pepsi Challenge, the public's yen for sweeter drinks, and the promise of the new formula. Goizueta met privately with Woodruff, with not even his ever-present assistant Joe Jones in the room. Hard of hearing and barely able to speak, Woodruff indicated a need to see one of his scrapbooks. Goizueta delivered it to him, and Woodruff worked his way slowly through the pages until he found what he was looking for.

It was a quotation Goizueta had seen before, one of Woodruff's favorite bits of Coca-Cola memorabilia. It was a browned and dog-eared copy of an article by William Allen White, editor of the *Emporia*

Gazette in Emporia, Kansas. Over the years White had stood firmly against patent-medicine quacks who had tried to influence his editorial positions and against temperance activists who in the late 1920s wanted to ban Coke as an addictive drink driving men to ruin. "Coca-Cola," White wrote after his seventieth birthday in 1938, "is . . . a sublimated essence of all that America stands for, a decent thing honestly made, universally distributed, conscientiously improved with the years." Woodruff's fingers lingered on the last phrase: "Conscientiously improved with the years." Goizueta had his answer, and the top-secret undertaking had a new nickname: Project Kansas.

THE DECISION MADE, IT WAS TIME TO GET THE PRODUCT TO MARKET. To be successful, New Coke would need to be on store shelves during the hot summer season, when sales and marketing outlays jumped and consumer sampling of new soft-drink products peaked. Plans already were underway for the huge centennial celebration of the invention of Coca-Cola in 1886, and Dyson insisted that the new product needed time to establish itself before the company started pushing a nostalgia theme in its advertising and communications with bottlers.

They wasted no time. On January 4, the bunker opened. It was a cramped, cement-floored room at 750 Third Avenue in New York City, adjacent to McCann's high-rise office building at 485 Lexington Avenue. Its most distinguishing characteristic: A shredder Zyman placed at the door, to destroy any handwritten note, memorandum, or other record of the top-secret advertising plans that a McCann-Erickson team developed under Zyman's very close supervision. At Zyman's request, McCann furtively assembled six high-level agency executives to work on advertising for the new formula. They had no secretaries, no creative staff to execute their ideas. To keep secrecy, Zyman demanded that the McCann executives work their regular hours, leave the office, then secretly design the advertising campaign for New Coke in the bunker. Zyman opened a second bunker in London, where production of commercials about a new formula for Coke would draw less attention than in the United States.

Although Zyman technically was outranked by Ike Herbert, The Coca-Cola Company's executive vice president of corporate marketing, it was clear to everyone in the bunker that Goizueta wanted this to be Zyman's show. "I'm here representing Sergio Zyman. I'm going to be your account representative, but Sergio is the guy," Herbert said during the first meeting. Although Herbert's instincts for grass-roots marketing were the best of anyone at Coke except perhaps Keough, Herbert deferred to Zyman's decisions throughout the nearly four months of work in the bunker.

Launching a new formula was tough under any circumstances. But Zyman made the bunker team's task even more complex by placing an ill-chosen campaign on the air in late 1984, even as the drive for New Coke was gaining momentum. Using Coke spokesman Bill Cosby, the ads attacked Pepsi-Cola for its sweetness. "Gooey," Cosby called it, rubberfacing an icky frown. The ad rolled out originally only in Pepsi strongholds, but bottlers nationwide demanded it. They, of course, had no way of knowing Coke was about to launch a new, sweeter Coca-Cola. Zyman did, and his decision to approve the "gooey" campaign remains baffling.

A few days after the bunker opened, Zyman with theatrical flair unveiled eight to ten aluminum cans. "This is your New Coca-Cola," he said. The bunker team poured the cola into paper cups, sniffed it, rolled it around in the cups, then poured it into their mouths. "They were not impressed," says John Bergin, then president of McCann-USA. "It's much more like Pepsi," Bergin told Zyman. "But Pepsi has a lot more spark to it. Pepsi's got a lot more carbonation."

The New Coke's poor taste test in the bunker was a bad sign. It is difficult for any advertising person to create a great campaign for a product they do not believe in. But the assignment got still tougher. Ever-sensitive about exposing themselves to counterattacks from Pepsi, Goizueta and his brain trust narrowly limited what the McCann people could and could not say in their ads for New Coke. Goizueta wanted no reason-why explanations of the new product, or comparisons with the old one. After all, Zyman said, shocking the bunker group, there would not be any "old Coke" on the shelves to compare with the new product. Coke was pulling the original formula off the market. "There will be no ad copy. Just, 'Here it is,'" Zyman declared.

Goizueta gradually enlarged the circle of people who needed to know about New Coke as the mid-April launch target approached. He allowed Keough and Dyson to inform key bottlers, including New York's Charlie Millard, who had sparked the Diet Coke kickoff. Coke farmed out work on a new can and new packaging. And one more time, Goizueta and his key team revisited the issue of withdrawing the original formula, but decided to stay the course. One key reason: They were convinced big fountain customers would never pour the original formula once the new formula was out. That rejection could doom old Coke to failure, and Goizueta could not stomach seeing the market reject the taste on which his company was built.

The February launch of a new product, Cherry Coke, provided cover in case of press or trade calls about the word "new" floating through the Coca-Cola system. Even before its launch, Cherry Coke had performed another unusual service by providing Coke an entrée into a relationship with a well-known investor by the name of Warren Buffett. During the Cherry Coke trial in the fall of 1984, Keough read a profile of Buffett in which the "Oracle of Omaha" was depicted drinking Pepsi-Cola, "preferably with a touch of cherry syrup in it." The next day, Keough sent a trial case of Cherry Coke and suggested Buffett switch brands. Buffett did, and in his own homespun style declared Cherry Coke the official soft drink of the annual meeting at Berkshire Hathaway, the insurance company Buffett used as his investment vehicle. Only three years later would Goizueta, Keough, and the rest of the world learn that Buffett had followed his palate and put his billion-dollar pocketbook behind an investment position in Coke.

NOBODY QUITE KNEW WHAT TO CALL COKE'S NEW CONCOCTION. Herbert had told the McCann-Erickson bunker team not even to experiment with the word "new" on the product. It was not an option. Goizueta and Keough wanted a simple redesign of the Coca-Cola can, but would not stamp "new" on the packaging or allow its use in the advertisements. Goizueta looked at the new formula as an improvement on a brand that The Coca-Cola Company had built for nearly a century, and did not want a name change to signal to consumers that Coke was throwing that investment away. Dyson and the handful of bottlers who had been brought into the process protested bitterly. Dyson in particular felt strongly that the product would move better if it was labeled as "new." The name would be a signal that the Coca-Cola that had lost in taste tests was no longer on the shelves, that Coke had replaced it with a flavor that beat Pepsi-Cola. The focus group studies showed that "new" made the fastest impact on consumers. Goizueta relented. "I caved in," he admitted later.

Nerves wore thin in the bunker. A combination of Zyman's overbearing manner and the use of senior advertising executives as little more than copywriters made a bad mix. Worse still, the client's demands were so constraining that the creative people could not come up with ideas that anyone truly liked. McCann's Bergin stopped working with Zyman, forcing Herbert to split the group into two teams. Zyman eventually decamped to London, where he oversaw the production of twenty-seven spots in three days. He personally took charge of much of the creative work on the ads, writing and editing on the fly. There were a number of Cosby spots and a musical theme that combined "Coke Is It!" with "Can't Beat the Real Thing"—evolutionary changes for a formula switch that clearly was a revolutionary event. A separate McCann group was assigned the task of thinking like Pepsi, anticipating the competitor's response, to help Goizueta and his team prepare for the counterattack.

Goizueta called a meeting in a conference room at the top of the Coca-Cola tower on April 1, 1985, to make the final decision on the launch. It was still possible, though hardly likely, to cancel the whole enterprise. Paul Austin certainly had done so, with both a new Coke and a diet Coke, but a change of heart was not in Goizueta's character. In a meeting that Keough would later describe as "tedious," Dyson laid out the factual case for a new formula, based largely on Roy Stout's research covering nearly 200,000 customers and costing $4 million. To keep the switch secret, Dyson would not inform all of Coke's bottlers until a day before the public announcement, with an assist from Stout. Zyman described the marketing plan, $10 million advertising budget, and possible Pepsi responses. He outlined possible problems: the new formula not meeting consumer expectations and bottlers getting edgy as a result. Consumer complaints were not expected, but any that did occur would taper off by mid-May, Zyman predicted. The next day, in a phone call to Dyson, Goizueta formally and finally approved the launch. Target date: April 28.

In the last two weeks before the launch, Goizueta focused on the announcement itself. He worked practically without sleep, as did most of the top executives on the project. The introduction of a new formula for Coke might be the most important announcement in the company's history, and would certainly be the biggest in Goizueta's career. Nothing could go wrong. But the announcement, above all, was important. As chief executive of Coke, this was the sort of public announcement that fell into the category of representing the company to the public, one of his three main duties. Every word would have to be perfect, because this was news the whole world would hear.

At least it seemed that way most of the time. There were times when Goizueta was not certain. He was losing perspective. The veil of secrecy thrown over the entire Coke empire had created a claustrophobic and otherwordly air inside fortress Coke. Caught up in late-night sessions, minute planning, and global orchestration, with the future of the company on the line, it was tough to stay connected to the outside world. Goizueta even had moments when he feared the public would greet Coke's big announcement with a collective yawn. During one planning session with Bergin, he looked up blankly and asked, "John, what will we do if no one cares?"

To make certain the public would pay attention, Goizueta scheduled the press conference in New York, not Coke's home turf of Atlanta. It was the best way to reach the world's media, just as the gala at Radio City Music Hall had debuted Diet Coke with a splash. Don Keough would join Goizueta at the podium for the press conference. Goizueta realized his speaking style lacked the sizzle Coke wanted for this kind of event. He wanted Keough to paint the press conference Coca-Cola red with his homespun style and stentorian voice.

The dry runs for the press conference did not go well. They switched between developing smooth answers to obvious questions, and moments of dumbstruck deliberation as Goizueta, Keough, and their image handlers tried to anticipate every question. The Coca-Cola public relations staff peppered the two executives with questions. The truth was the best response in most cases, so the answers came easily. But when the question arose about how the formula was first discovered, the Coke executives could not possibly admit the truth, that they had worked on a reformulation of Coca-Cola since the Pepsi Challenge ran roughshod over Coke's image in the late 1970s. The plan was to stick with an answer that was a small part of the truth—the taste was discovered during the search for Diet Coke—and hope nobody asked for a follow up. They prepared jokes designed to disarm the reporters. If Pepsi staged some kind of celebration, Keough would call it "an Irish wake."

Despite the game efforts, the key issue of New Coke's taste was problematic, largely because of Goizueta's ban against comparisons with Pepsi. When public relations man Carlton Curtis asked Goizueta to describe the taste of New Coke, the boss floundered. "Sweeter" was verboten. He might as well admit New Coke was a Pepsi knockoff. They could not boast that New Coke beat Pepsi. "Then someone will ask how old Coke did versus Pepsi," Goizueta said. Comparisons with Coke's original formula were out, too. Goizueta did not want to risk trashing the brand that had carried the company for nearly one hundred years. Goizueta and his minions puzzled over the question of New Coke's taste for more than an hour. Words like "full bodied" and "refreshing" would be OK. They are positive without making comparisons. Finally, though, Goizueta decided to attempt a dodge that would turn the question around on the reporters by indicating it was their job to describe the flavor.

Coke's true Achilles' heel had been laid bare and left bare. Goizueta's unwillingness to level on the taste issue became the core of the outrage that would develop over Coke's new formula. Goizueta realized later that if he had simply announced that the formula was better than Pepsi, the public and press would have taken up the line, and launched a series of Challenge-style inquiries. And Stout's research clearly showed New Coke should trounce Pepsi. Instead, by burying Coke's motivation, Goizueta unwittingly opened a second front in the Cola Wars. Instead of competing against Pepsi, as it was designed to do, New Coke wound up competing against the memory of the sainted original formula. "That became the issue, and we created it," Goizueta confessed.

WHILE GOIZUETA WAS WHIPPING HIS TEAM INTO A FURY OF PREPAration, his mentor Robert W. Woodruff was withering away quietly. A month after Goizueta's visit to unveil the plan to launch a new formula, Woodruff had stopped eating. By the end of February, Woodruff's aides took him on a rare winter trip to Atlanta, to check him in to the Emory University Hospital. In the midst of the Paul Austin succession struggle, Woodruff had recovered from near death to pick Goizueta to run his company, but this time there was no such revival.

Woodruff died March 7, 1985, at age 95. Tributes poured in from around the world, and his life was celebrated in a funeral attended by all of the business and political elite of Atlanta, as well as powerful corporate and government representatives from around the country. A quieter service also was held at Ichauway. Goizueta, who gave Coke employees a day off to honor the passing of Coke's preeminent person-age, felt empty that the old man had not survived to see New Coke unveiled. But he did not eulogize his mentor.

The annual shareholders' meeting was scheduled for April. Goizueta needed to line up board support before the meeting. Although the launch campaign practically was past a point of no return, Goizueta had not yet breathed a word of his plans to the board. Those who at-tended Woodruff's funeral would recall that James T. Laney, a new board member and the president of Emory University, had betrayed his ignorance of the impending announcement while eulogizing Woodruff, with a reference to The Boss's steadfast refusal to change Coke's formula.

Goizueta's first board call went to Jimmy Williams at Trust Co. Williams at first was astounded. "I can't believe that. That can't be right," he told Goizueta when informed of Coke's failures in relation to Pepsi. But Williams quickly came around when Goizueta rattled off some of Stout's numbers and reviewed the New Coke development ef-fort. Herb Allen argued for keeping the original formula on the shelves, but backed off when Goizueta explained the logistical difficul-ties. "Whatever you do, be ready to do it the other way," Allen advised.

At the board meeting, Goizueta placed cups of the old and new Coca-Cola at each of the director's seats, and invited them to a taste test. Goizueta himself had fallen in love with the new flavor. As a col-lege student at Yale, he had always enjoyed visiting a local drugstore and drinking chocolate Coke. After the soda man hit the pump two times, Goizueta always asked for one more dollop of syrup. The over-mixed soda of Goizueta's youth in New Haven had much in common with the sweeter, more syrupy taste of New Coke. In the boardroom that day, as he sipped New Coke, Goizueta felt certain he held a win-ning new formula in his hand.

Around the boardroom table, the flavor got a polite but unenthusi-astic reception. In deference to Goizueta, and out of hope that he knew what he was doing, the board reserved judgment. But many of them were skeptical of the sweet, thick, and somewhat flat taste of the new formula. Director Jimmy Sibley, who was raised drinking Cokes on the knee of Woodruff himself, did not like the taste as well as the original formula, but did not speak out. With Goizueta chairing the meeting and directing the discussion, the directors encouraged him to take no half measures, to make certain the new flavor succeeded. "We can't ease this in. We've got to take a full swat at it or nothing at all," said Richard J. Flamson III, chief executive of the California banking concern Security Pacific Corp.

Goizueta had worked on reformulating Coca-Cola for at least five years. He was about to make the most dramatic move of his career. The future of The Coca-Cola Company—the company to which he had dedicated his career, a place that became his home after he lost Cuba—was on the line. It was four days before the world would know of his plans. He already had telegraphed the news by summoning reporters to a press conference the following Tuesday, advising them that they would witness "the most significant soft-drink marketing development in the company's nearly 100-year history." At last, it was time for Goizueta to take an extraordinary step. He decided to tell his wife.

From the time he first began tinkering in the laboratories to the last hectic weeks of struggle, Goizueta had never discussed this radical move with Olguita. "She was shocked," he reported. Shocked at the news, no doubt, but not at the late date of its transmittal. Since the days when he first worked under Shillinglaw in the technical department, he had learned that the Coke way was to keep wives in the dark about business. Goizueta had typically kept Olguita more informed about his work at Coke than many other Coke executives. But it was a measure of the obsession with secrecy on New Coke that he had not trusted himself even to tell his wife what he was about to do.

THE DAY OF THE PRESS CONFERENCE, TUESDAY, APRIL 23, ROBERTO Goizueta's morning newspaper held a most unwelcome, full-page advertisement. "The Other Guy Just Blinked," it blared, over the signature of Pepsi USA president Roger S. Enrico. Pepsi's young president was preempting Goizueta's announcement by declaring victory in the Cola Wars. For Goizueta, the decision to ship invitations to reporters the previous Friday, in an obvious effort to generate maximum publicity, had been a major mistake. Pepsi headquarters was inundated with calls. And it took little detective work to determine what Coke had in mind. With a weekend to plan a counterattack, Enrico and his staff had enjoyed a creative outpouring of diabolical disruptions.

Pepsi had dropped the Pepsi Challenge in the fall of 1984, almost at precisely the moment Gianturco was delivering his final new formula to Goizueta. PepsiCo chairman Donald Kendall never felt comfortable with the Challenge's in-your-face style, and believed it was not an effective long-term market-share builder. He persuaded Enrico to concentrate on image advertising featuring singer Michael Jackson at the zenith of his popularity. But Enrico had not decamped from the Cola Wars, and advance warning of Coke's press conference was the equivalent of intercepting an enemy general's battle plan. Enrico made the most of the mistake. He placed the newspaper ad and gave Pepsi employees the day off to celebrate. Pepsi officials spent the weekend filling reporters' heads and notebooks with information and questions designed to fluster Goizueta and Keough at the press conference. And to generate Pepsi stories, Enrico staged a street festival a few blocks from the Coke event, giving away Pepsi-Cola products and drawing reporters to the carnival atmosphere.

As Goizueta stepped to the podium of the Vivian Beaumont Theatre at Lincoln Center on April 23, he should have felt supremely confident. The day before in Atlanta, he and Keough had won a standing ovation from bottlers after unveiling the news to them at the Woodruff Arts Center downtown. "Now we're back in the ballgame," an excited Goizueta told outside public relations consultant Harold Burson. At a conference with analysts the morning of the public announcement, the Wall Street crowd had seemed approving, and their quickie reports sent Coke's stock up more than $1 a share during the day.

The big show was the press conference. Goizueta knew the impression he left at the meeting would set the tone for coverage of New Coke in the vital first days. The scene was set just right. The stage in the Beaumont Theatre was awash in red, and the program began with a video montage interspersing shots of Americana with Coke imagery. Families, Eisenhower and JFK, the Grand Canyon and wheat fields, Bruce Springsteen and the Beatles, along with a retrospective of Coke commercials, all paraded across the screen to the beat of a patriotic ballad, "We are. We always will be. Coca-Cola. All-American history." Goizueta had approved Coke USA's hiring of pollster/speechwriters Richard Wirthlin and Patrick Caddell, strategists for Republican Ronald Reagan and Democrat Gary Hart, respectively, to consult on the New Coke launch campaign, and it showed.

As the lights came up, Goizueta did not storm the stage with an air of purpose and promise. In fact, as he approached the podium, he was wringing his hands, visibly nervous about the task at hand. "The best has been made even better," he announced, reading deliberately from his prepared text. And later, in a pose of triumph: "Some may choose to call this the single boldest marketing move in the history of the packaged goods business. We simply call it the surest move ever made."

Keough declared that "the best never rest," and pronounced The Coca-Cola Company confident of success before airing the first flight of New Coke commercials. Made in secret and reflecting Zyman's heavy hand, one showed a New Coke can rising, spaceship-like, from within a can of the now-retired Coke. There were several Cosby spots, and one featuring balloons in front of a billboard, which was shot on a deserted mountain pass in order to maintain secrecy.

The trouble began when the scripts ran out of words, and the press corps seized control of the agenda. "Are you 100 percent certain this won't bomb?" was the first question.

Fifteen seconds later came the first question about taste, and Goizueta did no better than he had in rehearsal. "When you describe flavor, it is a matter better left to poets or copywriters or members of the press," Goizueta said. Pressed, he responded, "I would say it is smoother, uh, rounder, yet, uh, bolder . . . it has a more harmonious flavor." The words might have meant something to a professional in Coke's taste department, but they drew blank stares from the reporters.

"Gee, you'd make a pretty good copywriter," Keough interjected jokingly, hoping to free Goizueta from his own verbal spider web.

The start was the high point. Reporters expressed skepticism about the supposed serendipity of "discovering" the new formula while inventing Diet Coke. They seemed to resent Goizueta's assertion that Coke's move was not prompted by the Pepsi Challenge: "The Pepsi Challenge? When did that happen?" he had deadpanned, ineffectually. It went on for an hour, and finally came to a close as a reporter asked Goizueta if he planned to reformulate Diet Coke if New Coke proved successful. "No. And I don't assume that it is a success. It is a success," Goizueta harumphed. On the way out of the theater, reporters tasted New Coke that had sat warming in paper cups on tables during the press conference. Many visibly grimaced, and some even spit the stuff out of their mouths.

FOR A DAY OR TWO, IT LOOKED AS IF GOIZUETA'S OPTIMISM FOR New Coke might be justified. The first barrage of press coverage, reflecting Coke's spin, was largely favorable. Coke's marketing staff figured news coverage of New Coke had as much impact as a $100 million advertising buy. More than 80 percent of the country was aware of the switch within days of the announcement. But the headlines, rather than talking about the exhilarating taste of New Coke, and explaining the old Coke's eroding market share, focused almost exclusively on New Coke's sweetness and the withdrawal of old Coke. This was precisely the opposite of what Goizueta had wanted, but hardly surprising given that Goizueta had failed to describe New Coke's taste and denied that old Coke was in trouble.

The good press, such as it was, lasted about one day. When *The Atlanta Journal-Constitution* ran a taste test in Atlanta on April 24, old Coke handily won, spawning stories in national media about New Coke's flop in its own hometown. The popular local columnist Lewis Grizzard lambasted New Coke, and the *Chicago Tribune*'s Bob Greene, whose column was syndicated nationwide, wrote paeans to the original formula, mourning its loss and decrying Goizueta's arrogance as "a sort of smugness—that if you don't like New Coke, you will." Goizueta fired off a letter to Greene, admonishing him for "typing when you should be tasting." After Goizueta ultimately relented and brought back Old Coke, Greene wrote that Goizueta and Dyson should be fired and, memorably, called them "soda jerks."

As pressure mounted, Goizueta sometimes had difficulty keeping order among his own team. In an interview with *Business Week* magazine, he stuck with his claim that New Coke was discovered by accident during the search for Diet Coke. "I wish the story could be sexier, but it is not," he told the magazine. Just days later, Dyson publicly contradicted him in the industry bible *Beverage World*. Asked if the discovery was a "happy accident" that developed during the Diet Coke research—precisely the circumstances Goizueta described—Dyson replied: "No, no. It was absolutely no accident. No, sir. In fact, in looking at all of our options, we directed flavor scientists to look at this issue based on the fact that Diet Coke had become such an outstanding breakthrough. They didn't stumble on anything."

The trickle of bad publicity turned into a flood. Negative calls to Coke's hotline began to mount, reaching more than 1,000 a day. Press clippings turned so nasty that Coke discontinued its clipping service.

One began with the memorable phrase, "Dear Chairman Dodo," a salutation that would become part of Goizueta's stock recounting of the New Coke debacle in later years. Others were no kinder. "It is absolutely TERRIBLE! You should be ashamed to put the Coke name on it," wrote one distressed Coke drinker. "I don't think I would be more upset if you were to burn the flag in our front yard," penned another. Goizueta was starting to see that he had accidentally tapped into something that meant more to the American consumer than a cold flavor on a hot day.

A Coke drinker in Seattle, Gay Mullins, declared himself head of the Old Cola Drinkers of America, and became a press favorite even though he chose New Coke over the original formula in repeated taste tests. Coke salespeople reported from the road that they were accosted in airports. Goizueta traveled by company jet, so he did not have any interaction en route. But when he checked into hotels, the Coca-Cola tags on his baggage tipped off staff and guests. "Why did you take our Coke away?" they asked him.

The protests struck home during Goizueta's talks with his father, with whom he still communicated almost daily. Living in Mexico City, Crispulo Goizueta had phoned, sometimes several times a day, to report on the local press' vilification of his son because of New Coke. And when Goizueta took a week off in mid-May for his son Robby's wedding in Miami, his father upbraided him. "This is terrible. You know they are calling you names," Crispulo Goizueta told his son.

"Dad, you'll just have to have patience. This is going to turn out OK, just have a little patience," the son replied.

THE SENTIMENT AMONG BOTTLERS HAD DARKENED DRAMATICALLY since the group cheered the launch of New Coke three weeks earlier. The calls pouring in to Keough's office enabled Goizueta and him to track where New Coke was the biggest failure, and where it was starting to make some headway. Disturbingly, the angriest calls came from the South, Coca-Cola's most solid region. "My god, this is costing us a lot of money," Crawford Johnson III, president of Coke United in Birmingham, Alabama, complained to Keough in mid-May. Johnson's sales figures plummeted from the day of the announcement, and "we knew we had a disaster within ten days," he says. Coke's leading domestic bottlers met in Atlanta, and even Frank Barron, the bottler from the Coke stronghold of Rome, Georgia, argued for bringing back Old Coke. People were hassling his delivery men at grocery stores, and his sales numbers were falling. Another old-time bottler, F.M. Bellingrath of Pine Bluff, Arkansas, visited Goizueta and told him that bottlers at a regional Texas meeting had signed a petition calling for the return of the original formula.

The complaints from some of Coke's most loyal bottlers caught Goizueta's attention. It worried him that the New Coke fury was starting to affect their business. "I can put up with flak when sales are up. Then flak doesn't bother me," he said. "But I can't put up with flak when sales are down."

Even though Goizueta and Keough were starting to voice misgivings, Dyson and Zyman remained steadfastly supportive of New Coke. They admitted people were taking longer than expected to embrace the new soft drink, but they insisted that the numbers would turn around. Stout had tracked consumer responses since the launch, and they were benign. But days had passed, and Goizueta wanted a new set of facts, so everyone involved could make decisions based on the same database. He sent Stout back to the marketplace to conduct another round of consumer surveys to find out what really was going on.

Stout leased space in a shopping mall, and set up a faux grocery aisle loaded with soft drinks, both Coke and its competitors. Different displays offered different product mixes: some with both New Coke and the original formula, some with only one or the other, all in combination with products from Pepsi and other competitors. Stout's staff recruited consumers from the malls, gave them ten poker chips, and asked them to place a chip on whatever brand they would buy to meet their family's needs. On June 20, the results came in. New Coke held a 3.5 percent market share, and the original formula won 19 percent of the market. Arguments about New Coke's better taste were becoming irrelevant. Consumers were rejecting New Coke as a concept.

While Stout was conducting his research, Goizueta and Keough traveled to a bottlers' meeting in Monaco, where they bravely declared their determination to stick with New Coke, and promised that the uproar would soon quiet down. Domestic bottlers implored them to bring back the old formula, but got only a polite hearing. Sitting in the audience, Coke-New York bottler Charlie Millard had the sensation of sitting at a Broadway play. The two Coke executives were selling their devotion to New Coke too hard. "Roberto and Don were putting on a hell of an act, but it was obvious to me that they knew the jig was up," he said.

After the meeting, Coke's top two executives took their wives to a six-table Italian restaurant on the hills overlooking Monaco. The seventy-year-old owner came to the table cradling a wine basket covered with a velvet cloth. Unfurling the cloth with a broad flourish, he revealed a 6½-ounce glass bottle of Coke. "This is the original Coca-Cola," the owner announced proudly. Goizueta eyed Keough, and in a glance they shared a revelation. Even in this remote outpost, people had an affection for old Coke that would not die.

ON THE FLIGHT BACK TO THE STATES, GOIZUETA, KEOUGH, MIL-lard, and their wives unwound in the company's plane. Everyone was talked out about New Coke. There literally was nothing more to say, so the conversation turned to personal matters and, for Goizueta, to a rare topic: Cuba. For more than an hour, he and Olguita told the story of their flight from their native land. Olguita was especially passionate, describing how she took off her jewelry, even her wedding ring, so the valuable trinkets would not attract the attention of Castro's customs agents. Goizueta spoke of the wrenching decision to leave his grandmother behind, to fly on a separate plane, again because a large family group leaving Cuba together might cause the guards to hold the Goizueta family at the border. "They were talking in the most intense, personal terms," Millard recalled. "It is the one time in all these years I felt personally close to Roberto."

By the time the Coke plane set down in Atlanta, it was time to quit acting bravely and start taking pragmatic action. When Dyson returned in late June from a trip to his family's estate in Argentina, Keough told him he had until July 8 to recommend whether to stay the course, wait a month, or bring back old Coke. While waiting for Dyson's response, Keough and Goizueta lunched in a dining room near their offices in Coke Tower. They looked each other in the eye and knew the end was at hand. "Why are we doing this?" Keough asked Goizueta.

Goizueta responded, "We'd better get started. We've got to do something."

On July 8, Dyson held another bottlers' powwow and left the meeting convinced he had no choice but to bring back the old Coke. As a group, bottlers stood to lose $30 million they had tied up in New Coke syrup, but none seemed to care. They wanted the original formula back.

There was one significant problem left. No one could agree what to name the old Coke. For two weeks, Goizueta, Keough, and Dyson had engaged in a traveling argument about the new moniker for the old drink. Calling it "original formula," as Dyson wanted, caused problems because of wording in the bottlers' contract. It was a through-the-looking-glass problem. "Original" in the contract referred to Coca-Cola, which was now New Coke, lawyer Robert Keller explained. The company could not market a product with that name without violating the bottlers' rights. Calling the drink "Classic" had its own problems, since it technically made old Coke a new product, and bottlers had the right to reject new products.

The legalistic discussion infuriated Goizueta. Nearly a month had passed since it became apparent that New Coke was not a success, and now his team was holding up the relaunch because of legal hair splitting. Coke's top two executives favored "Coca-Cola Classic," a name Goizueta and Harold Burson had dreamed up in a brainstorming session.

"The argument is over. It's 'Classic,'" Goizueta told Dyson.

The Coke-USA president sharply replied, "You let the lawyers name the product."

Goizueta left the meeting with Dyson, and spoke briefly with Burson. Together with Earl Leonard, Coke's top public relations executive, Burson had begun drafting out Goizueta's remarks for the re-launch of the original formula. Burson was impressed by Goizueta's cool temperament, especially near the end of a nine-week period in which he worked on little sleep and under immeasurable pressure. Now he was asking Goizueta to do something very difficult for the proud Cuban. "You've got to be humble, you've got to eat humble pie," he told Goizueta. Then, sitting at an old Underwood typewriter with two keys missing, Burson banged out the first words of Goizueta's mea culpa: "Today, we have two messages to deliver to the American consumer. First, to those of you who are drinking Coca-Cola with its great new taste, our thanks. But there is a second group of consumers to whom we want to speak today, and our message to this group is simple: We have heard you."

Ike Herbert asked Keough to tape a television commercial announcing the return of the old formula, but Keough and Goizueta did not like the idea. Goizueta preferred hiring actors to do the job, rather than burden Coke's president with a public atonement for the New Coke flop. Goizueta also was concerned about risks to Keough's personal security. The tone of the protest had grown sharper as time passed, and there was no telling what someone might do.

The next morning, July 10, Herbert again pushed for Keough to do the commercial. Two actors had tried, but the announcement sounded hollow coming from them. To win consumers back after such a bloodbath would require the talents of a man with Coca-Cola in his veins, Herbert argued. Keough shot seven takes of the commercial, and the winner was take number four. Goizueta looked at the Keough spot and one using an actor. "Use Don's," he ordered. Herbert beamed the television spot to New York, where it was rushed by helicopter to the three broadcast networks in time for their evening newscasts. Even as Keough taped his spot, ABC news anchor Peter Jennings interruped "General Hospital" to say the original formula was coming back.

At the July 11 press conference on home turf in Atlanta, the contrite tone seemed to win over a press corps that may have run out of steam in nine weeks of beating up on Goizueta and his crew. Dyson took a moment to boast that, despite the New Coke flop, nearly a third of the soft drinks sold in the United States still came from The Coca-Cola Company—a subtle prelude to the "megabrand" concept Goizueta would introduce a few weeks later. In an effort to salvage some positive spin on the biggest disaster of his career, Goizueta would argue that the entire Coke family of products constituted a single "megabrand," and that analysts should stop measuring the company's performance based on the performance of individual brands. To many, the idea of underplaying the importance of individual brands sounded odd coming from the world's most successful brand marketing company.

Keough took charge of the press conference and explained that the debacle was really good news for the company. "We love any retreat that has us rushing to our best customers with the product they love most," he said. Coke might be accused either of making the biggest marketing blunder in history, or of cynically concocting the whole brouhaha, he said. Keough's conclusion: "The truth is we are not that dumb, and we are not that smart."

The humility could last only so long. Toward the end of the session, reporters asked Goizueta if he would have gone ahead with the launch in April knowing what he did by July. His response was terse and to the point: "*Si mi abuela tuviera ruedas seria bicicleta.*" Translation: If my grandmother had wheels she would be a bicycle.

Spin control of the New Coke debacle began almost immediately. Stubbornly insisting that New Coke one day would triumph in the marketplace, Goizueta insisted on keeping it on the shelves, even though bottlers had warned they did not have the capacity to bottle and distribute yet another Coca-Cola product.

The bigger problem struck at the core of Goizueta's concern: The impact on Coke's finances and the desire to place first in every major measurement category. But with two Coca-Colas competing for market share, dominance in any category would be hard to win. If New Coke and Coke Classic were both successes, they would split Coke's share of the market, and Pepsi would look like a runaway winner even if the combined Coke products were walloping Pepsi.

"Megabrand," was Roberto Goizueta's solution to the problem. Rather than admitting defeat and letting Pepsi claim market leadership, Goizueta would try to change the way success is measured in the entire soft-drink industry. Instead of simply counting up Coke Classic's sales and comparing them to Pepsi-Cola, Goizueta suddenly wanted to focus "on the total corporate share of the total industry, as well as each of the components which make it up." New products might cut into the volume of the flagship brand, but as long as total corporate share increased, that's all that would really matter.

Analysts and beverage industry veterans greeted the idea with derision. For decades, the beverage industry had been built around the notion of carefully nurturing individual brands and helping them carve out the largest possible share. From the bottler to the brand manager to the advertising people to the analysts, everyone was focused on selling or measuring the success of individual brands. But suddenly that was not convenient for Goizueta, because with two Cokes on the market, his flagship brand might place second or worse, so "megabrand" was born.

"Megabrand was absolutely layered on after the fact to try to make us look good after New Coke," says Michael Beindorff, a former manager of Diet Coke. The reason was obvious. The Coca-Cola Company's corporate offerings owned 38.7 percent of the soda market in 1985, versus 30.7 percent for Pepsi. But Coca-Cola Classic still lagged, with a 14.1 percent share versus Pepsi-Cola's 19.5 percent.

Megabrand was a concept of convenience. It served Goizueta only so long as there was a risk that Pepsi would take the lead in all sales categories as New Coke and Coke Classic split share. As it turned out, the megabrand idea had a life span barely longer than the abortive New Coke. After Coke Classic regained the market-share lead by 1987, hardly a whisper was heard of the "megabrand" concept from that point forward.

By then, Goizueta was proudly trumpeting Coke's stunning victory in the New Coke debacle. "Management does not get paid to make the shareholders comfortable, we get paid to make the shareholders rich," he told analysts, tacitly allowing that New Coke had caused some discomfort, somewhere. "We do not get paid to be right, we get paid to produce results."

The claim was not quite literally true. Sometimes, even before the results are in, management gets paid handsomely, indeed. In the fall of 1985, before anyone knew how the New Coke debacle ultimately would sort out, Coke's board had moved to compensate Goizueta and Keough handsomely for placing the entire company at risk. At the behest of Herb Allen's compensation committee, the board created a new form of bonus called "performance units" that would award Goizueta and Keough for Coke's long-term stock appreciation. The bonus was a major factor in Goizueta's record $86 million pay day in 1991.

The claim of a great management victory—like the product New Coke itself—always had a tinny, flat taste. Like Roy Stout's early market data, Goizueta's New Coke postmortem had the virtue of being technically true, while missing a far larger and more significant point. The world's most successful marketing company had misread its customers, and risked the future of the world's most successful brand. But the salvation of Goizueta and his management team was the strength of the brand they nearly destroyed. Despite all that Goizueta & Co. had done to fatally weaken the brand, Coca-Cola was strong enough to save itself, and Goizueta, too.

6

Changing the Script: The Bottler Spinoff and Escape from Hollywood

In early October 1985, Roberto Goizueta sat down at his desk to do something he almost never did: Write a memo to Don Keough. The two had such a close working relationship, with their adjoining, nearly identical offices, that they almost never put their thoughts down on paper. When there was an issue on Goizueta's mind, he typically dropped in on Keough, discussed it, and dispatched it.

The substance of the note Goizueta wrote matched the uniqueness of the fact that he wrote the memo at all. In October 1985, while Coke's top managers were preparing their 1986 budgets for review by Goizueta, Keough, and chief financial officer Doug Ivester, Goizueta for a rare moment seemed willing to allow The Coca-Cola Company to briefly take a rest. "The year 1986, in my opinion, should be a year of consolidation and harvest," he wrote. "Let's not do anything new. We have to absorb the expenses of the centennial. Let's consolidate and extract some profits from the business."

The centennial, indeed, was a major item. Goizueta had earmarked $30 million to celebrate the invention of Coca-Cola, in 1886, and after

139

five years of planning was preparing to fly 14,000 Coca-Cola colleagues, customers, and bottlers from around the world to share the experience, or to join in by satellite from locations around the globe. But by the standards of Coca-Cola's $6.9 billion in 1986 revenues, even the centennial celebration's outlandish scale was nothing significant. The truth was, after five years of furious activity capped by the pressure chamber that was New Coke, Goizueta needed a break, and his company did, too. The almost passive tone of the note was highly unusual for Goizueta, who always prided himself on speed, aggression, and appetite for unfettered growth. This time, he seemed to realize that the energy of his drive was taxing the resources of The Coca-Cola Company.

The bottling consolidation, the international push, the launch of Diet Coke and New Coke, and the Columbia acquisition were pulling the company in at least a half-dozen different directions. And the costs of all these moves were stretching the company's financial resources in a way that seemed to verge on recklessness compared to the hyperconservative legacy of the Woodruff era. The company's long-term debt had jumped from virtually nothing before Goizueta took office to $867 million at the end of 1985, and its credit rating, while still Triple-A by 1997, would face its first downgrade in Coke's 100-year history. Coke Classic finally had overtaken Pepsi in all sales categories, but only at the cost of an expensive and exhausting marketing drive that taxed the company's creative output. For Goizueta and everyone else who worked under him, the time felt right for a brief breather.

Goizueta's harvest memo had a short shelf life. It was superseded almost immediately by an unexpected visit from John T. Lupton, owner of one of Coke's oldest bottling franchises, the JTL Corp. The harvest memo was barely filed when Lupton appeared at Keough's office and announced without warning that he wanted out of the bottling business. He was nearing retirement and his children did not want to take his place. "Out of respect for the company, I want to offer it to you first. But if I can't get a fair price from you, I'll have to go to the outside market," Lupton told Keough.

The price tag was a shocker: $1.4 billion. If Keough agreed and Goizueta approved it, it would be by far the biggest price for any bottler ever, worldwide. But without taking an extra breath, Keough had an immediate response for Lupton. "We want to buy it," he said.

When Keough quickly took the news to Goizueta after Lupton left, the chairman immediately approved the offer. He and Keough saw they had no choice. In the middle of the 1980s, with junk bonds and leveraged buyouts reigning on Wall Street, Lupton could easily find a pool of money that would purchase his company, with its string of strong operations in metropolitan Texas, Denver, Phoenix, and Daytona Beach, Florida. In a push to milk money from the operation, a financial buyer would keep prices high and would avoid investing in new bottling systems. Raising prices to increase margins would give Pepsi a big advantage. This would hurt syrup sales and could ultimately cost Coke big numbers in terms of overall market-share leadership.

The Lupton bottling interests were different than any Coke had bought before. Until this point, Goizueta and Keough had bought up struggling or poorly managed bottlers, fixed their problems, and then sold them again. Whenever possible, they had put the rehabilitated franchises into the hands of bottlers they trusted to do a good job building the Coca-Cola brand name. Goizueta called the process "refranchising."

The JTL properties were not in need of refranchising. They were among the best-run bottlers in the Coca-Cola system, and Goizueta found that attractive. Despite its experience buying, fixing, and selling bottlers, Coke had not distinguished itself as a long-term operator of bottling companies. The company-owned bottling operations in Boston, Atlanta, Seattle, Chicago, and San Francisco had underperformed under Atlanta's ownership. Executives who moved into bottling from other parts of the company considered bottling a career killer, so the company-owned bottlers never got the aggressive leadership they needed. If Lupton, perhaps the domestic system's most successful bottler, could be brought into the fold, perhaps the rest of the Coke-owned bottlers would benefit.

For Lupton, the offer to sell his family franchise to Coke was a sign of how much his opinion of Goizueta had changed since the crotchety Chattanooga bottler had led the push to unseat Goizueta during the summer of 1980 by recruiting Charles Duncan as a prospect for chairman of Coca-Cola. During the five intervening years, Goizueta had made Lupton a believer. As a board member at the start of the Goizueta regime, Lupton saw immediately that Coke's new chairman meant business. Beginning board meetings a half hour earlier was just the start. Goizueta also insisted that committees meet more frequently between board meetings. He provided detailed briefing papers to board members, and wanted their opinions, especially during one-on-

one conversations with favored directors before the actual meetings began. Austin had not done that. As early as 1981, Goizueta shrewdly steered the Fort Worth bottler to Lupton, taking it out of the hands of financial buyer AEA. Coke desperately needed help in the Dallas-Fort Worth area, ground zero for the Pepsi Challenge.

Lupton also found it impressive that Goizueta chose to delegate the job of dealing with bottlers almost entirely to Keough. He recognized that few CEOs would cede such an important duty to a lieutenant. He also knew Keough well enough to understand how difficult it must have been for Goizueta to win over Keough, a proud and capable executive who had been bitterly disappointed to lose the chairmanship. Rather than operating the company by gut feel, as both Austin and Woodruff often seemed to do, Goizueta and Keough seemed driven by spread sheets and forecasts. "They understand how to work together, with all kinds of forecasts and directions laid out by Roberto," marveled Lupton. "This is something we never had before. Even Woodruff ran it by feel and touch."

The surprise JTL offer was not foreseen in Goizueta's forecasts, but he was glad to have the chance to buy the big bottler. The Lupton franchise offered immediate operational advantages. Coupled with Coke-USA's operations in San Francisco, Seattle, and Spokane, the deal would give Goizueta control of many of the key markets in the western United States, in an arc from Dallas through Seattle. Rumors already were swirling that Beatrice Cos., the Chicago-based food and bottling concern, might be a takeover target. If Beatrice was taken out in a leveraged buyout, the new owner almost certainly would look to pay down debt by unloading the capital intensive bottling operation that was not part of Beatrice's core food business. Coke would have a clear shot at acquiring the key Los Angeles, San Diego, and Las Vegas markets, and it would have a bidding advantage over any other potential acquiror because of its strong bottling presence in the West.

Even so, it was not immediately clear to Goizueta how to structure the JTL Corp. deal. At a price tag of nearly $1.5 billion, the Lupton franchise was almost as large as all of the deals Goizueta had put together since becoming chairman in 1981, a record-setting $2 billion. Goizueta and Keough could not handle a deal like the Lupton transaction in quite the same way they had accomplished the rest of the refranchising effort. It was time for an entirely new approach to the refranchising of the bottling business.

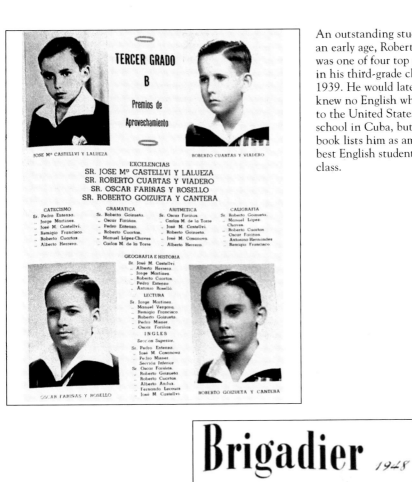

TERCER GRADO

B

Premios de

Aprovechamiento

JOSE Mª CASTELLVI Y LALUEZA

ROBERTO CUARTAS Y VIADERO

EXCELENCIAS

SR. JOSE Mª CASTELLVI Y LALUEZA
SR. ROBERTO CUARTAS Y VIADERO
SR. OSCAR FARIÑAS Y ROSELLO
SR. ROBERTO GOIZUETA Y CANTERA

CATECISMO	GRAMATICA	ARITMETICA	CALIGRAFIA
Sr. Pedro Entenza.	Sr. Roberto Goizueta.	Sr. Oscar Fariñas.	Sr. Roberto Goizueta.
„ Jorge Martínez.	„ Oscar Fariñas.	„ Carlos M. de la Torre	„ Manuel López-
„ José M. Castellví.	„ Pedro Entenza.	„ José M. Castellví.	Chaves.
„ Remigio Francisco.	„ Roberto Cuartas.	„ Roberto Goizueta.	„ Roberto Cuartas.
„ Roberto Cuartas.	„ Manuel López-Chaves	„ José M. Casanova.	„ Oscar Fariñas.
„ Alberto Herrera.	„ Carlos M. de la Torre	„ Alberto Herrera.	„ Antonino Hernández
			„ Remigio Francisco.

GEOGRAFIA E HISTORIA

Sr. José M. Castellví
„ Alberto Herrera.
„ Jorge Martínez.
„ Roberto Cuartas.
„ Pedro Entenza.
„ Antonio Roselló.

LECTURA

Sr. Jorge Martínez.
„ Manuel Vergara.
„ Remigio Francisco.
„ Roberto Goizueta.
„ Pedro Manet.
„ Oscar Fariñas.

INGLES

Sección Superior.
Sr. Pedro Entenza.
„ José M. Casanova.
„ Pedro Manet.
Sección Inferior
Sr. Oscar Fariñas.
„ Roberto Goizueta
„ Roberto Cuartas.
„ Alberto Andux.
„ Fernando Lecours
„ José M. Castellví.

OSCAR FARIÑAS Y ROSELLO

ROBERTO GOIZUETA Y CANTERA

An outstanding student from an early age, Roberto Goizueta was one of four top achievers in his third-grade class in 1939. He would later claim he knew no English when he came to the United States after high school in Cuba, but his yearbook lists him as among the best English students in his class.

Brigadier *1948*

Roberto Goizueta Cantera

In his senior year at Belen Academy in 1948, Goizueta was named Brigadier of his class, the school's highest honor. The award recognized achievements in academics, athletics, civics, and leadership. Fidel Castro, who graduated from Belen four years ahead of Goizueta, did not receive this award. Credit: Courtesy of Belen Jesuit School, Miami.

(Photo at right.) A basketball player and swimmer at Belen Academy, Roberto Goizueta (third from left in back row) was not a particularly gifted athlete. (Goizueta is third from the left, back row.) His father, Crispulo Goizueta, embarrassed him with overly vocal support during basketball games. *Credit: Photo courtesy of Belen Jesuit School, Miami.*

(Top) Roberto Goizueta was born November 18, 1931 in a mansion his father built in the wealthy Vedado section of Havana, Cuba's capital city. *Credit: Atlanta Journal-Constitution/David Tulis.*
(Right) The house features a two-story stained-glass window of Don Quixote jousting a windmill. In the yard, Goizueta's father kept some of the bulldogs he raised. *Credit: Atlanta Journal-Constitution/David Tulis.*

The chemical engineering fraternity at Yale, Alpha Chi Sigma. Goizueta was a diligent and successful student, known for studying hours at a stretch. But he wasn't tenth in his graduating class, as he sometimes claimed. Goizueta stands second from right in the third row from the front. *Credit: Photo courtesy of Richard Cook.*

Graduation day at Yale University, Class of 1953. Roberto Goizueta and Olguita Casteleiro had an understanding before they both left Cuba for education in the United States. Her father, a merchant, was one of the dozen richest men in Cuba. Goizueta never dated anyone else in college and saw Olguita virtually every weekend. *Credit: Photo courtesy of Richard Cook.*

The invitation to Goizueta's wedding. The leading Havana newspaper described the June 14, 1953, Goizueta-Casteleiro wedding as "the most spectacular wedding in years." Several hundred of Havana's social elite attended. Roberto's sister Vivien was maid of honor. *Credit: Courtesy of Richard Cook.*

Olga González de Casteleiro
Segundo Casteleiro Colmenares

y

Aida Cantera de Goizueta
Críspulo Goizueta Fernández

tienen el gusto de invitar a usted
al matrimonio de sus hijos

Olguita y Roberto

el Domingo catorce de Junio de mil
novecientos cincuenta y tres, a las
once y media de la mañana, en la
Iglesia del Sagrado Corazón,
Reina, La Habana.

Misa de Velaciones.

IMPORTANT
A FOOD ENTERPRISE
WANTS TO HIRE A
CHEMICAL
ENGINEER
A RECENT GRADUATE
Must speak and
write English correctly
Profitable Opportunity

On June 18, 1954, after working
for his father for a year, Goizueta
spotted this advertisement. He
did not know the company was
Coca-Cola until he arrived for
the interview.

Still not quite in Robert W. Woodruff's inner circle in the early 1970s, Goizueta (far right), tagged along on a plant tour led by his bow-tied boss, Cliff Shillinglaw. On a trip to London in 1974 to mix a batch of concentrate and collect cassia leaves that had been spirited out of China, Shillinglaw suffered a heart attack. Days later, Orville May made Goizueta only the third living person to know Coke's secret formula. *Credit: Special Collections Department, Robert W. Woodruff Library, Emory University.*

"The Boss" and his protégés: Although Roberto Goizueta (fourth from the left) was one of Robert W. Woodruff's protégés, he did not receive a coveted invitation to the Ichauway Plantation until after he was elected chairman and chief executive of the company. Jimmy Williams (far left) was the Trust Co. executive who helped boost him to the chairmanship and became one of his closest friends. Woodruff is at the far right. *Credit: Courtesy of Special Collections Department, Robert W. Woodruff Library, Emory University.*

In with the new. After more than two years of brutal corporate infighting, Roberto Goizueta at last was named as chairman and chief executive on August 6, 1980. Next up: Developing a strategic plan that reversed the course set by his predecessor, J. Paul Austin. No one knew it at the time, but Austin was suffering from Alzheimer's disease. *Credit: AP Laserphoto.*

(Top) Out with the new, in with the old. Seventy-seven days after the introduction of New Coke set off a nationwide consumer protest, Roberto Goizueta and Donald Keough on July 11, 1985, relent and bring back the original formula. Keough, skeptical of the new formula from the start, holds "Coca-Cola Classic." Goizueta toasts with New Coke, later renamed Coke II. It remained his favorite flavor the rest of his life. Credit: Robin Rayne/ZUMA.

(Bottom) King of the realm. With the New Coke debacle swirling around him in the summer of 1985, Roberto Goizueta descends the circular stairway that connects Coke's three-story executive suite. Credit: The Atlanta Journal-Constitution/Calvin Cruce.

In April of 1995, Roberto Goizueta and heir apparent M. Douglas Ivester toasted their fortunes on the tenth anniversary of the New Coke fiasco. Credit: The Atlanta Journal-Constitution/Phil Skinner.

Roberto Goizueta stands proudly in front of The World of Coca-Cola, the Coke museum he built in Atlanta, GA. *Credit: Copyright Ann States/SABA, November 1990.*

Olguita Goizueta looks on as her sons Javier and Roberto S. Goizueta (all wearing dark glasses) help carry the casket of her husband away from Holy Spirit Catholic Church in Atlanta. Roberto C. Goizueta died October 18, 1997, at age 65. A chain smoker since high school, he succumbed just six weeks after he was diagnosed with lung cancer. As the casket moved down the aisle, the Atlanta Symphony Orchestra played the tune, "I'd Like to Teach the World to Sing." *Credit: AP Photo/Ric Feld.*

Sparked by the Lupton offer, Goizueta and Keough picked up on a discussion of the bottling business that they had begun in 1981 as they formed their partnership at the helm of Coca-Cola. The demands of bottling, the high levels of capital and relatively low margins, were not a good fit for Coke. The core business of Coca-Cola had just the opposite profile: high margins on relatively little capital investment. With an appropriate balance sheet and good management, bottling could be a good business. But it consumed too much capital and took too much management time to thrive within Coke itself. Goizueta and Keough wanted to find a way to retain some control over the bottler's investment and marketing strategies, but still place the bottling operations into some sort of stand-alone entity, where investors would be more forgiving of the high need for capital and low margins that characterized that business.

If ever there was a time to start changing the structure of bottler deals, the JTL Corp. offer was it. Goizueta told Keough to propose that Coke would buy part, but not all, of JTL, and Lupton agreed. Keough proposed that Lupton remain as chairman of the bottling company, so Coke could draw on his expertise. He agreed. By early January, they had an agreement in principle. It was not yet a binding contract, but the two sides had moved along smoothly enough that they unveiled the talks publicly on January 27. "The handshake on the deal has already taken place. It's just a matter of working out the details at this time," Keough said, hopefully. Goizueta was so optimistic about JTL's unique place in the Coke bottling hierarchy that he named it: "The megabottler strategy."

Within a month, Lupton backed out. For no discernible reason, he suddenly was unwilling to move ahead. He wanted to maintain operating control, not serve as a non-executive chairman. At times, he was wary of selling altogether, and at other times he considered taking the bottler to buyers other than Coke. "We did quite a little rain dance with him," Keough would recall.

AND WHILE THE DANCE WENT ON, GOIZUETA AND KEOUGH HAD another important matter to attend to: Coke's 100th birthday bash, the largest corporate-sponsored party in history. In his last memo to Woodruff, celebrating The Boss' ninety-fifth birthday, in December 1985, Goizueta had stated that he looked forward to raising a beverage—in this case something with a little more alcoholic kick than a

Coke—to celebrate the 100th anniversary of Coca-Cola. Woodruff's death was the only void at the company's 100th birthday, a party Goizueta had planned for five years, beginning almost literally on the day he took over as president of Coke. From then until the party came to an end on Saturday, May 10, 1986, Goizueta took an inordinate interest in every last facet of the 100th celebration. His incredibly detailed, hands-on approach to the event marked his keen sense of Coke's heritage.

With a five-year lead time, a budget of $30 million before it was all done, and his strong personal interest in the event, Goizueta made certain no rational thought or preposterous proposal went unexplored. At the same time, he insisted that Coke not just throw away money on an orgy of corporate back slapping. Goizueta wanted every aspect of the meeting to focus the Coca-Cola system worldwide on four major themes: the company's heritage, the highly competitive North American market, the drive for international growth, and the company's future. Two points, Coke's heritage and Coke's future, were uppermost in Goizueta's mind as he attended several dozen meetings during the planning process. The impression, Goizueta noted during one session with the planning team, should be of Coke's development "from the outhouse to outer space." And he wanted to imbue Coke's bottlers with the notion that their business, by bringing capital investment to many underdeveloped countries, was on the vanguard of social change worldwide. A message of the exhibit, Goizueta pointed out, should be that, "Business will be the institution of the future. It's the only global institution."

The planners had plenty of time and real estate to work with. Goizueta wanted a four-day celebration that would include the largest parade in Atlanta's history and a million square feet of exhibition space in the Georgia World Congress Center and adjacent Omni sports arena. The main thoroughfare of the Congress Center complex carried the Coke story from 1886 to 1986 and beyond. It contained a replica of Doc Pemberton's drugstore and wound up in a laser-lit arena with an interactive computer display—a futuristic novelty in 1986. Some of Coke's classic advertising played continuously in one theatre, while Columbia Pictures blockbusters looped in another. A futurism exhibit featured holography, an actual NASA space satellite, and a car of the future from the Ford Motor Company, where Goizueta served on the board of directors.

A VIP party the night before the festivities marked the opening of the new atrium that Goizueta had built on the site of the old Plum Street headquarters that held Woodruff's office for years. Goizueta showed his engineer's mind and son-of-an-architect's breeding by sitting in on six major planning sessions for the atrium, personally selecting the marble and furniture, and even renaming the sculpture that greeted visitors before they entered the globe-shaped atrium. The George Rickey piece "Triple L Excentric Gyratory, Gyratory II," which featured three oversized L's moving independently in a 100-foot arc over a reflecting pond, he renamed "Leadership." In a brochure, Goizueta explained that the L-shaped pieces of the sculpture represented "Leadership in people, leadership in product, and leadership in integrity."

Although Goizueta had developed a reputation for being socially inadequate in large groups, he and Olguita boosted their energy and nerve for the event and played host in a way he had never done before, or would do afterward. At the close of the VIP party, Olga delighted the small crowd with a piano singalong straight from her days on the recreation farm in Cuba. Although Olguita had a reputation as a dynamic presence in small-group settings, it was unusual for her to draw attention to herself at such a large event.

In planning sessions for the big centennial events, Coke marketing chief Ike Herbert and his team decided Goizueta and Keough should be assigned different roles, almost like actors in a play. Goizueta, they said, should be cast as "the visionary, the mastermind, the person that understands every country in the world," one participant recalled. They cast Keough to type, as "the heart of Coca-Cola." The role playing was scripted down to the video beamed to large displays through the convention hall while the two men spoke. Goizueta, with his hollow cheeks, Latin nose, and deep-set eyes, came across cold on big screens, so the producers minimized use of his image. Instead, Coke slogans, images, and trademarks came in and out of focus as he spoke. Keough, on the other hand, was a jaunty and welcome face, and the camera shots would make the most of it.

On opening night, May 7, 1986, Goizueta gaveled the celebration to order with the same mallet Woodruff had used to open the company's first worldwide bottlers' meeting a half-century earlier. With the Woodruff slogan "The World Belongs to the Discontented" flashed on a huge screen behind him, Goizueta told the bottlers they had come to Atlanta from around the world to "celebrate the start of our second century." His 30-minute speech covered everything from boosting consumption around the world to leveraging the Coke trademark with as many new brands as possible. Pretty dry stuff, but the tightly choreographed dance show, highlighted by a miniature gas-powered delivery truck driving on stage, gave the crowd something to remember.

That night, Goizueta and Keough toured the regional parties, stopping first at a raucous Latin American bash where they were serenaded by a sombrero-wearing Mexican bottling contingent that Goizueta had named division of the year in 1985. Some had expected Coke-USA, after the trauma of the New Coke episode, might get the honor, in part as a reflection of Goizueta's stubborn insistence that in the end, New Coke had been good for the company by re-awakening the American love affair with Coca-Cola. By the time it was over, the bottlers would see Chuck Berry, Kool and the Gang, Merv Griffin, and even Vanna White on stage or in parades. By Friday afternoon, Goizueta was so worn down that he broke precedent and went home for an afternoon nap.

At the closing party three nights later, Coke capped the event by toppling 680,000 dominoes on six continents, in a globally transmitted broadcast hosted by Dick Cavett. They sang happy birthday to Coke in their native languages, with Keough exhorting everyone involved worldwide to join hands and "feel the power of the Coca-Cola system." Goizueta, in his last remarks at the meeting, sought to tie together his deep indebtedness to the past and his vision for the future. "May every moment of our future be as special as the memories of our past," he said. "As Mr. Woodruff said to me so many times, 'May all your luck be good luck.'"

GOOD FORTUNE FAVORS THE WELL-PREPARED. AND AS GOIZUETA turned his attention away from megaparties and back to megabottlers in the days following the centennial celebration, he found his luck and preparation paying off again. Keough in January had said only a few details needed to be "worked out" to complete the merger between Lupton and Coke. The details, alas, did not work out over time, thanks to Jack Lupton's second thoughts about the deal. This proved fortunate for Goizueta, because it left an opening through which he drove an overhaul of Coke's entire bottling strategy.

In April, the leveraged buyout firm Kohlberg, Kravis Roberts & Co. gained control of the Beatrice Cos. and ousted its chairman James L. Dutt. To pay down the sizable debt from the deal and rationalize the bloated operation Dutt had built, KKR hung a for-sale sign on Beatrice's bottling operation. For Goizueta, that sign spelled opportunity. With the Lupton deal not yet closed thanks to disagreements over control of the bottling operation and with Beatrice's entire BCI Holdings bottling unit available for sale, there was no point pushing forward with negotiations that, at best, would lead only to a merger with Lupton. Now Goizueta wanted an outright purchase—not just of JTL, but of Beatrice as well.

But the move to buy both the Lupton and Beatrice bottlers had a significant sticking point: the huge load of debt it would drop onto Coke's balance sheet. To get the two companies, Goizueta would have to add $600 million in long-term debt, an increase of nearly 70 percent. He had already signaled to Wall Street a willingness to boost Coke's debt beyond the current 18 percent of the company's total capital, but even he had not contemplated such a big move all at once. And with return on invested capital remaining one of the key benchmarks of his management style, Goizueta knew he would risk distorting key capital ratios on which he had trained Wall Street to base its valuation of Coke's stock.

The price of the two huge bottlers was less problematic to Goizueta. As he had demonstrated with the Columbia Pictures deal, he was not a particularly disciplined dollars-and-cents negotiator. In this case, as with Columbia, Goizueta was more concerned with gaining control of the company than dickering over every last dollar. He was willing to pay as much as 11 times the cash flow of both companies, far more than the average cash flow for bottlers at the time. He would not have much choice. Lupton had entertained offers from other bidders since the merger talks with Coke broke down, and Henry Kravis of KKR was keenly aware of the market price for BCI Holdings.

If he was to nail both of them down, Goizueta would have to pay a rich price, which he promptly did. On June 16, he agreed to buy the bottling interests of BCI Holdings for $1 billion in cash. Two weeks later, he agreed to pay $1.2 billion for JTL, and assume the bottler's $200 million in debt. The Beatrice deal must have been particularly hard to stomach. Three years earlier, Goizueta had a shot to buy the bottling operation in southern California for $300 million from its previous owner, Northwest Industries. Keough campaigned aggressively for the deal. But Goizueta failed to pull the trigger because he was worried about the impact on Coke's balance sheet. Three years later, Goizueta was paying more than three times as much as the price he had rejected as too rich.

Now Goizueta was in a bind. He prided himself on predictability, but in a span of two weeks he had thrown off Coke's bottler investment strategy by taking outright ownership of two huge bottlers. Wall Street analysts generally approved of Coke's refranchising program, but they did not want him tying up too much capital in owning bottlers. As recently as November 1985, Goizueta had promised not to get caught owning too large a chunk of Coke's bottler system. He had intended to remain primarily a minority equity investor in a few key bottlers. "As an equity investor, we will participate in the rising value of the entire system, as well as maintain a voice of influence without total direct ownership or complete investment," he had said. "Our goal is not to become a major player in bottling, but to facilitate a stronger and more efficient independent bottling system."

It was a classic case of Goizueta trying to meet several seemingly contradictory objectives—enjoying the fruits of investment, without quite becoming the owner; operating as a major equity owner, while still claiming the bottlers were independent. It would be especially tough to claim the bottling system was independent now that the combined Coke/JTL/BCI bottling operations would have a footprint covering 38 percent of the U.S. population. Goizueta had moved nimbly to seize the opportunity of two huge bottlers suddenly coming up for sale, but now he had to move just as fast to get them off his hands, and get Coke back on the course he had set.

Although Goizueta and Keough had begun the conversation about spinning off the bottlers in 1981, pressing matters like Diet Coke, Columbia, and New Coke had intervened. While planning a pep rally for bottlers in 1984, Goizueta had exclaimed that the refranchising of the bottling system "is the logical extension of everything we've done." But Keough and Goizueta had not dared to dream then that a franchise with the history and size of the Lupton bottlers would come up for sale. And they never imagined that a second bottler the size of the Beatrice operation would come on the market at virtually the same time. Now, after five years at the helm, Goizueta saw he had no choice but to finally launch the bottling program. "It made sense to us then, and it makes even more sense to us now," he told Keough.

To do the job, Goizueta called in chief financial officer Douglas Ivester. The charge to Ivester was simple. He needed to find a way to spin off the Coke bottling operation—to knock $3.1 billion in debt off of Coca-Cola's balance sheet, yet still retain control of the bottling operation. Moreover, Goizueta did not want to see Coke's debt climb above 20 percent of the company's total capitalization. While he recognized the benefits of leverage, there was enough of Woodruff in him that Goizueta still demanded an extremely conservative balance sheet, especially by the standards of the debt-crazed 1980s.

Ivester had worked all his career to get an assignment like this. A native of Gainesville, Georgia, Ivester had first shown promise as a numbers whiz in the fifth grade, when he tested at the 12th-grade level in a standardized math exam. He bagged groceries to help pay for college at the University of Georgia, eloped to marry his high-school sweetheart, Victoria Kay Grindle, and took a job with the Ernst & Ernst accounting firm after earning a bachelor of science degree. At Ernst & Ernst, Ivester impressed his bosses by his diligence—plodding through a muddy field to find serial numbers for a heavy-equipment company audit—and by his facility with complex tax laws in countries around the world. In 1976, he was assigned to the Coke account, one of the firm's most prestigious jobs. Three years later, Coke offered Ivester a job as assistant controller and director of corporate auditing. Mike Henning, chief executive of Ernst & Young International, wrote a farewell note to him that ended with the sentence, "I expect to write you another congratulatory note when you become CEO one of these days."

When Ivester went to Coke, he joked to a colleague about his parents' reaction to the move. "This is going to be so much easier for my parents because they never understood what Ernst did, but everyone knows what Coke does," he told fellow auditor Diane Janes.

He went to work with a flurry of financial moves that brought Coke's balance sheet into the modern age. First, he helped put together Coke's $100 million debt offering in 1980—the one that helped finance the construction of the Coke tower. In seven subsequent Eurobond offerings, Ivester three times made the Coke paper

more attractive to investors by attaching warrants to the bonds, enabling them to purchase a separate tranche of Coke's debt at a fixed
price for a fixed period of time. If Coke's fortunes kept rising, the warrants could have real value for investors.

Columbia Pictures' television operations had a huge, untapped re-
source in its receivables—the money it was owed from selling syndicated shows. It was Ivester's idea to bundle the receivables and sell
them to investors in the form of securities. Coke got $630 million in
ready cash far faster than it would have if it waited until the shows
aired on television—then the conventional practice in the industry.
Some of the money went toward the June 1985 purchase of two television production companies, Tandem Productions and Norman Lear's
Embassy Productions. When those deals created new streams of receivables for Coke, Ivester securitized them, too.

To Ivester, at least, the solution to Goizueta's quandary was fairly
simple. If Coke could own just 49 percent of its big bottling arm, it
could exert virtual control. But by remaining just shy of a majority interest, Coke could still treat the bottling operations as an investment
holding. It was a distinction with a big difference. It meant Coke
could dump $3.1 billion in debt from its balance sheet on to that of
the bottling entity. Just as significantly, the capital invested in bottling would also fall off of Coke's financial statements. If the bottling
operation paid a handsome dividend—a matter Coke could influence
through its 49 percent ownership of the bottling concern's stock—
that would give a lift to Goizueta's all-important measuring stick of
return on invested capital.

Goizueta dubbed Ivester's proposal "the 49 percent solution," but
he was not certain it would fly with regulators. To make certain there
would not be any hang-ups, that the debt would stay gone once Coke
bounced it onto the new megabottler's balance sheet, Goizueta sent
Ivester to meet with the Securities and Exchange Commission's chief
accountant, where he got an informal blessing on the deal. Goizueta
had the plan in place before he went to the board for final approval on
the Lupton purchase, and Keough publicly signaled the spinoff of the
bottling operation when he announced in mid-July that Coke had
struck a deal to buy John Lupton's bottling company.

The spinoff also enabled Goizueta to move Brian Dyson out of
Coke's executive suite. Just a few weeks earlier, Sergio Zyman had left

the company to open shop as a consultant to consumer products companies. Goizueta would never stop rationalizing the New Coke debacle as an ultimately successful mistake, but at the same time he did nothing to stop Zyman from leaving, and actively moved Dyson out of Coke's North Avenue tower. If he succeeded with CCE, Dyson could rehabilitate himself. But if he did not, then the two men who with Goizueta were most closely tied to New Coke would no longer be at work for the company.

GOIZUETA WAS DETERMINED TO LEAVE NOTHING TO CHANCE IN THE spinoff of Coca-Cola Enterprises. For investment banking counsel, he called in Herbert Allen, Jr., now a close friend and fellow Coke board member since selling Columbia Pictures to Goizueta in 1982. Allen was an odd choice for lead manager of the CCE public offering. Despite his reknown as a media dealmaker, he had virtually no experience underwriting stock offerings. Allen's investment banking arsenal lacked simple tools of the IPO trade like pricing, segmenting the target market, planning the road-show presentations to analysts, and timing the stock offering itself. He headed up a team that also included far more seasoned underwriting firms—First Boston Corp., Salomon Brothers, and Shearson Lehman Brothers. But it was Allen, Goizueta, and Ivester who made all the major calls on the CCE sale.

Goizueta had a very strong idea of how he wanted the deal done. First, he told the underwriters at an organizational meeting to start the IPO process, it was imperative to launch CCE before the end of 1986. Coke had borrowed the entire purchase price of the Lupton and BCI properties, and Goizueta could not afford to leave that much debt on Coke's financial statement when he closed the year. Next, to make it clear to investors that CCE was stepping out as an independent entity, Goizueta wanted no direct Coke involvement in any public aspect of peddling the IPO. Most importantly, he wanted to get top dollar for the bottler. And he wanted the CCE deal to be the largest public offering in history. "Everybody at Coke had a bad case of 'biggest-deal-ever-itis,'" says one investment banker who attended the planning sessions.

Allen ran the numbers on CCE and came up with a price range from $21 to $25 per share. Goizueta wanted more, as much as $27 a share, but the investment bankers persuaded him the CCE launch would fail if he stuck to that price, because nobody would pay it. Even in the range of $21 to $25 a share, it was clear even to Allen and his associates that CCE's shares might be priced too high. At that price, the stock would go public at 62 times earnings—a higher ratio than most high-technology growth stocks could fetch, let alone a capital-intensive business like bottling. It would dwarf even Coca-Cola's hefty 18 times earning. Publicly held bottlers tended to trade at something closer to 14 times earnings.

But Goizueta wanted his $24 a share, so he decided that the best way to sell CCE was to change the way that Wall Street looked at the deal. Rather than focusing on earnings, investors should focus on cash flow. Measured that way, Coke was asking investors to pay only about 12 times cash flow for CCE, only slightly more than the inflated price the company itself had paid as a defensive move, to stop these two key bottlers from falling into the wrong hands. The emphasis on cash flow was in keeping with the lessons Goizueta had learned from his grandfather in Cuba. "Spend much less than you need to live with, and always have a strong cash position in the bank. That way you can take advantage of opportunities as they arise," his grandfather had said.

To Wall Street, the sudden talk of cash flow from Goizueta seemed like a shell game. Bottlers had always been measured with the same tools as other companies, with net income, operating earnings, price/earnings ratios, and the like. The cash-flow sales approach drew only scorn from Wall Street. "They were talking about it on a cash-flow basis," sniffed one analyst. "They had no earnings because they were busy covering all the debt." As CCE conducted road shows in Boston, New York, Chicago, and other major markets, the analysts and investors who came to hear the pitch walked away scratching their heads, and holding tight to their wallets. In Boston and Chicago, attendance was thin, in part because the deal was getting a bad reputation, and partly because Allen scheduled the sessions at out-of-the-way hotels, a rookie mistake.

Dyson proved incapable of selling the deal. Analysts believed the cerebral Coke executive was ill-suited to the rough-and-tumble of running a bottling company, despite his success in renegotiating the bottlers' contracts in the late 1970s. Dyson underscored those concerns with his choice of presentation materials in the CCE road show. Rather than going into detail about distribution systems, bottling technology, and financial forecasts, the Dyson presentation relied heavily on Coca-Cola commercials, promotional programs, and other bells and whistles that had little measurable impact on the bottom-line results of a big bottler like CCE. "The company came off as being very aloof. They did not give a lot of financial information," says Martin Romm, a beverage analyst with First Boston who was part of the team trying to peddle the deal. "There was a sense of them saying, 'We're the Coca-Cola Company, and you either believe us or you don't.'" For some in the audience, it was unsettling to see Dyson in charge of the new bottling company, regardless of his poor handling of the road show. With his high profile as a career Big Coke executive who had orchestrated New Coke, it underscored that the parent company was setting up CCE as a puppet it could manipulate from outside.

In the end, the analysts did not buy the CCE story. With the year-end deadline approaching and the deal still getting negative reviews, the investment bankers caucused, and Allen delivered the news to Goizueta that he was never going to get the price he wanted. Reluctantly, Goizueta agreed to let Allen & Company knock down the price on the deal, lowering the expected offering range by $3 per share. That meant CCE would go public at anywhere from $18 to $24 a share, reducing the total value of the IPO by $215 million. It irked Goizueta, but the investment bankers believed he and Keough could not bear seeing CCE stock go public and immediately drop so soon on the heels of the New Coke disaster.

Three days later, when the stock at last went on sale for the still-lower price of $16.50 a share, Dyson and his fellow CCE salesmen still had not convinced many skeptics. "We were thinking about $15," said James Martin, executive vice president of the College Retirement Fund. The nation's largest stock portfolio just could not buy Dyson's cash-flow sales job for CCE. "We look at things on a fundamental basis, and it did not seem that it was going to sell well. It was hard to picture when the earnings would come out in a visible way."

Indeed, Lehman Brothers, which had told Allen it could sell around 30 million shares to the retail investors it was targeting, wound up unloading only 15 million shares of CCE. Shearson was stuck holding some of the CCE shares in its own account. And even in Atlanta, retail broker Robinson-Humphrey had to struggle before finally finding buyers for its 3.2-million-share allotment. Rather than bumping up slightly and giving investors a quick feel-good effect that most underwriting firms try to build into the pricing of IPO shares, CCE actually fell in its first day of trading.

The CCE launch cleared $3 billion in debt off of Coca Cola's books, but in most other respects, Goizueta's experiment in launching Coke's huge bottling transformation proved a debacle. He did not come close to the price he had wanted, and he failed to set the record for an IPO. At $16.50 a share, the deal brought in only $1.18 billion—behind the $1.2 billion offering by the Henley Group. Rather than being a growth stock, as he and Ivester had insisted CCE would become, shares of the Coke offspring languished. He set the company adrift with a management team, led by Dyson, that was unprepared to handle the rough, low-margin, capital intensive business of bottling his company's sugared water. Ultimately, he would be forced in 1992 to replace Dyson with a new team more capable of running the world's largest bottling company. At least he could take pride in the fact that several other firms followed the 49 percent solution strategy, including Sonat Corp., where Goizueta was a board member. And he again gave Herbert Allen a big pay day, enabling him to pocket more than $10 million of the $59.3 million in investment banking fees that arose from the deal.

GETTING CCE OFF THE TABLE CLEARED THE WAY FOR GOIZUETA TO focus on the one noncore company still cluttering Coke's balance sheet: Columbia Pictures. From the very start, when Wall Street analysts jumped on Goizueta for paying too much for Columbia, the foray into Hollywood had proven more difficult than Goizueta could imagine. At the outset, Columbia Pictures seemed to have enough domestic revenues to help Goizueta achieve his goal of bringing domestic revenues into parity with returns from overseas. What he did not take into account was the cost of bringing in those extra sales—the cost in management exertions, in bad publicity, in capital outlays, and in the boom-and-bust impact on Coke's earnings statements.

Goizueta considered himself a capable and perhaps even gifted manager. He scoffed at people who considered management a science. "It's an art, not a science," he said. And he felt that his artistry as a strategist and bottom-line manager should somehow be able to create a masterpiece out of his Hollywood adventure. Good things would come of the effort. He would get ideas that led to the creation of CCE and, after he sold Columbia in 1989 at a sizable profit, he would get the funds needed for Coke's big push into eastern Europe in the early 1990s. But from 1982, when he first acquired the studio, until 1989, when he finally unloaded it into the arms of an unsuspecting Sony Corp., Goizueta never quite mastered the art of playing corporate chieftain in the byzantine world of modern movie-making.

It was never widely known, but Columbia actually had played an important part in helping Goizueta and Ivester come up with the notion of the spinoff of 51 percent of Coca-Cola Enterprises. The deal exposed him to the notion of creating an off-balance-sheet enterprise, pooling capital from outside parties, and booking any profits as investment income rather than operating profits. At the time he acquired Columbia, the movie studio's management team already had negotiated a partnership with the cable television service Home Box Office and the CBS broadcast network to jointly finance a new movie studio, Tri-Star Pictures. As part of the deal, HBO and CBS committed to pay from 30 percent to 50 percent of the cost of every film Columbia or Tri-Star produced. The more successful the movie, the more the partners paid in, with no ceiling on their total payments. Capitalized at $1 billion, Tri-Star would help Coke's entertainment unit boost its total output of movie titles, spread the average $15 million cost of producing a movie among the three partners, and bring in funds that would help Columbia pay down debt.

Goizueta immediately recognized the Tri-Star deal as a huge boon to Columbia and Coke. The Tri-Star deal already was in the works, though not yet publicly announced, when Goizueta bought Columbia. Besides exposing him to the benefits of an off-balance-sheet entity, Tri-Star also enabled Goizueta to protect Coke's results from some of the financial risks of the movie industry's boom-and-bust profit picture. At the time of the CCE offering four years later, Goizueta told Columbia executives that the strategy for spinning off CCE was inspired directly by the thinking behind Tri-Star.

Tri-Star was the one pleasant surprise that Columbia gave to Goizueta. For the most part, the others were shockers. Before it was over, by the time he endured Hollywood's boom-and-bust cycle of blockbusters and flops, the microscopic scrutiny of the entertainment press, the sometimes fascinating sometimes enraging vagaries of dealing with

Hollywood talent, Goizueta would learn lessons about himself and about his company. Goizueta personally would learn that he was better off sticking with the one business he knew well, rather than dabbling in those he did not understand. And he became convinced that his company was better off investing all its money in soft drinks and related products, where earnings were predictable and manageable, growth could be fairly certain, and the future did not depend on the fickle entertainment tastes of the public or the unfathomable egos of stars.

From the beginning of Coke's dominion over Columbia, with a kick-off management meeting, Goizueta's actions set the tone for an uncomfortable and sometimes unproductive relationship. When Goizueta invited Vincent and his executive team to a meeting in Vancouver, British Columbia, the Columbia crowd expected an informal get-acquainted session, with a smattering of strategy and heavy dollops of corporate bonding. And Goizueta's opening remarks seemed to confirm their expectations. "We have just acquired Columbia Pictures, so it is best that we meet in British Columbia," he joked lamely, to a polite if unenthusiastic chuckle from one or two of the Columbia team.

That ended the levity for the day. During the next four hours, Goizueta, Ivester, and marketing chief Herbert guided the way through an exhaustive, highly polished, multimedia introduction to The Coca-Cola Company. They covered an extensive strategy statement laying out performance goals for Coke's new entertainment unit, and sent a clear message that Coke meant business and Goizueta meant to call the shots. "It was a deliberate and successful attempt by Roberto to put on such a fantastic presentation as to, if not embarrass, at least put in place the Hollywood crowd," recalled Peter Sealey, a Coke marketing executive at the time. That night, Vincent's team stayed up late trying to spruce up their presentation to the level of what Coke had just put on, but the power game already was won.

IT WAS APPROPRIATE THAT THE RELATIONSHIP START OFF WITH COKE ambushing Columbia, for unpleasant surprises would characterize Columbia's relationship with Coke during Goizueta's entire seven-year flirtation with movie moguldom. Almost from the start, it was apparent that Coke's expectations—as outlined in the study A.D. Little had prepared in building the case for Coke's acquisition of the studio—were not in line with the realities of modern Hollywood. And because

Goizueta had relied heavily on Little's work in selecting his acquisition target, he was impatient and discouraged when the early returns did not come in as planned. Over time, he would find that earnings were not predictable, and Coke's marketing expertise was not as valuable as Little had expected.

Finally, tired of hearing about the study, Vincent asked Goizueta to let him see the damn thing. Beholding it, he was shocked at the ten reasons Little had used to claim that Columbia made sense for Coke. "Two of the ten are total bullshit," Vincent said in a meeting with Goizueta. Studio chief Frank Price was not, as the study claimed, one of the studio's great assets. And movie making, with its wild profit swings and exorbitant costs, was not itself a great business. The rest of Little's findings proved at best only half right. And the vaunted consulting firm had missed altogether what Vincent considered Columbia's biggest asset—its extensive holdings of syndication rights for popular television programs. "The TV business is the business you wanted here," Vincent told Goizueta.

Such plain talk was typical of Vincent, a man who himself was a fairly new player in Hollywood. Francis T. Vincent, Jr., grew up in New Haven, Connecticut, the son of a Yale-educated telephone company employee. A standout high school football player, Vincent suffered a debilitating back injury during his freshman year at Williams College. After a roommate locked him in his dorm room, Vincent slipped on an icy window ledge while trying to climb to the roof, and fell four stories, crushing two vertebrae. He learned to walk again, graduated from Williams, then from Yale Law School. After starting a promising career as a lawyer, first in New York and then with the Securities and Exchange Commission in Washington, DC, Vincent in 1978 received a surprise call from a Williams College classmate, Herbert A. Allen, Jr.

Allen needed help because the Hollywood studio he had purchased was thrown into turmoil when its studio chief, David Begelman, was found to have forged checks and misappropriated company money. He hired Vincent, who moved overnight from his $47,000-a-year SEC job to running one of Hollywood's major studios. Vincent quickly took charge, instituting new management and accounting procedures to cut down on the petty graft that he found throughout the system, and fending off raider Kirk Kerkorian. Recognizing that paying greenmail to ward off Kerkorian had put Columbia into a tight financial position, he encouraged Lewis Korman, a Columbia executive, to push ahead with his plan to create Tri-Star as a means of reducing Columbia's film-making costs. When Coke bought Columbia, Vincent saw that his immediate cash concerns were solved, but also quickly recognized that Coke's cash came at a heavy cost because Coke's plans for the studio often did not measure up to the reality of the business.

Despite Vincent's blunt disparagement of the Little study, Goizueta was not quite ready to completely dump its precepts. But Vincent's concerns were enough to convince him he needed a Coke man on the scene to bring some soft-drink discipline to the unwieldy and unpredictable movie operation. The man for the job: Peter S. Sealey, Coke's number two marketing executive. At the time, Sealey served both Goizueta and Vincent by stepping into his new role. After the Vancouver meeting, Vincent recognized that he would need someone from Atlanta to help interpret the world of Coke as it applied to Hollywood. Goizueta, meanwhile, was learning enough about Hollywood's runaway costs and million-dollar personal services contracts to recognize he needed a Coke man in Hollywood to lend a dose of reality.

In transferring Sealey to Columbia, Goizueta got his first taste of a part of the Hollywood scene he would never understand: the trappings of Hollywood, the personal services contracts and huge entertainment budgets that everyone in the movie business seemed to take for granted. As Sealey settled in his new job, he quickly learned that he would not be taken seriously in Tinseltown unless he worked under an employment contract. Instead of a Coke salary, he wanted guaranteed pay and a few of the requisite perks of Hollywood life. Goizueta was repulsed at the idea, and when Keough informed Sealey of the rejection, the marketing man was distraught. "I don't know how I'm going to be treated like anything but a corporate spy unless you do it," he said. Ultimately, Goizueta and Keough relented, signed a contract, and resigned themselves to the fact that Sealey had gone Hollywood.

Sealey set immediately to work laying the Coke marketing template over Columbia's movie-making operations, following the strategy Goizueta had laid out when he bought the studio. Sealey pushed to bring sophisticated consumer surveying techniques refined in soda-pop marketing that went far beyond the focus-group research already common in Hollywood. He began by identifying "heavy users" of entertainment. He tested their responses to advertising campaigns, even to story lines for prospective film projects. In several instances, Sealey even tested the relative merits of individual actors in given roles. He tried hard, but could not succeed, with one of Goizueta's favorite schemes, the push to distribute video cassettes through Coca-Cola's bottlers. The idea proved a nonstarter when bottlers complained that tapes on their trucks would crowd out the far-more-profitable soda pop.

Sealey pushed an emphatic cost-reduction program that reflected Goizueta's strong push for an economic return on his investment in Columbia. He noted that the Columbia Pictures release *Gandhi*, which won the Academy Award for best picture, barely eked a profit because the studio overspent on marketing. He cut radio spending to advertise sneak previews. He pushed to give Columbia access to Coke's television advertising schedule, enabling the studio to take advantage of Coke's bulk-rate purchasing. That move alone boosted Columbia's advertising time by 5 percent without increasing spending beyond the budgeted $30 million in 1983.

Not surprisingly, the strong Sealey input, coupled with occasional directives from Goizueta and Keough, began causing troubles with Hollywood. It bothered Goizueta when Price refused to boost movie production, as called for in Goizueta's studio plan. The old-line Hollywood producer claimed an increase in production would affect his ability to turn out artful movies. When Tri-Star began operations in 1983, Price complained that the new studio would give HBO a virtual monopoly in cable, reducing Columbia's cable revenues by killing off competition for cable rights. Goizueta did not buy either complaint. And the talk about quality sounded hollow from the man who had greenlighted *Howard the Duck,* and who had such a tin ear to audience taste that he told Goizueta *Annie* would be a success.

On the receiving end of Frank Price's complaints, Goizueta grew short-tempered. He wanted results, and he felt Price could not deliver. Price's constant carping annoyed him. After a lengthy discussion with one studio executive about problems with Price, Goizueta summed up his opinion succinctly. "Frank Price makes me puke," he said.

Vincent decided Price had to go, but he still was nervous when he phoned Keough with the news in the fall of 1983, because the A.D. Little study had made such a big deal about Price's great value to Columbia. Keough was nonplused. "Fay, you don't understand. Whatever your problem is, it's not a problem for The Coca-Cola Company," Keough said. "Frank Price is not a problem. Frank Price is a personnel issue."

The far bigger issue for Coke was the lesson it learned when Columbia's 1983 results came in, and Vincent was vindicated in his warnings about the shoddiness of A.D. Little's research into the movie business. Earnings from television, which Little completely missed in its evaluation of Columbia, comprised four-fifths of Columbia's total return of $91 million, and contributed nearly 10 percent of Coke's entire 1983 operating income. The results were encouraging, but Vincent and Goizueta were hardly satisfied. Vincent set his immediate sights on catching Minute Maid and Goizueta announced that Columbia should contribute 25 percent of operating income by 1990.

As positive as the television numbers were, it was obvious that Columbia needed to boost returns from the movie business, and Goizueta and Vincent approached the problem by dumping studio chiefs more often than baseball owners oust their managers. As much as anything, the troubles with Columbia's studio heads soured Goizueta on the movie business, but there was plenty else for Goizueta not to like. He despised the personal services contracts, in which studio chiefs were paid like movie stars, where demands for chauffeurs, private jets, and the construction of private screening rooms were commonplace. It bothered him that a multimillion-dollar investment like a movie could thrive or fail based solely on how it performed in its first weekend in theatres. It irked him that, even though Columbia's movie operation was only a tiny part of his company, it attracted more media attention, and nearly as many analyst queries, as the rest of the Coca-Cola system combined.

Frank Price clearly was not the man to make Roberto Goizueta like Hollywood. When he refused to boost Columbia's production to meet Goizueta's strategy of getting more movies on the market, Price had to go. At first blush, it looked like Guy MacElwaine might be the man. Vincent in late 1983 promoted the well-known Hollywood producer to studio president, and he immediately turned heads in Atlanta by doubling the production target for 1985 to 18 movies. Goizueta and Keough showed their appreciation by showering MacElwaine with attention and support. Keough at one point tried to introduce MacElwaine to the concept of lifetime employment that was standard issue for most high-level Coke executives. "You've docked your boat with

Coca-Cola for the rest of your life," Keough told MacElwaine early after his promotion. And in a telephone conversation, Goizueta assured MacElwaine he had complete authority in running the studio. "There is only one head of the studio, and you are the head of the studio," he said.

Goizueta had promised himself he would not get hung up in Hollywood. Not long after he bought Columbia, when a reporter accused him of an undue fascination with the movie business, Goizueta disagreed. "The closest I've ever come to Brooke Shields is when our pictures appeared together in the same issue of *Newsweek*," he said. But the trouble with the studio chiefs, along with the allure of the klieg lights, seemed to draw him into the fray at Columbia more than he ever intended. When Goizueta did try to rub shoulders with the Hollywood talent, he was sometimes comically out of his element. Visiting the set of *Ghostbusters* in 1983, the pinstriped and uptight Goizueta made an odd pair when trying to talk movies with a beer-swilling, shorts-wearing Dan Aykroyd.

When he bought the studio, Goizueta had pledged not to censor the creative content of the movies, so long as Columbia never produced an X-rated film. But he got nervous about Coke's image when he heard Columbia was producing a feature-film treatment of comedian Richard Pryor's raunchy stage act, *Richard Pryor . . . Here and Now*. Inviting Pryor and studio boss MacElwaine to Atlanta for a talk, Goizueta opened the conversation by complimenting Pryor on his film *The Toy*, a farce in which he played a live toy awarded to a spoiled rich boy. Then he launched into a five-minute talk about the importance of family entertainment, and the impact of movies on American morality. "There comes a point when someone has to stand up for morality and ethics in our society," Goizueta told the movie men.

Coca-Cola's chairman stopped talking, and an uncomfortable silence filled his cavernous office. Then Pryor turned to MacElwaine. "Well," he said. "I guess we don't get laid tonight."

Pryor's joke drew a chuckle from Goizueta, but it did not erase for him the growing concern that Coke was out of its element in movie land.

It was not yet clear to Goizueta, but by the end of 1984, he already had reached the high-water mark for his Columbia excursion. *Ghostbusters*, released that summer, grossed $220 million at the box office. Better still for Columbia, Tri-Star partner HBO had to kick in $35 million to help cover Ghostbusters' production costs, because HBO was committed to pay Columbia fees based on its movies' box-office results. When Frank Biondi, the HBO executive who negotiated the Tri-Star deal, lost his job over Ghostbusters' bust for HBO, Vincent got Goizueta's approval to hire Biondi to help run Coke's television operations.

Despite the financial success of Ghostbusters, it marked the end of Goizueta's first-blush fascination with movie-making. "It's intoxicating at first, and no one can resist it. But the smart people soon find out it's a business like anything else, and not much of a business at that. Roberto went through the whole cycle," said one executive who worked with Goizueta throughout his evolution in the movie business.

The cycle peaked for Goizueta in 1984 because he began to realize that Columbia would not solve his problem of obtaining predictable results from Coca-Cola's domestic operations. Rather than logging 1984 as a big success because of Ghostbusters and Karate Kid, Goizueta recognized it as a sign of trouble. In everything he did, Goizueta valued predictability and reliability. The movie business was proving a reliably unreliable income source. If income could more than double in a single year, as it did in 1984, it could drop just as fast, as it nearly did in 1985. And it irritated Goizueta that the movie business in particular drew so much attention from the business press and Wall Street analysts, even though it never came close to his target of contributing 25 percent of operating income.

Goizueta urged Vincent to find a way to smooth out Columbia's earnings, and Vincent complied by paying out $485 million in 1985 to add Embassy Entertainment, syndicator of "Who's the Boss?" to the entertainment unit's lineup. When Frank Biondi told Doug Ivester in early 1986 that he wanted to buy Merv Griffin Enterprises for another $200 million, he got a chilly reception. Ivester was skeptical about "Wheel of Fortune" and "Jeopardy" as the bedrock for such a big purchase. "How do you know the shows are going to last?" Ivester asked about two programs that have remained two of the most valuable properties in the history of television syndication. Besides, the Merv Griffin deal carried the added benefit of bringing both Griffin and letter-turner Vanna White to Coke's centennial bash that May.

Still trying to iron out the Columbia earnings, Vincent also purchased the Loews theatre chain. The idea seemed to make sense as a form of vertical integration—owning another part of the movie distribution chain. Goizueta approved the deal, but quickly discovered it was a mistake. Theatre operators threatened to cancel their Coca-Cola contracts because they resented purchasing soda pop from the company that owned their competitors. Coke's struggling fountain business could ill afford such losses, but for Goizueta it was a valuable lesson. When Pepsi diversified into restaurants with the purchase of Pizza Hut and Taco Bell, Goizueta confidently and correctly predicted trouble based on his own experience. "It's bad business to compete with your best customers," he said.

Even that shortcoming might have been acceptable if the entertainment division did not suffer from the ultimate failing of its inability to meet Goizueta's demand that his company produce, reliable quarter-by-quarter results. "Every quarter has to be better than the next. The movie business is very hard to manage, and it doesn't work that way," said one former studio executive. "Doug Ivester would call and tell us he needed a few more pennies per share. There was a big tension between us and Coke, because we just couldn't do that." Except for the *Ghostbusters'* bonanza in 1984, the movie studio itself never made money. Even when combined with Tri-Star's films the total share of box office sales remained near the bottom of the Hollywood heap. Goizueta added it up, and found that the deal had not obtained his minimum objective of helping Coke's domestic operations account for 50 percent of total operating income. Despite Columbia's contribution, domestic results remained stuck at just above 30 percent.

There was a flaw in Goizueta's strategic vision for Columbia that was at least partly responsible for his ultimate failure to make entertainment work. He wished the studio well, but only if it abided by the prerequisite that the entertainment division could not outgrow soft drinks. "Coca-Cola is, and will always be primarily a soft-drink company," Goizueta said. Goizueta was asking his executives to manage the entertainment companies for slow growth, something he never would have condoned in the soft-drink business, and a tactic that was certain death in a marketplace that demanded quick action and big investments in order to succeed.

Vincent recognized the fallacy in Goizueta's plan, and struggled against it. As if to test Goizueta, Vincent began presenting proposals that he thought would help Columbia reach its natural size, and enable it to be one of the half-dozen studios with a chance to survive as the movie industry consolidated. He suggested buying a movie lot, but Goizueta refused. He preferred to lease space instead. At a meeting in Toronto, Vincent told Goizueta and Keough that Coke needed to buy either Warner Brothers or Time Inc. The two companies were en route to an eventual merger that created the world's largest entertainment enterprise. Goizueta immediately rejected the idea. "Coke has to be a soft-drink company," he insisted. Later, after Time and Warner merged, Goizueta rejected outright a Biondi-Vincent proposal to buy Time-Warner's cable operation. Vincent got much the same response when he suggested purchasing Viacom Inc., the cable television operation.

Vincent's biggest test of Goizueta's strategic plan came in the fall of 1986. Thomas Wyman, the chairman of CBS Inc., approached him at a lunch in early September with a proposal that Coke should buy CBS. The two agreed to pursue the notion. Vincent flew to Atlanta and told Goizueta and Keough he thought he could buy CBS for around $160 a share.

This time, Goizueta said he was willing to consider the deal. "We're not sure we want you to do it, but we owe it to you to think about it," he told Vincent. There was no point going any further, he noted, unless Vincent was certain it would be a friendly deal. Goizueta had not changed his position on hostile takeovers since rejecting consideration of a Disney merger in 1982, fearing the damage he might do to Coke's reputation.

For a more experienced Coca-Cola executive, the caveat "We're not sure we want you to do it" would have been a clear warning. But Vincent was determined to grow the entertainment sector. Vincent reported the nonrefusal to Wyman, who broke the news on September 10 to his board that Coke might be willing to acquire CBS. Powerful board members Laurence A. Tisch and William Paley promptly rejected the plan, and the board immediately fired Wyman for carrying on merger discussions without authorization. When Tisch took Wyman's place, one of his first telephone calls was to Goizueta. "Is it true you're going to bid for CBS?" he asked.

"Absolutely not," Goizueta told CBS's new chief executive. "We've never had a discussion about it." Perhaps he had forgotten the fact that he had given Vincent approval just a few days earlier to at least discuss the possibility with Wyman.

THE INEFFECTUAL CBS DALLIANCE MARKED A WATERSHED IN Goizueta's thinking. From that point forward, every move he took was designed to reduce Coca-Cola's direct connection to entertainment, to dress up the business for future sale. He understood at last that he could not commit to entertainment on a scale to succeed, and it was not in his nature to be involved in any business that he could not dominate. More and more, it looked like time to leave Hollywood.

If Goizueta had any second thoughts, definitive proof of the need to recede came in the form of a British producer named David Puttnam. Vincent hired Puttnam, best known for the low-budget success *Chariots of Fire,* as Columbia's third studio chief in four years, his last best hope to find someone who could make movies work for Coke. He purposely selected an outsider, someone not tainted by the Hollywood system of huge contracts and costly perks. Puttnam was a strange fit from the start. He made it clear from day one he would leave Columbia at the end of his three-year contract, and he flew to Hollywood to announce to Goizueta and Keough that movie-making should not be subject to "the tyranny of the box office."

Goizueta was not interested in movie-making philosophy. He wanted to know if Puttnam could deliver domestic grosses. When Puttnam said he could not promise significantly higher domestic grosses, but thought the market for international sales was wide open, Goizueta warned the new studio chief to keep focusing on the U.S. market. "If you can deliver fifty-fifty, we'd regard that not just as a breakthrough, but also as the correct balance," he said.

On his next trip to Atlanta a few months later, Puttnam got on the wrong side of Herbert Allen. "Hollywood is a despicable place," Puttnam told Allen, opening a conversation.

"If it's so despicable, why did you ask to work there?" Allen responded. Later, Allen told Puttnam that he could do what he wished, but as a three-year journeyman at Columbia, he had better do nothing to risk the long-term future of the studio or its library of films. When he got back to Hollywood, Puttnam seemed unable to utter a well-chosen word. He railed against big agency packages, big stars, and big salaries in an October 1986 meeting with Creative Artists Agency, the font of such things in Hollywood. He criticized *Ghostbusters'* star Bill Murray for selfishness and made longtime Coke pitchman Bill Cosby practically grovel before agreeing to produce *Leonard Part VI*. He dumped a host of Columbia's veteran directors, including the venerable Ray Stark, one of the few in the Hollywood establishment who had befriended Goizueta. Stark maintained a regular telephone relationship with Goizueta, delivering a blow-by-blow description of Puttnam's faux pas. Ultimately, Puttnam would get a $3 million severance package from Coke as part of his ticket out of town.

Puttnam's last measure of revenge on Goizueta and Coke was his approval of the epic flop *Ishtar*. Filmed in Morroco, the farce of a Bob Hope-Bing Crosby road movie featured outlandish budget items such as $6 million each for stars Warren Beatty and Dustin Hoffman and a $5 million nightclub set. Goizueta was shocked at the excesses, and sent Peter Sealey to Morocco to find out what was going on. Goizueta knew he had lost control when Sealey showed up in a publicity photo in *People* magazine, lounging between Hoffman and Beatty, a smirking grin peeking out from an unkempt beard. When the tab was tallied, Coke took a $25 million writeoff in 1987 on losses from *Ishtar*.

By the time the final tally for *Ishtar* came in, Goizueta already was well into executing his exit strategy. In January 1988, he combined Tri-Star and Columbia Pictures, and spun off the new Columbia Pictures Entertainment as a taxable dividend to shareholders. He retained 49 percent of the company for Coca-Cola, applying the 49 percent solution to the movie industry. By distributing the $3 billion studio as a dividend, he avoided the dog-and-pony show for analysts and investors that had turned the CCE spinoff into such a stock-market dog.

It was a wise decision, because there was plenty not to like in the Columbia Pictures Entertainment deal. Before he spun off the company, Goizueta all but looted the movie company, allowing Coke to retain $300 million in cash, $240 million in receivables, and $125 million worth of real estate that included 711 Fifth Avenue in New York, where Columbia, Tri-Star, and Allen & Company all had offices. Herbert Allen once again struck gold on one of Goizueta's deals. Ignoring the conflict of holding a bundle of Columbia and Coke stock and sitting on Coke's board, he issued a fairness opinion on the deal, earning $5 million in fees. Goizueta left the new film company with a $1.36 billion inventory of films in development, a huge number that led to more than $100 million in writedowns, most of it in Columbia's first year of freedom from Coke.

Even though Goizueta already had made it clear inside Coke that the company was on its way out of the movie business, he chafed when a *Los Angeles Times* reporter characterized the Columbia Pictures Entertainment deal to him as a disinvestment. "That's totally inaccurate," he shot back.

Goizueta was preparing to get out of the entertainment business. Although he denied it, that's precisely what he was doing. He still enjoyed the Hollywood social scene and was excited to attend the 1988 Oscars with Olguita and watch *The Last Emperor*—ironically, one of David Puttnam's films—become the first movie since *Gigi* to win in every category for which it was nominated, including best picture. Dawn Steel, the fifth and final Columbia Studio boss under Coca-Cola's reign, hosted a party beforehand, at which the Goizuetas and Keoughs mingled with the likes of Dustin Hoffman, Arnold Schwarzenegger, Sean Connery, and Glenn Close. Hollywood still had its charms, but the movie business had lost all its sparkle.

Fortunately for Goizueta, the old Hollywood studios were hot properties, with MGM/UA Entertainment Company, Warner Communications, and 20th Century Fox all selling during the final years of Coke's involvement with Columbia. Within months of the Columbia Pictures Entertainment spinoff, Goizueta encouraged Victor Kaufman to meet with Michael P. Schulhof, who was representing Sony Corp. in its search for a trophy Hollywood property to add to its extensive consumer electronics and real estate holdings in the United States. Schulhof first offered a price in the mid-$20 range, but Goizueta would not even consider the offer. He suspected there was more money to come for the studio, from Sony or from someone else.

It took a year before he was proved right. But Schulhof returned, met with Herb Allen, and in September 1989 made a landmark $3 billion bid for Columbia Pictures Entertainment, the largest price ever paid for a Hollywood studio.

For Goizueta, it was a total windfall. He had already taken nearly $700 million out of the business with the Columbia spinoff alone, not to mention the entertainment division's profits over the seven years

Coke owned the studio. Coke's $1.2 billion share of the Sony sale itself made the controversial foray into movies look good. Goizueta might have done much better had he bought Disney in 1982. The studio he had rejected in favor of Columbia had a much more profitable and predictable performance during the years Goizueta held Columbia. But Sony's desire to make a splash in Hollywood at any cost had extracted Goizueta from a frustrating, time-consuming, and poorly performing foray into the land of movie madness. Goizueta had made the same mistake many chief executives made during the 1980s, diversifying into businesses they did not understand, never quite learning how to make them work, and dumping them unceremoniously, often at a loss. Goizueta was lucky to bag a profit with Columbia, and he was cagey enough to learn not to repeat the mistake.

In the end, the Columbia purchase had failed in the chief mission Goizueta set out for it when he bought the studio: Building profits from Coke's domestic operation to parity with its international returns. In 1989, Coke earned only 27 percent of its operating income from its U.S. businesses, not the 50 percent Goizueta had envisioned when he bought the studio. But by 1989, the world was a different place, as was The Coca-Cola Company. From the perspective of the late 1980s, it seemed almost trite that Goizueta ever would have wanted to make domestic returns keep pace with the international market. The real problem, he now recognized, had been the disarray in Coke's bottling system. The refranchising effort and launch of CCE had fixed that problem.

After Columbia, Goizueta knew exactly where Coke's future could be found. It was not in movies, and it was not in trying to force the U.S. operations to match Coke's remarkable international growth. Almost as soon as he had the Sony money in his pocket, Goizueta made the world his target. With democratic revolution brewing in Europe and capital development increasing in the Pacific and other regions, the opportunities overseas were more appealing than anything Goizueta had seen in his career. And Roberto C. Goizueta was ready to seize them.

7

Coca-Colonization

In the spring of 1993, Roberto Goizueta climbed aboard Coke's Gulf-stream IV corporate jet for a trip to get a firsthand glimpse at a region to which he recently had committed $1.55 billion of Coke's money: Eastern Europe and the former Soviet Union. Nearly four years after he took the windfall from Columbia Pictures and invested it into an aggressive European expansion, the trip offered a glimpse of the results. In a larger sense, it was a window into Coke's strategy for investment overseas and development of untapped markets from Europe to Asia and beyond.

He visited a new $28 million bottling plant in Prague, a production line operated not by Coke, but by one of several major multinational joint venture bottling partners, the Australia-based Coca-Cola Amatil. Goizueta had invested $500 million in Amatil in June of 1989, then his largest investment in an international bottler, taking a 60 percent stake in the company and representation on Amatil's board so he could control the company's expansion program. Amatil had spent much of the 1980s improving its bottling business in Australia, and now was ready to look far afield, even to Eastern Europe. Financially strong and influenced by the Coca-Cola executives on its board, Amatil shadowed Coke's moves in Eastern Europe by investing its own capital in building a new Coca-Cola bottling system. Taking leave of Czech Prime Minster Vaclav Klaus in Prague, Goizueta flew directly to Warsaw, rode downtown in an escorted motorcade, and listened to Polish Prime Minister Hanna Suchocka discuss her difficulties in trying to pass privatization legislation. Suchocka was eager to see Coke Light—the international version of Diet Coke—distributed in her country. "As soon as your government approves it, we will sell it," Goizueta told her. Two weeks later, the Polish government did just that.

After opening a Warsaw plant operated by another coke bottler and visiting a promotional giveaway in Warsaw's town square, Goizueta flew to Romania, target for an $80 million Coke investment. Coke lawyers had drafted the laws Romania used to clear the way for Coke's bottling investment, and Romanian officials hoped aloud that Goizueta's visit was a portent. "Coke brings jobs and color to our streets, and now that you are here, we are confident other businesses will come," Romanian official Misu Negritoiu told Goizueta. "You have that power." From there, it was on to Dusseldorf, while others in his party split off for destinations including Sofia, Bulgaria, and even Albania, which still welcomes Coca-Cola despite being one of the most xenophobic nations on earth.

Goizueta's grand tour had all the spectacle of a state visit, complete with motorcades, flags, and even a few cheering crowds. It was a far cry from his job four decades earlier, making solitary sojourns to Cuba's five plants, checking water purity and fighting the incursion of rust rings around the necks of Coke's 6 ½ ounce glass bottles. In those days, if anyone took notice, it was simply because he was one of the most smartly dressed bottling technicians the industry had ever known.

The progression of Goizueta's career and the development of his company's international power can be measured in the distance and nature of his business trips. Moving to Miami, he toured the Caribbean. And from Atlanta, he expanded to all of South America, traveling often with Cliff Shillinglaw on quality control and product development missions. He flew to Egypt with Paul Austin, then president of AquaChem, in the unsuccessful push to offer the transfer of water purification technology as an inducement to get Coke's carbonated beverages through the Arab boycott. On that trip, Goizueta and the rest of the delegation were struck by the pomp of their reception when an Egyptian band struck up the French national anthem just as Austin was about to descend from the plane. Goizueta and board member Jimmy Sibley helped Austin brush off his coat and make certain he was presentable for such a reception. Then, as Austin stepped out, he and the rest of the Coke traveling party realized the serenade was meant for a French government official, whose plane was parked nearby. The Coke crowd cracked up laughing, realizing for a moment that perhaps they had overestimated their importance in Egypt.

As president of The Coca-Cola Company, Goizueta visited China, opening Coke's first bottling plant in Peking, and timing the opening of Coke's Canton plant to coincide with Robert W. Woodruff's 58th anniversary with the company. As chairman, Goizueta visited the Philippines, where he was making his first significant investment in an international bottler. Travel was as much a part of his job as sitting in the chairman's office dictating letters, attending meetings, and speaking to employee groups. During busy periods, he spent more than a third of his time on the road, a kind of soft-drink missionary carrying the Coca-Cola product and way of life to the farthest reaches of the globe. It pleased him to see Coke become the largest single employer on the African continent, or to watch Coke trounce Pepsi in such competitive markets as Japan and Germany, year in and out.

Goizueta did not have Paul Austin's knack for turning a quiet meal into a mega-dollar opportunity. He could not claim a triumph like Austin's famous lunch with a Chinese trade officer that opened that vast country to Coca-Cola. Nearing the end of his first decade as chairman, he could not put his name to any major overthrows in Pepsi's established strongholds. From the vast reach of the communist world to holdout countries like Venezuela, there were still pockets Goizueta had not yet painted Coca-Cola red. But Goizueta was much less the flashy deal maker than the unstoppable strategist, a technician who made moves so quietly and so far in advance of events on the ground that it was easy to overlook them, or underestimate their importance. In 1985, he had coined the phrase "affordable, acceptable, accessible" to describe how Coke should go about achieving Woodruff's grand vision of putting a Coke "within arm's reach of desire." He spent the rest of the decade trying to realize that vision.

THE CAMPAIGN LEADING UP TO GOIZUETA'S GRAND TOUR OF EUROPE began long before his G-IV took off from Atlanta in early 1993. It began behind the scenes well before Mikhail Gorbachev precipitated the collapse of the Iron Curtain in the late 1980s. It began, really, as Goizueta and his top management team in the mid-1980s began focusing on the need to improve Coke's international operations. After spending half a decade shoring up Coke's domestic bottling system, Goizueta saw something he recognized in Coke's international system: neglect and disarray resulting from the same lack of investment and strategy that had weakened so many domestic bottlers. In 1984, as he was laying plans for the launch of New Coke, Goizueta recognized he had trouble in Coke's international business. Coke's domestic soft-drink volume grew nearly 10 percent that year, while international volume grew only about 4 percent. Goizueta was not happy with either figure. But the poor international performance was doubly irksome because it lagged the expectations he had set forth in his initial strategy statement in 1981. "We haven't grown overseas volume like we said three years ago we were going to do," he complained.

Goizueta was so determined to change the game, he was willing to sacrifice an opportunity for a short-term earnings boost created by the declining value of the U.S. dollar. When Goizueta was learning the intricacies of currency hedging, he and chief financial officer Sam Ayoub bet a dollar a day on the price of the dollar relative to the Japanese yen, West German mark, British pound, and other major currencies. If Ayoub had not retired, he and Goizueta would have spent much of 1985 trading bets as the buck fell against major currencies. That created a huge opportunity for a currency-related earnings boost, when the stronger international currencies were converted back into the weaker U.S. dollar. Goizueta saw an opportunity developing for a large one-time gain that would please Wall Street by boosting earnings for 1985, but as he strategized about Coke's future needs in international markets, he decided he should reinvest the money in operations overseas. "Rather than report a 30 percent increase in earnings because the dollar has weakened, I would throw it into the international marketplace," he predicted at the outset of the dollar's decline.

As well he did. In meetings with bottlers in Europe and around the world, Goizueta and Keough carried the message that they were done carrying suitcases for the international bottlers. It was essentially the same message they had carried to the domestic bottlers in the early 1980s, before the launch of Coca-Cola Enterprises. Although Goizueta was not yet planning a CCE-style consolidation of the bottling systems, he recognized a need to do something to shake the international bottlers from their lethargy, and to make them accountable to Atlanta for their results. Until now, Goizueta had talked often of the Coke system as a multi-local company. That description was true, to a point. As his international bottling strategy played out over the next few years, it became clear that he wanted strong local bottlers, but with controlling authority emanating from Coke's central headquarters, as a means of coordinating strategy and enforcing standards—centralized decentralization applied to international bottlers. In France and other countries, the process would come to be known derisively as "Coca-Colonization."

With Keough doing much of the leg work, Goizueta began taking charge, holding bottlers accountable for their results, ousting weaker bottlers and allowing stronger bottlers to absorb their territories. "We don't want to do business with anyone who's interested in doing less," Keough warned again and again as he toured the system. The unspoken threat of the aggressive new policy lay in Goizueta's ability to make changes almost at will. Unlike in the United States, where many of the bottlers still held the old 1921 contracts that guaranteed their franchises in perpetuity, Coke's 950-odd international bottlers operated under short-term contracts that held no renewal guarantees.

The continent in most immediate need of attention was Europe. The European Community had laid plans to knock down international trade barriers by 1992, and the push for a common Europe had significant implications for Coca-Cola's bottling, marketing, and distribution systems. In the mid-1980s, Goizueta and Keough began a roving series of meetings with top executives responsible for European operations, especially Claus Halle and, eventually, M. Douglas Ivester, the accountant who had created the now-famed "49 percent solution" that led to the establishment of Coca-Cola Enterprises. The upshot of the strategy sessions was that Coke would not be ready for a unified Europe unless it moved quickly and aggressively across the continent to shore up bottling operations and increase market penetration.

Goizueta set out to do just that. By 1990, he would spend more than $380 million upgrading and consolidating bottling operations in Britain, France, Belgium, the Netherlands, and West Germany. The cash and management infusions paid off in each individual market, but ultimately, he made the most important single investment in a bottling plant in Dunkirk, France. For Coke, the site of the dramatic Allied retreat from Nazi forces during World War II would become a staging ground for his campaign to free Eastern Europe from Pepsi's strong grip after the fall of the Berlin Wall in 1989.

Nowhere on the continent was there more demand for immediate change than in West Germany, Coke's largest market outside of the United States, though not its most profitable. Goizueta knew why West Germany fell short. Coke's bottling system there was divided into more than 160 tiny fiefdoms, small bottlers who often lacked capital resources and frequently failed to coordinate their activities with Atlanta. Some were professional and resourceful bottlers, but others were holdovers from the Woodruff days, such as former heavyweight boxing champion Max Schmeling. By 1992, Goizueta would reduce the number of bottlers to just 60 well-capitalized and well-run operations.

France had its own, contrasting problems. Just one company dominated the Coca-Cola bottling business, the liquor company Pernod Ricard S.A., and the bottler seemed intent on moving its own soft-drink product, Orangina, which competed directly with Coke's Fanta and was strong enough to take away market share from Coca-Cola itself. Goizueta suspected Pernod Ricard intentionally priced Coke's products high in order to give Orangina a chance at dominating the market, and sued to stop the practice. He recognized that litigation was more costly and time consuming than negotiations, but was not hesitant to use lawsuits as the ultimate recourse when persuasion failed.

Virtually half of Europe's geography lay out of Goizueta's grasp: the Soviet-dominated states of Eastern Europe and the populous western region of the Soviet Union itself. The Soviet Union had been the showcase for Pepsi's international ambitions ever since Pepsi-Cola chief Donald Kendall signed a pact in 1972 with the Soviets granting Pepsi an exclusive ten-year franchise in that country. By the time the deal expired, Pepsi-Cola had built 23 bottling plants in the Soviet Union and 40 in the rest of Eastern Europe. Pepsi's polyglot corporate structure was perfectly suited to the countertrade deals that often were necessary to transfer revenues from operations in the Soviet countries back to the United States. In return for Pepsi-Cola concentrate, Pepsi received Stolichnaya vodka, which it sold through its Wine & Spirits International unit. It used Polish-made furniture in its Pizza Hut stores, and took wine as pay in Hungary and Bulgaria.

Goizueta had not come close to matching Pepsi's success, either in the Soviet Union or the satellite countries it dominated. And the few deals he had to work with were vestiges from the Paul Austin era that were not among Austin's better efforts. When Austin negotiated

Coke's first entry into the Soviet Union in 1979, the best he could get in return for Coke concentrate was Lada cars. The soft drink itself was bottled in Pepsi's Soviet plants, and distribution was a nightmare. The situation was no better in other socialist countries. In Poland, Coke gained a toehold in 1977 only by guaranteeing it would export one million cases of Polish beer by 1982. And the ill-fated Avia wine it took in countertrade from Yugoslavia had marked the low point of Goizueta's effort to boost Wine Spectrum's results by selling cut-rate wines to build sales volume and revenue.

Hard as he tried, Goizueta could not find a way to penetrate Pepsi's dominant share in the Soviet countries. And though he would not admit it, he had his hands full turning around the situation in Western Europe, launching major investments in China and the rest of the Pacific Rim, minding Coke's stock repurchase efforts, and rebuilding the Coca-Cola brand in the aftermath of the New Coke experiment. He was pushing for a renewed emphasis on increased margins, especially in big but relatively low-profit markets like Mexico. The continued retrofitting of the bottling system took less time than before the launch of Coca-Cola Enterprises, but by 1988 CCE was faring poorly, and needed increasing amounts of Goizueta's attention.

By 1988, the reorganization of the domestic bottling system would lead Goizueta to lay off 200 employees from Coke-USA—the first and only layoff of his tenure as chief executive. The downsizing was minor by the standards of a company Coca-Cola's size, but it marred Goizueta's otherwise spotless record of restructuring and growing his company without tossing employees aside in the process. In private conversations with business colleagues years later, he sometimes criticized chief executives who had to resort to layoffs to manage their way out of trouble.

WHILE GOIZUETA TURNED HIS GAZE INCREASINGLY TO COKE'S INternational operations, his efforts in the global arena were drawing attention from a place not very far from the geographical center of the United States: Omaha, Nebraska. At the nondescript offices of Berkshire Hathaway, a man by the name of Warren Buffett had quietly placed The Coca-Cola Company on his trading radar. The product Coca-Cola had been part of Buffett's life since childhood, when in 1936 he bought six packs of Coke for 25 cents, divided them and sold the individual bottles for a nickel each, a 20 percent markup. "In this excursion into high-margin retailing, I duly observed the extraordinary consumer attractiveness and commercial possibilities of the product," he wrote in the 1989 installment of his annual report to Berkshire's shareholders.

Buffett does not say exactly what kindled his investment interest in Coca-Cola. Until 1985, Buffett favored the flavor of Pepsi, with a dollop of cherry flavoring mixed into it. Then, as Coca-Cola test marketed Cherry Coke in late 1984, Don Keough sent Buffett a case of the new drink. Buffett fell in love, and in 1985 declared Cherry Coke the "official soft drink" of Berkshire's annual meetings. The Cherry Coke episode makes a nice story, but it was probably the other major product introduction of 1985, New Coke, that truly piqued Buffett's interest by reminding him how strongly the world felt about the Coca-Cola brand name. Buffett believes a great brand name builds a moat around a product that protects it from upstart competitors.

By 1988, Goizueta's efforts in the international arena were starting to pay off, and the impact of the CCE spinoff had begun producing a significant boost in Coke's return on invested capital. When the stock market crash of 1987 knocked Coca-Cola shares down 25 percent from their pre-crash high, it did not take an investor of Warren Buffett's genius to recognize Coke as a buying opportunity. As the stock started regaining its lost ground, an inordinate amount of the activity came from a relatively obscure midwestern brokerage. Goizueta and Keough were studying Coke's stock activity one day in the fall of 1988, when Keough suddenly saw the light. "You know, it could be Warren Buffett," he told Goizueta.

Keough picked up the phone and connected with his old Omaha chum. "Well, Warren, what's going on?" he asked. "You don't happen to be buying any shares of Coca-Cola?"

"It so happens that I am," Buffett said. He asked Keough not to disclose the investment until SEC rules required Buffett to do so after he acquired a 5 percent stake in Coke, and Keough readily agreed. By March 1988, when Buffett disclosed his Coca-Cola investment, the "oracle of Omaha" had spent $1.02 billion to pick up 7.7 percent of The Coca-Cola Company at an average price of $10.96 a share, the second largest holding behind the venerable Trust Co. Bank.

Buffett was characteristically playful, and less-than revelatory, when reporters asked him to describe his interest in Coca-Cola. "It's like when you marry a girl. Is it her eyes? Her personality? It's a whole bunch of things you can't separate," he said. He was slightly more direct with a group of business students a few years later when he said, "I like businesses that I think I know what they will look like in 5 or 10 or 20 years. I think I know what Coke will look like."

When Buffett made his first visit to Atlanta after investing in Coca-Cola, he joined Keough and Goizueta for lunch. But instead of dining in Goizueta's private dining room, at the Capital City Club, or at any of a number of Atlanta's top restaurants, the trio feasted at The Varsity, a landmark diner a few blocks from Coke's North Avenue headquarters that's best known for its greasy onion rings and chili dogs. They don't serve Cherry Coke from the fountain at the Varsity, so Buffett brought his own six pack.

Buffett seemed to have an innate appreciation of the value of the Coca-Cola franchise around the world. He could not exactly put a price tag on it, but he at least set the floor on where the bidding would have to start. "If you gave me $100 billion and said take away the soft-drink leadership of Coca-Cola in the world, I'd give it back to you and say it can't be done," he said.

There is little doubt that one of the key issues in Buffett's investment decision was the potential for Coke's international business. He quickly committed to memory the per-capita consumption rates in markets around the globe and liked to point out Coke's huge potential for growth. He believed that Coca-Cola's consumption rates could grow virtually without limit, unlike Hershey bars, another well-known digestible brand name. "People are going to drink eight servings of something every day, and history shows that once people are exposed to it, and I'm living proof, they like drinking it," he said.

Goizueta wasted no time in placing Buffett on Coke's board of directors. In other companies, Buffett took an activist role—tutoring Katherine Graham at the Washington Post Co. on the benefits of share repurchases and actually taking charge at Salomon Bros. after a trading scandal nearly destroyed the firm. But Buffett admired Goizueta's management acumen. His devotion to share repurchases was Buffettesque. Several times, Buffett cited Coke's stock repurchase programs as an example of his concept of "look-through earnings." The funds used for stock repurchase were transparent, Buffett noted in his famed annual letter to Berkshire Shareholders, because they were spent buying up more shares rather than in pumping up Coke's reported earnings. Goizueta could just as easily have paid out the funds in dividends to shareholders, and that strategy would most likely be used by a less capable management. But Goizueta, Buffett argued, was reinvesting a sizable chunk of Coke's earnings in the Coca-Cola franchise, boosting the stock price with his repurchases and strengthening the Coca-Cola system with capital investment. In Buffett's view of investing as a long-term relationship with a company, there was no better strategy for building shareholder value, and Goizueta was unequaled in deploying his "look-through earnings."

Buffett seemed respectful of the close tie Goizueta had forged with Keough, a man Buffett knew and respected. He remained an informed but passive director, and over time became one of Goizueta's closer friends in business. After one of Buffett's famed annual meetings, during which investors flock to Omaha like pilgrims to Mecca, he jibed Goizueta. "There was only one question about Coke," he told him over the phone, "and it was about management."

GOIZUETA, LIKE BUFFETT, WAS CAUGHT IN THE THROES OF A LOVE affair with Coca-Cola stock. The 100 shares he had purchased while living in Cuba still sat in a New York trust account, and he had never sold a share of his own holdings that now amounted to nearly 9 million shares worth some $600 million. Coca-Cola equity, he proudly announced, comprised "99 percent of my net worth." And with the sale of Coke's share in Columbia Pictures Entertainment, Goizueta at last had squared his corporate investment policy with the approach he used in his personal portfolio, turning away from diversions like movie making in order to concentrate on the one business he knew: Coca-Cola itself. The sale of Columbia to Sony Corp. for $3 billion had left Coke with a $509 million windfall, free cash to invest in addition to the $1.2 billion income in 1989 from Coke's worldwide operations, and he planned to put a sizable chunk of it toward an investment in Coca-Cola stock.

Goizueta did not tinker when it came to repurchases. Just after reporting on the Columbia sale at the October 1989 board meeting, Goizueta persuaded the board to approve a new 20 million-share repurchase that marked a milestone: 100 million shares of Coke stock bought since Goizueta initiated Coke's share buybacks in 1984. All told, the company under his orders had spent $3.4 billion buying back Coke shares, one of the most aggressive and extended repurchase programs in the history of corporate America. The purchases had the effect of increasing Coke's earnings per share and return on equity, two key indicators Goizueta used when assessing his own performance as CEO, and two of the most important yardsticks measured by Wall Street analysts. With Coke trading around $67 a share at the time the repurchase was approved, Goizueta would eat up $1.34 billion in capital by the time he completed the two-year buy-back program.

Columbia in the end had paid off handsomely, but it also had provided a harsh lesson. With its comedy-and-tragedy mix running the gamut from the magnificently profitable *Ghostbusters* and "Wheel of Fortune" to the comically disastrous *Ishtar*, the Hollywood interlude had taught Goizueta that it was too costly and time consuming to learn a new business, and at the end of the day, he either would not be able to manage it very well, or, if he did manage it well, it would take away precious time from his main job selling Coca-Cola to the world. His smartest investment was in the soft-drink industry he knew best. Goizueta now recognized that anything outside of Coke's core business would be a distraction for management, and worse yet, would stand little chance of matching Coke's rate of return on invested capital. "There's a perception in this country that you're better off if you're in two lousy businesses than if you're in one good one—that you're spreading your risk," he grumbled. "It's crazy."

Contrary to common wisdom about diversification as a means of spreading risk, Goizueta now believed that he could best reduce risk by placing all of Coke's financial, physical, and managerial assets behind the brand that had built the business. The end of the Columbia interlude marked a key turning point, on par with his "special assignment" work in the late 1960s and early 1970s, or the creation of the Mission Statement for the 1980s. Goizueta was done with diversification. From Columbia onward, he never invested in a business that did not directly relate to quenching the thirst needs of the world's population with Coca-Cola or one of the company's other beverages. It was as if it took the sale of Columbia for the ultimate lesson of the New Coke debacle finally to sink in. Approaching the fifth anniversary of New Coke, for the first time reassessing his company without Columbia Pictures blocking his view, Goizueta now clearly understood that his fortunes would rise or fall based solely on how he did making certain that his company sold more Coca-Cola than ever before.

The refranchising of the domestic bottling system under Coca-Cola Enterprises was a significant part of the redefined focus on Coke's brands, but for the time being CCE was a domestic bottler only. If Goizueta wanted to succeed with his new emphasis on brand building, he would have to turn to the markets that by now provided well over 70 percent of his company's operating profits, the international arena. Indeed, it made little sense to continue pouring the bulk of his cash into developing Coke's domestic market. Tough competition with Pepsi and restrictive pricing contracts with bottlers meant Coke's profit margins in the United States were only about half of the average 30 percent margin in most overseas markets. Alongside the attractive opportunity to buy Coke's own shares, the international market dawned as his most obvious and lucrative strategy.

Goizueta abruptly initiated a series of major investments in international bottlers that placed challenging new demands on his resourcefulness and capital. In June 1989, he had initiated the investment in Amatil of Australia. As a prerequisite to that $500 million investment, Goizueta and Keough had lobbied hard with Amatil's management to persuade them to dump their non-soda businesses and focus on Coca-Cola. He swooped in on another deal, after learning that bottlers in Hong Kong, China, and Taiwan were discussing a possible joint business arrangement. Goizueta quickly hammered out arrangements with all three, investing in each company and overlaying that with a new joint venture structure called Coca-Cola Swire Beverages Ltd. Coke again took a major share. In each case, he placed Coca-Cola executives on the boards of directors and pushed through operational and management changes to bring the companies into line with Coke's global standards. The strategy had evolved dramatically since the first investment in the Philippines in 1981. In the mid-1990s, Goizueta began calling this his "anchor bottler" strategy. It would become the key development of Goizueta's Coca-Colonization of the world.

Investing in bottling and in Coke's own stock fit a new concept of business that he began to call "the post-conglomerate era." As he assessed the 49 percent solution approach to Coke's investments in Columbia and Coca-Cola Enterprises, Goizueta developed a new view of how Coke should look in the future. Nearly a decade into his chairmanship, and with the confidence he obtained from Warren Buffett's explicit endorsement of his management abilities, Goizueta increasingly began to consider his vision for The Coca-Cola Company as a template for major companies worldwide. The shareholder letters in Coke's annual reports began taking on an almost Buffett-like philosophical tone, and his public pronouncements sounded more the part of the corporate statesman than the business tactician.

In one of his most far-ranging expositions, Goizueta declared that the day of the conglomerate was over. Businesses of the future must focus on their core areas of expertise and ruthlessly realign operations to maximize whatever those core capabilities might be. "The company's structure itself is a variable, subject to change to the same degree as its personnel, products, plans, and strategies," he wrote in an article he published in *Leaders* magazine. Conglomerates were "as awkward as tailfins and just about as functional." Goizueta advocated a hybrid, in which a company operated from a core business, while making financial investments and exerting management influence over companies in related industries. In other words, companies should follow the CCE example and the bottler investment program he was implementing in the international markets.

AT THE BRANDENBURG GATE IN EAST BERLIN, THOUSANDS OF EAST Berliners streamed through the Berlin Wall that had divided them from the West for nearly 30 years. On November 10, 1989, Goizueta's ground forces were already in motion. Driving upstream against the flood of smog-belching East German Trabant passenger cars, hulking Coca-Cola delivery trucks worked their way into position, opening their doors to the communist crowds, and giving them their first taste of freedom in the form of a bubbly brown beverage called Coke. At one checkpoint, delivery trucks dispensed more than 70,000 cans in just a few hours.

Television news reports duly noted Coke's marketing coup. Jumping to the Wall that way exposed the boisterous, freedom-seeking East Germans to the ability of aggressive capitalists to transform great moments in history into quick-hit marketing gimmicks. Goizueta enjoyed the attention his marketing forces received and was peeved a month later on December 7, when Pepsi beat Coke to the punch by airing the first U.S. commercial filmed at the opening of the Berlin

Wall. Coke the same night came in a distant second with a retooled version of a spot developed to coincide with the Reykjavik summit between President Ronald Reagan and Soviet President Mikhail Gorbachev in Iceland.

The Cold War was over, but at Coke's North Avenue headquarters, the Cola Wars were about to rage again, this time in the international arena. Pepsi was never far from Goizueta's mind. Although major endeavors like the CCE spinoff and the Columbia exit had occupied large chunks of his time, he still carefully checked the Nielsen rankings of domestic supermarket sales and still kept a summary of Pepsi's global strategy alongside his summary of Coke's strategy in the top drawer of his desk. He never missed an opportunity to make a dig at his chief competitor while speaking with analysts or reporters. When reporters asked him why Coke was able to respond so quickly to the collapse of communism, he explained that it was because he was not distracted by restaurants or snack foods, a not-so-veiled reference to PepsiCo.

In most regions of the world, Coke was so far ahead that Pepsi was barely a factor. Rather than focusing on competition with Pepsi, Goizueta told his executives to key on the larger challenge of growing the market and pushing per-capita consumption to increase Coca-Cola's overall sales volume. Coke's market share ranged as high as 70 percent in some countries, so there was little upside to stealing share away from competing soft-drink products. "The name of the game isn't to increase market share, but to grow the market, to take share from juices, milk, coffee, tea, and beer," Goizueta said. It was a prelude to a strategy he would later crystalize into the phrase "share of stomach," Coke's effort to control the liquid portion of what goes into a person's mouth.

There were markets where trench warfare was necessary, and indeed desired, and Eastern Europe was shaping up as one. Pepsi's position in Eastern Europe had once seemed almost as unassailable as the Berlin Wall itself, but now that the Wall was down, Goizueta was ready to take a whack at Pepsi's long-held position as the dominant supplier of soft drinks to the fast-crumbling communist world—the nations of Eastern Europe and the Soviet Union. The collapse of border controls first in Hungary and later in East Germany had brought one of the largest migration tides in human history. To Goizueta, they all looked thirsty.

GOIZUETA HAD THE RIGHT MAN ON THE SPOT: M. DOUGLAS IVESTER. Coke's former chief financial officer had nursemaided the launch of CCE in 1986, something Goizueta recalled as a major accomplishment despite the embarrassing on-again, off-again nature of the initial stock offering. Since then, Ivester had focused on a $150 million project to modernize Coca-Cola's information systems. A notoriously impatient communicator, it frustrated Ivester that sales reports and other financial figures from Coke's vast enterprise often did not make their way to Atlanta for six weeks and more. He persuaded Goizueta to invest the money, and spearheaded a modern data-gathering, e-mail, voice mail, and video conference network that brought Coke into the modern age. He liked to joke that he did it "by getting to know everyone in the typing pool on a first-name basis."

With so much attention focused on Europe, Goizueta selected Ivester knowing that it was the first step toward picking a successor for Keough, who was set to retire in 1993. Keough and Goizueta had mapped out an executive succession strategy in late 1987, when Claus Halle had told Goizueta he wanted to retire three years earlier than the company's mandatory age of 65. Goizueta moved Ike Herbert to run Coke's North American operations and John Georgas to run international. But both men were set to retire in 1991, so the moves were a temporary way for Goizueta to take the measure of players including Ivester and John Hunter, then Coke's head of Pacific operations. And to lay the groundwork for Ivester's jump to the European slot, Goizueta also had realigned Coke's international operations, creating a special management group that would handle Coke's business in the common market after European economic unification in 1992.

He was not just picking Keough's replacement. Goizueta was consciously if quietly designating his own successor, as well. At the end of each year, Goizueta had asked Keough to write a memo to him laying out a succession strategy in the event Keough suddenly was incapacitated and unable to run the company. Since the launch of CCE, Keough had pegged Ivester as the man who should succeed him, and Goizueta endorsed this choice. He discussed the choice with several other close confidantes, to make certain he was choosing the right man, and that there was no fault of Ivester's he was overlooking. He told associates he planned to remedy Ivester's lack of experience as line manager by assigning him to Europe.

When Ivester did not immediately jump at the notion of moving to the European sector, Keough sat him down for a talk. "Doug, you're going to have to make a decision," Keough said. "Everyone's comfortable with you as CFO, and you're damn good at it. But if you're not careful, that's what you're going to be the rest of your career."

"Have you got the guts to leave something you're comfortable with and go run Europe?" Keough concluded.

When Goizueta announced that Ivester was moving to Europe, it sent a clear message to anyone who followed Coke and had an interest in the careers of top management. Harold Burson, the public relations strategist who often served as Goizueta's sounding board, could read between the lines. "I suspect you've got your successor picked out," Burson said in a conversation with Goizueta at the time.

Without answering directly, Goizueta made it clear to Burson that he had hit the mark. "I would not like my successor to not have operating experience," Goizueta said. "I got away with it, but I don't want my successor to have to." Goizueta had no intention of putting Ivester through the same second guessing of his credentials that he had endured when he became president of Coke.

Ivester had never travelled overseas before his appointment to the Europe job. But there seemed little doubt about his capacity to succeed. In everything he had done, Ivester had proven himself a driven manager and blood thirsty competitor. He had shown his financial creativity in everything from converting movie receivables to spinning off CCE. Now that it was time to demonstrate he could do it on the ground, too, Ivester hit the job hard.

His first challenge was France, where Coke's results were suffering in the hands of a difficult bottler, Pernod Richard. Coke had accused the company of favoring its own brands over Coca-Cola's, and Coke's lawsuit forced the bottler to sell its soda assets to Coke for $140 million. The rest of the move on France was vintage Ivester, brash, aggressive, and not particularly concerned with fine details such as cultural sensitivity. Cutting against Goizueta's typical instinct of adopting, as much as possible, the style of the host country, Ivester pushed Goizueta and Keough to approve the importation of William Hoffman, Coke's Atlanta bottler who had never before visited France and did not speak the language. With an initiative called Project Farsight, Hoffman provoked café owners in Bordeaux to boycott Coke when he placed vending machines outside their doors with cut-rate prices for Coke. He riled French sensibilities by plunking one at the base of the Eiffel Tower. He introduced the concept of large in-store displays and ran up costs by hiring more than 500 new employees to execute Coke sales promotions throughout the country. Hoffman also booked racy ads that included a topless model with a strategically positioned arm standing between Coke and full frontal nudity. He got results: Volume in France rose 22 percent a year, and per capita consumption jumped 25 percent during his time in France, to 49 bottles per year. But Hoffman's gonzo style also won him a return ticket to Atlanta; Goizueta called Hoffman home after just 18 turbulent months in France.

Halfway through Hoffman's tenure, the Berlin Wall fell, and suddenly the other major plank in Ivester's French redevelopment effort came into play: the new bottling plant in Dunkirk. The plant was not designed as a crowbar for busting through the Wall. Rather, the huge, technologically advanced $55 million canning colossus located just a few miles from the channel linking France and England was designed to improve distribution in the United Kingdom, France, Belgium, the Netherlands, and Germany. Goizueta planned to use the plant, in part, to persuade reluctant German bottlers of the need to modernize, merge, or drop out of the bottling business altogether. But once the Wall came down, its production headed east.

THE FAST PACE OF CHANGE IN EASTERN EUROPE AFTER THE BERLIN Wall fell provided an object lesson in the wisdom of Goizueta's management technique of giving his top managers maximum flexibility in making major decisions. Goizueta studied the business carefully and had his own network of trusted colleagues who provided him with on-the-ground information. He provided guidance, often in the form of body language or a pointed question that made it clear what his opinion was. But he rarely told an associate what to do or directly vetoed a proposal. With the communist world quickly collapsing and the markets in a state of flux, the strengths of this system paid off in the form of Coke's ability to respond quickly and aggressively whenever opportunities presented themselves.

As the East German crowds still were streaming into West Germany, Goizueta and Keough had agreed that they would be able to invest as much as $500 million in building up the East European market. Then, in mid-November, Keough received a visit in Atlanta from a prominent German bottler, who told him that Coke needed to move more quickly, that the opportunities in Eastern Europe demanded more than the half a billion dollars Coke was ready to invest. Keough flew to Europe in mid-December, touring East Germany and assessing the outlook for the poorly consolidated West German market. On the spot, he agreed that the bottler was right. By February, he was back in Europe, at a conference in Davos, Switzerland. Without consulting Goizueta, Keough announced that the Coca-Cola system would spend $1 billion in Eastern Europe.

When Keough told Goizueta, the chairman immediately backed his decision. "Roberto didn't blink an eye," Keough recalled. "We had not been a leader in eastern Europe, but now we were ready to move with the speed of light."

Still, there was a difference between laying out major investment goals and making those investments work on the ground. As Coke attempted its blitzkrieg through East Germany, Ivester quickly learned there were no distribution routes, no modern canning plants, and few trucks of any quality. In early January 1990, he had opened negotiations with the East German government with an eye toward bottling Coke in six major East German cities. But there was one sticking point: East German companies and customers could deal only in East German marks, and it was unclear whether that very soft currency would ever be convertible into West German marks. Walking along Berlin's suddenly bustling Alexanderplatz, amid the construction cranes that were just starting to pop up in anticipation of German reunification, Ivester listened as the president of Coke's German division urged him to accept the Ostmarks, regardless of their ultimate value. Even if Coke never could exchange the money, the company would benefit by building a new customer base. The argument rang true to Ivester, but he wanted to consult with Goizueta before moving ahead.

Ivester argued to Goizueta that Coke needed to do business in the local currency in order to kick start retail trade. But there was no guarantee Coke would ever see a pfennig until the West German government made a decision on currency convertibility. Like most financial analysts, he seemed to believe that the West Germans would make the Ostmark convertible, perhaps even at a 1-for-1 exchange rate. But no one knew for certain. "We don't have the slightest clue how we are going to get paid, none whatsoever," Ivester told Goizueta.

"I don't care," Goizueta said. "Just ship the product. Sooner or later we're going to get paid somehow." Three months later, the West German government did agree to a 1:1 exchange rate, an inflationary move for the German economy but a lifesaver for Coke.

The company's vaunted international intelligence had all but guaranteed that result, and Goizueta had banked on it in laying out plans to invest $140 million to upgrade Coke's distribution system throughout eastern Germany. Already, Coke had sold 2 million cases in East Germany and had reversed Pepsi's leadership position by a wide margin, outselling the onetime market leader by ten to one. By year end, so-called "Osties" had bought 21 million cases, and per capita consumption in eastern Germany had jumped to 30 servings. Goizueta was building toward an investment commitment with the Eastern German redevelopment agency Treuhandanstalt by which he would triple his initial investment, ultimately committing Coke to spend $450 million overall to upgrade and improve Coke's bottling and distribution system in the country.

The planning team in Atlanta went crazy. The plants in Germany, they argued, were not in the right places, and were hopelessly out of date. Spending money on upgrades was a waste. But Goizueta would have none of it. "We've got to move quickly," he said. "We don't need to put a Coke sign up in front of all the plants, but it's essential to be flexible and be in first."

Ultimately, Goizueta could not resist hanging Coke's famous Spencerian script on all six of the company's bottling plants in eastern Germany. "They're not the best looking plants in the world, but we put the name Coca-Cola outside," he said. What really mattered was the output from the plants: 80 million cases by 1991, quadruple the volume the year before.

LIBERALIZATION MOVEMENTS WERE SPREADING THROUGHOUT THE Soviet bloc, and Goizueta intuitively recognized that Coke had to be ready to step over the Iron Curtain as it fell to the ground. In Atlanta, Goizueta chaired a series of planning meetings aimed at capitalizing on the opportunities. The upshot was Project Jumpstart, a three-year program to reverse Pepsi's leadership in the eastern bloc countries.

Goizueta viewed eastern Europe as more fertile ground for Coke's investment than the Soviet Union, because of the capitalist heritage in those countries before the Soviet domination that began after World War II. "Russia never knew capitalism," Goizueta explained.

Eastern Germany had made sense as the first line of attack because of the guiding hand coming from the government in Bonn. But Goizueta and his Jumpstart team laid aggressive plans for the rest of the region: the Polish and Romanian plants that he would visit on his grand tour in 1993, as well as others dotted throughout the region. They even introduced modern marketing techniques like sweepstakes and neon signage in Hungary, the most westernized country of the former communist bloc. Project Jumpstart proved a success, even if not every individual investment panned out. Goizueta was forced to abandon a $12.5 million investment in a plant in Brasov, Romania after the antiquated bottling plant produced some full bottles, some half-empty bottles, and leaks in the roof defied repair. By 1992, Coke's market share would top Pepsi's in every country except Poland and Czechoslovakia and before long, those countries would fall, too.

For Pepsi, the eastern German episode was a landmark disappointment in the company's effort to compete against Coke in the international arena. Once the dominant player in eastern Europe, Pepsi virtually missed the chance to attack when the Berlin Wall fell because it was too busy mopping up from an ill-advised decision in mid-1990 to take control of all its independent bottlers in Germany. The move tied up capital and distracted management from the cataclysmic market changes occurring just across the fast-disappearing border between the two Germanies. But PepsiCo was not unilaterally dropping out of the competition for all the markets behind the old Iron Curtain. In 1990, PepsiCo chairman Wayne Calloway moved to cement his position in the Soviet Union by striking a $3 billion pact, a ten-year deal to barter Pepsi-Cola products in exchange for vodka and freighter ships. On a more tactical scale, Pepsi in late 1991 announced plans to invest $1 billion in an effort to seize market leadership away from Coke in Spain, where Coke held a 7-to-1 advantage, on the theory that Coke would be too consumed with Project Jumpstart to protect its flank in southern Europe.

Growing increasingly confident over time, Goizueta did not bother concealing his contempt for Pepsi's mishandling of its European operations. And firmly committed as he was to his newfound allegiance to soft drinks as the unchallenged core of Coke's business, he enjoyed swiping at Pepsi's strategy of investing in snack foods and restaurants. "They tend to think with their mouths open and they don't always do what they say," he scoffed, sending a missile via an interview with *The New York Times.* "That money has not been invested yet, and I'm sure a lot will go into restaurants and snacks. It's wonderful to have a good competitor. But I just hope they don't get too distracted with potato chips."

It was a good time to gloat. In 1991, Coke earned operating income of $800 million from the European Community—as much as the entire company had earned during the New Coke year of 1985. Ending his first decade as Coke's chairman, Goizueta felt proud that the company that had a market capitalization of $4 billion when he slid behind the chairman's desk now was worth $35 billion. With dividends reinvested, $100 invested in Coke stock in 1981 was worth $976 on the day Goizueta celebrated his tenth anniversary as chairman. The stock price jumped from $6 per share to more than $80 a share. In the second half of his first decade as chairman, Coke's stock delivered a 35 percent compounded annual return to its shareowners a title Goizueta had adopted in preference to the more commonly used "shareholders," intentionally emphasizing the stable and proprietary connotations associated with ownership.

FOR ONLY THE SECOND TIME IN COKE'S MODERN HISTORY, GOIZUETA held the 1992 annual shareholders meeting in Atlanta, marking the hundredth year of the company's incorporation. But the 4,000 shareholders who flocked to the Georgia World Congress Center did not come to hear Goizueta celebrate the occasion or boast about accomplishments of the prior year. They came to hear what the chairman had to say about his huge pay package for 1991. Goizueta had spent the better part of the last two years breaking through the Iron Curtain, and now he was about to break down walls in his march toward a world-record payday. The deal, shareholders had learned a few weeks earlier, was this: Goizueta's total pay package for 1991 totaled $86 million in pay and bonuses. The largest compensation package ever, it topped the $78.1 million paid to Time Warner Chairman Steve Ross the prior year. In addition to his $2.96 million cash payment, Goizueta received a bonus of one million shares of Coca-Cola stock.

As if the size of the package were not breathtaking enough, share-holders and executive compensation experts were put off by the insult-ingly sneaky way in which the package was explained to shareholders in the company's proxy materials. Goizueta had final approval on a proxy statement that seemed designed to mislead investors. A table listed his compensation at $2.96 million. Then, in the body of a com-plicated passage explaining Coca-Cola's complex stock-incentive pro-gram, the proxy noted that the board of directors had awarded Goizueta a one-million-share bonus. The words "one million shares" were written out, rather than in numerals, concealing the award from all but the most careful reader. Indeed, the normally studious *Wall Street Journal* missed the award completely in its first reading, and re-ported the specifics of Goizueta's deal only after *The New York Times* scooped the *Journal* on the details of Goizueta's pay package.

Three years earlier, Goizueta crony Herbert A. Allen, Jr., had pushed through a plan to award as many as ten million shares as in-centive to Coca-Cola's top executives. The rules Allen laid down al-lowed for the awarding of as many as two million shares to a single person, if performance warranted that large an award. In other words, Goizueta 's 1991 pay could have reached a breathtaking $160 million in restricted stock if he had had a truly exceptional year. Even more confounding, the package included an innovative arrangement sad-dling taxpayers with the burden of paying Goizueta's personal income taxes on the deal. Coke made the payments on an annual basis, but did not take annual deductions on them. By the time Goizueta died in October 1997, the company was due more than $1 billion in deferred tax credits related to Goizueta's compensation.

The huge pay package for 1991 drew criticism not just for its scale and the underhanded method of its announcement, but also for the role played by Allen. Since the 1982 Columbia Pictures deal, Allen & Co. had earned $24 million in investment banking fees alone from Coke-related transactions, in addition to the millions Allen earned from the equity stakes it held in Columbia and other Coke deals. Allen was un-abashed. "Our firm has done a lot of work, and every transaction we were involved in was beneficial to Coke shareholders," he explained.

Goizueta hated talking about his compensation and refused to comment about the deal even as a debate swelled in the press about the notion of a single person receiving such a huge paycheck. Goizueta

had long ago become accustomed to the requirement that shareholders had a right to know how much money their top executives were
earning. But he could never stomach the American fixation with a
person's income. He had found it offputting as a young Cuban immigrant and found it deplorable now.

GOIZUETA WAS STARTING TO APPEAR ON LISTS OF THE COUNTRY'S
wealthiest and highest paid executives, but his lifestyle had changed
little since he first moved to Atlanta in the mid-1970s. He had lived
in his first home—the modest, four-bedroom white-framed house in
an upper middle-class neighborhood on Atlanta's northwest side with
an estimated market value of $180,000 the year before he sold it—
until 1988. And although he was worth more than $100 million by
the time he moved, he paid only $975,044 for his new home. The
brown-stucco, 1.5-story house had five bedrooms, four full and two
partial baths, and was encircled by a wrought iron fence on one acre
of property. Still, even though the new home was less than a mile from
the palatial Tuxedo Road estate where Robert W. Woodruff had held
court, it was in an entirely less substantial economic stratum. The two
houses were the only pieces of real estate he would ever own.

When asked why he moved out of his longtime homestead he explained that he needed room for his grandchildren to stay overnight.
His daughter Olga Maria, who had attended law school at Emory University, was now a mother. His eldest son Roberto S. Goizueta had
abandoned preparation for the ministry when he fell in love, and now
was a professor of theology at Loyola University of Chicago and a father. His youngest child, Javier, worked for Procter & Gamble, and at
the time of his father's death was stationed in Brazil.

Indeed, Goizueta's lifestyle hardly matched that of the multimil-
lionaire, jet-setting executive that typified this "Masters of the
Universe" era in corporate history. He was privileged to ride the corporate jet to his favorite vacation spot at Sea Island, Georgia, but
once there he stayed in a rented villa, and spent most of his time
reading at the pool or on the beach. Calls from the office were forbidden during the two weeks of vacation time he took each year.
When not traveling the globe on business, often in the company of
Olguita, he spent most evenings at home reading or listening to
country music. Country music was what he listened to when he was

driven home, usually sitting in the front seat with the driver of his company-owned Lincoln Town Car. A member of the Woodruff Fine Arts board, he attended Atlanta Symphony Orchestra concerts. But other than that, Goizueta was rarely a part of Atlanta's active social scene.

Success had not spoiled Goizueta. But it also had not dimmed his appetite to cash a paycheck that was as large as his work deserved. As he stepped before Coke's annual meeting. Coca-Cola's chairman was ready to deal. Firmly, but without defensiveness, he reminded shareholders that they had approved the compensation program by a 93 percent to 5 percent margin in 1989. He recounted Coke's financial performance under his direction, and the huge increases in the company's stock price. Without a touch of irony, Goizueta quoted John D. Rockefeller, one of the wealthiest men in American history: "Every right implies a responsibility, every opportunity an obligation, every possession a duty," he said, implying that the giant paycheck was compensation for his outstanding performance in a job of almost overwhelming pressure. Goizueta concluded the topic by pledging his best to the company and society, "knowing that these efforts will be for the benefit of all."

Even compensation critics caught Goizueta's point. The numbers were huge, but Goizueta was not picking anybody's pocket. "Who among his shareholders will pick up a paving stone and march with me to the boardroom? His shareholders are bursting their buttons with fine food and drink," said executive compensation expert Graef S. Crystal, who first focused attention on the tax advantages of Goizueta's compensation package in his book *In Search of Excess*.

Four times during his remarks, shareholders interrupted Goizueta with applause. Many of them had become millionaires thanks to Coke's incredible growing stock price. They seemed intent on thanking Goizueta for his work to date, and waited with anticipation for results yet to come. Little did they know that a drama of almost Shakespearean magnitude was about to play out before them. For half a century, Coke had built its corporate soul around advertising from a single agency, McCann-Erickson. But suddenly, and almost completely without warning, Roberto C. Goizueta was ready for a change.

8

"Always" a Great Shootout

McCann. *A Play in Three Parts:* The Warning, The Shootout, and The Choice. In which Roberto Goizueta dumps the McCann-Erickson advertising agency, taking away most of Coke's $600 million worldwide ad spending. The interloper is the Creative Artists Agency, its stable of Hollywood talent, and its utter lack of advertising experience.

The setting: The year 1991. Something is rotten in the state of Coca-Cola's advertising. Coke's current ad campaign, "Can't Beat the Real Thing," is a bust. Market share is falling, and Pepsi-Cola once again is outselling Coca-Cola Classic in supermarkets. Consumers are losing their connection with the brand, cannot recall the ads. While Roberto Goizueta takes bows for pushing Coke aggressively into European markets, especially the former Soviet bloc countries, he's concerned because the home fires are barely smoldering. Danger lurks behind every aisle display and vending machine.

Dramatis Personae: Goizueta, the king of the realm knows Coke's ads are troubled, but doesn't know how to fix them.

Donald Keough, the lion in winter, he hopes to revive Coke's advertising before retirement. Transfixed by CAA's lustrous talent list, he'll junk McCann if necessary.

M. Douglas Ivester, the bloodless, ambitious prince, waiting for his chance to step next in line to Goizueta's throne.

Peter Sealey, Coke's brooding, cerebral courtier, he'll make the change, then off with his head.

Sergio Zyman, Ivester's Rasputin. Flamboyant, mesmerizing, perhaps dangerous.

John Bergin, an advertising legend who created "Coke Is It" while president of McCann-USA. He's near retirement, and out of favor at McCann.

Gordon Bowen, a cerebral and remote ad writer, one of the most hotly sought talents on Madison Ave. because of his success with American Express' "Portraits" ads. But he's a stranger to Coke, and will never catch on.

Michael Ovitz, the head of CAA. A dark spirit, full of promises about star power and and a new approach to advertising, but he's never produced a spot in his life.

The story begins at the offices of the Interpublic Group of Companies, parent of McCann-Erickson, on 6th Avenue in mid-town Manhattan. In the summer of 1991, Don Keough paid a visit, and he was not happy. He had called the meeting of top executives at McCann and IPG, and flown from Atlanta to New York for a specific purpose. A message needed to be delivered, in person and in blunt terms. For several years, Keough and his top advertising staff had complained about the "Can't Beat the Real Thing" campaign. It lacked zip, was not memorable, and did not move product. It was clearly just a place holder until something original came along. The trouble was, there was nothing new in sight.

Phil Geier, the chairman and chief executive of IPG, headed the group of a half-dozen executives, each of whom bore some responsibility for the problems with the Coke account. As they listened to Keough speak, it was clear that the jocular side of Don Keough had stayed in Atlanta. The Keough who appeared before them was all business, a dissatisfied and demanding client with narrow eyes and a commanding voice. It was a Keough that the public never saw, but one that his close business associates often confronted. This Keough wanted action.

"We are frustrated by the lack of progress on this campaign," Keough said. He saw no reason why McCann could not bring its global resources to create a world-class advertising campaign to match Coke's huge profile and its unique status as the world's most recognized trademark. "We want the best in the world, and we won't settle for anything less," Keough said.

He wanted McCann to succeed, he said, but if it did not, Coke would not keep waiting. "If you don't pull this off, folks, you are staring at a loss of the business," he said. It was the first time Keough explicitly threatened to break up McCann's half-century monopoly on Coca-Cola's advertising account, and it spoke volumes that he had traveled personally to New York just to deliver this simple message.

In a follow-up meeting a few weeks later, Keough was less direct, and almost doleful about the inability of Coke and its agency to solve the advertising problem. He was forced, he said, to take the next step. Coke planned to bring in some "help" from an outside agency. Help from outside the advertising industry. From Hollywood. He would soon announce plans to hire the Creative Artists Agency, the most powerful talent agency in show business, as a creative consultant for Coke's marketing programs. "You know the people who have their fingers on the pulse of America?" Keough did not so much ask as declare. "It's Hollywood. Those people have their fingers on something. They have something we don't know about."

"Those people" at the Creative Artists Agency were led by Michael Ovitz, then the most powerful force in the Hollywood movie industry. Perhaps the people at CAA did indeed have their fingers on the pulse of America. Most certainly, Ovitz had his paws all over Coke. He had a line directly to Keough, and to Goizueta. And he could influence them both through his close friendship with Coke board member Herbert Allen Jr.

No one needed to be told that Goizueta was backing the push to break Coke's dependence on McCann. Keough would never go this far without input from Coke's chairman, and he had made it clear that Goizueta shared his unhappiness with McCann's recent work. A simple, bald statement from Goizueta had set the entire process in motion. Early in the fall of 1990, during an advertising strategy session, Goizueta grew weary of the excuses he was hearing about

Coke's lackluster advertising. He shared the impression of his market-ing staff that "Can't Beat the Real Thing" did little to prompt people to buy more Coke, and when one of Coke's marketing executives com-plained that Pepsi's advertising was always "hipper" than Coke's, Goizueta had a simple retort. "Then go to a hipper source," he demanded.

Goizueta would handle the agency shootout in his typical style, keeping apprised of every intimate detail, but intervening personally only at strategic points, in this case, at the very beginning and very end of the process. His remark about hipness and his ear for Ovitz's inducements had set the process in motion. Once Keough, and be-neath him, Peter Sealey, began studying a possible switch, Goizueta would step out of the way. He would let Keough be the key actor in the drama, the one who orchestrated the competition and recommended a final call.

To Keough and Goizueta, there was little doubt where this was all leading. Ovitz had already approached both men, and had also quietly lobbied Allen, selling them all on the notion of hiring CAA to con-sult on Coke's advertising. He had known Keough since Coke bought Columbia in 1982, and had spoken frequently about what CAA could bring to Coke's advertising—Hollywood stars, movie directors, and big ideas. He had represented Sony when it took Columbia off Goizueta's hands. By the fall of 1990, Ovitz was desperate to burnish CAA's image, and his own, by claiming that CAA was more than just a talent agency, even as it was the most powerful agency in Hollywood. He wanted to expand CAA into a broker for big Hollywood mergers, and as a provider of creative talent to major advertisers. Ultimately, Ovitz believed, he might take over a major entertainment company, perhaps one the size of Time Warner or Sony itself.

OVITZ GREW UP IN CALIFORNIA'S SAN FERNANDO VALLEY, BUT world's away from the glitz of Hollywood. His father was a liquor sales-man. As class president at Birmingham High School, he knew class-mates Sally Field and Michael Milken. The closest he got to being inside Hollywood was when he rode his bike to the RKO Studio lot and sneaked in to watch films being shot. He studied premedicine at the University of California at Los Angeles, but took more of an in-terest in his summer jobs leading tours at Universal Studios and

Twentieth Century Fox. His first Hollywood job was in the mailroom at the famed William Morris Agency. He rose quickly and at age 29 left Morris to set up his own agency with four colleagues.

At the launch of Creative Artists Agency in 1975, Ernest Borgnine and Rich Little were the best-known stars on Ovitz's roster. Without a brand name of his own or any major success to speak of, he decided he could break into the Hollywood power structure by going after the more easily lured talent, screenwriters and lesser-known directors. His most revolutionary idea was the notion of "packaging:" putting together the screenwriter, director, and actors, and presenting them as a unit to a movie studio. After much hard selling, he finally broke through. His first major hit was *Silence of the Lambs,* and by the mid-1980s, CAA was Hollywood's largest agency, and Ovitz was regarded widely as Hollywood's most powerful man.

Ovitz was legendary for routinely calling all of his major contacts once every few months, just to keep in touch. In 1990, his persistence paid off with Coke as it had with so many other relationships over the years. Keough, with the subtle push from Goizueta motivating him, decided it was time to take a serious look at hooking up with the man who by now was a Hollywood legend, featured on the cover of the *New York Times Magazine* and whispered chronically about on the back lots and casting rooms of moviedom.

For tactical reasons, Keough did not want to approach Ovitz directly. He feared appearing overly eager. And he knew better than to rely on Coke marketing chief Ike Herbert, who had no experience dealing with Hollywood. Instead, he decided to track down Peter Sealey, the former marketing executive who had built a Rolodex full of Hollywood connections when he was exported from Atlanta to oversee Coke's investment in Columbia Pictures. Keough had a personal policy against rehiring people who had left the company, but in this case he made an exception.

Sealey was never a quintessential Coca-Cola organization man. He started his career at Procter & Gamble, where he redesigned the Jif peanut butter label. He joined Coke in 1969 as brand manager for Sprite, and before long he had transferred to the wine business, where he first learned to savor the California lifestyle. He was back at Coke headquarters in 1982 when Goizueta bought Columbia Pictures, but in 1983 when Fay Vincent was having trouble integrating Columbia into the Coca-Cola culture, Sealey volunteered to serve as Vincent's guide. At Columbia, he took charge of Coke's efforts to apply its expertise in market research and brand building to the movie business, with mixed success. In 1985, Sealey hired a former Paramount Picture Corp. marketer, Shelly Hochron, on the advice of actor Warren Beatty. When Ovitz was setting his sights on Coke five years later, Hochron was the first person he hired to head up his nascent advertising agency.

When Goizueta sold Columbia Pictures in 1989, Sealey stayed in California, raised some venture funds, and started two small companies. He had tried his hand at publishing, with a failed local magazine called *Monterey Life,* and enrolled in doctoral studies at the Peter F. Drucker Management Center at the Claremont Graduate School in California. Over the Labor Day weekend in 1990, during his final semester at Claremont, Sealey received a telephone call from Herbert, calling him back home to Coke.

After telling Herbert he was interested, Sealey quickly phoned Keough, who wasted no time getting to the point. "I don't think our advertising has been up to the level of the brand, and, second, I don't think it's been up to the level of Pepsi-Cola," Keough told Sealey. "They've always been seen as having better advertising. I don't want to retire with that legacy." Keough, 63, planned to retire by the end of 1994, two years past Coke's customary retirement age of 65—not much time to rescue a Coke advertising machine that had not turned out a winner since Bergin penned "Coke Is It!" in 1982.

Sealey did not mince any words. "I don't know if I can do it with our current advertising counsel," Sealey told Keough.

Keough told Sealey of the Ovitz overtures, which came as no surprise. Ovitz had talked to him, too, about Coca-Cola advertising when he was working at Columbia. Keough told Sealey he was the best person to make a decision on whether or not CAA was for real. "You understand the community headquartered in Hollywood," he said. "Let's see where this goes." Keough told Sealey to get to Atlanta as soon as possible.

THE DECISION TO CONSIDER A SHIFT AWAY FROM McCANN WAS THE culmination of several years of frustration Goizueta felt over Coca-Cola's marketing efforts. Looked at in isolation, the ads by McCann were far less than great, with their unremarkable tag line and indifferent graphical treatments. "Can't Beat the Real Thing" scored Coke's lowest ratings ever on the trade publication *Advertising Age*'s ranking of major campaigns, and had negligible impact on the key measurement of consumers' intent to purchase Coca-Cola. Worse still, the McCann advertising suffered tremendously in comparison with the rest of Coke's operations, which were moving toward hyperspeed as Goizueta's makeover of the late 1980s began to take effect. "We got all the back shop in place. Then we took a look at marketing," Goizueta would say.

In typical fashion, once Goizueta took a look, he wanted immediate action. Starting closest to home, in 1989 he ordered Ivester and marketing chief Ike Herbert to restructure the U.S. marketing operations. The restructuring came right from Ivester's playbook: breaking down problems and opportunities into component parts, making all of them work to their maximum, and reassembling them into a more powerful, more profitable whole. Ivester and Herbert divided the promotions department, which formerly had treated opportunities in a virtually ad hoc fashion, into three parts: prestige accounts, a sports group, and a new products group. From that came a host of new joint-venture-style deals, with partners ranging from a Super Bowl halftime show Coke co-sponsored with Walt Disney Co. to sponsorship deals with Major League Baseball and the National Football League.

Some of the experiments were outright failures. In the summer of 1990, Coke launched a promotion called MagiCan, featuring cans with a built in, spring-loaded device that popped a prize of scrolled cash, up to $200, out of the mouth of the can. The gadgets appealed to Goizueta's technical side. In a fit of enthusiasm eerily reminiscent of the unwillingness to listen to the New Coke market research, Coke officials ignored warnings from the can's manufacturer that the MagiCans could malfunction. A chlorinated liquid added as ballast might leak into the money chamber at the top of the can, and people might accidentally drink it. That's exactly what happened shortly after Coke launched its 750,000-can promotion. The marketing was not totally thought through, either. Even winning customers sometimes complained when they got currency instead of Coke, and were still left thirsty in the deal. After less than five weeks, Goizueta made the $100 million MagiCan promotion disappear.

Goizueta also made one more ambitious, but ultimately disappointing go at New Coke, dubbed Coke II in its final incarnation. There were other new products on the plate during this period—the sports drink PowerAde and a caffeine-free version of Coke among them— but Coke II held a unique place for Goizueta. Five years after the greatest mistake of his career, he still drank New Coke, and could never fathom why it would not catch on with consumers. When he chose to test the brand's mettle against one of Pepsi's strongest bottling and marketing operations, in Spokane, Washington, Pepsi rose up in defiance. Coke's competitor pumped $1 million into the Spokane market on everything from television advertising to a campaign to stop retailers from placing Coke II on their shelves. A few months later, as Pepsi's counterattack funds ran dry, Coke II jumped to a 2.5 percent share of the Spokane market. A test in Chicago, where Coke's bottling operation is more dominant than in Spokane, fared about the same. It was respectable, but not enough to give Coke II legs for a national rollout. Goizueta's dream for a successful revision of the classic formula were dashed again.

The exertions and promotions for Coke II, MagiCan, and a series of new products launched during late 1980 was a sideshow when stacked up against the essential task of fixing Coke's advertising, especially in the crucial U.S. market. Although operating income from non-U.S. markets had jumped to 77 percent of Coke's $2 billion total in 1990, from only 53 percent when New Coke was launched in 1985, the U.S. market still owned a position of superiority in the minds of Coke's top executives. With his "centralized decentralization" concept of management—adapted from the days of redesigning the corporate engineering department with Chap Tyler in the late 1960s—Goizueta had created a structure in which the rest of the world was affected directly by the lessons learned in Coke's domestic market. "The U.S. is the test market for the world," Keough explained. "When good things happen, we can export them around the world. And when things don't work, we can make sure they don't get exported."

KEOUGH EXPECTED GOOD THINGS TO COME FROM BRINGING SEALEY back into the Coke family. It was Keough's second shot at finding a fixer for the marketing troubles. He had searched for two years before finding Ted Host, who had worked as the president of a consumer products company before coming to Coke. But Hosts's risk-averse management style and a lack of beverage experience did not fit the job. Herbert enthusiastically endorsed the hiring of Sealey. Only later would Herbert, 63, discover that Ivester planned to use the hiring of Sealey as an excuse to push for Herbert's early retirement. Ivester believed it was important to give Sealey free reign in his important new task of redesigning Coke's advertising.

But before Herbert could bring Sealey back on board, he had to ink a deal with the former Columbia pictures executive. First, there was the matter of pay, always a sensitive point between Coke and Sealey since the time Sealey had shocked Goizueta by requesting an employment contract for his post at Columbia as a means of improving his standing in Hollywood. "I'm not going to negotiate with you on what I'm paid," Sealey told Herbert. "You're going to decide what I deserve." And Sealey would be the first to claim the new title of director of global marketing, a subtle way of telling the world that Sealey was expected to break Coke out of its marketing miasma.

Herbert left the salary question open and grudgingly acquiesced to Sealey's request to remain in California until year end, to complete his class work at Claremont. There was just one more matter to nail down. "Peter," Herbert said, "shave the beard before you come back." To Sealey, it was a bracing reminder of how little had changed at Coke. If Goizueta's prohibition against facial hair was still in effect, how many of Coke's old habits were still in effect? If Sealey did not have the power to keep his beard, would Goizueta really let him discharge McCann?

When Sealey protested mildly, Herbert offered an explanation. "Well, it's Roberto," he said. "It's a thing he has about facial hair. I think it's related to Castro." Sealey shaved the beard.

Once back inside fortress Coke, Sealey began a systematic review of Coke's advertising for all the major brands, especially the domestic campaigns. Ivester as head of Coke-USA was hungry for results, and Sealey responded to the pressure. Even at the outset, it was clear to those who worked with the men that there might be trouble in the mix. Sealey's deliberate style seemed to irritate Ivester, who seemed to consider the speed with which a decision was made almost as important as whether or not the decision was right. As much as he tried to push himself, the cerebral, deliberate Sealey never seemed to meet Ivester's timetable, or his rigorous, bottom-line ethos.

Still, Sealey did take action. Within months of arriving in Atlanta, he invited the Backer Spielvogel Bates advertising agency to present some ideas for a Coca-Cola Classic campaign, but nothing came of those discussions. Sealey also initiated a review of Diet Coke's $65 million advertising campaign, with an eye toward making a change, even though that would be almost as risky a step as rewriting the Mc-Cann relationship. Diet Coke had become the most successful new product in Coca-Cola's history, based largely on the strength of the "Just for the Taste of It" campaign. But now Diet Pepsi was back on the march, thanks to an immensely popular new campaign featuring former Coke pitch man Ray Charles and a catchy slogan, "You've got the right one baby, uh huh."

The hip Ray Charles campaign for Diet Pepsi effectively underscored Pepsi's emphasis on youth and freshness, a theme Pepsi had worked successfully since the Pepsi Generation ads first aired in the 1970s. By contrast, Diet Coke's competing campaign practically underscored its inability to connect with youth. Paula Abdul and Elton John were laced into classic black-and-white film footage with old time movie stars like Mickey Rooney and Humphrey Bogart. And while Charles' face emanated pure joy as the blind pianist sang to the accompaniment of three beautiful women in deeply scoop-necked black dresses, Diet Coke seemed plain peavish with a campaign bad-mouthing Diet Pepsi from the likes of "Wheel of Fortune" letter-turner Vanna White and frequently retired boxer Sugar Ray Leonard.

THE WORK ON A NEW DIET COKE CAMPAIGN, DRAMATIC AS IT WAS, still paled before the prospect of a possible switch for brand Coke. Even though he clearly had been brought back at Goizueta's behest, Sealey still had not had a direct conversation with Coke's boss about the advertising strategy, and that bred a sense of foreboding about the dramatic move he was contemplating for Coca-Cola Classic. After all, the Diet Coke switch meant only a change in slogans, not dumping a long-standing agency. For Diet Coke, Sealey planned to continue allowing Lintas: New York to work on the account. That would keep all the major Coke brands under the umbrella of the Interpublic Group of Companies, which held both Lintas and McCann in the umbrella of agencies it owned worldwide.

With brand Coke, Sealey was ready to change both the slogans and the sloganeers. He was ready to move away from McCann and the other shops owned by IPG. He freely talked about the traditional agency-client relationship as "outmoded," and called the agencies "dinosaurs." Goizueta, Keough, and Ivester all seemed to back such thinking, and Keough had told Sealey and McCann that he was prepared to bring CAA into the mix to introduce a new level of creative expression into Coca-Cola's advertising. But it is easy to favor change before the change occurs. Before the New Coke launch, practically everyone was behind the switch. If it failed, Goizueta and Keough would not be the only ones to shoulder blame. For Sealey, there was no telling where Goizueta, Keough, and Ivester ultimately would be—and where Sealey would wind up—if a swap flopped.

STILL, IT WAS QUITE CLEAR THAT CAA WAS HEADED TOWARD BIG things at Coca-Cola. In the fall of 1991, preliminary talks with Ovitz had grown serious enough that it was time to bring him to Atlanta for a formal meeting with Goizueta. Ovitz came well prepared. As well as he knew Coke from nearly a decade of talks with Keough and Sealey, he still took the time to attend several sessions in which Coca-Cola marketing executives taught him the lore of the brand. He studied Coke's advertising over the years, and began to sketch out ideas for transforming the way the world's best-selling soft drink was presented to the public.

In Goizueta's stately office on the twenty-fifth floor of the Coke tower, Ovitz was all polish and sell. He appealed to Goizueta's pride in his product, and to the frustration he knew Goizueta and Keough shared about the inadequacy of Coke's advertising. "Here we've got the greatest star in the world, Coca-Cola," Ovitz said. "It's instantly recognizable, the most bankable star in the world. The beautiful thing about this star is it won't talk back to you, won't renegotiate its contract."

Ovitz's idea was simple. He would create mini movies, casting Coca-Cola as the star. His roster of Hollywood talent—actors, directors, and writers—would support the product and show it in the best light. His agency, as well as anybody in the world, knew what the public wanted. His sense of the people was tested on a weekly basis, as movies he packaged opened in theatres across the country.

Goizueta mostly just listened. There was no discussion of money and no specific talk of precisely how a relationship with CAA might work, whether it would mean dumping McCann-Erickson outright, or forcing an uneasy alliance between the two agencies. But his last words to Ovitz were encouraging. "We need a new direction in Coca-Cola advertising," Goizueta said. "I'm happy that we're in some discussions about what that might be."

THE IMMEDIATE PLAN WAS TO TRY TO MAKE MADISON AVENUE AND Hollywood coexist. Keough and Sealey felt it would be unfair, highly risky, and practically impossible to dump McCann overnight. Even if Coke used no ads from the agency—an almost unthinkable prospect at the time—Sealey would still need McCann's global distribution network to buy air time, set advertising schedules, and otherwise implement the Coke program. Sealey invited CAA in as a consultant, but did his best to sell executives at both firms on the idea that McCann and CAA did not face an either/or proposition in their dealings with Coke.

Sealey told the McCann and CAA people that he had a "new paradigm" in mind. "The traditional advertising agency is like the movie industry in the 1950s, when the studios put actors under contract, hired directors, produced the movies, and owned their own theatrical distribution," Sealey told the McCann team at one meeting. "Today, the factory called McCann-Erickson is the same as Columbia Pictures of 1955. It's got to change." Coke, McCann, and CAA would work together in a triangle, with Coke describing the target audience and advertising goals, CAA providing ideas, and McCann producing ads and distributing them into the marketplace.

The notion of a harmonious triangle of cooperative production might have sounded good in one of Sealey's postgraduate business classes. In the real world, it was a gong show. From the start, the relationship between McCann and CAA was defined by suspicion, jealousy, resentment, and one-upmanship. Worse still, the same sentiments soiled relations within the McCann team itself, making it impossible for the group to unify in an effort to get along with CAA.

To make the "new paradigm" work, and to save McCann's hide, would have required a strong leader and visionary ad man. Unfortunately for McCann and its corporate overseers at IPG, McCann had neither at this crucial moment in its history. At the time that Keough brought Sealey back to Coke, McCann had recruited Gordon Bowen, an aloof and sometimes brilliant ad man. Bowen was one of the hottest names in advertising, after creating the American Express "Portraits" series that featured the likes of retired House Speaker Tip

O'Neil and jockey Bill Schumaker in Annie Liebovitz photographs with advertising copy implying that their American Express cards somehow added to their personal lustre.

McCann's recruitment of Bowen from rival shop Ogilvy & Mather had become a cause célèbre on Madison Avenue, and when he finally started work at McCann in October 1991, Keough welcomed him with a verbal embrace. "Do for me what you did for American Express, and I'll name a boardroom after you," Keough told Bowen.

Sealey could not quite muster Keough's unblemished enthusiasm. "Are you willing to put your reputation on this work?" he asked Bowen in a separate meeting. "This is the agency's last chance."

Bearded, a westerner, and lacking any major experience selling consumer products, Bowen had hardly come from Coke central casting. The relationship started on sour notes for both Coke and Bowen. Bowen's first job when he started was editing a reel of commercials for Coke's 1992 campaign, ads he had said should be killed when he first saw them while McCann was recruiting him the summer before. The result did not satisfy him or his client. Then Sealey and Keough summarily rejected Bowen's next idea, a "We are the World"-style ad for the 1992 summer Olympics, to be directed by Quincy Jones and featuring do-gooder artists like Sting, Phil Collins, and Eric Clapton. They knew Goizueta was not about to approve paying the tab for a costly campaign that might save a rainforest or two, but would not be likely to move much Coke.

Bowen's initial troubles were easy to explain away as just a rough start. It was far more important that he make good when he and his team began focusing on the project that had caused McCann to hire him in the first place: Creating a new theme for Coke's advertising. And he would have to do it, Bowen learned in the fall of 1991, with at least some input from the folks at CAA. That meant, chiefly, Shelly Hochron, the former Columbia Pictures marketing executive during Coke's ownership whom Ovitz recruited as the first employee of his start-up advertising unit. Her partner was Len Fink, a veteran ad man recruited from Ogilvy & Mather in New York.

THE FIRST JOINT MEETINGS, HELD AT COKE'S ATLANTA HEADQUARTERS and McCann's New York offices, were uncomfortable and sometimes testy. Things got worse from there. Although CAA officially was hired only as a creative consultant, it was obvious to the McCann people that Ovitz's team planned to dig into the entire creative end of the business. Hochron and Fink wanted do everything, from brainstorming broad themes to drawing up storyboards for specific commercials. A confrontation of some sort was virtually inevitable.

The unavoidable ego showdown came early in the summer of 1992, as both sides prepared for an important presentation of the new campaign's theme line to Coke's top brass in Atlanta. Keough wanted the McCann-CAA "team" to present a marketing theme at a meeting scheduled for June at Coke headquarters, and the two sides were doing their best to pull together to meet the deadline. Hochron and Fink flew from CAA's modern I.M. Pei-designed office in Beverly Hills to McCann's headquarters in a midtown Manhattan highrise. Sealey flew in from Atlanta.

McCann had put out a worldwide call for ideas for the Coke theme, and Hochron liked one of the returns: "Real Things Last." But Bowen pronounced that the word "last" was hardly uplifting. "Last gasp of life," he said, making a fair point. And the line would expose Coke to clever counterattacks from Pepsi. "The Last Thing you Want to Drink," for example.

Instead, Bowen preferred "A Spark of Life," a theme he felt was an extension of "The Pause That Refreshes," one of Coke's most venerable and successful slogans, a creation of none other than the late Robert W. Woodruff. An associate explained that the "spark" theme was ambiguous enough that it could be used universally, for a variety of purposes, just as Pepsi had transformed the Pepsi Generation into so many meanings. The room fell silent, as even the McCann operatives seemed to distance themselves from The Spark of Life. For some, the metaphor did not work. Soda pop should put out fires, not ignite them. Others again feared Pepsi's likely rejoinder. "They're down to their last spark of life," was one concern.

Then Hochron savagely tore into the suggestion. "I will tell you right now that that is the worst advertising idea I've ever heard of," Hochron said.

The room silenced again, as everyone waited for the client to weigh in. "She's right," Sealey said. Until then, Sealey had not stated a definitive opinion on any of the ideas that were floated in the weeks of meetings since all the parties joined in the advertising overhaul. But

Hochron's outburst seemed to awaken something in him. "I think we all need to think long and hard about what Shelley just said, because this is not going to work," Sealey concluded.

THE LAST THING SEALEY WANTED TO HEAR WHEN MCCANN MADE its presentation to Coke headquarters the next month was any reference to the "spark" idea. In the weeks since Bowen flubbingly floated "spark," Sealey had seen dozens of storyboards for commercials, with many incorporating the spark theme, but he could not stir up any enthusiasm. "We don't have it yet," he said repeatedly. CAA, meanwhile, was hard at work fleshing out "Real Things Last," even though that, too, had barely hobbled out alive from the June meeting. While Sealey had a difficult time explaining exactly what he wanted, he was quite clear about what he did not want, and Sealey thought he had made it clear that "spark" would not work.

By mid-July 1992, it was time for the shootout. Except in this case, the contest between McCann and CAA was not yet the main event. Instead, a civil war broke out between two warring factions in McCann, a dirty family feud on stage as Keough, Sealey, Ivester, and other Coke brass watched in horrified amazement. Goizueta was not present for the meeting. His blessing at the outset had been all the approval Keough needed to conduct the total overhaul of Coke's advertising. Having set the decision in motion, Goizueta did not want to get involved personally in meetings with vendors like McCann and CAA until a final series of advertisements was proposed.

It was fortunate for everyone involved that Goizueta decided not to attend. Although McCann and CAA were still, technically at least, working together to develop a new campaign for Coke, the disastrous meeting would finally prove that there was no hope of keeping McCann from rending itself into bits, much less forge a team of CAA and McCann.

The CAA crowd was at least all pulling in the same direction. Coke sent a plane to Los Angeles to pick up Ovitz, his second-in-command Ron Meyer, Hochron, Fink, and ten other CAA people who made up Ovitz's ersatz advertising agency. Everything was happening so fast that the entire CAA team was preparing for the seminal Coke session literally on the fly. En route to Atlanta aboard a Coca-Cola Gulf-stream, they reworked advertising copy, rearranged the order of ads they would show, drew up new storyboards, and refined the pitch that Ovitz, Hochron, and Fink would make. "It was a high-pressure, time-sensitive creative atmosphere. There was an electricity about what we had the opportunity to do," recalled one of the CAA team.

The CAA team had combed through old Coke advertising as far back as the 1950s. "Their ads were world calibre and highly memorable, until the last five-and-a-half years, when they lost their way," one of the CAA people recalled, in assessing McCann's work. The new ads were out of date. Hochron and Fink had decided to devise fresh and original images that would break through as something unique and memorable. The team arrived in Atlanta and shuttled directly to Coke's headquarters.

To open the CAA pitch, Ovitz introduced Fink and Hochron, who showed glimpses of the works in progress. Fink amused the Coke brass by barking like a dog as he introduced one spot showing a pooch determinedly digging up a Coke bottle buried in a suburban backyard. There were no over-arching strategy statements, no big thinking about the future of Coca-Cola advertising. CAA kept it simple: just the work to date, and a promise to capitalize on CAA's extensive Hollywood contacts to create the most original and memorable advertising in Coke's history.

CAA DID LITTLE MORE THAN DROP OFF A BUSINESS CARD COMPARED to what McCann had on the line. The real show on this day would be McCann. McCann's 40-year relationship seemed to weigh on the team that stepped to the front of the room to unveil its plans for the next big turn in Coke's advertising strategy. And the opening pitch of the McCann blitz was, shockingly to Sealey, Keough, and Ivester, "Spark of Life." David Warden, Bowen's fellow traveler on the "Spark" idea, declared that Coke had lost touch with its target audience. "Spark" was the best way to reconnect.

The shock parade was just starting. Next up was one of the great power plays in advertising history, staged before the biggest consumer products advertiser in the world, by one of the industry's consummate inside players. John Bergin had set his table nicely. In the days before the Atlanta showdown, Bergin had sent a "white paper" to Sealey outlining a totally different pitch from Bowen's "Spark." Sealey had passed it on to Keough and Goizueta, leaving the Coke brass with the impression that McCann had settled on something different and more traditional than "Spark."

The white paper was a masterful touch of gamesmanship, one worthy of a legendary Cola Wars veteran. Bergin was one of the few who actually had fought on both sides of the battle. During his 23 years at Pepsi's agency, BBDO, he had created the "Pepsi Generation" advertising that had sparked the number two cola's assault on Coke. A native of New Haven, Ct., who had been thrown out of both preparatory school and Amherst College because of discipline problems, Bergin had talked his way back in to Amherst after spending World War II as an artillery officer on the island of Guam. From Amherst, he won his job at BBDO by writing 80 proposed advertisements for a hypothetical product in the space of a few hours. When IPG in 1980 bought up his second agency, Sullivan, Stouffer, Caldwell & Bayliss, Bergin promptly went to work on the Coke account. By penning "Coke Is It," he had earned Roberto Goizueta's undying admiration, and Keough's friendship.

By 1992, though, Bergin's was past tense at McCann. Even before Bowen arrived, with the Coke account in crisis, he was invited to make little real creative input. He was involved in the Coke account only because of his personal ties to Keough. In meetings leading up to the first showdown with CAA, he had suggested an alternative to "Spark of Life" that played on the theme of Coke's universality and its consistent popularity worldwide. The key word was "Always," as in "Always Coca-Cola." But Bowen did not like it, and Geier himself had rejected it out of hand. To them, the old war horse seemed ready for pasture.

As Warden stepped away from the podium with the words "Spark of Life" hanging in the air, Bergin bounded to the front of the room. The first words from his mouth were, "That's bunk." The Spark idea was reaching too hard, trying to make Coke something it is not. "Let the brand be itself," Bergin pleaded. Then he laid out his alternative theme. Coca-Cola, Bergin said, has a taste that is at once universal and indescribable. He quoted Coke's flavor scientists, "in Atlanta, of course," claiming that, "We do not have a Coca-Cola memory."

Bergin had developed the appeal as if he were pitching to Roberto Goizueta himself. Goizueta, after all, had come up through the technical side of the business, and Bergin and Goizueta had spoken frequently about the inability to describe Coke's taste, about the lack of "taste memory" that made Coke distinctive. Indeed, the indescribable nature of Coca-Cola's taste was exactly the problem that had caused Goizueta so much trouble at the New Coke press conference, when he stumbled over every word in his effort to describe the flavor of New Coke. "It's my theory that Coca-Cola has no taste memory," Goizueta had once said. "Hi-C, iced tea, they're all in your taste memory. Coke doesn't taste like anything."

Goizueta saw Coke's lack of taste memory as one of the product's great strengths. And Bergin decided to take that thinking a step further. The lack of a memory, he explained, meant that the product is universal. Because its taste is nowhere in particular, it's everywhere at once. The flavor, and the brand, surround the consumer. They connect with consumers in unlimited ways. Coke's ever-changing taste profile makes it "always new." Its ubiquity, "always there." Its familiarity, "always real." Its uniqueness, "always you." Bergin strung the phrases together: "Always there. Always new. Always real. Always you." He showed that the string of words worked in French, and claimed it would sell in other languages, too. The white paper had described one potential ad, featuring an American little leaguer traveling with his team to Tokyo, thrilled to find the Coca-Cola logo amidst the neon clutter of the Ginza strip. But for the live presentation in Atlanta, Bergin had secretly created a "steal-a-matic"—a mock-up of a commercial with video images stolen from someone else's advertising. The idea was to give prospective clients a visual taste of what their advertising might look like. Without telling Bowen, Bergin had pirated video from an old McDonald's commercial of a Taiwanese little league team visiting the United States. The lilty tune in the background accompanied lyrics that said, "Wherever you go, wherever you've never been before, the face of a friend is all that you're looking for, and how many times has it happened to you, a friend called Coca-Cola happens to be there, too?" Then the punch line: "Always Coca-Cola."

Again, the appeal was targeted directly at Goizueta. When the Coke chairman would talk about his fondest wishes for Coke's global expansion, he often would muse about a family from China, the Philippines, Indonesia, or other far-away land paying their first visit to the United States. "They come to Times Square and see a Coke sign, and they say to each other, 'I didn't know they had Coke here, too, he would say.'" Bergin's little leaguer was playing exactly that part.

With Bergin finished, McCann's multiple-personality pitch again turned to Bowen. In the preplanning, he was designated as McCann's closer. Instead, it was a salvage operation. Even though Bergin's gambit had laid waste to "Spark," Bowen was still pitching the idea. Bowen was relaxed, and even effusive. He launched into an expository of everything he had learned about Coca-Cola marketing in his nine months on the job, the unique Coke brand and the Coke culture. Bowen's laid back and confessional demeanor was the opposite of Bergin's aggressive and earnest hard sell. His dummy ads, which were supposed to be 15-second spots, were too complex for that format and were 30-seconds instead. One featured a motorcyclist, knocking on the door of a friend, who turns out to be blind. "That wasn't a soft-drink spot," a McCann executive later groused. "There are very few commercials that feature the blind, except those that say, 'Help the Blind.'"

Keough observed the spectacle with a mixture of shock and anger crossing his face. Bowen's ode to Coke was precisely wrong for Keough, who liked to take the hot air out of overly effusive Coke marketers when they tried to turn soft-drink marketing into astrophysics. The product, Keough reminded them, is "a small pleasure on an average day." With three decades of selling Coke behind him, Keough was insulted to hear such a simplistic pitch. "It was marketing 101," he harumphed when recalling the episode.

Keough stood, ready to leave the room, but halted briefly to unleash an attack on Bowen. Sweeping his arm across the Coke, CAA, and McCann people in his midst, Keough said, "Gordon, there are people in this room with more knowledge about the soft-drink industry and its advertising than you will ever know the rest of your life. I am offended and I am distressed that you think you can teach us about it." Keough turned and left, with Ivester and Sealey close behind.

Bowen followed Keough to his twenty-fifth floor office at the Coca-Cola tower. He wanted to explain himself to Keough, to use his finely honed persuasion powers to make Keough understand his ideas on Coke, to score even a small win from a jarringly lousy meeting. Though he arrived moments behind Keough, Bowen was told that the Coke executive was too busy to see him. Goizueta's office was just a few steps away, but Bowen knew better than to ask to see Goizueta. He had not yet met Coke's chairman, and this certainly was not the time. He sat down in a couch in Keough's anteroom. There he waited, forlornly and in vain, and when Keough did appear he laid out the whole sad saga of McCann's infighting over the Coke account. But Keough was not interested. The result at the meeting had spoken for itself.

The outrageous pitch meeting at Coke's headquarters yielded immediate action. Keough recognized the dysfunction at McCann, and its impact on the agency's failure to bring Coke a winning new marketing slogan. But he was nervous about changing shops, and even told Sealey he was concerned about the impact on IPG's stock if Coke summarily dismissed McCann, the publicly held company's biggest operating unit. Besides, he liked Bergin's "Always" theme, and had run it by Goizueta for a reaction.

Sealey and Keough agreed that by adopting "Always" they could still sell the new Coke campaign as a collaboration in which McCann played a key role. A day later, Sealey called Bowen and declared, "You will execute 'Always Coke' exactly as laid out by John Bergin." The CAA crew got the order to work "Always" into their ads, but to pursue the ideas sketched out at the meeting.

THE MOST IMPORTANT AND FAR-REACHING RAMIFICATION OF THE meeting was less obvious. Fresh from the disaster, Ivester put out a call—to Sergio Zyman. Ivester knew Coke needed a backup campaign, in case the untested CAA could not deliver the goods. And he knew that bringing Zyman into the loop was a move that Goizueta would easily approve. Goizueta had always liked Zyman, going as far back as his work on the formulation of Diet Coke in the late 1970s. He admired Zyman's work on New Coke, and seemed to appreciate Zyman's willingness to take the fall for the debacle by leaving the company in 1986. To show his appreciation, Goizueta had made certain to keep Zyman busy with consulting work even during his exile. His other clients during the time included Microsoft, Miller Brewing, General Mills, and McDonald's, but $100,000 a month in consulting fees made Coke his biggest client.

By the time he got the call from Ivester, Zyman knew the chief of Coke-USA quite well. Keough in the summer of 1990 had called Zyman to his office to talk about a unique assignment. "I want you to talk to Doug about marketing," Keough said. "I want Doug to get to know marketing as well as he knows numbers."

For more than a year, Zyman had spent Saturday mornings tutoring Ivester on the finer points of marketing. It pleased Goizueta that

Ivester had burnished his strong financial credentials with a stellar turn in Europe, his first operating post. But his early run at Coke-USA was proving less than impressive, given Pepsi's recent strength. Even after building distribution systems in Eastern Europe and ousting the uncooperative French bottling partner, Ivester clearly still needed experience in the core activity of The Coca-Cola Company: marketing. Goizueta, Keough, and Ivester realized that the University of Georgia accounting major needed a crash course and they immediately recognized Zyman as just the man for the job.

While playing the Henry Higgins role, tutoring Ivester in the finer points of marketing, Zyman took the opportunity to pepper Ivester with criticisms of Sealey's advertising and marketing programs. He especially targeted the important and moribund Diet Coke. And he worked to sell Ivester on one of his biggest brainstorms during his period of exile from Coca-Cola, a concept called momentum marketing, which calls for a company to speedily move brands into the marketplace at a minimum of cost, using advertising tactically to quickly build word of mouth. At that point, he explained, the marketer should assess how the brand fares before increasing investment in it.

Both men knew Zyman was, in essence, auditioning for Sealey's job. By this point, the mutual dislike between Ivester and Sealey was an open secret at Coke's headquarters. Zyman and anyone else who cared knew it was only a matter of time—in fact, probably just the remaining months until Don Keough retired—before Sealey would get fired.

Ivester at the end of his tutorial delivered a simple, though politically risky assignment to Zyman. He wanted Coke's former marketing chief to develop a backup campaign, in case CAA's "Always" work was not right for Keough and Goizueta. Both Goizueta and Keough had given lip service to the notion of turning Coke's advertising behavior inside out, but there was no guaranteeing they would go through with the plan once the ads were placed before them in an auditorium the final of the big shootout between CAA and McCann.

Ivester had an unorthodox notion of how to create an alternative. He wanted Zyman and Bowen to work together, on an idea that was not far away from some of Bowen's musings about Coke. It was a busy time for Bowen. Despite the debacle in Atlanta, he was still technically in charge of assembling McCann's answer to CAA. Also during this period, he spent time unsuccessfully trying to persuade his bosses at IPG to allow him and Bergin to fly to Los Angeles with an eye either toward acquiring the CAA advertising agency, or working out a creative partnership with Hochron and Fink. Phil Geier, the chairman of IPG, reportedly nixed the idea.

Ivester wanted Zyman and Bowen to focus on the theme of "Feel It." It was obvious that the CAA ads were going to be an abrupt departure from the past, so he ordered an update to Coke's classic style of Norman Rockwell America advertising. They never got past the storyboard stage, but the Zyman-Bowen ads seemed likely to serve as an antidote to CAA's fast-moving, mold-breaking work. One featured a teenage girl who breaks up with a boyfriend and is consoled by her brother while drinking a Coke. Another pictured a group of whale watchers, quaffing Cokes to calm their nerves before diving into the water to swim with the beasts.

By the time of the final shootout meeting, October 15, 1992, CAA was fully in control. Sealey even flew from Atlanta to California the day of the meeting to pick up Ovitz, Hochron, Fink, and a handful of their colleagues. After landing at Los Angeles, while waiting for the CAA limousines, the pilot told Sealey that the Coke plane had broken down. Sealey nearly panicked. To make the meeting with Goizueta and Keough back in Atlanta, he would have to find a replacement in virtually no time. And second, he would have to somehow convince Ovitz, who was afraid of flying, to accept on faith the safety of a plane Sealey had rented on the spot. However, the crisis seemed to ease the tension everyone felt for the flight to Atlanta. In contrast to the harried flight to Atlanta before the July showdown, this time the CAA team was ready and confident.

Though they had flown in together earlier in the day, Sealey greeted Hochron with a kiss on the cheek when the CAA group entered the Coke conference room for the decisive showdown. Ovitz opened, drawing on Sealey's concept of a "new paradigm" by explaining that CAA was prepared to bring Coke a new form of advertising. The agency would serve as a producer, enlisting directors, writers, and actors create the 15-second and 30-second mini movies that would become Coke's new advertising message.

Ovitz knew enough of Coca-Cola's experience with Columbia Pictures to understand how starstruck Goizueta, in particular, had become. He dropped some big Hollywood names. Director Rob Reiner, who had made the sleeper hit *Stand by Me* for Columbia, would create one of the ads, and Francis Ford Coppola another, he promised. He rolled the Reiner ad, a chronolog of a couple aging from youth to retirement age, always within arm's reach of a Coke, to the tune of the Beatles song "When I'm 64." Other spots followed: The dog digging up the Coke bottle; Coke as perceived by Renoir and Picasso; a crew of space warriors trying to catch an alien imposter by asking questions about Coke trivia; polar bears admiring the northern lights.

Bergin, Bowen, Geier, and nearly 40 people from McCann and its parent company IPG crowded behind Keough and Ivester, with the hope of picking up something from their body language. They were shocked by what they saw. Except for the polar bear ad, none of it appeared to them to be worthy of a client the calibre of Coke. The pieces were creatively uneven and lacked any coherent line. Even more shocking to them: The Coke brass loved it. Their shoulders heaved with laughter at the humorous spots, and when the "Always" theme song rose—a distinctive stoccato beat that jumped up and down the tonal register—Keough visibly bounced in his seat.

Bergin scratched a note onto a pad he had brought with him to the meeting and passed it to his colleague Marcio Moreira. Bergin made it short and to the point: "We are dead."

BEFORE THE FEBRUARY 10 ROLLOUT OF COKE'S NEW ADS AT A LANDmark press conference in New York, Goizueta assembled Coke's senior management team to view the ads. The tally showed just how devastating CAA's win had been: 24 ads produced by CAA, only 2 by McCann. Goizueta and his executives watched quietly as a new era began. They were replacing the long-time Coke strategy, "one sight, one sound, one sell," with a rifle-shot approach that would aim ads at specific niche audiences, unifying the group only with the "Always" tag line at the end.

Next came the press conference in New York. Although he had driven the process with Coke's bottom line in mind, to the very end Keough seemed personally conflicted by the switch to CAA. Loyal as he was to Goizueta and to Coca-Cola, Keough also was turning his back on a career-long friend, Bergin, and on years of relationships at McCann's parent company. Throughout the long process, he had given

McCann every opportunity to stay in the game. Even so, Keough recognized that if the ads were a hit, he would achieve his goal of remaking Coca-Cola's advertising before he retired. "Don did not fully buy in or realize the extent of the campaign until February 10 in New York," Sealey said. "When the polar bears came on, you could hear the audience switch from being objective observers to just admiring the ads. That's when we won Don Keough."

The imprint of Goizueta's bottom-line thinking was present in the new strategy. Sealey boasted about CAA's use of freelancers and other cost-cutting measures to produce the spots quickly and cheaply. Ovitz joined in, claiming that the total cost of CAA's initial flight of 24 ads was equal to what Coke spent on the 7 ads McCann had produced in 1992.

The CAA spots won immediate acclaim from the popular press at Coke's initial showing. Then the beatings began. Advertising executives and critics hated the new "Always" campaign, recognizing CAA's incursion as a possible Trojan horse that would imperil the future of their industry. In a review panel organized by the *Adweek* trade publication, J. Walter Thompson executive Peter Kim seemed contemplative about the ad industry's complicity in the CAA triumph. "The industry has to take a great deal of the responsibility for the sad state we're in, the fact that CAA's even in the mix," he said. But Andy Berlin, president of DDB/Needham N.Y. was more typical in his peevishness. "What we see here is the result of a creative gang bang with no strategic centrality and not enough gate-keeping to keep the good stuff away from the bad stuff," he said. "They're not CAA spots, they're just spots brokered through CAA."

Even Bergin joined in the criticism, publicly breaking with Coke and his friend Keough for the first time. "When you look at the commercials, you just say, 'Well, my God, where's the corporate identity? Who made that one. When you perceive the author in your mind's eye, you need to say 'Coca-Cola' or you're not doing the full job."

But the ads worked. By the end of the year, the tracking firm Video Story Board Tests ranked Always as the third most popular and most remembered advertising campaign of 1993. Coke's supermarket sales picked up, and the ads proved successful in their international roll-out—one of Goizueta's key aims in developing a new, universal advertising theme.

Goizueta was pleased by the smoothness with which Sealey had commanded the switch. "Peter Sealey did an extremely good job on the Always campaign," he said. "That's exactly what he was brought on to do." But the job was done. Keough would soon retire. CAA was in place and McCann was out the door as Coke's key ad creator. Sealey did not know it yet, but his Coke days were numbered. The switch to CAA was a moment deserving of handshakes all around. But the job was done. Coke had a world to conquer, and Goizueta would have to finish the job with Doug Ivester, not Don Keough at his side. It was time to move on.

9

The Big Brand Machine

At the beginning of 1991, Don Keough and Roberto Goizueta had sat in Goizueta's office for an earnest discussion about the future. Keough would turn sixty-five in September, and company policy dictated that he should then retire. But Goizueta had other ideas. "I don't want you to retire," he had told Keough. "I want you to stay as long as I'm here."

He paused a moment, letting Keough do the math in his head. Goizueta would not turn sixty-five until November of 1996, meaning Keough would be at least seventy by the time they could retire in tandem. "I know you're not going to do that," Goizueta continued. "But I'd like you to stay two more years."

Keough agreed. And at the January board meeting, Goizueta put it to the directors this way: "It isn't true that Keough is going to be 65 in September. He's going to be 63." The board puzzled for a moment, then got the message. They voted unanimously to let Keough stay on.

Nearly two years later, as Goizueta and Keough met between Christmas and New Year's in late 1992, Keough came to the meeting with a surprise announcement. "I'd like to step down at a logical point early in the year," he said, cutting short their plan for him to stay at least through September. Keough explained that he had felt uncomfortable sitting through the last budget cycle in October, when he knew he would not be there to see the plans fulfilled. For the first time in his career, he felt he was keeping people below him from reaching their potential. His time was up.

218

The partners discussed their options and agreed that the April board meeting would make a sensible retirement date. Then, with a bittersweet sense of nostalgia, they went through the traditional agenda: reviewing financial goals for the coming year, discussing the performance of their top 150 managers one by one, and sketching out the next career moves for those with the most promise. They agreed that Keough's job should not immediately go to Doug Ivester, even though he topped both of their succession lists. Ivester still needed seasoning before any official anointment.

Keough's imminent departure marked a significant watershed. The partnership of the two men, a true marriage of convenience in the midst of their bruising fight for the chairmanship, had started like a wedding in which half the congregation is betting the union will not last. But it lasted for more than a decade. Outwardly, the two had seemed to have little in common. Keough, the gregarious middle-class midwesterner, the masterful negotiator, and natural salesman who had befriended bottlers while taking away their exclusivity contracts, was nothing like the aristocratic, cerebral, and introverted Goizueta, who had played an insider's game to climb to the top of Coke. But they shared a passion for their work, and for Coca-Cola, and they built their relationship from that common point.

Keough always respected Goizueta for sticking with the deal the two had forged to work together, regardless of who won the fight for the corner office. And he returned the favor with loyalty to Goizueta. For several years after Goizueta climbed past him to take the chairman's slot, Keough could not go anywhere among his big business peers without someone pulling him aside and asking if he would be interested in the chief executive's job at one or another consumer products company. Finally, Keough turned them down too abruptly, too consistently, and too frequently, and people stopped asking. Coke's Spencerian script seemed sewn across his breast.

Goizueta was able to keep Keough, and keep him happy, because he went far beyond the pledge to bring Keough to the top with him. He stuck with the division of labor the two worked out early in their partnership. Marketing and operations remained Keough's domain, and strategy, Wall Street, and the significant personnel decisions remained primarily Goizueta's playground. Working together on the twenty-fifth floor of the Coke tower, they formed a kind of roving executive office that was situated wherever the two happened to meet—at the stock ticker near their offices, in Keough's or Goizueta's office. There was constant overlap and consultation, but the spheres of influence remained largely unchanged over 11 years together.

Goizueta and Keough kept nearly identical offices, separated by a shared dining room. During a deposition in a lawsuit, a plaintiff's lawyer skeptically asked Keough why there was no record of the chief executive's decision to grant him authority to make a decision in the matter. The lawyer said documents must have been destroyed, since there were no memoranda memorializing any of the communication. "I went through that door first," Keough said, pointing to the dining room. "I asked him for authority, and he said, 'Yes, go ahead.' And I came back through the door to my office."

In more than a decade of partnership, their only major policy disagreement focused on the New Coke launch. Keough played the good soldier, but had remained privately skeptical about New Coke despite Goizueta's yen to launch the new brand. Still, he shared the heat with Goizueta when it was time to reverse course. At the press conference announcing the return of Coke Classic, and starring in the mea culpa commercial, he admitted Coke had erred in taking away the nation's favorite soft drink. When asked in later years about New Coke, he liked to joke that he "was on vacation" when the decision was made. It was his subtle way of distancing himself from the decision.

Perhaps Keough could have served as Coke's chief executive, he acted like one in so many ways. But even he came to recognize that Goizueta's unique genius for strategy and long-term thinking probably made him the better choice. Just as certainly, Goizueta could never have done Keough's job: rallying bottlers, creating esprit de corps among Coke's forces worldwide, playing second fiddle to a strong-willed boss. Goizueta did the right thing by turning to Keough after he nosed out the Irishman for Coke's top job. Keough filled Goizueta's voids of substance and style in a way that perhaps no other person could have.

Goizueta, for all his authority, strategic vision, and leadership skills, still could never muster the kind of heartfelt devotion from Coke's rank and file, and even some of the company's top executives, that fell so naturally to Keough. If Goizueta was Eisenhower, Keough was Patton. People respected and admired Goizueta's capabilities, his ability to plan and execute major campaigns wherever the Cola Wars happened to rage, but Goizueta always remained aloof. Keough was an old blood-and-guts warrior, the kind of leader who could march troops across Europe in the middle of winter with barely a complaint, as he had in fact done during Coke's assault on eastern Europe after the Berlin Wall fell. Robert Woodruff had recognized this intuitively and betrayed his unspoken assessment by inviting Keough to Ichauway years before Goizueta received the coveted invitation.

It's easy to call Keough a back slapper, because the sharp pat between the shoulder blades came as naturally to him as a handshake. Some called him Coca-Cola's Ed McMahon, and it fit because he both looked and sounded like Johnny Carson's sidekick. Keough was such a natural at what he did that it nearly concealed what a rare talent he had. No one else could have laid out a mea culpa for New Coke that was at once humble yet confident. No one could bring a crowd to tears at the Coke centennial by talking from the heart about the love in the room without sounding overly corny.

When Keough told Coke-New York bottler Charlie Millard he really would retire in April, Millard penned a tribute to his friend. "KO without Keough?" it asked, using the company's New York Stock Exchange ticker symbol. "Say it ain't so, Joe! It's like peanut butter without jelly, like Ireland without a Kelly! KO without Keough? It's like eggs without ham, like Army without Spam! Keough not at KO? It's like New York without the *Times,* like a poem without rhymes! It's like Costello without Abbott, like Easter without a rabbit!" This isn't the sort of tribute anyone would have written about Roberto Goizueta.

Goizueta frequently heard Keough described as "the heart of Coca-Cola" or "the keeper of the trademark," while people more often referred to him as "the brain of Coca-Cola." It pleased Goizueta to be thought of as smart and shrewd, but there was part of him that coveted Keough's unique ability to win the affection and personal loyalty of the people who worked for them at all levels of the company. Goizueta betrayed this resentment in rare and unseemly outbursts.

At an executives' retreat at the River Oaks Country Club in Houston in the late 1980s, Goizueta launched into a description of the division of duties between himself and Keough. "The difference between Don and me is that Don is the president and I'm the chairman," Goizueta explained. "The difference between the president and the chairman is, the chairman can fire the president." It was an attempt at humor, but with Keough squirming in front of the crowd near the dais, few found it funny. One top executive even bravely called Goizueta afterward to complain, and Goizueta was stricken that his attempted joke had gone so wrong.

With Keough retiring, Goizueta could have pushed to keep him on Coke's board of directors. Other past presidents of the company had stayed on the board following retirement, most recently Luke Smith in the late 1970s. But early in his tenure, as part of a series of bylaw changes that sought to rejuvenate the board, Goizueta had pushed through a bylaw change that prohibited a past president from remaining on the board. The restriction appealed to corporate governance experts who believe retired executives often exert unproductive influences as board members by criticizing their successors. Instead, Goizueta retained Keough as a consultant to the board. Goizueta's friend Herbert Allen, Jr., rewarded Keough for his years as one of corporate America's leading statesmen with a job as the non-executive chairman of the Allen & Co. investment banking firm.

GOIZUETA SOON FOUND HE COULD NOT EASILY REPLACE KEOUGH. No single person could take on the multifaceted role of Coke's top war whooper, its operations chief, its marketing genius, and its strategic sounding board. Even though Goizueta understood he needed to anoint a number two, he knew just as clearly that he would have to get other top executives to pick up some of the load that Keough had borne so effortlessly. As far back as 1989, Goizueta had told Harold Burson and other close associates that Doug Ivester was likely to be his top choice. After the short but successful run in Europe, he had moved Ivester back to head up Coke's North American operation, and let him play a role in the switch from McCann-Erickson to Creative Artists Agency. He had filled the operations and marketing gaps in Ivester's resume, but Goizueta was not inclined immediately and publicly to appoint a single individual to be his top lieutenant. Some sort of competition for the job would keep open his options, keep the 45-year-old Ivester hungry, give Wall Street analysts the satisfaction that Goizueta was deliberately evaluating the decision, and save face in case Ivester did not develop the leadership and strategic vision required of his heir apparent.

As Ivester's corporate consort, Goizueta chose John Hunter. The gruff Australian native had started with Coke as an advertising manager in Japan, and never strayed from the Pacific region until Goizueta called him to Atlanta as president of Coke's international business sector in 1991. On the same fall day, he promoted Ivester to head Coke's North American operations—a step that set up the Keough succession moves two years in advance. Hunter had made his first companywide impact in 1981, when he dreamed up Coke's landmark $13 million investment in the Philippines that led to the development of the anchor bottler program. The bald-pated, leather-faced Hunter won notice for keeping Coke on top of the fast-changing, hypercompetitive Japanese market of the late 1980s, and leading early development work in the Far Eastern region of the globe. Spending 60 percent of his time on the road, he learned to say "Have a Coke" in twenty-one languages.

While Goizueta technically had two people vying for the job, he clearly had a first and second choice. Age favored Ivester, who would be only 49 years old when Goizueta turned 65 in November 1996, while Hunter would be 59, and at best could serve only as a caretaker CEO if he succeeded Goizueta. Ivester had a far more varied portfolio, from auditing to movie financing to the bottling spinoff to European development to domestic operations to marketing. In many ways, Ivester was appealing to the boss because, unlike Keough, he was a flesh-and-blood copy of Goizueta in so many ways. His strong financial background and uncurbed aggressiveness appealed to Goizueta's technical and competitive nature.

Just as Goizueta had spent most of his career at the Atlanta headquarters, Ivester had worked all but one year from offices on North Avenue. Goizueta had no operating experience when he became chief executive, but Ivester's had come just in the last three years—after Goizueta already had focused on him as his choice for the top job. Like his boss, Ivester would never draw notice in a crowd, was not much of a public speaker, and was singlemindedly dedicated to his job. Ivester did not even have children to distract him from work. He voraciously consumed newspapers and magazines, but read few books, and had few outside interests. Former Coke executives speculated that Ivester's narrow world view was a factor in Goizueta's unwillingness ever to formally designate him as his successor.

By the time Keough retired after Coke's April board meeting, Goizueta's succession plan was obvious even to those outside the company. The annual meeting proxy statement put it in numbers. In 1993, Ivester earned a $520,000 salary and a $270,000 bonus, 110 percent more in aggregate than Hunter's $486,250 salary and a $240,000 bonus. Although Goizueta would never publicly designate Ivester as his successor, it was clear on Wall Street and wherever else people cared that the low-key, high-strung Georgian was Goizueta's man almost from the day Keough retired.

IN JANUARY 1993, JUST DAYS AFTER KEOUGH'S QUIET HOLIDAY RE-tirement talk with the boss, Goizueta called Ivester and Hunter to his office for a major planning session. He discussed Keough's departure, and his plan to proceed with promoting the two men. Ivester would take charge of North America and marketing, and Hunter would handle international.

Then he got down to the real business of the meeting: Goizueta was downright unhappy. Over the holidays, he had studied Coke's 1992 performance, and liked very little of what he saw. Coke's stock grew just 4.4 percent in 1992—exactly in line with the overall stock market. This mortified Goizueta. Since August 1988, when investors first caught on to the earnings power Goizueta had unleashed by unloading Coca-Cola Enterprises, through the end of 1991, Coke's shares had quadrupled. The compounded annual growth rate was nearly 55 percent. Then the stock died. A dividend increase helped boost total shareholder return to 5.8 percent for the year. But compared to 1991's 75 percent return, Goizueta felt like he was practically taking money away from his shareowners. The year 1992 would go down as the worst sustained stock performance and one of the worst business results of his career as chairman.

Plenty of factors explained the malaise. From the United States to Europe to Japan to Mexico to Brazil, every major market in 1992 experienced economic slowdown or recession. European growth was half its average in recent years, and Latin America was a flat line. World-wide case volume grew at just 3 percent, far short of the target Goizueta demanded in the fall budgeting session. In the United States especially, there was more than just bad economics at the root of the trouble. New age beverages, bottled teas, private-label brands, and non-cola soft drinks like Dr. Pepper and Barq's root beer suddenly began drawing significant sales. Snapple bottled tea was everywhere. Flavored seltzers, juice drinks, and "natural" soda pops suddenly had retail sales that approached $600 million, hardly a threat to Coke, but too big to ignore. As a group, all of these non-cola interlopers were drawing unreasonable amounts of attention from the press. If not handled properly, they could one day put a real dent in cola hegemony.

Goizueta scoffed at the New Age, private label, and bottled tea craze. "I read a lot about Snapple," he complained to a reporter. "Mello Yellow sells more than Snapple." Pausing for a moment, he spit out the name of the most aggressive private-label company. "Cott. We sell more Coke in Nigeria than they sell worldwide."

Measured against the scale of Coke's cola business, the convoy of new drinks might seem less than even a minor annoyance to the common person. Cola's share of soft-drink retail-store sales had fallen since the peak of 63.6 percent in 1984, but still held a commanding 60 percent share of the total non-alcoholic beverage market—a position worth $27.6 billion in total retail sales. But Goizueta was hardly complacent when he saw Snapple's pastel tones taking up shelf space in stores where Coca-Cola products could be. "I want it all," he said. "I don't want them to have even these niche products."

It was time to do something about the trouble. Goizueta wanted an all-out marketing offensive. The primary purpose: To activate the Coca-Cola brand. Diet Coke, a product always close to Goizueta's heart, needed immediate attention and perhaps a new marketing program. Anything with the Coke name on it or attached to it should be pushed with new aggression. As part of the effort, Goizueta would focus new attention on two joint ventures, a British-based bottling alliance with Cadbury-Schweppes and a separate arrangement for selling bottled tea alongside Nestlé SA. The Creative Artists Agency advertising would strengthen Coke's image.

As the discussion concluded, Goizueta laid out the plan of attack, ticking off the points on his fingers one by one. He wanted a flurry of new products, developed and launched in record time, to combat the sudden rash of New Age drinks. New information systems—video conferencing, e-mail, and the like—should be employed to improve coordination between Atlanta and the field. Coke needed to leverage its advertising spending and shuffle the use of agencies around the world to find messages that worked. Hunter picked up on Goizueta's message. "I don't care if they like the people, I don't care if they like the cast we use," he said. "At the end of the day, the consumer has to say, 'I want to go out and buy a Coke.'"

ONCE AGAIN, GOIZUETA WAS AT A MAJOR TURNING POINT IN HIS career and in his company's history. In the past, he had attacked big problems with dramatic and unorthodox solutions: dumping Aqua-Chem, the Wine Spectrum, and the rest of the Paul Austin menagerie, buying then selling Columbia Pictures, launching New Coke, and creating CCE. The net effect was that Goizueta had peeled his company down to its very essence. At its core, The Coca-Cola Company really was just one thing: a trademark. The word Coke, the fancy script, the unique bottle, the red disc logo all emanated from the trademark. Coke's soft drinks themselves each had unique recipes. But their real value in the marketplace came when The Coca-Cola Company lent its name to the products.

As he, Ivester, and Hunter set Coke's course for the near future, Goizueta was taking a dramatic step, but not the sort for press conferences and headlines. Those would come later, when the financial results came in and Coke's stock price once again bounded forward. There really was no way to gather a crowd and announce that the time had come to do the little things right, to wring maximum value from Coke's brands, to focus on the company's core, and to provide Coke people around the world with the resources to do so. There were essential competitive advantages on which he wanted to capitalize: speed, information, global reach, and access to capital.

The times demanded that Goizueta focus on continuing the building of the international system while shoring up Coke's operations in the United States. Internationally, the biggest promise was on the continent of Asia. Goizueta was enthusiastic about prospects for Coke's return to India after an absence of nearly 20 years, the investment program in China, the development of the market in Indonesia, and the successful attack on Pepsi's stronghold in the former Soviet Union. The anchor bottler program was taking shape, with companies designated as Coca-Cola's partners in expanding its reach and influence in key markets around the globe. Some of the anchor bottlers, such as Coca-Cola Amatil, themselves were developing a presence on more than one continent, an expansion of the concept beyond Goizueta's original notion. The invasion of eastern Europe was paying off, and Coke's dominance in Latin America was marred only by its inability to make headway in Venezuela, despite millions in new investment that Goizueta had approved in that country.

While the international scene absorbed much of Goizueta's time, Coke's domestic unit as always commanded attention because of North America's important impact on the mindset of the entire Coca-Cola system. North America was an incubator for trends both good and bad throughout the company's global operation, had an impact on Wall Street's attitude toward Coke's stock price. Besides, Goizueta and the rest of his executive team woke up and went to work most days in the United States and were influenced by everything from the selection of billboard advertising in Atlanta to the choice of advertisements for Coke's commercials in the Super Bowl.

If he wanted to get people focused on the minutest aspects of Coke's business, Goizueta knew he needed to do so himself. The target he chose was Tab Clear—a gimmickly, colorless soda about which Goizueta could barely muster enthusiasm. Normally, he would have steered clear almost entirely of such a tiny undertaking. But Tab Clear, which Goizueta personally named because he did not want to risk the Coke brand name on such a chancy product, gave Goizueta an opportunity to make a point about speedy action, decisiveness, and risk taking at a time when little such activity was percolating up from the ranks of his company.

When Coke got wind that Pepsi was laying plans to launch a new, colorless version of Pepsi-Cola by early 1993, Goizueta sprang into action. He ridiculed the "clear" category as a fad, but he wanted to prove a point internally about how fast the system could move if directed properly. Rather than allow the ponderous Peter Sealey to spearhead the project, Goizueta brought in Sergio Zyman. Conventional wisdom had it that Goizueta exiled Zyman for his role as marketing mastermind of the New Coke debacle. But Goizueta never admitted that was the case, and he admired Zyman's work on other new product launches, especially Diet Coke.

For the new clear cola, Goizueta laid out a simple task: Get it done, and get it done fast. He was pleased when Zyman moved from formulation to the store shelves in 60 days, even if he still had no confidence in the ultimate success of the product. Pepsi, meanwhile, beat Coke to market with a costly Super Bowl launch of its own colorless version, Crystal Pepsi. "Pepsi has made a huge mistake calling it Pepsi Clear," Goizueta said, getting the name wrong. His regard for the category was so low that he hadn't even bothered to commit the name of Pepsi's offering to memory. "I doubt there is a clear cola category, and we don't want to put the Coke name on it."

Less than a year after the launch of Tab Clear, Goizueta correctly forecasted the fate of both the Pepsi and Coke clear drinks in an uncharacteristically frank assessment to a group of New York analysts. "Both Tab Clear and Crystal Pepsi are about to die," he said. And he was right. In early 1994, he finally pulled Tab Clear from the market.

There was more to Goizueta's ill will toward Tab Clear than just the fact that he did not believe the product would succeed. It irked him that he personally had to be involved in too many details of launching what was obviously a very minor brand. Tab Clear was created for the wrong reason—as a defensive move to counter Crystal Pepsi. It lacked an effective marketing plan. And the advertising slogans were poor. He finally settled for "The ultimate diet soft drink" and "Not what you think," but did not like either of them. Doug Ivester reflected his boss' ambivalence about the clear cola when he told reporters, "It will be marketed for what it is—a study in contradictions. We talked to consumers, and they told us, in no uncertain terms, that they don't want products just because someone labels them 'New Age.'"

EVEN SO, THE EXPLOSION OF NEW DRINKS WAS SENDING A SIGNAL that consumers wanted to experiment, and Goizueta could not afford to ignore the trend. In early 1993, he set up a new products group at Coke-USA. He wanted to develop the capability in the United States that Coke had long exercised in Japan—the ability to launch new products quickly and effectively. In Japan, Coke launched more than twenty new products a year. The United States was far more stable than Japan's flavor-of-the-month market, but the influx of New Age drinks was opening a new competitive dynamic that Goizueta felt he could not afford to ignore. He also laid plans to revamp Coke's entire marketing operation by joining U.S. and international marketing into one global marketing unit.

Goizueta felt strongly that he could not carry out the job of focusing intense effort on the global marketing and new product functions with the wrong person running the operation. Keough had brought Sealey back to Coke to dump McCann and hire Creative Artists Agency, and he had done the job. But the days ahead needed decisive, inventive action. That part was not written for Sealey. Besides, Ivester wanted Sealey out. The two men had clashing notions of what Coke's advertising should look like. With the hiring of CAA, Sealey seemed enamored of the glitz he was bringing to Coca-Cola while Ivester became fixated on the trouble with Diet Coke. The landmark new product of Goizueta's chairmanship saw its growth slip in 1992 for the first time since its launch a decade earlier. Sealey scrambled to reverse the disaster in January of 1993 by dumping celebrity endorsers like Paula Abdul and Elton John and adopting an unorthodox new campaign with a tag line "Taste It All." But bottlers hated it. "I saw Diet Coke on the screen for maybe one second," complained one. And consumers did not respond, either. The market erosion continued.

The Diet Coke campaign proved so ineffectual that Goizueta would not approve any additional spending after the initial flight of ads. Outlays on Diet Coke advertising in 1993 fell more than 50 percent to $24 million. "You didn't see any Diet Coke advertising last year, because the campaign didn't work," Goizueta said in 1994. "Why spend the money if the advertising doesn't work? You pay the same money whether it's a great commercial or a lousy one."

Ivester was intent on dumping Sealey, and Goizueta was not about to stop him. Coke's CEO was just as comfortable with Zyman as Ivester was. Goizueta admired Zyman's hard driving style and respected the man's marketing genius. And he felt empowered by the fact that both Ivester and Hunter shared his view. Ivester had grown close to Zyman during his Saturday morning marketing sessions, and Hunter knew him well. He had hired Zyman to help launch new brands in Latin America, and asked him to lay out a blueprint for a new organization of Coke's international marketing, an assignment on which Zyman traveled the globe meeting marketing executives at top consumer goods companies.

For Goizueta, the hiring of Zyman would also signal to the outside world that he was ready to shake up Coke again. The general public had no idea that Zyman had worked intimately at the highest level of Coke almost since the day he left the company. Rehiring Zyman would send a message that he was willing to take risks to rebuild Coke's marketing programs.

Keough retired in mid-April. In mid-July of 1993, Goizueta had arranged to be out of town on business when Ivester called Sealey into his office and told him, matter of factly, "This isn't working out. You'll have to clean out your desk, and we'll work out the separation terms later." Sealey asked for time to wind up a project, but Ivester shook his head. "You'll have to be gone by the end of the day," he said. It was the last high-profile sacking of the Goizueta era. Goizueta was not afraid to confront people over strategic or tactical issues, but he seemed incapable of personally firing people from the Coca-Cola family. Although dozens of high-level executives had lost their jobs under Goizueta, he never personally fired a single one.

When Ivester announced to Coke's marketing staff that Zyman would replace Sealey, one secretary could not stifle a horrified, "Why him?" Goizueta recognized why people were startled to see Zyman back because of his reputation for abrasiveness and arrogance. Ivester and others went to work assuring nervous staff and managers that Zyman had grown and would not indulge in the temper tantrums and personal attacks that had marked his first tour at Coke. "I quite well understand that Sergio has the outside reputation of 'the Ayacola.' But you have to put that in the context of time," Goizueta said, defending his new hire. "Sergio is no longer the enfante terrible." Goizueta might put the best face on it, but rehiring Zyman involved an intrinsic tradeoff. He would brook Zyman's occasional autocratic excesses in return for the man's marketing genius and ability to get things done. Once Zyman's changes started to take effect, Ivester and Goizueta printed a t-shirt with the slogan "Get Used To Sergio" on it—GUTS.

There was little real risk in bringing back Zyman. As mercurial as he was, he also had an ability to arouse an intense sense of loyalty among a corps of committed believers, and Goizueta gave Zyman free rein to hire a staff that he could turn into just such a clique. Over time, he even allowed Zyman to place his marketing people at key operations centers around the world. Rather than reporting to the country chief or division chief in the place they worked, they reported directly to Zyman. In an enterprise often consumed by palace politics, this gave Zyman strong political advantages, in addition to on-the-ground marketing information.

Goizueta brought back Zyman for a number of reasons. The Sealey-Ivester rift made it obvious a change was needed. But he also was frustrated that Coke's marketing machine had failed to capitalize on the success of the first flight of CAA ads, and that Diet Coke was doing so poorly. There were other annoyances, too. It irked Goizueta that Coke nearly lost its long-time sponsorship of the NFL in early 1993 because the league felt Coca-Cola was ignoring it. Ivester just barely saved the NFL sponsorship by personally intervening and designing an innovative co-marketing deal with McDonald's and the NFL that made the three partners in promoting the league over the course of a five-year, $250 million program.

Inside and outside the company, Zyman was greeted with a mix of hope, fear, and consternation reminiscent of Napoleon returning from Elba. Zyman quickly made a dramatic move, dumping Diet Coke advertising agency Lintas:New York. Zyman junked the "Taste It All" campaign. He hired Lowe & Partners, like Lintas a unit of the Interpublic Group, and ordered the agency to update "Just for the Taste of It," a campaign Lintas itself had created in 1982. Goizueta showed his approval by returning Diet Coke advertising spending to traditional levels. Zyman also flirted with dumping CAA in favor of Madison Avenue stalwart Fallon McElligott, and even cut off most direct communication with the CAA advertising executives Shelly Hochron and Len Fink. But CAA chieftain Michael Ovitz intervened with Goizueta and staunched the maneuver.

It was an easy sell for Ovitz. Goizueta loved the CAA campaign so much that he stopped at Gucci in New York in spring 1993 and bought polar bear ties and scarves to distribute among his senior staff back in Atlanta. He was not inclined to walk away from the people who had produced the polar bear campaign. Indeed, Goizueta wanted to draw closer into the Michael Ovitz orbit. When Ovitz left CAA in early 1995 to take a job at Walt Disney Company as Michael Eisner's second in command, he took the advertising business with him. Within weeks, Goizueta and Ovitz were negotiating a Coke investment in Disney's new advertising unit. The deal raised eyebrows when it was announced the next November because Goizueta was investing in an agency owned by one of his largest customers, the Walt Disney Company. Goizueta decided he could live with the conflict that might occur between riding herd on his advertising agency and keeping one of his best customers happy.

TO DRIVE COKE SUCCESSFULLY THROUGH THIS KEY PERIOD OF BRAND deployment, Goizueta needed every bit of marketing creativity he could muster. Brand-name products were in retreat everywhere. In April 1993, Philip Morris set off a stock-market nosedive when it reduced the price of its cigarettes 25 percent, citing an inability to compete with off-brand cigarettes. Wall Street analysts hammered Coke and other branded-goods companies, and Coke's shares lost nearly 10 percent of their value over the next two weeks. Goizueta complained to analysts that they were punishing his company for a mistake that Philip Morris had made, but he also understood the stock market's lesson. Unless he continued differentiating Coke's products, the company and its stock would be vulnerable to the private-label and new-product onslaught.

By happenstance, Goizueta had an almost immediate response to Marlboro Friday. On April 19, he sent Doug Ivester to Terre Haute, Indiana, site of the Root Glass Co. that had developed the famous Coca-Cola bottle in 1919, to introduce a new 20-oz. plastic contour bottle. To Goizueta, the contour bottle represented the essence of the Coke brand. It viscerally connected the consumer to physical and visual cues that are part of the powerful pull of the Coca-Cola trademark. The contour bottle notched double-digit volume increases in every test market, and Goizueta had to delay the national rollout by several months because Coke's supplier could not meet demand. Thrilled with the success, Goizueta ordered that the cover of Coke's 1994 annual report be adorned with a billboard featuring the contour bottle's silhouette and the brief tag line, "Quick. Name a soft drink."

The contour bottle succeeded by every measure, but Goizueta recognized he needed to do much more than repackage Coke's flagship brand. He needed to take on the growth of alternative beverages head on. By the end of 1993, New Age drinks had claimed 12 percent of the total beverage market, a $6 billion chunk of retail sales. Traditional colas controlled 58.8 percent of the retail market, down nearly five percentage points from their share a decade earlier. The evidence was mounting that New Age drinks were not the fad that Goizueta had first thought them to be. He now recognized that alternative drinks as a group were going to continue commanding a sizable chunk of the market. He could not ignore the segment, yet he needed to find a way to approach it differently, to make good on his demand, expressed frequently to his staff, that The Coca-Cola Company always be "special, different, and better."

The New Age attack was a rare instance in which Goizueta could not find a way to play to his strengths. His native conservatism combined with the dismal experience of the New Coke launch had made him reluctant to introduce new brands in the United States. And Tab Clear's failure had reinforced his lack of confidence. But Goizueta recognized the demands of this era, and resolved to toss products into the market even if they had mixed chances of success. "Some may be home runs, others simply hits, others have to be sacrifice bunts. You don't have Diet Coke every time you come to the plate," he said. The new-products initiative he established in late 1992 had kicked in, and Goizueta greenlighted a trio of new drinks: a family of fruit-flavored drinks called Fruitopia, a Generation-X soda called OK, and a sports drink called PowerAde.

The new-products initiative required a delicate balancing act between Goizueta's abhorrence of copycat marketing and his pragmatic need to compete in the growing non-cola segment. His solution was to redefine the role of new products in Coke's overall competitive strategy. The new rules of the marketplace dictated that Coke's new drinks were not important in their own right, as Diet Coke and New Coke had been. Instead, they were expressions of Coke's strength as a purveyor of brands. As Coca-Cola evolved into a pure brand marketing company, it could succeed only by introducing an array of new brands that would satisfy the growing customer demand for an ever changing banquet of liquid flavors. He said he wanted to fight for "share of stomach," to make Coca-Cola products account for as much as possible of whatever it was that people poured down their throats. "Sometimes I think we even compete with soup," he said.

By necessity, Goizueta was entering market segments created by his competitors—an uncomfortable competitive posture he had always avoided. But if he was going to play defense, Goizueta was determined to bring all of Coke's other competitive advantages to bear. He especially sought to capitalize on the power of Coke's distribution and marketing systems, and the strengths of Coke's capital structure. The marching orders were simple. "To be successful, we've got to make it impossible for the consumer to escape The Coca-Cola Company," Goizueta announced. He changed the barrier for launching a new product. Coke would no longer insist that a product be a guaranteed success. Instead, he promised to listen to any new-product proposal that promised to deliver more than an 11 percent return on Coke's investment, about half his usual target. "If you can get your money back in a couple of years, I think that's fine," he said.

He also sought to develop entire new styles of brand creation. Fruitopia, the line of sweet, fruit-flavored drink with the psychedelic packaging and funky names like "Strawberry Passion Awareness" and "Citrus Consciousness," broke with Coke's traditional method of creating a brand and attaching it to a single drink. By design, individual flavors would come and go, based not just on sales but on seasons and other factors. "Fruitopia will be the brand, the individual products won't be," Goizueta explained. "It's a lasting brand with an unlasting line of products." And the Fruitopia line conformed with Goizueta's new emphasis on speedy development. Although the concept was first created before Zyman returned to Coke, Zyman's forces were able to launch the entire line three months after Goizueta approved it in December 1993.

At the same time, Zyman also was developing OK Soda, an experiment in minimalist marketing. Designed to taste like the old "suicide" drinks mixed from all the flavors at a soda fountain, the drink appealed to Goizueta because he felt it had no "taste memory." That was a description he bestowed on only one other soft drink, Coca-Cola itself. But when Zyman unveiled the product's name and gave Goizueta an early glimpse at the marketing program, he got a cold response. "I guess I'm not the target market," Goizueta said. He was right, of course. The target was teenagers and others included among the post-baby boomers called Generation X. Zyman was tickled by the response, printed up a host of t-shirts with the notation, "I'm not the target market," and distributed them among his staff of more than 100 mostly young, highly educated Coke marketers. The slogan emphasized the fact that Coke's marketers had to break with tradition, identify market opportunities, and meet them, regardless of their own tastes or biases.

Goizueta never did like the product's name and had no confidence in the marketing campaign, which sought to adopt the diffident mood of Generation X. The marketing plan called for Coke to send letters to high-school students promoting "OK-ness" and inviting them to dial a quirky 800-number to share their Gen-X experiences. Despite his misgivings, Goizueta agreed to launch OK in April, but gave it only minimal financial resources. OK commanded only a 3 percent share in its test markets, a clear failure by Coke's conventional new-product standards. It lasted just more than a year. But Goizueta gleefully reported to the board of directors that it was still a profitable success because the investment was so small.

To attack the tea segment, Goizueta decided to go outside the company for expertise. In 1991, three years after Snapple virtually created the ready-to-drink tea segment, Goizueta had inked a deal with Nestlé SA for a joint venture to create and market teas and coffees in the United States, Japan, and elsewhere. Each company invested $100 million, and neither got its money's worth. Bound by rivalries and indecision among the partners, the joint venture proved remarkably lead footed. Nimble smaller competitors like Arizona Iced Tea developed products far more quickly. And, most embarrassingly, a PepsiCo joint venture with Thomas J. Lipton Co. fared better than Coke, introducing a low-priced canned tea more than two years before the Coke-Nestlé venture did. In August 1994, discouraged by his lack of success, Goizueta all but folded the venture, salvaging only a marketing and distribution pact between the two companies.

In the midst of this new product activity at Coca-Cola, Goizueta's attention was drawn forcibly away from the action at the North Avenue tower for an extended period of time for perhaps the only time in his career. All his career, only significant family matters had distracted him from the affairs of Coca-Cola, and even those distractions were kept to a minimum. Associates had marveled at the dignity with which he handled the death of his son Carlos of leukemia in 1970, and he had fit his children's weddings into breaks in his work schedule. Indeed, his son's wedding had come in the midst of the New Coke debacle. He vacationed for a week only during the month of August, and then only at Sea Island, Georgia, where he and Olguita rented a well-appointed unit not far from the villa Don and Mickie Keough used. Friends marveled at the sight of Goizueta in a beach chair, lounging with a book in his lap, momentarily oblivious even to Coke's stock price.

The distraction in the middle of 1993 came from Goizueta's role as a board member at Eastman Kodak Co. Goizueta sat on seven corporate boards: Coke, Kodak, the Ford Motor Co., Sonat Inc., SunTrust bank, and two of its subsidiaries. That was more than double the amount that corporate governance experts recommend for board members. But even as the issue of board governance took on an increasingly high profile in the 1990s, Goizueta remained intensely loyal to the companies and never stepped away from a directorship.

There are perquisites that go with directorships, and Goizueta was not immune to such pleasures. On the Ford board, he enjoyed borrowing the company's latest high-performance models for his personal use, and relished the board's regular trips to the company's test track to hot rod Ford's latest sports cars. But he did not let his enjoyment of the board outings get in the way in the fall of 1996, when Goizueta felt Ford chairman Alexander J. Trotman was losing momentum with a reorganization plan called Ford 2000. He joined a group of hardliners on the board who wrote Trotman a sternly worded letter warning him to correct the problems. Goizueta had not pushed the matter to a resolution by the time he died in the fall of 1997.

The Ford episode was one of several that indicated how seriously Goizueta viewed his obligations as an outside director. Directorships had assumed outsized importance very early in his own career, when the invitation to join the SunTrust board had helped push him over the top when Robert Woodruff was wavering over the decision to name Goizueta chairman and CEO. Once in charge at The Coca-Cola Company, he took up a revamping of the board as one of his first projects, introducing a mandatory retirement age of 75 and bringing more business before the directors. He did not always achieve his goal of totally open communication with directors. He gave the board ample warning of the Columbia Pictures deal, but sprang New Coke on his directors only at the last minute, when the launch virtually was a fait accompli. But still, Goizueta philosophically believed boards should be informed, engaged, and active, and that's how he tried to conduct himself on all his boards.

His commitment to outside board work reached its apogee with the crisis at Eastman Kodak Co. that culminated in the summer of 1993. Over a period of two years, Goizueta had grown increasingly concerned about shrinking market share, bloated bureaucracy, and falling profits at the legendary photographic equipment company. Almost from the time that Kay Whitmore took the chairman's job in 1990, Goizueta and former New York Stock Exchange Chairman John Phelan led a group of directors who grew increasingly critical of

Whitmore's stewardship of the company. Whitmore seemed unable to draw any benefit from a major transaction he had championed, the $5.1 billion purchase of Sterling Drug in 1988. He let Fuji seize the innovation edge in the film marketplace, and seemed unable to reduce Kodak's bloated workforce or trim costs.

Inside Kodak, Whitmore was perhaps best known for falling asleep at important meetings. But Goizueta and Phelan got his attention when they broke Kodak precedent, began second guessing him, and pressured Whitmore to devise a strategy that worked. Whitmore hired noted corporate cost cutter Christopher J. Steffen in January, 1993, but fired him four months later, threatened by Steffen's apparent ambition for the top job. Under fire from shareholders at the annual meeting that spring, Whitmore promised action but did not deliver. For Goizueta and the rest of the growing anti-Whitmore faction, the end came when Kodak's chairman opened a July meeting with institutional investors by asking them for advice. Within days, the board told Whitmore he was through.

Goizueta took charge of the Kodak search committee. Although Coca-Cola under Goizueta had never turned outside the company for a high-level executive, he quickly declared the need for new energy at Kodak's Rochester, New York headquarters. "This company is very much inbred," Goizueta said. "That tends to accentuate the faults and also the virtues to the point where virtues become faults. We need a third party to look at Eastman Kodak." Goizueta tapped Gerard R. Roche, chairman of the Heidrick & Struggles recruiting firm, to head the search for an executive with strong drive, proven ability to cut costs, marketing know-how, and international expertise.

The first man they identified was George M. C. Fisher. As chairman of Motorola Inc., Fisher had won acclaim for building the company's cellular telephone business and successfully invading the virtually impenetrable Japanese market. But there was just one problem. Fisher in early 1993 already had turned down the chance to succeed John Akers as chairman of IBM Corp. Despite IBM's troubles, the Big Blue job was then seen as the most attractive CEO slot to open up in years. If Fisher would not leave Motorola for IBM, he seemed unlikely to jump to the equally demanding but less prestigious job at Kodak.

That did not deter Goizueta. He asked a mutual friend, Goldman, Sachs & Co. partner John Wineberg, to set up a meeting with Fisher.

Flying to Chicago on Coke's Gulfstream IV, Goizueta secretly met Fisher over coffee in a conference room at the O'Hare Airport Hilton hotel. He opened the meeting by laying out the troubles at Kodak. "The Kodak company has not been well managed for a number of generations," Goizueta said. "We need somebody to come and rehabilitate the company, and we think you're the guy to do it."

Several hours passed as Goizueta quizzed Fisher on possible approaches to Kodak's problems, and on his record of success. Fisher pleased Goizueta by expressing a hope that Kodak could grow its way out of trouble, rather than resorting to major layoffs. Fisher seemed intellectually stimulated by the challenges at Kodak, but his body language and cerebral approach to the questions gave little hint of any real desire for the job. He also was intensely worried that his name might leak, as it had at IBM, perhaps ruining his opportunity to take the helm at Big Blue and causing trouble at Motorola. "If my name leaks, I'm out," he warned Goizueta.

Goizueta finally wound up the meeting by telling him that the opportunity to save a great American company like Kodak was nothing less than a patriotic duty. "There are certain companies that are national assets. Coca-Cola is one. Kodak is one," he said. It was a schmaltzy argument that only Goizueta could make because of his dramatic history as a Cuban refugee.

It worked on Fisher. The two men spoke several times by telephone over the next several weeks, and met a second time in Washington, DC, to discuss the pay package—which ultimately included a hefty base salary and a $5 million signing bonus. In late October, Goizueta proudly announced the completion of the search. "Our number one candidate was God, and we stepped down from that," he crowed with a touch of self-congratulation.

Fisher acknowledged that most of his ideas probably would not work, but that "10 percent will be killers." He was half right. Fisher's move into digital imaging proved ineffective, and he could not effectively parry Fuji's push into film processing and sales. His cost-cutting program fell short. Four years almost to the day after Goizueta touted him as second only to God, Fisher in November 1997 announced yet another major restructuring. He turned to job cuts. There would be pink slips for 10,000 Kodak employees, the largest layoff announcement of 1997.

Even though Fisher had not been able to devise an immediate turn-around, Goizueta remained steadfastly behind his recruit. Besides, whatever Fisher's ultimate shortcomings on the job at Kodak, Goizueta had done a tremendous job on behalf of the board. He had recruited the hottest CEO candidate in the country, persuaded him to take a less attractive job than the one he had mulled just a few weeks earlier, and encouraged him to remedy Kodak's troubles without knee-jerk recourse to layoffs and other quick fixes. Even though Goizueta had been forced to resort to layoffs at Coke just once, and then only for about 200 employees, he was not philosophically opposed to layoffs per se. In 1996, in the wake of layoff announcements by AT&T, IBM, Digital Equipment, and other corporate giants, Goizueta wrote a two-page letter to company employees explaining that he thought he could continue increasing shareholder values without layoffs or a corporate restructuring. But he refused to rule out either option completely. "There are any number of situations that could change tomorrow—even this minute—that would force us to make hard decisions we've never had to make," he wrote.

When Fisher in 1997 finally had to resort to both layoffs and re-structuring, he admitted his disappointment. "We are really mad at ourselves that we got into this situation, but we are out of denial and determined to get back on track," he said. Goizueta, the meticulous strategic planner who prided himself on looking at the cold realities of the business world, would have cringed to hear one of his proteges de-scribe himself as recovering from "denial." Worse still, he would have had a hard time condoning the announcement Fisher made barely a month later, when he nearly doubled the number of layoffs and raised the write-off to $1.5 billion, 50 percent higher than the original fore-cast. The huge increases in such a short time revealed a sloppiness in forecasting that would have been poison to Goizueta.

NOT LONG AFTER HE FILLED KODAK'S TOP SPOT, GOIZUETA TOOK stock of his own succession plans. When Coke's board decided in April to ask Goizueta to stay "indefinitely" past November 1996, when he would turn 65, Coke executives whispered and Wall Street analysts shouted that the extension was a sign that neither Ivester nor Hunter suited Goizueta and the board. Goizueta did nothing to re-solve the matter when he told *The Wall Street Journal*, "No one has the inside track." Then he paraphrased a Japanese novelist and added, "Until I act, it's as if I didn't know." The extension made it obvious that Hunter, 56, would not last to become CEO. In July 1994, Goizueta made the inevitable official and promoted Ivester to be Coke's president and chief operating officer, in part to calm speculation about succession that had brewed since the board extended his own tenure on the job. At the same time, Goizueta made a point of demonstrating just how vigorously he was approaching his work by inviting the *Atlanta Journal-Constitution* just before his sixty-fifth birthday for an interview that discussed his busy travel and work schedule and his compelling interest in the day-to-day work of his job.

As Ivester prepared to keynote a beverage industry conference in October, he knew the speech would mark his coming out as Goizueta's heir apparent. In the insular soft-drink industry, events like the Inter-Bev '94 conference take on outsized importance as major events, so Ivester knew this speech would be significant and Goizueta wanted him to make the most of this one chance to make a first impression as the leader for Coke's next generation. "Tell them, 'Be different, or be prepared to die an agonizing death,'" Goizueta advised.

Ivester took the advice perhaps too literally. He delivered a swaggering, aggressive speech in which he labeled Coke as a wolf hunting its prey, its brand-name competitors as sheep, and private-label soft drinks as parasites. Talking about Coke's plan to protect its market share, Ivester invoked a quote of General Colin Powell when asked his strategy for launching the ground war against Iraq in the Persian Gulf War: "First, we're going to cut it off. Then, we're going to kill it." Ivester seemed aware that he was shocking his audience. "Now, none of what I've said this morning may sound very uplifting. And it hasn't exactly been statesmanlike, either," he admitted. But then, he pointed out, even Roberto Goizueta was not always a statesman. He quoted one of his boss' favorite sayings, "If you can't be different, you might as well be damned." He left the stage as a series of tape-recorded wolf howls serenaded him. "That's just a friendly pack of competitors over at The Coca-Cola Company having a good time," Ivester concluded.

The InterBev attendees should not have been too shocked by Ivester's provocative speech. Everybody in the industry already had heard about Ivester's first talk to a Coke managers' meeting after he was named president. Ivester talked about the importance of competitiveness, and referenced a famous saying from Ray Kroc, the man who built McDon-ald's into a global colossus. If he found a competitor drowning, Kroc had said, he would get a hose and stick it in his mouth. Reaching be-hind the lectern, Ivester grabbed a length of garden hose and held it into the air. "Well, I've got the hose," he said. "I think you know what to do." Even at hypercompetitive Coca-Cola, many in the audience thought the remark went beyond the pale of good taste.

Goizueta had his own moments of undiplomatic conduct, although they were normally in the private of his office rather than before several thousand industry colleagues. For the most part, he had given up the fits of temper that had so rattled division managers dur-ing the Spanish Inquisition. In its place, he had mastered the whith-ering stare and dismissive brushoff. "If he was unhappy with you, or if he no longer needed something from you, he would walk right by you as if you were not there," said a former colleague. "You did not exist as far as he was concerned."

He relished throwing barbs Pepsi's way, jibing the company for di-versifying out of soft drinks, and mocking their attempts to compete in the international markets. He even attacked Pepsi's taste. When a student at Georgia Institute of Technology asked him if he ever drank Pepsi, Goizueta cut sharply. "Only when I've eaten something I don't like and I want to throw up," he said.

Goizueta did not limit himself to criticizing competitors and col-leagues. He developed an art for communicating his opinions—some-times of approval, but more often of reproval—to the securities analysts on Wall Street and the financial press who covered his com-pany. An avid letter writer by nature, Goizueta developed a zeal for epistolary commentary that had its roots at the very beginning of his chairmanship. Oppenheimer & Co. analyst Roy Burry had followed Coca-Cola's stock market performance since the days of Paul Austin, when the company's chief financial officer Fil Eisenberg had refused to talk to Wall Street. Burry was pleased when Goizueta made a point of inviting a group of analysts to lunch after he became chairman, and enjoyed the apparent thaw in relations. But when Burry wrote his first stock report of the Goizueta era, he quickly received a lengthy letter critiquing in detail every aspect of his report. Burry replied in writing, "Your letter was obviously written by the hand of an expert."

A few days later, he received a response, hand written by Goizueta. Years later, Goizueta was still writing to Burry, congratulating him on an award by a securities industry group, but concluding gratuitously, "your research on Coca-Cola doesn't warrant it."

In Goizueta's reviews of analysts' reports, the world broke down into distinct groups: the incorrigible idiot, the misguided but redeemable, and the genuine genius. In order, they fell into those categories by (1) downgrading Coke stock, by (2) underestimating Coke's potential, or by (3) highly recommending continued purchases. When Allan Kaplan of Merrill Lynch & Co. wrote critically of Coke's declining margins, Goizueta replied as if scolding a wayward child. "How many times have you heard that in a business like ours—the gross margin is measured per gallon of syrup sold, not per dollar of revenue?" he challenged. He sent a companion letter to Kaplan's boss, threatening to "freeze him out" of Coke's communications with Wall Street. Indeed, during his tenure, Goizueta gave several analysts the silent treatment for months at a time in retaliation for reports that fell short of his lofty assessment of Coke's prospects.

Glowing reports received equally glowing reviews. "You are to the writing of analyst reports what Warren Buffett is to the writing of 'Letters to Share Owners,'" Goizueta wrote to Joseph Doyle of Smith Barney & Co. after one positive review. Goizueta went so far as to send a token of his esteem. Doyle had written that Coke's results blew his socks off, and Goizueta responded by sending a pair of white socks engraved with the Coca-Cola logo.

Reporters, too, became the targets of Goizueta's poison pen. After years of working closely with Goizueta, and even writing a balanced book about the New Coke debacle that served Coke's interests by presenting a counterweight to Pepsi president Roger Enrico's scathing declaration of victory in the Cola Wars, *Atlanta Journal-Constitution* reporter Thomas Oliver offended Goizueta with a story the Coke chairman considered unfairly negative. Goizueta pounded out a scathing, multipaged missive, and terminated the journalist-source relationship with Oliver.

Goizueta had a long memory for everything that was written about the company. At the end of 1995, *Atlanta Journal-Constitution* reporter Chris Roush found that he was insufficiently optimistic about Coke's prospects when he predicted the stock would rise to $60 by the end of the year. When the bull market's momentum actually carried Coke shares to $75, Goizueta photocopied the 10-month-old article and goaded Roush in a crisp note, "Dear Chris: So much for predictions."

The biggest press blooper came, ironically, from *Fortune* magazine, the periodical that chronicled Goizueta more frequently and favorably than any other publication during his tenure. A copy of the article became a prop in a ritual part of the visit to Goizueta's office for reporters, analysts, and even other business executives. Goizueta would carefully pull the tattered story from his desk drawer, and in his deep, Cuban accent would read aloud:

About 10 years ago, one of the shrewder financiers in the country made a thoroughgoing investigation of Coca-Cola, with a view to taking a heavy long-term position in the stock. After several weeks of unusually careful study, he decided to buy another company stock instead. Since then, Coca-Cola stock, allowing for splits, has been selling three-and-a-half times higher—while the other stock actually declined.

This episode, in one form or another, has often been repeated. Several times every year a weighty and serious investor looks long and with profound respect at Coca-Cola's record but comes regretfully to the conclusion that he is looking too late. The specters of saturation and competition rise before him. He hears dire rumors of the inroads made by Pepsi-Cola and some new up-and-coming soft drinks—and he reluctantly passes Coca-Cola by.

But Coca-Cola steadily sweeps on.

Then came Goizueta's punch line. "That was from the December issue of *Fortune* magazine," he would say. Then, after a pause, "December of 1938." The article actually referred to the rise of Dr. Pepper, not "up-and-coming" soft drinks. But Goizueta's edit did not alter the broader point: People doubted Coca-Cola in the present just as they had doubted Coke in the past. The competitive challenges, as always, looked bad, and Coke's strategies, limited. The clear moral of the story for Goizueta was that the luckless investor of 1938 missed a rare chance to buy into one of the world's great franchises. Any reporter, investor, or business colleague who dared sell Coke short in the modern era should do so at their peril. "No matter what the decade or what the situation might be, we always take great satisfaction in proving these people wrong," Goizueta said.

GOIZUETA INDEED HAD THE WEIGHT OF EVIDENCE ON HIS SIDE. HIS emphasis on the financial aspect of Coke's business—one of the CEO's three chief responsibilities to his company—had produced obvious and consistent results. At the end of 1995, a decade after the launch of New Coke, Coke's profits had more than quadrupled during his tenure, to $2.99 billion, outpacing the growth in revenues, which tripled to $18 billion. Several of the company's division presidents were running operations that were larger than all of Coca-Cola when Goizueta took charge. The debt to capital ratio of 43 percent was high by Coke standards, but still below its peaks of 48.4 percent in 1987 and 45.2 percent in 1992.

By the two measures that Goizueta watched most closely—stock performance and economic value added—Coke's great march forward continued unabated. Since 1980, Coke's shares had grown at a compounded average annual rate of 24 percent, more than double the increase in the Dow Jones Industrial Average and the Standard & Poor's 500 stock index. The stock's inexorable climb had created $89 billion in shareholder wealth, a fact that won Goizueta accolades as the greatest wealth creator of all time. Proud as he was of Coke's share performance, Goizueta knew that the stock market results were driven largely by his single-minded dedication to economic profit, or Coke's after-tax operating profit minus an implied charge for the cost of capital. In 1995, Goizueta figured his company's economic profit at $2.17 billion, a nearly ten-fold increase from the $266 million his company logged in 1985.

Hosting analysts for a two-day conference in Atlanta in the spring of 1996, Goizueta described his three-step process of management. "One, state expectations. Two, meet or exceed those expectations. Three, repeat," he said. "Now, of course, the hardest part is repeating," Goizueta informed the more than 400 analysts and investors who traveled to Atlanta to hear the world according to Roberto.

In the effort to repeat Coke's strong performance, Goizueta announced, he was amending the Coca-Cola mission of making the drink "available, affordable, and acceptable." Instead, he suggested, the new emphasis would focus on "the three P's." Coke would be "pervasive," would have the best "price relative to value" and would be "the preferred beverage everywhere." It was a clumsy poke at alliteration, but the vow seemed full of serious intent. Coming just months before the Olympic torch would at last reach Atlanta for the 1996 Summer Games, the statement resonated strongly. Atlanta already had been painted Coca-Cola red with the erection of a Coke plaza the size of a city block just a few blocks away from where the analysts were gathered. Goizueta had worked quietly and forcefully behind the scenes to bring the games to his adoptive home town. And when his friend Juan Antonio Samaranch officially opened the centennial games, Goizueta's legion of Coca-Cola emissaries would give new meaning to each of those Ps.

At the Atlanta Games, Roberto's beverages would be everywhere, the price sky high, and the preference beyond compare. Coke seemed to control every cold drink sale in the state of Georgia, and all but banished Pepsi and every other non-Coca-Cola beverage from the city of Atlanta. It was an appropriate payback. Although he had struggled mightily to disguise his role in bringing the Olympics to Atlanta, Goizueta had played a bigger part than anyone outside the organizing committee itself. It was inevitable that the 1996 Summer Games became known as the Coca-Cola Olympics. But had it not been for the key role played by Roberto Goizueta, the games might never have called Atlanta their home.

10

The Games Roberto Played

William Porter Payne was not the kind of guy Roberto Goizueta typically did business with. Until early 1987, Goizueta never knew the man existed. Payne made his living cutting real estate deals, converting apartment buildings into condominiums and syndicating commercial property. But even as a successful real estate lawyer and former University of Georgia football star, Payne operated in a different world from Coke, and by all accounts he seemed unlikely ever to approach Goizueta's cloistered aerie on the twenty-fifth floor of Coca-Cola's North Avenue tower. Still, like most native Atlantans, Payne grew up with an immense sense of pride and a proprietary interest in Coca-Cola. He drank cases of it as a kid and felt that Coke represented the best of Atlanta, and that a small part of him traveled around the globe with Coca-Cola's red-disc logo and caramel-brown syrup.

Thanks to an outrageous notion Billy Payne had that Atlanta should host the summer Olympics, Goizueta and Payne were in fact destined to meet. On February 8, 1987, Billy Payne decided that Atlanta should host a summer Olympics. The notion first struck him, and then possessed him, immediately after the dedication of a new sanctuary for St. Luke's Presbyterian Church in the posh northern suburb of Dunwoody. Payne had chaired the church's $2.5 million fund-raising campaign, and his first significant effort at volunteer

246

work had taught him plenty about getting involved in something bigger than himself, something good. At 4 A.M. the next day, his usual starting time, Payne bowed over a scratch pad in his law office and searched for a mission. He considered, then discarded relatively mundane and commercial ideas like hosting a political convention or Super Bowl, or building a huge amusement park. Then the Olympics popped into his head.

It struck Payne as an idea "founded in goodness." It also, inexplicably, struck him as something he could conceivably do. Never mind that he had never set foot outside the United States, never attended an Olympic games, never circulated among the power elite in Atlanta who would need to get on board—yesterday—for Atlanta to have any chance of hosting an Olympics. And Payne did not want to host just any Olympics. He wanted to host the 1996 Olympics, the Centennial Olympic Games, a feat that would call for him to beat out sentimental favorite Athens, Greece, and a half dozen other serious contenders to make history by becoming the first city ever to win a bid for the Olympics on its first try.

Payne did know enough to be certain he would need Roberto Goizueta if he was going to succeed. Nothing good happens in Atlanta without The Coca-Cola Company involved somewhere, at some level, Payne believed. And Coke would not get behind an Olympics bid, he sensed, unless the chairman was squarely behind the effort. Ultimately, Goizueta would help Payne bring the games to Atlanta, and the Atlanta Olympics in turn would cause Goizueta to invest $350 million in the games alone, and focus virtually the entire Coca-Cola marketing strategy on the world of sports. In the end, Payne and his vision would have an impact on Coke and Goizueta that few external factors ever could.

It was a Coke man Payne first turned to the same day he decided Atlanta needed to host the 1996 summer Olympics. But the Coke man he sought out was not Goizueta or Don Keough, nor any of the dozens of Coke executives who had helped turned the modern Olympic movement into the most bankable sports property in the world. In fact, the Coke man he turned to was connected to Coke through blood, not sweat. His very name—Peter Candler—was the essence of Cokeness. Candler is the great-great-great-nephew of Asa Candler, who bought the original Coke formula from Doc Pemberton not long after he created it in 1886. In the South, the past still means something. And in Atlanta, the names Candler and Coke still are as inseparable as the red from the clay.

Payne at first did not seek out Candler for his Coke connections; rather, he wanted a dose of reality. Candler was the soberest, most clear-headed friend Payne had, and he was counting on the Coca-Cola heir to talk him out of pushing ahead. But Candler was no help whatsoever. When Payne reached him by telephone that morning, Candler did not talk sense, as Payne had expected he would. Rather, he egged Payne on. "If this is going to go any further, you have to have in our corner the Four Musketeers of Atlanta: Emory University, King & Spaulding, SunTrust, and Coke," Candler told Payne. "Let me get an appointment with the one guy who's wired in to all four."

Days later, Payne and Candler were sitting in Jimmy Williams' office at the top of the SunTrust Tower on Peachtree Street. A decade and a half after playing a key role in Goizueta's succession to the chairmanship at Coke, Williams was more entrenched than ever in the quiet corridors of corporate and political power where the real decisions are made in the capital of the new South. In addition to his board membership at Emory and Coke and his company's role as a major client to King & Spaulding, his bank's vaults held the secret formula for Coca-Cola, and something else almost as valuable: the shares of Coca-Cola stock that Trust Co. bank had taken as payment for bankrolling Coke's initial public stock offering.

SunTrust's Coke stock was a great investment, never more so than during the years since Goizueta had taken the helm. But it gave Williams more than just earning power for his bank and a voice in affairs at Coke. Because of the appreciation of Coke's stock price, the shares artificially inflated SunTrust's value and made the bank virtually immune as a wave of mergers in the late 1980s claimed every other Atlanta-based bank of any size. Secure from overtures by acquisitive Charlotte bankers like Hugh McColl of NationsBank and Edward E. Crutchfield, Jr., of First Union, Williams would soon be the lone surviving chief executive of a major Atlanta-based lender. A blessing from Williams could open the door to Goizueta's office—the person Payne knew he would need above all to give his dream a chance.

The blond-haired, blue-eyed Williams sat quietly behind his desk as Payne spun out his vision of an Olympics in Atlanta. When Billy stopped talking, Williams stopped him short. "You know, that's not a new idea," Williams said, momentarily emptying the room of Payne's energy.

In the early 1970s, a local Atlanta businessman had caught Olympic fever, and pitched the idea to Coke chief executive Paul Austin. "They kicked him out of the office," Williams told Payne. "Paul wouldn't touch the idea with a ten-foot pole, because of the certainty that it would be laid squarely in the lap of The Coca-Cola Company." Austin did not want his company saddled with running an Olympic games. And he would not allow Coke to risk alienating customers around the world by giving the impression it had used its influence as the oldest and biggest Olympic sponsor to bring the games to Atlanta.

Then came the words that chilled Payne's spine. "Nothing's changed that would allow Coke to distance itself from your effort," Williams said.

It must take an actual bolt of lightning to knock Payne off his feet, because in a heartbeat he changed gears, adjusted his pitch, and talked fast to prevent a moment of silence from terminating the meeting. "Think of the benefits that would accrue to this community just from trying," Payne told Williams, hoping to strike the native Atlantan's deep chord of civic pride. "It's the journey and not the destination that counts."

But Williams was not buying, and Payne was out of time. Candler and Payne shook hands with Williams, and made their way to the door. Then, as they reached the threshold, a funny thing happened. From a pace behind the two men, Williams placed his hand on Payne's shoulder. "If I were you, Billy," he said, " I wouldn't give up."

Payne looked over his shoulder, and into Williams' eyes. "Thank you, I wasn't intending to," he said. In a moment, Payne's mood shifted from despair to destiny. He felt Williams had heard or seen something that had warmed him to Payne's vision. Walking to the elevator, Payne told Candler he thought Williams was on board. And though he had not asked directly for the favor, Payne figured Williams would phone Goizueta and pass along his impressions of the Olympic quest. If Williams was with them, Payne felt, Goizueta and Coke could not be far behind. And with Coke as a backer, the Atlanta Olympics would be a sure bet.

A FEW DAYS LATER, PAYNE WAS IN THE COKE TOWER, A FEW HUN-
dred feet from Goizueta's office, but he could just as well have been
miles away. Despite phoning nonstop in an effort to climb through
Coke's corporate hierarchy, the best Payne could do was an appointment with Randy Donaldson, one of the company's platoon of public
relations executives. Ten minutes passed, then twenty. Payne waited
ninety minutes and finally gave up. He was trying to get to the chairman, and a public relations guy had just stood him up. It was the low
point of Payne's early quest for the games. "I did my best not to try to
read anything into it," Payne says. "I was impressed he was so busy.
And if I were (Donaldson), I don't think I would have met with me
either."

It was no accident that Goizueta was so elusive. Indeed, Williams
was not right in his assessment that nothing had changed that would
enable Coke to distance itself from an Atlanta bid to host the
Olympics. The whole truth was that profound changes had occurred—
changes that would make it even riskier for Coke to get behind a bid.
In Austin's day, the Olympics were little more than a two-week track
meet that briefly attracted the attention of sports fans around the
world. Typically, only a couple of cities competed to host the games.
Austin probably overestimated the likely negative impact of backing an
Atlanta Olympics bid. Given the relatively low commercial and economic stature of the Olympic Games during the early 1970s, customers
and business partners around the world probably would not have cared.

By 1987, as Payne mounted his Olympics bid, the world of sports
sponsorship had changed, thanks to Coke. Paul Austin had taken
sponsorship payments into the big time when he paid $8 million to
sponsor soccer's World Cup. For the 1984 Olympics, Coke in 1979 had
paid the International Olympic Committee $12.6 million for sponsor-
ship rights and was irked to learn that national Olympic governing
bodies were performing a stickup on Coke. The countries were demanding an aggregate of $15 million in extra payments before they
would allow Coke to use the Olympic rings in its advertising and marketing inside their borders. Keough ordered an internal study that
found the costs of sponsorship soaring, and the value in decline.
When he, Ike Herbert, and Coke sports chief Gary Hite reported the
results to Goizueta, they got simple marching orders. "See if you can
change it," Goizueta said.

Sports sponsorships, like everything else at Coke, had to achieve a 20 percent return on capital, or they were not worth doing. Hite began traveling the globe, persuading individual countries to join a program by which sponsors could buy up rights in one package. When he reported his efforts to IOC president Juan Antonio Samaranch, Hite was surprised to learn that the IOC was doing the same thing. Samaranch needed a way to save the Olympics from the economic disaster that resulted after the Montreal Olympics left Canadian taxpayers a $1 billion bill, and the boycotted Moscow Olympics of 1980 left corporate sponsors angry.

Samaranch hoped to build a global sponsorship plan in which individual countries would give up their rights to the IOC, which would then package them together and sell them. But Coke would not back down from its efforts to develop a similar program that put Coke in charge of consolidating all the rights. "We can't afford to take a chance at winding up nowhere," Hite told Samaranch. Ultimately, the IOC's program won out, and created The Olympic Program (TOP). Outmaneuvered by the IOC, Coke became the first TOP sponsor, paying $15 million for rights to the Seoul and Calgary Olympics in 1988. For Coke and companies like Kodak, Visa, and IBM that followed suit, the TOP program streamlined the purchase of rights to the Olympics. It put the Olympic movement on a solid financial platform that enabled the IOC to become a huge global financial enterprise that struggles, not-so-mightily, to maintain the balance between the founding ideals of amateurism and the modern demands for economic profit.

Just before the IOC beat out Coke in the race to modernize the Olympic sponsorship program, Goizueta attended his first Olympics, the winter games at Sarajevo, Yugoslavia. There he first met Samaranch, and the two became fast friends. They had much in common both personally and professionally. Samaranch was born in the Catalonian region of Spain, just east of the Basque region that was home to Goizueta's forebearers. He left his father's textile business to pursue a life in sports, taking his first job in the government of Francisco Franco, the fascist dictator who had been so popular among Goizueta's teachers in Spain. Working behind the scenes, Samaranch moved quietly up Spain's sports hierarchy, won a spot on the International Olympic Committee, and pushed to the top, taking over the

IOC presidency after the Moscow games, as the IOC's economic slump hit bottom. Samaranch mounted an intense political battle to unseat Olympics purists, who saw any encroachment on amateurism as a threat to the entire Olympic movement. He inserted in their place pragmatists who saw a need to cash in on the value of one of the world's great trademarks, the Olympic rings.

By the time Billy Payne and his team of nine devotees began criss-crossing the globe selling the IOC on their ability to host the best Olympics ever, the TOP sponsorship program and runaway television network spending had dramatically changed the fortunes of the Olympic Games. The Los Angeles Olympic Committee's remarkable $223 million profit from the 1984 summer games—achieved the year before TOP was launched—put other cities on notice that there was money to be made from hosting the world's largest track meet. After Los Angeles, cities around the world suddenly viewed the Olympics as a chance to rebuild decrepit downtowns, stage a two-week global tourism promotion, and lay claim to being one of the world's premier international cities. The number of cities competing to host the games ultimately held in Seoul in 1988 and Barcelona in 1992 increased each quadrennium, to the point that Atlanta competed with six finalists in its bid to host the 1996 games.

The TOP program and financial success of the L.A. Games almost overnight had turned the Olympics into the biggest sports property in the world. Coca-Cola and eight other TOP sponsors together paid a combined $100 million for rights to the 1988 Seoul summer games and Alberville winter Olympics. They were part of a global boom in sports, with properties like the World Cup, the Tour de France, and even American football and basketball attracting more interest and more money worldwide than ever before. As he listened to presentations from Hite and Keough about the promise of sports as marketing properties, Goizueta saw an opportunity to build the Olympics into a key component of a strategic transformation aimed at making sports the centerpiece of Coke's worldwide marketing efforts.

BECAUSE THE OLYMPICS WERE A WORLDWIDE PROPERTY AND COKE was a global company, Goizueta could not look at the Atlanta bid to host the 1996 games purely in parochial terms. If he publicly backed Payne's bid, he would risk irritating local bottlers and customers around the world, and possibly jeopardize Coke's long-range marketing objectives. PepsiCo had made that mistake, sponsoring the American entry in the America's Cup yacht race and losing business in Australia and New Zealand as a result. And if Atlanta did win, people around the world inevitably would complain Coke had "bought" the games for Atlanta. The term "Coke Olympics" was not yet in vogue, but soon would be, thanks to overly zealous marketing plans Goizueta approved for the 1988 Calgary winter games.

Sports writers dubbed Calgary the "Coca-Cola Olympics" after a choir it sponsored, called the "Coca-Cola World Chorus," appeared in opening and closing ceremonies and sang "Can't You Feel It?" The games' theme song echoed in both wording and tune Diet Coke's "Can't Beat the Real Thing" campaign. And Coke penetrated the IOC's "clean venue" policy when television coverage of the ceremonies featured shots of spectators wearing plastic ponchos with the Coke logo emblazoned on them, a gift placed under their seats by Gary Hite's sponsorship team. Outside the venues, the introduction of the "Coca-Cola Pin Trading center" ushered in Coke's newest effort at democratizing its sponsorship.

Goizueta recognized that the Calgary overkill had created an opening for Olympics purists, and he did not want to further jeopardize the value of the Olympic rings by giving the impression that Coke was trying to control the awarding of the centennial games. Besides, Goizueta was wary of risking Coke's heavy investment in the Olympic movement by backing an unknown and unpredictable quantity like Billy Payne and his high-stakes Olympics bid. That is the position he made clear to Payne and everyone at Coke when Payne walked into Goizueta's office in the summer of 1987. Goizueta laid it out: Coke-USA and the bottler Coca-Cola Enterprises would be Payne's only sources of financial support from the company, just as Coke bottlers and national organizations in other countries were free to contribute to their own Olympics bids. Goizueta made it clear he was serious. "I am not willing to and am not able to go any further in a statement of support," he said.

In Payne's judgment, Goizueta never wavered from that position. "He never ever once, even with a wink of an eye, let me know or even allowed me to speculate whether he had a private position that was different than his public position," Payne says.

That was true, to a point. For while Goizueta talked a good game, no one at the top of Coke, including Goizueta, ultimately could resist the temptation to back the home team. For starters, Coca-Cola entities gave Payne's bid more money, by far, than they gave to the other bid cities. By the time the IOC finally chose Atlanta in September 1990, Coke USA and CCE together had donated $350,000 to the Atlanta bid, made corporate jets available free of charge, hosted lunches, and fielded hundreds of volunteers. By contrast, Toronto, Canada, received only $125,000 from Coke entities, and Melbourne, Australia, got only $80,000. A letter to the Manchester, England, bid committee betrayed to many in the Olympic movement exactly where the heart of The Coca-Cola Company really was, despite its stated neutrality on Olympic bids. It would be "inappropriate for us to be supporting a bid in opposition to that prepared by Atlanta, given the standing that our company has in that city," Coke's U.K. bottler explained. Coke officials reasoned that the disparity of financial support among the various bid cities reflected market size in the bid countries, but that must have served as little consolation to cities bidding against Atlanta's Coke-besotted war chest.

GOIZUETA HIMSELF QUIETLY JOINED THE GAME. HE INVITED PAYNE to his office once a quarter during the bid process, for updates on the Atlanta bid's progress. Payne worked hard to win Goizueta's confidence. The local media could not decide between dismayed courtesy or caustic lampooning of the Olympic effort, and Payne needed to prove to Goizueta, he says, "that I was something deeper than the way I was being described in the newspapers, as a crazy young lawyer pursuing an impossible dream." Beginning early in 1990, as the date approached for the IOC's meeting in Tokyo that September, Goizueta began monthly meetings with Bob Holder, a construction company executive who had joined Payne's team at the outset. Holder was among Goizueta's few personal friends in Atlanta, and Goizueta had a respect for Holder as a businessman that Payne would never quite earn.

To Payne, Goizueta's biggest help in those early meetings was the advice he offered about how to read Samaranch and other top IOC officials. When Payne consulted with Goizueta before he took a trip to IOC headquarters in Lausanne, Switzerland, for his first meeting with Samaranch, Goizueta warned him that the IOC president is famous for speaking in elliptical phrases that carry hidden but important messages. "Try not to read literally what he is saying to you," Goizueta warned. "There will be a message if you listen for it."

The advice immediately paid off. Payne traveled in late 1987 to Lausanne with Horace Sibley, a prominent Atlanta lawyer, half-brother to the former Coca-Cola board member and son of the late Woodruff crony John Sibley. Following the complex courting ritual of gift giving that is part of the art of mounting a successful Olympic bid, Payne presented Samaranch with a set of mint julep glasses. Uncertain whether the Spaniard would recognize their purpose, Payne explained, "They're for drinking mint juleps."

Samaranch responded, "Can you drink Coca-Cola out of these?" A slight smile crossed his face, and raised the spirits of Payne and Sibley. Samaranch was similarly succinct when he suggested Payne should meet "my friend Leopoldo Rodes." Payne recognized immediately the name of the Barcelona banker who masterminded Barcelona's successful bid, and he took this advice as a signal of tacit support, just as he had seen Jimmy Williams' encouraging words as proof that Williams would back his bid.

GOIZUETA WAITED FOR A DO-OR-DIE MOMENT IN ATLANTA'S BID process to interject himself personally, if not quite publicly, behind Payne's bid for the games. In doing so, he created an object lesson in how power relationships work at the highest level of corporate society. Goizueta carefully maintained his official public neutrality, while still sending unmistakable signals about what he truly wanted done.

By March 1990, the Atlanta Olympic Committee was tapped out. It had burned through the $5.5 million that a dozen Atlanta Chamber of Commerce companies had contributed to the bid. Traveling around the world to meet at least twice with every IOC member, staging a huge volunteer rally in Atlanta including a 10-kilometer race with several thousand participants, hosting lavish southern-style hospitality houses at all the IOC meetings, and inviting IOC members for all-expense-paid personal visits to Atlanta, complete with overnight stays in the city's finest homes, the nine Atlanta Organizing Committee members had covered expenses with their own money and lived as frugally as possible. But the initial $5.5 million was still gone.

To finish the bid, Payne needed another $1.5 million to produce the final bid presentation for the Tokyo meeting. He turned to Holder, and Holder turned to Goizueta. "Let's go talk to Roberto and see what ideas he may have," Holder told Payne.

Goizueta's support to this point was entirely private, just something between him, Payne, and Holder. It was an act of friendship to Holder as much as anything, and even his friendship had limits. When Holder invited him to a dinner for Samaranch at the home of a bid committee member, Goizueta let him know he had crossed the line. Dinner with Samaranch, even in a private home, went too far. "I told you we're not going to get involved," Goizueta bluntly replied.

But a meeting in his own office, with just Holder and Payne, was a different matter. Sitting on the couch not far from his desk, Goizueta listened as Payne and Holder hashed out various plans for raising funds. Borrowing money was out of the question. If Atlanta lost its bid, they would never raise the money to repay a loan. They could either try to raise $1.5 million from the community at large, or go to the Chamber members who had created the original kitty. At last, Goizueta offered his opinion. "Well, it seems to me that I would go with the people who have already shown the interest," he said.

It was the answer Holder expected, and he immediately had a reply for his friend. "Would you help us do it?" he asked.

"No," Goizueta said. "We're not going to take sides in this. But I will host a lunch in my dining room to let you make your pitch."

The same day, Holder drafted a letter of invitation stating that Roberto Goizueta was hosting a lunch for the Atlanta Organizing Committee, and faxed it to Goizueta for approval. His phone rang twenty minutes later. "You still don't get it," Goizueta said. "What I'm trying to say is, I'm not going to do any of this. I'm not inviting them, you are. I'll come along since you're going to have it at my place."

Goizueta clearly was splitting hairs, but Holder worried that even that small difference might jeopardize the success of the lunch. "If you invite them, Roberto, they'll all come," he said. "If I invite them, I'm not sure they will." But Goizueta would not budge. The invitation went out with only the names of Holder and Payne on it. But the site— the chairman's dining room, One Coca-Cola Plaza—was the draw.

They all came. As the leaders of household-name companies like BellSouth, Georgia Pacific, Holiday Inn, and Equifax listened, Holder laid out the situation. "Gentlemen," he opened. "We've got a little bit of a problem here. We told you the bid was going to cost $5.5 million, but it's going to be a little more." He explained that creating presentation materials meant far more than printing up a few pamphlets. In the modern game of Olympic bidding, it meant computer-generated images of not-yet-built stadia, compact disc tours of cities, all the bells and whistles modern technology could bring to such things. All the other cities would have it, and Atlanta needed it, too.

Then, like any good fund-raiser, Holder went for the ask. "If everybody in this room who's been so generous up until now would give just 50 percent more, we'd be OK," Holder concluded.

Goizueta rose to speak. Word for word, they probably were the two most important sentences in the history of the Atlanta bid. "I really appreciate everybody being here," he said. "I think these fellows are doing a good job and may be worthy of your support."

Payne got his $1.5 million within days.

Six months later, Juan Antonio Samaranch stepped to the podium at a hotel in downtown Tokyo and announced that the International Olympic Committee was awarding the centennial Olympic games "to the city of At . . ." He hesitated just a second, perhaps to tease the overly confident bidding team from Athens who had squandered a sure thing. Then he concluded with two distinct syllables, ". . . lanta." Payne and his bid team erupted with hugs and cheers. A few feet away, the Athens wannabes stared, slack jawed. Then they watched, amazed, as a Coke factotum made his way across the dais, pinning lapel pins on everyone, Samaranch included, bearing the inscription "Atlanta 1996" and the unmistakable Coca-Cola bottle. The Greeks and the world press cried foul, apparently unaware that Coke had prepared similar pins for each of the six finalists.

A few feet from the dais, Rob Prazmark, a TOP salesman, congratulated Gary Hite on Atlanta's win. "You don't understand," Coke's top Olympics operative responded. "Everybody is going to be thinking that Coke bought the Olympics for Atlanta. If anything, we did not want it in Atlanta. We wanted it somewhere else."

Hite hit the mark. The Greek delegation refused to recognize that their own sense of entitlement and inability to make plausible guarantees about security and logistics had torpedoed their bid. It was much easier to blame Coke for stealing the games from Athens, where the first modern Olympics had been held in 1896. In retaliation, the Greek Olympic delegation made themselves a nuisance throughout the planning process, and were particularly resentful of Coke's sponsorship of the Olympic torch run, which Greek Olympic officials consider a sacred symbol. Until the last moment, Greek officials left Payne in suspense about whether they would allow ACOG to use the Temple of Hera for the traditional ceremony to light the Olympic torch from rays of the sun.

Still, Hite's disclaimer about Coke's ambivalence to the Atlanta Olympics became the official Coke position—no matter how much the facts belied it. Company executives privately explained their mixture of pride for their hometown, but consternation about being tied to an undertaking over which they had so little control. Coke's internationalists seemed to find it vaguely insulting that anyone would put such a parochial fix on their global enterprise. Keough gave voice to this frustration when a reporter asked how he felt about the Olympics coming to Coke's backyard. "We've got a pretty big backyard," Keough said.

PAYNE RETURNED FROM TOKYO TO A TICKER TAPE PARADE DOWN Peachtree Street and to a gargantuan job. To make the games work, he would have to make good on his boast that he could sell a dozen sponsorships for $40 million each, about ten times the amount raised by Los Angeles, that he could sell U.S. television rights for $600 million, build $515 million of sports venues and housing, and donate them to the community, and conclude the Atlanta Olympics with a $250 million profit. That figure also conveniently bested L.A.'s result, by $50 million. And he would have to do it all without government funding or loan guarantees, and with nothing but trouble from the city of Atlanta, which suddenly saw the Olympics as a major cash windfall after refusing to support Payne throughout the bidding process.

First, Payne had to keep his job. The Chamber of Commerce types—first bemused, then amazed by Payne—suddenly were startled that this real estate lawyer with no management experience might be left in charge of their Olympic games. Payne at various times had hinted he would step down if Atlanta won, as had been the custom with all prior Olympics in other cities. But when Payne showed no sign of leaving, a cabal of the corporate elite met, and decided to suggest

that a change should be made at the top of the newly christened Atlanta Committee for the Olympic Games.

And they had a successor in mind, according to several sources familiar with the putsch effort. The name: Don Keough. Coke's number
two executive made sense. At age 63, he was expected to retire from
Coke in 1992. He had headed Coke's Olympics programs since before the TOP program was created. He had the political, business,
and social connections in Atlanta that would be necessary to make
the games succeed. And alone in the city, he could match Payne's
charismatic preacher's style of speaking, word for word. To this day,
Payne says he was prepared to fall on his Olympic pin and resign if
Holder and Atlanta's inner circle told him he was through. But
Holder stood by Payne, and the rest of the Atlanta Nine rallied
around him.

Although some Olympics sources say Coke was backing the Keough
candidacy, the company never made an overt effort to push Keough
atop ACOG, and the dump Billy effort died. Keough says he was never
aware of a bid to put him in charge of the games.

WITH THE OLYMPICS COMING TO ATLANTA, GOIZUETA FACED TWO
major jobs: Preparing both his company and his city for the 1996 summer games. A realist as always, Goizueta knew Coke's image would be
linked to Atlanta's success or failure. It was a done deal that Coke
would jump to be the first worldwide TOP sponsor, meeting Payne's
$40 million asking price on February 2, 1992. Eventually, Goizueta
would invest nearly eight times that much in marketing related to the
Atlanta Olympics. Yet he faced the tough job of capitalizing on the
unique marketing opportunity of a hometown Olympics without lend-
ing validity to the inevitable "Coke Olympics" epithets by oversaturat-
ing the games with Coca-Cola red. Meanwhile, as an adoptive
Atlantan, he wanted to make certain that his city did not flop in its
first significant turn on the international stage since Martin Luther
King, Jr., won the Nobel peace prize.

Now that Payne had won the Olympics and survived the effort to
oust him, he was as important to Goizueta as any business partner in
the company's global operations. Coke's public relations efforts to
distance itself from the Atlanta Olympics, never very successful, were
doomed. Payne was now Goizueta's partner—an unmanageable,

untested, and technically unsophisticated partner on whom The Coca-Cola Company's reputation suddenly rested. "I know Billy looked at Roberto as an elder statesman offering sage advice, but Roberto never really got past looking at Billy as a kind of puppy, all full of good intentions, but likely to dump over a potted plant or two," says a high-level Olympics source.

Payne's early management style, such as it was, was the opposite of Goizueta's. Coke's chairman strove to be the master of the strategic step, leaving the rest to those beneath him on the organization chart. He encouraged studied risk taking. He was adamant about delivering on forecasts, especially those involving money. Payne in the early days tried to be the entire organization chart. Instead of delegating trivial decisions and focusing on strategy, Payne tried to do everything. He arranged seating at dinners and decorations at public events. A decision about the color of a brochure once took more than a day. He upbraided employees—many of them still volunteers. His manner could be at once high-handed and aloof, and in the early days after winning the bid, his office became a bottleneck for decisions big and small.

Payne increased the frequency of visits to Goizueta's office, and Goizueta sharpened his focus on the man and the games. The days of the pep talks and strategic advice were behind them. Now it was bottom line. At each meeting, Goizueta wanted to see Payne's financial numbers and hear the latest about sponsorship signings, bank credit, and construction schedules. After McKinsey & Co. drew up an organization chart for Payne, he hired A.D. Frazier, a native Atlanta banker and former Carter aide who had moved to Chicago to work in the executive suite at First National Bank of Chicago. Goizueta seemed pleased by the appointment, because Frazier was a known quantity in Atlanta's business circles. In fact, he had overseen financing of Coke's successful Chicago bottler for years.

But Payne did not seem to know how to work with a second in command. Rather than embracing Frazier as Goizueta had Keough, Payne did not trust him. When Frazier held his first staff meeting without inviting Payne, an irate Payne called Frazier into his office and in a profanity-laden tantrum questioned his loyalty. When Ivester invited Frazier to Coke's headquarters for a get-acquainted lunch, it irritated Payne. "How do you know these guys?" he demanded. Frazier explained that he had lent Coke bottlers hundreds of millions of dollars while banking in Chicago and pointed out that he had started off well in his meeting with Ivester by showing off his understanding of the bottling business.

The two ACOG executives even competed at arriving at work ahead of each other—a remarkable contest, given that Payne's typical work day already started at 4 A.M. The tension passed after Payne suffered a heart attack in April 1993, and Frazier ably and loyally managed ACOG during the month Payne stayed home to recover. Over time, with some prodding from Holder, Payne and Frazier developed a working relationship that was consciously modeled on the hand-in-glove association between Goizueta and Keough.

Payne's biggest departure from Goizueta's style was his penchant for bold, seat-of-the-pants pronouncements that proved embarrassingly wrong. His initial boasts about his ability to raise money, sell television rights, build sports venues, and turn a record profit all veered off target. In the end, he was $85 million short of his sponsorship forecast, $144 million short of his U.S. television target, brought the Olympic Stadium in at more than twice its original budget, and barely broke even.

He could not blame Coke. A few weeks after Coke had signed on as the first TOP sponsor of the Atlanta games, Payne visited Goizueta's office and admitted for the first time that his goal of selling $500 million in sponsorships was beginning to look unattainable. The economy was weak, and few sponsorship offers were coming in. If it kept up, there was a risk the Atlanta Games could lose money.

Goizueta was horrified. "You have said you will do this," he told Payne, firmly. "You will do it, at all costs and at the invoking of all required disciplines. You must break even whatever you do." To put muscle behind his words, Goizueta urged Keough to help Payne arrange meetings with the chief executives of potential sponsors, a task the well-connected Coke executive took on with relish.

Despite Keough's help, there was no quick way to turn Goizueta's stern warning into gold. Desperately in need of cash in July 1993, Payne settled for $456 million from NBC for the U.S. television rights, nearly $150 million shy of his forecast. When no U.S. automaker would buy worldwide rights, he was forced to break the category into domestic and international pieces, and never did make the $40 million target for the automotive category. In the end, he parsed the sponsorship packages into tiny pieces of property—categories like "official game show" ("Wheel of Fortune," once one of Coke's Columbia Pictures properties) and "official automobile antitheft device." Some companies paid as little as $1 million for the right to call themselves official sponsors of the Centennial Games—irking the loyal Atlanta companies like Coke, Delta Air Lines, and United Parcel Service that had paid $40 million for the right to make the same claim.

BESIDES LOOKING AFTER THE WELFARE OF ACOG, GOIZUETA ALSO needed to make certain Atlanta itself was ready. In May 1994, after a referendum for $149 million in bond improvements was withdrawn before a vote in part because business leaders had not lined up to support it, Goizueta made a rare appearance before the Commerce Club of Atlanta. He chided those in the business community who feared the social and financial burden of the Games and feared they would "embarrass us in front of the world." Such thinking, he warned, could become a self-fulfilling prophecy. "Like it or not, we in this room are facing a wide range of issues that will do much to determine the future of our city," he said.

In a self-congratulatory riff, Goizueta called for the kind of commitment to Atlanta's urban center that had led him to build a museum of Coke memorabilia and history, The World of Coca-Cola, near a struggling downtown shopping district called Underground Atlanta. A remarkable exercise in capitalist excess, The World of Coca-Cola delivers the Coca-Cola story in glitzy multimedia displays, endless loops of Coke's most famous commercials, a life-sized reproduction of Doc Pemberton's drugstore where the first Cokes were served, and, during Goizueta's lifetime at least, a videotaped welcome from the chairman himself. Remarkably, it is one of Atlanta's most popular attractions and has fared far better financially than the troubled government-subsidized shopping center that Goizueta had hoped it would save.

Goizueta put energy behind his Commerce Club call to action by playing a key role in creating one of the most memorable legacies of the Atlanta Olympics: the Centennial Olympic Park downtown. Payne in mid-1993 had proposed the downtown park after looking out his office in downtown Atlanta at the warehouses and abandoned buildings that stood between the hotels and the Georgia Dome and Omni where gymnastics, basketball, and volleyball would be played. But to make it happen, he would need public and private support to help buy the property, bulldoze the buildings, and turn the area into a park that could be the main gathering place for the games. Payne knew one person, Goizueta, would be key to whether the idea would fly or fail. He commissioned an architect to create a rendering of his idea, and ordered him to draw the park as if seen from the point of view of Goizueta's office at Coke's North Avenue tower.

A few days later, Holder and Payne visited Goizueta and showed him the drawings. The gambit worked. Goizueta backed the plan. And in a rare fit of face-to-face arm twisting, he buttonholed Georgia Governor Zell Miller at a Woodruff Arts Center reception, and urged him to support the park plan. With Miller behind the proposal, offering state condemnation powers but no money, private enterprise quickly lined up to help buy the land. Goizueta played the good citizen, but only to a point. While he lobbied for the park, he refused to attach Coke's name directly to anything so freewheeling as Payne's idea of an open space accessible to anyone who visited Atlanta during the Olympics. Rather than contributing to the park along with other companies, Goizueta ordered Coke's real estate people to buy adjacent land and develop an attraction that would live up to Coke standards, under Coke control.

Not everyone fell in line with the idea. A handful of small businesses refused to sell out to Coke, and mounted an embarrassing public campaign against the company's efforts to shut them down. Ultimately, the company bought 12 acres of property and turned it into an attraction called "Coca-Cola Olympic City." In a $20 million complex anchored by an 80-foot-tall Coke bottle, customers who paid the $13 admission could entertain themselves with a variety of interactive experiences, such as a brief dash against a video version of heptathlete Jackie Joyner Kersee or a virtual basketball shootout with Dream Teamer Grant Hill.

Goizueta's decision to mount an exhibit separate from the Olympic Park annoyed Payne and Frazier. "When we came up with the Olympic Park idea, Coca-Cola Olympic City came right behind it, but on their own property, under their construction, with ticketed admission," beefs ACOG's Frazier. "It was antithetical to what Billy had in mind." Frazier extracted some pleasure when AT&T, which supported Payne's concept by building a venue for free concerts at the heart of the park, designed its entertainment tent to stand nearly three stories tall—just enough to hide Coca-Cola Olympic City from the view of the millions who came to Olympic Park to celebrate the games. It was the AT&T pavilion, not Coke's Olympic City, that became the focal point of celebration during the Olympics and, sadly, the target of a terrorist who tried to destroy the Atlanta games by detonating a bomb late one night during the first weekend of the games.

GOIZUETA COULD NOT WORRY ABOUT HURTING PAYNE'S FEELINGS with his Olympic City, because he had an Olympics of his own to run. The stakes for him were larger than just how downtown Atlanta looked during the games. Goizueta looked to the Atlanta games to mark the debut of a strategic shift in Coke's global marketing strategy. For years, Goizueta had pushed Keough and then Ivester to make certain that Coke's sports sponsorship programs were cost effective and fit the marketing mantra of "special, different, better." And ad maker Sergio Zyman, with his return in July of 1993, had moved sports ever closer to the center of Coke's global marketing strategy. For the Centennial Olympics alone, Coke would spend more than $350 million for sponsorships, advertising, and marketing. Incredibly, according to Gary Hite, the company when he retired in 1994 was sketching plans to spend even more on the Sydney Olympics in 2000—even though the games half a world away are in a time zone half a day different than Coke's key U.S. market.

From the Atlanta games onward, sports would become the driving force, the centerpiece, of Coke's global marketing efforts. Zyman persuaded Goizueta and Ivester that sports more than any other activity connects with consumers practically in the stem of the brain, rather than in the front lobe where reasoning and calculation take place. And most sports appeal to an active, young person who neatly fits the profile of Coke's target demographics.

Zyman began selling the world on the idea of sports as the ultimate marketing vehicle. "Sports lets you get into a dialogue with the consumer without having to buy into the gestalt of our brand as one big thing," Zyman told a reporter a week before the Opening Ceremonies in Atlanta, where he had alighted after a whirlwind trip that took him to the Tour de France to shoot television commercials, the European Cup soccer championships, and a meeting with Primo Nebiolo, head of the International Track Federation. After prodding from Ivester and Zyman, Goizueta approved a plan to put the Coca-Cola imprint on every major sport in every continent on earth. "We're doing it like lava," Zyman boasted. "We keep on moving slowly but inexorably in every sport."

The year 1994—with a Super Bowl in Atlanta and the World Cup in the United States—provided a perfect run-up to the unveiling of the new strategy at the Centennial Olympics. In orchestrating the strategic shift, Zyman and Ivester worked on different tacks, but to the same purpose. Ivester pushed to make certain that Coke made money on every dollar spent on sports sponsorship, advertising and marketing. "We need to activate our sponsorships," Ivester said again and again, as he urged Coke's marketing troops to make certain that stadium displays, promotional programs, billboards, and advertising all supported the investment in sports. Zyman, meanwhile, worked to create new properties and marketing strategies. Acting on the advice of Creative Artists Agency, Coke produced its own cable television show, "Coca-Cola Big TV," an elaborate pre-game show for the Super Bowl and the World Cup. The Super Bowl show cost $1.6 million to produce and air, about $200,000 less than the cost for a minute of advertising during the game, but offered hours of programming with a healthy list of CAA clients making cameo appearances. Coke backed its huge television and print advertising campaigns with other on-the-ground promotions at the events themselves, including a lavish Super Bowl bash in Atlanta for bottlers and customers, and interactive sports for the public exhibits at both events.

At the World Cup Big TV show in Los Angeles in 1994, the night before the soccer final, smarmy sports announcer Pat O'Brien introduced guests like the singer Toni Braxton in a sheath dress featuring Coca-Cola logos, and the anti-hero actor Dennis Hopper, whose black socks were highlighted by Coca-Cola-style red disks. As the comic Sinbad roamed the Big TV audience with a live microphone, he stopped at Ivester's table and toyed with Coke's second in command. "Now here's a man who has no clue of what he's doing for Coca-Cola," Sinbad said, as the chronically stiff Ivester fidgeted uncomfortably in his seat and forced a strained smile to his lips. "He might lose his job," Sinbad concluded.

NOT HARDLY. IVESTER'S JOB WAS SECURE. AND WITH THE KEOUGH'S retirement in 1993, the Atlanta Olympics had placed him at the center of Coke's strategic shift to sports. Except for Payne's meetings in Goizueta's office and Goizueta's selected interventions on behalf of his company or ACOG, the Olympics became Ivester's baby, and he treated the games in his typical tough, take-no-prisoners style. When Coke failed to meet its January 1994 target for getting all its Olympic programs in place and ACOG complained about an inability to get decisions from Coke, Goizueta told Ivester to fix the problems. Ivester eased Hite into retirement and moved his cerebral but slow-acting lieutenant where he could not do any harm: running the World of Coca-Cola.

In came Stu Cross, who had spearheaded Big TV and the Super Bowl bash. ACOG had run out of patience with Coke's inability to make decisions and its knee-jerk desire to control everything it touched, along with its constant carping about getting maximum brand-name exposure on every square inch of the Olympics. When Cross came on the scene, he immediately tried to make peace with ACOG. "It's our view that you feel that the relationship between The Coca-Cola Company and ACOG is adversarial, and we want to change that," Cross told Frazier during their first meeting. His peace offering: a cooler in Frazier's office, continuously filled with Tab for the remaining two years until the games concluded. Cross was not a total panacea. In several of the disputes involving Coke's overly zealous efforts to put its trademark on everything Olympic, especially involving the torch run, the arguments between Frazier and Cross were so fierce that Goizueta and Payne personally had to mediate, but on the whole, Cross and Frazier developed a relationship that mostly aligned the efforts of Coke and ACOG.

Cross' arrival marked the point at which Coke's Atlanta program at last truly sprang into action. With Ivester and Cross calling the shots, Coke sprang to action. It concluded the deal to pay $15 million to sponsor the Olympic torch run, built the $20 million Coca-Cola Olympic City, laid plans to spend $25 million entertaining more than 6,000 guests, bought up $62 million of NBC's television time for its ad campaign, and put $35 million into an array of activities like a pin trading center, on-site advertising, commercial production, and a radio network. Ivester also pushed Zyman to finally decide on an advertising theme for the games. The result: "For the Fans" kicked off Coke's effort to build a pipeline into consumers' brains by emphasizing the fans' eye view of the big Olympic events, en route to becoming a tag line for other sports around the world.

Coke did more than just throw money at the events. Consider the torch run, which AT&T had sponsored for the L.A. games, asking runners to contribute $3,000 to charity in exchange for the privilege of carrying the Olympic flame. Even though the contributions were made to charity, the AT&T run had drawn complaints from people who were offended that the Olympic flame was put up for sale to fat cats with the cash to pay for a brief moment of Olympic glory. Ivester decided to push the program toward grass roots. Linking with United Way, Coke ran an elaborate contest for selecting "community heroes" to run with the torch, a shrewd move that won the company publicity during the selection process, and also from the hundreds of emotional and heartrending stories of torch bearers as the flame crossed the country.

Typically for Goizueta's detail-mad management style, Coke delivered a 91-page guidebook even to the tiniest towns on the 15,000 torch route, which the local merchants and bottlers were ordered to use to make the torch's visit to their towns a success. Among the must-dos: Hanging Coke banners throughout town, policing for any Pepsi banners that mysteriously appeared, recruiting upwards of 200 volunteers to sell soda from backpacks shaped like Coke bottles, and reading a proclamation from Payne and Ivester memorializing the torch's visit to town. Goizueta personally reviewed the details of the plans, and the corny scripts for the ceremonies, before they were shipped.

Coke's ground troops responded like zealots to orders from Goizueta and Ivester that the company wanted its money's worth out of its Olympic sponsorship, especially so with the torch run. ACOG's Frazier was waiting on the dais at Olympic sponsor Anheuser-Busch's big Budweiser plant in St. Louis in mid-June when his cell phone rang. Ginger Watkins, the ACOG executive in charge of the torch run was calling. "A.D., you've got to take the Anheuser-Busch logo off the dais," she told him. "Stu Cross knows it's up there, and Coke's going ballistic." Frazier looked behind him, and saw the logo, and it definitely did not belong. But on his left was the president of Anheuser-Busch, on his right was the head of marketing, and in front of him were 2,000 Busch employees, enthusiastically waiting for the torch to arrive. "Ginger," Frazier told her. "The odds of me getting up and taking down that A-B logo are quite remote. Tell Stu he'll have to do it himself."

En route to the games, Goizueta's Olympic team overreached in other, more serious ways. A court ultimately struck down a city ordinance they pushed through that allowed for a city ordinance allowing billboards the size of a nine-story building, and offered them for sale only to Olympic sponsors. They never stopped trying to persuade the IOC to allow them to put advertising at mid-field of the soccer venue, as Coke does at World Cup matches. They agreed to conceal the logos on PowerAde bottles provided to athletes on the field only after weeks of tense meetings. When Cross and Ivester learned that the Home Depot chain had purchased the right to distribute Olympic tickets as part of its sponsorship, they engaged in a bitter custody fight, complaining to ACOG that Coke alone had the capability to distribute enough ticket brochures nationwide for ACOG to have a shot at reaching its goal of selling 10 million tickets. Frazier refereed the dispute, and ultimately convinced Home Depot to give up the rights if Coke picked up the printing bill for the 40 million brochures.

WHILE IVESTER AND CROSS PLUCKED AWAY AT THE DETAILS THAT would put Coke's stamp on the Atlanta games, Goizueta was focusing ahead—far ahead. In an unprecedented step, he proposed to Samaranch that Coke wanted to renew its TOP sponsorship. NBC had shocked the sports world in December 1996, when it announced it would pay a total of $3.5 billion to broadcast every Olympics not already sold through the 2008 summer games, for which the host city is not yet known. But that was an eye blink compared to what Goizueta wanted. Moving so quietly that the press following the Olympics never discovered the scope of his Olympic ambitions, Goizueta proposed that Coke should sign on as a TOP sponsor through 2028, in other words, for the next 32 years. The offer was for eight Olympic quadrennials at a price that topped $500 million. Other Olympic sponsors were amazed when advised about the size of Coke's huge Olympic bid. "Other sponsors don't have that kind of confidence in themselves," marveled David D'Allesandro, chief executive of John Hancock Life Insurance Co. and a veteran TOP sponsor. "Coke is betting that the Olympics are going to be practically forever. Most executives don't like putting their company on the line for that long."

Goizueta had his eye on Atlanta's future, too. Again taking the podium in front of Atlanta's business community, this time just three months before the games, Goizueta warned the Chamber of Commerce that the city needed to act quickly and decisively or it would never capitalize on the Olympics. He still was concerned by a lack of investment downtown. "It is our city's very core, and it cannot be like a doughnut. A great city cannot have a hollow center," Goizueta said. To some, the emphasis on downtown was a touch hypocritical, given that Coke had started the corporate flight from the urban center in the 1970s when it chose to build its headquarters in Atlanta's mid-town district. He urged a program of urban renewal after the games, and underscored his commitment to the future by agreeing to serve on the board of Mayor Bill Campbell's Atlanta Renaissance Program, which was designed to make Atlanta's post-Olympic plans.

Like Woodruff before him, Goizueta enjoyed inviting Atlanta's mayors to lunch at his office at regular intervals, to talk shop and discuss the future of the city. During the riots in Atlanta following the acquittal of white Los Angeles police officers who were videotaped beating motorist Rodney King, Goizueta faxed then-Mayor Maynard Jackson and urged him to do whatever necessary to stop rioting in Atlanta. It was an echo of Woodruff's offer, on the night Martin Luther King, Jr., was shot, to pay for King's funeral so that the famed civil rights leader would have an appropriate burial in Atlanta. When Campbell asked Goizueta to serve on the Atlanta Renaissance Program, Goizueta said yes even though he had turned down other mayors for similar projects. Despite his good intentions, though, Goizueta failed to make much of an impact on the Renaissance program, and it made little impact on the city. More than a year after the Olympics, people in Atlanta would point to the still unfinished Olympic Park and mismanagement of enterprise zone funds that were won in part because of the Olympics as evidence that the city had not heeded

Goizueta's warning at the Commerce Club that the city should not "take a nap after having such a big lunch."

Ironically, it was Atlanta's mayor himself who would do more than anyone to cut short any chance Atlanta had of capitalizing on the Olympics. Bill Campbell tried to cash in on the Olympics by selling vending licenses to hundreds of small business people, giving them rights to hawk trinkets, t-shirts, and other cheap wares on the streets of Atlanta wherever Olympics spectators were likely to walk. The mad scene of raw commercialism, while adding to the excitement of the games for some, struck many spectators and the international press as a grotesque distortion of the spirit of amateurism that had created the Olympic movement. Of course, with $40 million commercial sponsorships and a twelve-acre Coca-Cola City just down the street from the main bazaar, it was not just the street vendors who were turning the Olympics into a money machine.

As the Opening Ceremonies approached, the overlap between ACOG and Coke intensified. The torch run was winding down, and the park was about to open, but there was one last matter that caused Stu Cross to call A. D. Frazier: Roberto needed a place to park. "I'd like the same parking pass for Roberto that the mayor has," Cross said. Frazier listened, slack jawed, then rejected the request. "Listen," Cross continued. "He'll have heads of state visiting, and he'll need this." Frazier refused again, and told Cross that his boss would have to ride the Olympic transportation system's sponsor busses along with other mortals.

With some 6,000 guests in town for the games themselves, Goizueta and the rest of Coke's brass busily hosted major customers, bottlers and, yes, heads of state. Experienced as Coke is at playing host at major world events, the games themselves were hardly extraordinary. Until, that is, 1:45 A.M. on July 28, when a bomb exploded in Olympic Park, killing a woman visitor, causing a Turkish cameraman to die of a heart attack, and injuring dozens. The next day, as Frazier and Payne scrambled to keep the games on schedule and lay plans to reopen the park, Frazier received a call from Cross, who announced that Coke wanted to help out. Rather than delaying the announcement that Coke was signing to be an Olympic sponsor until the year 2008, the company was ready to hold the ceremonial signing immediately, to show the world that the Olympics could not be defeated by terrorism.

On August 2, Samaranch and Ivester signed the contract. The deal Coke finally reached was shorter by twenty years than the pact Goizueta had first proposed. For an undisclosed sum, it made Coke a sponsor through the year 2008, as long as NBC's broadcast pact. Frazier chuckled to himself about the Coke-centric view of the world, the notion that the signing of an Olympic sponsorship would calm the fears of a city upended by a bombing downtown while all the world watched. Bitter experience during the games had taught him that only at Coke would anyone believe that their signing of a sponsorship agreement would rebuild the public's confidence in the Atlanta Games. "It was great they did that, but it didn't make a damn bit of difference to anyone in the world but Coke and the IOC," Frazier said.

Frazier apparently had missed the point of his long service side-by-side with Cross, Ivester, and, occasionally, even with Goizueta. Inside the world of Coca-Cola, there is no event too large not to become a moment for Coca-Cola. If Coke could help win World War II by building bottlings plants abroad, if it could celebrate the collapse of the Berlin Wall by sending trucks to East Berlin, if it could export jobs and opportunity to underdeveloped markets by forming alliances with anchor bottlers, then surely Coke could bring a sense of solace to its home city by signing an Olympics contract a few days after a bomb exploded in Olympic Park. Under Roberto Goizueta, at least, the world was, after all, The World of Coca-Cola.

11

"It's Coca-Cola Heaven"

During the three weeks of the Atlanta Olympic games, Roberto Goizueta and Doug Ivester shook hands with more than 2,000 guests of Coca-Cola—the bottlers, customers, employees, and politicians who came to pay homage to the unofficial hosts of the Atlanta Games. After the flame was extinguished on August 4, 1996, Goizueta and Ivester dutifully signed photographs of the handshakes, and sent them as mementos to their guests who had returned to their homes at the farthest reaches of the globe.

Ten days after the Olympic flame died out in Atlanta, Goizueta and Ivester again stood with their wives Olguita and Kay before the pond and the "Leadership" sculpture outside the rotunda at Coca-Cola's headquarters. Again, they were waiting to greet guests from abroad. And again Goizueta knew he would soon put pen to paper. But this signature would mean much more than an autograph on a photo, a fleeting remembrance of some sporting entertainment. It would mark Coca-Cola's triumphal conquest of an entire country and with it, symbolically at least, a continent and perhaps the world.

A line of limousines came up the circle drive, filled with the heads of one of South America's leading industrial clans, the Cisneros family of Venezuela. Stepping out of the limousines, cousins Oswaldo and Gustavo Cisneros first shook hands, then gave bracing Latin hugs to Goizueta and Ivester. The wives made small talk. And the group of more than a dozen Cisneros executives and their wives, matched by a smaller group of Coke couples, made their way to the twenty-fifth floor

272

of Coca-Cola's North Avenue tower. There in the shrine of Robert Woodruff's old office, on the desk from which he had asked Goizueta to take control of The Coca-Cola Company, Roberto Goizueta signed a contract that bound him together with the Cisneros clan. For $500 million, Goizueta's Coke claimed a 50 percent stake in *Coca-Cola y Hit de Venezuela*, a joint venture with the Cisneros' bottling company, Venezuela's largest bottler. Overnight, Coke controlled a 98 percent share of Venezuela's soft-drink market.

The Roberto C. Goizueta scrawl on Woodruff's desk symbolized Coke's dominion, not just over the country, or the South American continent, but of the entire soft-drink world. Napoleon kept fighting after Waterloo, and Lee stayed afield after Gettysburg. Taken alone, neither town was of major strategic significance. But for both generals, the losses there ended dreams of conquest, and ultimately, of contention in the great war of their lives. Venezuela held little strategic significance in the war for global soda hegemony between Coca-Cola and PepsiCo. Coke owned every other country in South America, and was not hurt by Pepsi's control, since 1940, of the bottler that dominated the Venezuelan market. But for symbolic purposes, Venezuela marked the Waterloo and Gettysburg of Pepsi's pretense toward contention with The Coca-Cola Company for soft-drink leadership in markets around the globe. After Venezuela, Pepsi seemed only to be going through the motions, declining gradually toward irrelevance.

Over his 15 years as Coke's chief executive, Goizueta had outplanned, outspent, and outhustled Pepsi in country after country around the world. He fired his first shot in the Philippines in 1981. Pepsi rallied with its successful push into the Soviet bloc countries, where it held sway until the Berlin Wall fell. Quickly, Goizueta seized Eastern Germany, then the rest of the satellite countries. For some time, Russia remained a holdout empire, with PepsiCo's 60 percent corporate share leading Coca-Cola's 38 percent as recently as 1994. But with $500 million in new-plant investment and a strategy focused on new capitalists instead of Pepsi's old bureaucrats, Coke quickly overturned Pepsi in Russia, too. By the time of the Venezuela contract signing, Goizueta was just days away from declaring victory in Russia. "While achieving leadership in Russia has been a long time coming, the turnaround came even more quickly than anticipated when we launched our investment," Goizueta would crow. Only in the Pacific region were major markets still up for grabs, mainly because they still were largely underdeveloped.

GOIZUETA SAVORED EACH TERRITORIAL CONQUEST, BUT VENEZUELA was personal. It was a Latin country, and like Goizueta, the Cisneros family had Cuban roots. The fathers of Oswaldo and his cousins Gustavo and Ricardo left Cuba in 1928 to seek their fortunes, and by 1940 became Pepsi's sole bottling franchisee in Venezuela. For Goizueta, Venezuela represented a chance to reverse that history and, above all, to settle a score with Roger Enrico, PepsiCo's chairman who was Oswaldo's personal friend. Enrico was dancing with Oswaldo's wife when stricken by a heart attack in Istanbul in 1990, and when American Express courted Enrico in 1993, he turned to Oswaldo for counsel. Oswaldo's advice: Turn it down. Enrico did, and by 1996 had become chairman of PepsiCo.

Although Goizueta had never met his counterpart at Pepsi, he resented Enrico's chutzpah ever since the man declared victory in the Cola Wars after the New Coke debacle with a rollicking, boastful book titled *The Other Guy Blinked: How Pepsi Won the Cola Wars*. In the second edition, after it was clear that the Wars were still very much engaged, Enrico toned down the subtitle, but it was too late. He had earned Goizueta's personal enmity by breaking the code of gentlemanly conduct that had typified the Coke vs. Pepsi relationship since the days when Goizueta was in Cuba. Until Enrico's outrage, both Coke and Pepsi executives almost never let the name of the rival drink cross their lips. In public, at least, at Coke's headquarters Pepsi was always "our competitor." After Enrico's book, any shot was fair game. Any victory over Pepsi was sweet for Goizueta, but because of Enrico's close ties with Oswaldo Cisneros, Venezuela was sweet revenge.

Enrico actually had the first shot at buying into the Cisneros Group. Oswaldo dangled the prospect before him in 1990, but Enrico said he would be interested only in a 10 percent stake, and would want only the Cisneros' flavor concentrate business, not the entire bottling operation. By that point, Cisneros was already uncomfortable with Pepsi. In 1989, Pepsi had begun investing in a costly and aggressive push into Brazil by Argentine bottler Buenos Aires Embotelladora SA (Baesa). The Cisneros Group had wanted to grow outside of Venezuela for years, and were astounded to see Pepsi back Baesa's assault on

South America's biggest market and neighbor to the south. "Pepsi was never friendly to the idea that our group could grow out of Venezuela," said Oswaldo Cisneros. "Perhaps they thought we would get too big for them—something they could not control." Worse still, after Enrico left soft drinks in 1990 to run Pepsi's snack foods business, Pepsi chairman Wayne Calloway never visited Venezuela and international chief Chris Sinclair, the architect of the Baesa strategy, swung through only once.

Cisneros hired New York investment bankers and in 1994, Oswaldo, Gustavo, and Ricardo Cisneros traveled to Atlanta for a furtive meeting with Goizueta and Ivester at Coke's headquarters. Coke's Project Swan was born, *cisne* is Spanish for swan. Goizueta assigned Ivester to negotiate the deal, and warned him not to talk about the negotiations even with Weldon Johnson, then president of Coke's Latin American operations. Ivester complied with that request, but did not keep his dealings secret from everyone in the executive suite. He brought marketing chief Sergio Zyman in on the planning, to help with an assessment of Pepsi's marketing programs in the country.

The deal was laborious. Ivester and Oswaldo Cisneros met at least ten times, always in airport hangers, hotels, or other clandestine places to avoid any security breach. Cisneros wanted to sell as much as possible of the company. Concerned about his high cholesterol and stress, he wanted out because his three daughters did not want to follow him into the business. But Goizueta did not want an outright buyout. He wanted to limit Coke's stake to 25 percent. Experience with seven anchor bottlers around the world had proven that was enough to gain significant voting control while still limiting the size of Coke's investment. Rattled when Cisneros walked out of a meeting early in 1996, Goizueta gave Ivester the OK to raise Coke's stake to 50 percent, and they had a deal. The Cisneros had hired the small New York investment banking firm Violy Byorum & Partners, but Goizueta had chosen to deal without bankers. With more than 100 domestic and international bottling deals behind him, Goizueta thought Coke's dealmaking team was stronger than anything any firm could put together, even his old stalwart Allen & Co.

By the time Enrico got wind of the deal when he became PepsiCo's chief executive in April 1996, it was too late. Oswaldo Cisneros at first did not return his calls. In early summer, Enrico finally offered to buy a quarter of the Cisneros Group bottling operation in early summer, but by then Coke and the Cisneros were finalizing terms of their deal. For Enrico, it was a double defeat. The bottler on which Pepsi had placed its big South America bet, Baesa, was on the verge of bankruptcy, in part the result of Goizueta's personal lobbying with Argentine president Carlos Menem to reduce the tax on imported cola from 24 percent to 4 percent. Eliminating the tariff virtually erased Baesa's pricing advantage, and opened the door for Coke's all-out assault on Argentina. When Goizueta ordered up a ground attack on retail outlets in Brazil— a plan to shut out Pepsi from retail outlets by placing Coke coolers in stores throughout the country—he injured Baesa again. By September, Enrico was forced to take a $525 million special charge, primarily to write down the value of its 25 percent stake in Baesa.

Coke and the Cisneros Group had a deal by April, but Goizueta knew his raid on Pepsi's one remaining foreign outpost would grab headlines. With more than $350 million invested in the Olympics, Goizueta would not risk distracting anyone in the Coke system, the press, or Wall Street from the culmination of the years spent planning for the Atlanta Olympics. By this point, rumors of a Coke-Cisneros deal were rampant at Pepsi, and waiting nearly two months would give Enrico an opening for a last-minute attack. But Goizueta was confident. He had Oswaldo's word and was willing to wait.

With the Olympics over, Goizueta was more than happy to play the Cisneros takeover as a public relations bonanza. He personally did not make himself available to reporters to talk about the deal. Given that a lawsuit or other legal action from Pepsi was expected, it would have been risky to chance making any unscripted public statements. Oswaldo Cisneros spoke out briefly, until he learned his first lesson of Coke image management when the Coke publicity machine bottled him shut. Goizueta ordered the public relations army to puff the news that Coke had charted a 727 jetliner, had it fueled and ready to fly to Caracas from Mexico with a nation's worth of Coke bottles in its belly. Or there were the crews ready to repaint 2,500 trucks, and the overnight transformation of store displays, bottle racks, and the rest of the distribution infrastructure from Pepsi to Coke. A month later, Goizueta flew to Venezuela and toured the Caracas bottling plant as a conquering hero before visiting with Venezuelan president Rafael Caldera that evening. "There is a lot of space to grow here," Goizueta said. "The last time I was here was 1978. Now I will be coming back more often."

To Goizueta's delight, Pepsi executives and public relations people wore out their vocal chords whining about the treachery of Coke's Venezuela raid. Just days after losing the Cisneros Group, Craig Weatherup, chief executive of PepsiCo's soft-drink division, complained in a letter to bottlers that the Cisneros deal was "a new low, even for The Coca-Cola Company." PepsiCo indeed filed a complaint with Venezuela's anti-monopoly commission that the Cisneros deal created a monopoly and illegally broke a contract with Pepsi that ran through 2003. Shrewdly, Goizueta a few months before the deal had purchased a group of bottling plants, six of which he offered to sell to Pepsi so it could claim a toehold in the market. The offering had the effect of undermining Pepsi's claims that Coke wanted to own all of the Venezuelan market. Coke ultimately paid a $2 million fine. It was a small price for the economic and especially the psychological advantages that came with the deal.

Enrico was blistered by the debacle in Caracas and the loss of a friend. Immediately after the deal was announced, he picked up the phone to call Oswaldo Cisneros, but his old compadre did not return several calls. "Ozzie took his 30 pieces of silver and ran," Enrico complained bitterly.

The business fallout was not any easier to handle. Enrico ordered Weatherup to begin a restructuring of Pepsi's international operations, and by mid-October the two chastened Pepsi executives announced that their new strategy would focus on markets where Coke was not dominant. There was enough room in up-for-grab markets and those in the developing world for Pepsi to thrive, Enrico claimed. "Most of the time we don't need to beat Coke to have a huge and growing (international) business," Enrico told analysts in a late-September conference call.

Emboldened by his theft of "the Swan," by Pepsi's stuck-pig reaction, and by Enrico's retreat from competing against him on a global basis, Goizueta could not resist some in-your-face trash talking. "It appears that the company that claimed to have won the cola wars is now raising the white flag," he told *Fortune* magazine. Wall Street had rewarded Coke for the coup, and boosted Coca-Cola shares to an all-time high of nearly $54 a share. This, coupled with the personal dimension of the victory over Enrico, made Goizueta both jubilant and cocky. Asked by a reporter to pull out of his desk drawer the Pepsi business strategy he had stored there for years, Goizueta jabbed his Pepsi foe again. "I threw it out," he said. "As they've become less relevant, I don't need to look at them any more." Goizueta got a good laugh at Enrico's expense when the *Fortune* story featuring this comment was fronted by a retouched cover photograph depicting Enrico confined tightly inside the familiar shape of a Coca-Cola bottle.

There was more to Goizueta's point than just an in-your-face barb for Enrico. Pepsi had become less relevant to Coke's strategic planning for a number of reasons. International sales was perhaps the biggest. By 1996, 70 percent of Coke's revenues and 80 percent of profits came from international markets, while Pepsi drew virtually identical numbers from its domestic operations. Much of Pepsi's revenues and profits came from businesses in which Coca-Cola did not even compete— snack foods and restaurants. Goizueta loved to chide his competition for distracting itself with running so many different businesses, and in 1997 Pepsi finally succumbed and spun off the restaurant operation, acknowledging that the capital-intensive business hurt Pepsi's soft-drink sales because other restaurant customers did not want to buy soda from the company that also owned Pizza Hut. While industry rumors had it that Pepsi planned to spin off its bottling operations à la Coca-Cola Enterprises, by early 1998 Enrico still had not taken that step. As a result, Pepsi's reliance on capital-intensive businesses like bottling and snack foods made it difficult to compete with Coke's return on equity. Pepsi tended to give investors a 20 percent return, while Coke's return on equity typically was more than double that, at about 55 percent.

VENEZUELA WAS PERHAPS THE MOST DRAMATIC STEP IN GOIZUETA'S campaign for global dominance. And together with Pepsi's Baesa debacle it marked the point at which Pepsi finally gave up the pose of trying to compete on equal terms with Coke in markets around the globe. This dramatic victory just a few months before his sixty-fifth birthday was one of the major achievements of Goizueta's career, and he owed it in large part to his strategy of designating anchor bottlers around the world to take charge of bottling and distributing Coca-Cola in their native countries, adjoining nations, and, ultimately, in widely diverse geographies so long as they could effectively manage their business. By this point, the anchor bottler program was reaching maturity and Goizueta had developed it into a profit machine that was the ultimate in adding economic value to the Coca-Cola system.

Goizueta developed the anchor bottler concept in a way that was not typical for him. He had unveiled his other landmark strategies—from Diet Coke to Columbia to CCE—with fanfare and flash. But he built the anchor bottler concept gradually, if inevitably, by modifying and refining it along the way. This low-profile approach served the useful strategic purpose of enabling Goizueta to build his network of anchors without gaining much attention from Pepsi, or from competitors in the native countries where its partners resided. The strategy originated with Coke's partnership with the likes of Amatil Swire Beverages PLC in the mid-1980s, and was an extension of the notion of minority investment that was the bedrock of the Coca-Cola Enterprises deal.

At maturity, the program looked like this. First, Coke's finance staff made certain that their initial investment in the bottlers would yield Goizueta's standard target of a 20 percent return on invested capital. This meant Coke chose partners who were strong to begin with, and looking to expand. By placing Coca-Cola executives on the anchor bottlers' boards, Coke could direct investment capital, enforce financial discipline, make certain the bottlers supported marketing programs introduced by Atlanta, and otherwise maximize return on Goizueta's capital. Because the bottlers themselves were prominent businesspeople in their own countries and regions, Coke benefited from the image of local ownership and the street smarts of entrepreneurs who already knew how to succeed in local market conditions.

The anchor bottlers multiplied the impact of Coke's investment in them by investing capital of their own in growing their markets, giving Coke a huge advantage especially in underdeveloped markets where it was racing PepsiCo and other competitors to establish dominance in the midst of fluid market conditions. Not only did Coke sell more of its syrup to anchor bottlers, it also benefited from the return on its equity investment in them. The only apparent shortcoming of the anchor bottler program was the risk that Goizueta might expand it too quickly, and diminish the importance of the designation, as bottling partners around the world clamored for anchor-bottler status.

Oswaldo and Gustavo Cisneros certainly wanted to be anchor bottlers, and Goizueta had indicated that might be a possibility. There were ways in which the Cisneros fit the bill. Goizueta had declared that anchor bottlers be substantial multinational businesses, experienced bottlers with capital available to invest in their existing markets and expansion abroad. It was a tall order, and a rare designation. At the time of the Cisneros deal in 1996, a decade after the anchor bottler program began, Goizueta had designated only eight companies as anchor bottlers, operating in 40 countries around the world and comprising nearly 70 percent of the Coca-Cola system's international volume. Even so, the Cisneros enterprise fit that basic definition, so it is in some ways understandable that Oswaldo and Gustavo Cisneros took Goizueta at his word during negotiations when he told them privately that they might have an opportunity to become anchor bottlers if they switched from Pepsi to Coca-Cola.

A close look at the map should have told them otherwise. After all, Goizueta already had an anchor bottler in South America, Pan American Beverage Co. (Panamco). Goizueta had no prohibition against more than one anchor bottler per continent, but he did want his anchors to have room to expand in contiguous territories. And since Panamco's footprint already covered Brazil, Colombia, Costa Rica, and parts of Mexico, the Cisneros operation was virtually surrounded by another anchor bottler. This made it highly unlikely that the new Coke-Cisneros bottler could become an anchor. Within a year after the Cisneros clan merged the family bottling operation into the joint venture with Coke, Panamco swallowed up Coca-Cola y Hit de Venezuela in a $1.1 billion gulp.

THE ANCHOR BOTTLER PARTNERSHIPS WORKED BECAUSE THERE WAS little overlap between the bottling operations that dominated the anchors' business and the concentrate and brand-marketing functions at the core of Coca-Cola. Goizueta did not do nearly as well with partners that were more closely competitive with Coke. Goizueta had failed to find common ground in his joint venture with Nestlé, which he had been forced to downgrade from a partnership to simply a licensing deal. His luck with a second high-profile partnership was just as bad. A highly touted joint venture with Cadbury Schweppes collapsed in 1996 even as Goizueta was coming to terms with the Cisneros family in Venezuela.

The Cadbury partnership had worked at first. When the deal first was set, Cadbury was known primarily as a bottler of seltzer water with a few niche brands in the United Kingdom. Goizueta wanted to combine Coke's marketing savvy with Cadbury's distribution to make inroads into the U.K. market. And in its first three years of operation, Coca-Cola-Schweppes Beverages doubled sales and transformed Britain into one of Coke's fastest growing markets.

But the sweetness did not last. There had always been differences in operating philosophy, with Cadbury pushing for high returns from bottling and Coke emphasizing the somewhat contradictory objective of maximum margins on syrup sales. Coke's insistence on controlling all advertising and packaging decisions irritated Cadbury Schweppes Group chief executive David Wellings, but those disagreements were not unexpected, and clearly were not enough to kill the deal. The relationship hit the skids when Cadbury in 1993 acquired A&W brands and boosted its existing stake in Dr. Pepper/7-Up to 25.9 percent ownership of the company. Suddenly, Cadbury owned a big chunk in one of Coke's primary competitors, and Goizueta could not get comfortable doing business with the owner of products that were attacking Coke's brands in markets across the country and around the world.

The fractured relationship carried on like a bad marriage until the middle of 1994, when rumors swirled in the United States that Cadbury was maneuvering to buy the 75 percent of Dr. Pepper/7-Up that it did not already own from Prudential Insurance Co. Goizueta was outraged to learn that his U.K. joint venture partner was vying to become his second-largest competitor in the United States.

Goizueta flew to the U.K. to attend a Cadbury plant opening and deliver a message to Wellings. Stepping outside for a private chat after the ribbon cutting, Goizueta saw Welling reach inside the breast pocket of his finely tailored suit for a pack of Dunhill cigarettes. "You smoke?" he asked. "I smoke, too." Goizueta lit a True Menthol, and the two men smoked their cigarettes in silence.

Finally, as he stubbed his cigarette under foot, Goizueta delivered his message. "David," he asked. "Do you want to be my partner or my competitor?" Without another word to Wellings or anyone else, Goizueta slipped into the back seat of his Porsche sedan and headed back to the States.

Despite the warning from the chairman of Coca-Cola, Wellings proceeded with the purchase, tripling Cadbury's share of the U.S. soft-drink market to 16 percent, and 45 percent of the non-cola market. Goizueta turned on Cadbury. When Coke launched Fruitopia in 1994, it signed a separate U.K. distributor, claiming Cadbury's alternative beverage Oasis left no room for Fruitopia. In March 1996, at the start of the key summer selling season, CCE abruptly dumped Cadbury's A&W, 7-Up, and three smaller brands from its delivery trucks. Finally, with Goizueta's approval, CCE approached Cadbury with an offer to buy out its 50 percent stake in the joint venture.

The partnership had come to a bitter end, making Goizueta zero-for-two in joint venture partnerships with Nestlé and Cadbury. The breakdowns highlighted a lesson about Goizueta's inability to work with people he could not control. With the anchor bottler investments, which comprised major equity holdings in the partner's core business, Goizueta always made certain to own a high-enough stake that he could have some equity control. In addition, the anchor bottlers were closely aligned companies, totally dependent on Coke for their syrup, and were contractually very weak in their partnerships with Coke. That is how Goizueta liked it. Conversely, when he found he had no means of control over his partner, as was the case both with Nestlé and Cadbury, Goizueta quickly gave up.

INVESTING DIRECTLY IN PARENT COMPANIES DID NOT ALWAYS WORK either, as Goizueta learned, more than once, in India. Coke had abandoned India in 1977, grinding up all its glass bottles and abandoning its plants rather than acquiesce to demands that it reveal the secret formula for Coca-Cola to the socialist government that deposed Indira Gandhi. Pepsi, which also was forced out, had returned in 1988. But it was able to do so only after signing one of the most expensive barter deals ever, agreeing to export $5 of Indian-made products for every $1 of materials it imported into the country, and agreeing to fund research aimed at diversifying Indian farmers away from wheat and rice as part of a planned $1 billion overall investment. In 1990, the Indian government refused Coke's request to build a plant in India without a local investment partner, so Coke got back into India by purchasing a 10 percent stake in a joint venture with an Indian businessman, J.M. Rajan Pillai. The two companies busted their deal just days before the first Coca-Cola bottle rolled off a production line in October 1993 in Agra, India, home to the Taj Mahal. It is unclear why the partnership broke up, but Pillai later was convicted on unrelated fraud charges in Singapore, fled the country, and later returned to India, where he died in jail.

Goizueta soon found a bigger and much stronger partner, one that immediately gave Coke a huge presence in India, though not without some significant difficulties. It was a mark of Goizueta's management capabilities that he was able to retain John Hunter even after passing him over to select Ivester as Coke's new president. Hunter was peddling hard in India, and inked a deal to invest $40 million in Parle Exports, India's biggest bottler, as part of an overall $70 million investment. Overnight, the deal gave Coke control of 60 percent of the Indian soft-drink market, although all of it was in Parle brands, not Coke's, especially the top selling Thums Up. The deal also gave Coke immediate bottling clout, thanks to Parle's 54 plants distributed around the country. But the partners almost immediately ran into trouble, and Parle earned Goizueta's ire when Coke managers in India caught Parle continuing to make concentrate in its plants even after selling the rights to do so to Coke.

The partners resolved the dispute, but Goizueta seemed never to trust the Parle management again. In an act of retribution, he goaded Coke's managers in India to pull marketing support for Thums Up, and put all of Coke's marketing muscle behind developing the Coca-Cola brand. Perhaps it was a smart long-term move, but in its initial three years of operation, the spending shift still proved unable to vault Coke anywhere close to leadership in India's soft-drink sweepstakes. Even without meaningful marketing support, Thums Up remained India's strongest brand, with a 40 percent share. Coca-Cola's 20 percent trailed both Thums Up and Pepsi-Cola's 30 percent. "Thums Up got neglected by Coke, but the brand was so resilient it still sells more than Coke," gloated Parle chairman Ramesh Chauhan.

THE ANCHOR BOTTLER RELATIONSHIPS PROVED FAR EASIER TO HANdle and far more successful in building Coke's presence around the globe. Coke and its anchor bottlers seemed able to find strategies that benefited them both with little significant acrimony like the sort that destroyed the relationship with Parle. The anchor bottlers played a significant role in building Coke's market share throughout the world, in places as varied as Mexico, eastern Europe, South Africa, and Australia. As he turned his attention to the hugely attractive but incredibly expensive developing markets of Asia and the Pacific Rim, Goizueta turned to the anchor bottlers as a key to Coke's future, a source of connections and capital in places where Coke and its partners often had to build an entire soft drink industry—bottling, distribution, retail outlets, and customers—literally from the ground up.

China represented the most massive potential opportunity, if only it could be developed. The world's most populous country had special importance for Goizueta. It was one of the countries he first traveled to after jumping to the top echelon of Coke's management, and one he particularly enjoyed boasting about to Robert Woodruff in notes home from those trips. American executives for years have mused wistfully about the economic potential of China's 1.2-billion population. "If everyone bought one pair of shoes . . ." the thinking goes. But Goizueta proved to be one of the few who was making a good business out of China, thanks largely to partnerships with two anchor bottlers, the Swire Group of Hong Kong and, later, the Kerry Group of Malaysia.

Coke had struggled in China through most of the 1980s, constrained by the inability of local governments to provide enough capital to fuel a meaningful building program. In 1988, Goizueta turned to Swire, one of his first formal anchor bottlers, and asked them to help Coke develop bottling plants particularly on the coast of China. In 1990, Coke turned its first profit in China, and in 1993, Goizueta gave powerful evidence of the potential he saw in China by agreeing to a host of concessions in negotiations with the Chinese government. He promised to develop local soft drinks that would give cash income to Chinese farmers by including their produce as part of the flavoring, and he vowed to assist in transferring technology ranging from hygiene procedures to packaging to distribution improvements. In return, Coke earned the right to build ten new plants in China as part of a $500 million investment program. Goizueta's objective: have 23 plants operating in China by the end of 1997.

To build in China as quickly as he wanted to, Goizueta realized, he would need more than the combined capital resources and political skills of Coke and Swire. He turned quickly to Robert Kuok, a reclusive Malaysian billionaire who is one of the best connected businesspeople in Asia. Kuok's Kerry Group is one of the world's largest sugar traders, and Kuok has strong connections in China's interior, while Swire is best on the coast. To woo Kuok, Goizueta relied primarily on Doug Daft, head of Coke's Middle and Far East region. Daft first met with Kuok at the Kerry-owned Shangri-La Hotel in Hong Kong, then quickly developed their relationship by emphasizing their shared interest in Asian art. Goizueta, meanwhile, found a simple way to bond with the reserved sugar magnate. In choosing the Chinese translation for his name, Goizueta adopted exactly the same characters as Kuok as a sign of honor, and he indulged Kuok's passion for golf whenever possible.

JUST AS HE HAD QUICKLY TAKEN TO OLYMPICS CHIEF SAMARANCH in part because of the similarity in their backgrounds, Goizueta quickly befriended Kuok in part because the two also had fairly parallel life stories. Kuok was raised the eldest son of entrepreneurial fathers, sent away to school, and was expected to return to the family business. After the Japanese took control of Malaysia in 1941, Kuok struck out on his own after college by taking a job with a huge multinational corporation, Mitsubishi Corp., in a trading company office in his home province. Kuok went back to work with his father after the war and was left to run the family business practically on his own after his father died suddenly in 1948. From fairly unimpressive origins, he built a regional superpower through his entrepreneurial drive and strategic vision. He carried the courtliness of his prepschool upbringing, yet an engaging and disarming personality when working in partnership with peers. Like Goizueta, Kuok believed in the idea that a business must operate as if it were locally owned in every country where it has a presence. "I adapt like a chameleon to the particular society where I am operating at the moment," Kuok declared, in words that echoed Goizueta's desire for Coca-Cola to be a multilocal company.

Despite their similar backgrounds and outlooks, Goizueta and Kuok had different strategies for building their huge, highly profitable enterprises. While Goizueta narrowed Coke's focus to essentially one line of products, Kuok was an aggressive conglomerateur, diversifying away from the sugar and rice trading that built his initial fortune into hotels, commercial and residential real estate, beverages, and publishing. While Goizueta worked hard to develop a complex system for measuring the economic value of individual business lines, Kuok focused on sales volume as a measure of a business' health. Both men took naturally to people who could express an inner humility, although Kuok unlike Goizueta bore a natural suspicion of anybody who touted an M.B.A. as a credential of business know-how. Ultimately, one of the most important shared characteristics between Goizueta and Kuok was their belief in the value of joint ventures as a way to share risk. "When I'm in doubt, I chat," Kuok explained to *Forbes* magazine in a rare interview. "One of the best ways is to offer a cleverer man than yourself a joint venture deal, and if it's poison, he'll say it's an awful thing."

It is impossible to know whether Kuok recognized the tactic when Goizueta turned it on him in 1993, but Kuok saw the opportunity as anything but poison. Kuok was thrilled when Daft invited his investment into Coke's China adventure. "I thought, 'My god, this is a gift from heaven,'" Kuok recalled. Within weeks of signing his deal with Coke, Kuok had signed letters of intent to build bottling plants in Sechuan province, China's most populous, in the central province of Hubei, and in Shenyang in the northeastern part of the country. By 1995, thanks largely to Kuok's rapid deployment, Coke and its anchor bottlers had ten plants under simultaneous construction in China, the most ever in one country.

For some Chinese, the growth smacked of colonization and was too rapidly changing the social fabric of the areas surrounding the plants. A group of Chinese politicians in 1996 began targeting Coke as an undesirable foreign influence. Chen Bixia, a legislator from the Guangdong province in the southeastern part of the country, led a group of 32 lawmakers who proposed that China "appropriately restrict" Coke's future expansion. They scoffed at Coke's claim that soft-drink plants represented an important transfer of technology. "Beverages are not high technology or new technology," said Bixia. "It is unnecessary to give Coca-Cola and Pepsi market access in exchange for technology. We should protect traditional beverages and help them get on their feet."

Goizueta had seen in India and other countries how even a fairly localized political protest could have devastating national implications. And since China remained a delicate situation even 15 years after Coke's return to bottling on the mainland, he pounced to protect his investment and opportunity there. He commissioned Peter Nolan, an economics professor from Cambridge University, to study the impact of Coke's investment on employment and efficiency in specific markets where Coke and its anchor bottlers had constructed bottling plants. Nolan's study found that in Tianjin, a plant modernization increased production by 250 percent from 1990 to 1994, while profits per worker jumped nearly 400 percent. Every job at the plant created six supplier jobs and nearly 3.5 permanent retail jobs, the Coke-commissioned study claimed.

Not satisfied to rely on the academic report, Goizueta personally traveled to Beijing in September 1995 to meet with Chinese President Jiang Zemin. Goizueta never publicly discussed specifics of the Jiang meeting. But he seemed self-assured when he talked about his impression of Coke's popularity in China. "We are now very much welcomed, very much liked, and not only by the consumers but also by government officials," he said. "They view us as American, but also as local. Coca-Cola is ours, but to them it's also a symbol that to become more like Americans they consume Coca-Cola."

To Goizueta, it was important that Coke not lose momentum. Already in southeastern Asia, Goizueta and Ivester had made speed a primary objective as Coke moved to develop new markets. Ivester had made the point dramatically in a 1995 trip to Vietnam. When he learned during a meeting with Coke's joint venture bottler in Hanoi that a plant under construction was only half the size it needed to be to meet projected demand, Ivester grabbed a telephone, tracked down a second bottling line sitting on a ship in Singapore, and had it sent to Hanoi. "We push hard on discipline and precise communications," he explained. "Know the facts and be honest about the facts. Once you get the facts, the decision is pretty easy." The bottling line went into operation a year faster than originally planned. The point was made. Coke's top brass wanted nothing to stand in the way of growth. People in the field needed to identify obstacles to growth and find ways to remove or vault them.

Goizueta wanted that kind of thinking in the ticklish job of exploiting Coke's opportunities in China. Instinctively, he knew that he could hold up China as a model of speedy success against all odds if only he could make a blitz into the huge, underdeveloped market on the coast or in the interior. In China, with its history of mercurial political change, Goizueta pushed for quick action to take advantage of the openings at hand. By 1996, he boasted that Coke had built ten plants in three years, in addition to the ten that were currently under construction. It was the fastest building program in any country ever. One of the plants in central China went up in nine months—a world record. The rapid deployment occurred despite occasional delays caused by negotiations and other, less predictable factors.

Coke was building so fast, it had a hard time finding people qualified to run its plants and manage distribution and sales. "Our biggest challenge is finding people," Goizueta mused in the summer of 1996. To facilitate the hiring of 100 people each week in China, Goizueta approved the creation of a training program at the respected Fudan University in Shanghai as the leading edge of a $2 million investment in training some 1,800 Chinese employees in 1996. Reports that reached Goizueta's office indicated that Coke's people on the ground in China considered the Chinese to be ambitious and serious about their work, but indecisive and not very creative.

In late 1996, Goizueta saw no need to slow down, but the Chinese government did not see it that way. Chinese officials would not guarantee additional building beyond the current memorandum of understanding with the government. "We want to put in ten new plants every three years for as long as we can," Goizueta said. And he wanted his negotiating teams in China to push hard and fast. "Plants take nine months. Negotiations take years, sometimes five years. Many of the people we work with have no concept of time," he complained. Even so, the anti-Coke legislators in the National People's Congress won, at least temporarily, their battle to put a stop to new development by Coke. The government would make no promises about future development beyond those agreed to in the original 1993 understanding, though Goizueta fully expected to win new expansion rights once the current building program was complete.

China was valuable in its own right, and had huge potential. But it also had payoffs that Goizueta had not anticipated, foremost among them the introduction to Robert Kuok. By 1996, Goizueta had drawn the sugar billionaire ever deeper into the world of Coca-Cola. He invited Kuok to the Olympics, assigning Doug Daft as his personal escort through the maze of sporting and social events, and the next year satisfied one of Kuok's fondest wishes by introducing him to Warren Buffett when Kuok visited Coke's annual meeting in Wilmington, Delaware. The Olympic visit gave Goizueta an opportunity to persuade Kuok to move ahead with a plan to invest in Coke anchor bottler Coca-Cola Amatil. Just a few days after leaving Atlanta, Kuok announced he would pay $530 million for an 8.4 percent stake in Amatil, which had just taken over Coke's bottling plants in Indonesia. The Kuok investment would add both connections and capital to Coke's drive to develop the vastly attractive but extremely frustrating Indonesian market.

THE ISLAND NATION OF INDONESIA HAD ALWAYS BEEN AN UNRE-quited love for Goizueta. By rote, he could tick off the factors that made the market attractive. The Indonesian archipelago of nearly 200 million people straddles the equator and has a humid year-round temperature of 80 degrees Fahrenheit. Because the Indonesian population is predominantly Muslim, Coke does not have to compete against alcohol in trying to capture as much as possible of the average person's daily consumption of liquids. "We call it soft-drink heaven," Goizueta concluded.

While the potential may have been heavenly, Goizueta was realistic enough to know that Indonesia looked a lot more like purgatory at the bottom line. Nearly a decade after he began spending heavily in Indonesia in 1987, he had succeeded only in boosting per-capita consumption of Coca-Cola products to nine eight-ounce servings a year. That was an improvement from the 6 ounces the average Indonesian drank in 1991, but still the third-lowest among the 30 most-populous nations in the world. In fact, the two other large nations that trailed Indonesia's per capita consumption also were in Asia: China, at 5 drinks per year and India, at 3. The Asian strategy had huge potential, but there clearly was plenty of work to do.

The Indonesian per capitas were not high, but competition, at least, was virtually non-existent, with Coke soft drinks accounting for more than 70 percent of the Indonesian industry. The market had proven notoriously resistant to development. Distribution often relied on ferry boats, water taxis, and bicycle carts. Goizueta grudgingly approved the development of massive marketing programs, including a sampling project that set a Coca-Cola record by distributing 100,000 servings in a single week. But he knew sampling would not have any long-term effect until after Coke made a sustained capital investment in putting Coke bottles into more Indonesian hands. "No amount of savvy marketing or fancy commercials or sponsorships will do anything for you unless you have the trucks, the vending machines, and the warehouses," Goizueta figured. "There's no sense in having a marketing program if you don't have a bottling plant." He hoped Kuok's investment would create an opportunity for Coke to export its marketing know-how.

The anchor bottler system had racked up a strong performance since the concept first took shape in the 1980s, and he hoped Kuok's investment in Amatil would help generate the same kind of action in Indonesia. By 1996, Goizueta was expanding the anchor bottler idea strategically around the globe to strengthen Coke's hold on local markets and to advance a global strategy of penetration and performance. With Coke's return to South Africa, he designated an anchor bottler to develop that country and the rest of sub-Saharan Africa. The brewer and bottler, Carlsberg A/S, openly and successfully campaigned for designation as Coke's Nordic anchor bottler. The final new anchor of Goizueta's tenure was Coca-Cola Erfreschungsgetränke, with its territory designated as eastern and southern Germany. The move raised eyebrows both because Coca-Cola Enterprises was the key investor behind Erfreschungsgetränke, and beverage analysts were watching closely to see whether CCE ultimately might become as big an acquirer overseas as it had been in the domestic market, where it now owned nearly 70 percent of U.S. production.

Goizueta clearly was pleased to see the anchors use sports-themed advertising throughout the developing markets. He pushed for a plan to bring athletes from China to carry the Olympic flame in the torch run in the United States, and he endorsed the use of sports sponsorships to redevelop Coke's presence in South Africa through its new anchor bottler in that country. In 1997, just days after boxer Evander Holyfield lost part of his ear to the jaws of Mike Tyson en route to regaining the heavyweight championship of the world, Coke shipped Holyfield, a former Pepsi pitchman, to South Africa for a promotional tour that climaxed with Holyfield's meeting with South African President Nelson Mandela.

WHILE HE WAS OBSESSED WITH BUILDING COKE'S GLOBAL SYSTEM, Goizueta still took a direct, personal interest in the minutia of day-to-day decisions at the level of individual markets and products, even individual personnel moves. He approved the decision to launch Surge in early 1997, a high-sugar, high-caffeine competitor to the fast-growing Mountain Dew, in markets across the country without formal test marketing. The decision bought Coke a day in court, as a Chicago-based soda company complained that the Surge slogan, "Feel the Urge," was stolen from its own campaign for a line of ginseng-based drinks. Flush with the success of the 20-ounce contour bottle, one of Goizueta's few new-product successes since Diet Coke nearly 15 years earlier, he pushed for the launch of a contoured can. The steel-sided cans performed acceptably, if not remarkably, in a test in Germany. But U.S. bottlers' concerns about cost and quality delayed the domestic rollout.

On the international front, Goizueta's interest in the nitty gritty of the Coca-Cola system extended to Russia, where Coke had seized market leadership from Pepsi in late August 1996, and where Coke in a single day opened four plants—highlighting Coke's ongoing $600 million investment in the country. Japan was a different case. In his company's most profitable market, Goizueta pushed to use Coke's strong presence in vending machines and other marketing tools to blunt a generic-brand onslaught in 1994, and also called for high-speed development of new, noncarbonated, noncola brands to appeal to fickle Japanese taste buds. Goizueta recognized that the unpredictable Japanese palate could turn to any new fad, and wanted to make certain Coke was there to please it. The company's Japanese marketers responded, pushing up sales of teas and coffees 25 percent in 1996, while carbonated beverages remained flat. In Japan and other markets, fermented milk or canned coffee were fine substitutes for Coca-Cola, so long as a Coke product was making its way down consumers' throats. "We're after a share of stomach," Goizueta pronounced.

The complexity and variety of decisions reflected the widespread nature of the Coca-Cola system and the overwhelming substance of Goizueta's job. During his 16 years as chief executive of Coke, the company had more than quadrupled in size, to an expected $19.5 billion for 1997. Goizueta had dumped all of Coke's extraneous businesses, and realigned the foods operation, now dubbed Minute Maid

Co., to focus on strengthening its juice drink brands. Two of Coke's division presidents were operating companies that were larger than the entire Coca-Cola Company when Goizueta took charge. Goizueta had continued driving the dividend payout ratio down, to nearly 30 percent of earnings, which left more capital for him to invest in bottler deals, product research, and other opportunities around the globe.

GOIZUETA DID NOT PLAN IT THIS WAY, BUT BOTTLER DEALS WERE becoming an increasingly substantial part of Coke's financial performance. "We became an investment banking firm specializing in bottler deals," Don Keough recalled about his era, and after he left in 1993, the pace of the deals accelerated substantially. In the first half of 1997 alone, Coke had put together more than $7 billion in deals involving anchor bottlers, an all-time record. It was a big number, and even though Coke's share of the deals was far less than the total price tag, the impact on Coke was large enough to draw increasing scrutiny from Wall Street analysts wary of the impact that Goizueta's burgeoning bottler brokerage business was having on Coke's operating results.

Goizueta liked to view the bottler deals as a predictable and routine part of Coke's ongoing business strategy, and had worked hard to train Wall Street analysts to accept that thinking, treating the credits or charges from bottling transactions as part of Coke's regular operating results. In a way, it was sensible to look at the numbers that way because Coke's big participation in bottling deals had established a fairly regular stream of income over the years. But as the numbers grew larger, and the risk to the analysts' reputations increased as the price/earnings ratio on Coke's stock climbed ever higher, a cadre of Coke watchers on Wall Street began complaining that Goizueta and Ivester were manipulating Coke's financial numbers and risking future earnings disappointments with the way they accounted for the bottling transactions.

In his 1995 letter to shareholders, Goizueta had pointed out that his aim in communicating Coke's strategic vision was fairly simple. "State expectations. Meet or exceed those expectations. Repeat," he wrote. "The third step, of course, is the toughest." Some of the analysts believed Goizueta was trying to make the third step less difficult by adding or subtracting hundreds of millions to Coke's operating results simply by accelerating or slowing the size and number of bottling deals. Analyst Roy Burry of Oppenheimer & Co. led the charge in identifying and criticizing this decision. In 1996, he noted, Coke listed outlays of $645 million and sales credits of $1.3 billion from bottler deals alone, for a gain of $657 million. That represented a significant 17 percent chunk of Coke's total operating income of $3.9 billion. And the early results from 1997 indicated the impact of bottling deals would grow over time.

The transactions themselves were a significant factor, but they bred inconsistencies in other aspects of Coke's financial results. To massage the numbers, Burry figured, Coke could influence cost ratios and sales growth figures simply by the timely purchase or sale of bottling operations. And when that did not work, Ivester and Goizueta often made significant one-time purchases or inventory adjustments so that one-time gains from bottler deals would not blow Coke's earnings stream out of whack. In 1997, Burry and other analysts focused on a $200 million inventory writedown as an example of Coke's financial legerdemain. All companies massage their income statements, but Coke stood out in its aggressive and consistent approach and its listing of such major transactions as part of its operating performance. "Coke's accounting has raised substantial questions," Burry complained.

The criticism from Burry and others reached a crescendo during the summer of 1997, and began to have an impact on the price of Coca-Cola stock, as did price competition and fears about the impact a strong dollar would have on Coke's financial results. After tripling from June 1994 to June 1997, Coca-Cola shares fell back from their peak of nearly $73, and traded steadily downward. The stock barely budged when Goizueta fell ill with cancer in late August, a tribute to Wall Street's comfort with Ivester as an heir apparent, but it would continue falling in late October as concerns about the strong dollar escalated. Near the midpoint of the decline in the stock price, before Goizueta fell ill, Coke finally agreed to place bottler transactions into the capital gains section of Coke's income statement. Burry and others groused that the company had done so only because Coke was now facing a period of diminished activity in bottler transactions, so the old accounting method had little use.

GOIZUETA SPENT INCREASING AMOUNTS OF TIME FOCUSED ON THE world at large. Always a philosophical person, he took to heart a book by Christian philosopher Michael Novak. He gave a copy of it to Andrew Young when the former United Nations ambassador and Atlanta mayor visited his office, and he proselytized the book so much at the Coke tower that it became virtually required reading for anyone who came into contact with Goizueta. One of the book's main themes focused on the obligation of business to society, the impact that corporations do and should have on the lives of their customers, employees, and society at large. To make its point, the book opened a chapter with a quote from none other than Roberto Goizueta. "While we were once perceived as simply providing services, selling products, and employing people, business now shares in much of the responsibility for our global quality of life," Goizueta had said at Yale in 1992. "Successful companies will handle this heightened sense of responsibility quite naturally, if not always immediately." He concluded the Yale speech, at which a donation from Coke had funded an academic chair for interdisciplinary studies at his alma mater, by noting that the success of customer-driven businesses was changing the nature of power in the global economy. "I believe this shift will lead to a future in which the institutions with most influence by and large will be businesses," Goizueta told his Yale audience.

Five years later, Goizueta still saw those forces at work, but feared that business was failing to meet its responsibility. If this continued, he warned, government would step back into the vacuum, and limit the opportunity of business to spread the benefits of investment efficiently in underdeveloped markets around the world—not just Indonesia and South Africa but in places like Los Angeles and Detroit. "The danger of corporate business downsizing we see today is that at the very time government's role in economic affairs is being scaled back, as urged by business executives, many businesses appear unwilling to step up their commitments to anything but profits," Goizueta wrote to Jeffrey Sonnenfeld, a well-regarded Emory University business professor who headed the famous CEO College at which executives from around the world gathered to seek solutions to their common challenges.

In Goizueta's view, business would have only one shot at taking a leadership role in promoting the broader welfare of society. If business leaders fail in this, he warned, "businesspeople will become marginalized and without the moral authority to demand a hearing from government or the people. If business becomes so marginalized, it will help confirm the view held in many quarters that business executives are interested only in furthering selfish aims and are insensitive to the wider concerns of society. This would become a sad but accurate commentary of our times for future historians to make." Sonnenfeld was impressed not only by the depth of Goizueta's thinking, but by the fact that he personally had written the thoughtful two-page epistle after a brief encounter at a luncheon earlier that mid-summer day in 1997.

Roberto Goizueta demonstrated throughout his career that he could set an agenda for his business and execute it. And he emerged as an unlikely leader when other executives at other companies noticed, then followed suit. He had made economic value a fashionable calculus of strategic planning, and pushed the notions of the streamlined organization and the multilocal business to profitable extremes. For five years, he had refined his beliefs about the leadership role that businesses can and must take in addressing society's ills. He hoped that modern businesspeople would prove up to the task, and still bravely declared that he felt they would.

HE TRIED TO MAKE CERTAIN THAT COKE AT LEAST SET THE RIGHT example in its own backyard. When the Boys & Girls Clubs of America presented him with a request for a major gift in early 1997, Goizueta expressed interest. He was, after all, a board member. But he would move forward only if the gift could be structured so that Coke got some business benefit from the donation. This was vintage Goizueta philanthropy: getting bang for the buck, even while giving the money away. Contrary to Robert Woodruff's approach of making anonymous donations throughout his life, Goizueta wanted Coca-Cola to take bows whenever the company made a donation. Early in his tenure, he had organized all of Coca-Cola's corporate gifts under a new entity, the Coca-Cola Foundation, and he specifically charged it to get publicity whenever possible. "We always kept our giving in the closet," the foundations' first president Donald Greene explained. "We reflected Mr. Woodruff's discreet style and never took credit. It's not that we plan to be boastful now, but we plan to step out in our name and give at a level we can be proud of." Goizueta particularly favored giving that benefited children—Coke's target market—and in 1989 approved a ten-year, $50 million giving program targeted at public and private elementary and secondary schools.

Coke's corporate gift to the Boys & Girls Clubs in the summer of 1997 perfectly fit Goizueta's desire to get credit for what Coke gave away, and to tailor giving to Coke's key customers. Goizueta was leading a movement called "strategic philanthropy." In exchange for Coke's commitment to help the Boys & Girls Clubs raise $60 million over ten years, the company won the right to push Pepsi out of most clubs across the country and launch fund-raising programs tied into Coke's promotions. Goizueta turned down the original request for a $100 million program, but approved $60 million, and then strived to make certain that Coke made its biggest donation ever as he called for companies to focus on strategic philanthropy. "This initiative is simply about creating value," he told the Boys & Girls Club convention in July of 1997. "This initiative is about raising $60 million for your clubs over the next ten years." Translation: There was plenty of money available, but the Boys & Girls Clubs would have to earn it.

While he believed in corporate philanthropy, Goizueta himself was not known personally as a giver. Unlike Woodruff, who anonymously gave millions away for causes ranging from eradicating malaria in southern Georgia to the fine arts in Atlanta before finally owning up to his charity in the last few years of his life, there is no indication that Goizueta ever anonymously gave his money away, no instance of sizable anonymous donations and no parallel to the open secret in Atlanta about a "Mr. Anonymous" that everyone knew was Robert W. Woodruff. When Emory named its business school for Goizueta, that was in recognition of a $10 million grant in Goizueta's honor given by the Woodruff Foundation, on which Goizueta served as a board member. Likewise, the money behind the creation of the endowed academic chair at Yale University came from Coke, not out of Goizueta's pocket. Ever since fleeing Cuba, Goizueta had placed great emphasis on the importance of education, and education remained the focus of his philanthropic urges. But just as consistently, he relied on his company, and not his own pocketbook, to provide the resources for him to realize his goals in giving.

As Goizueta reached retirement age, people involved in Atlanta's charitable foundations wondered aloud when and if he would begin bestowing largesse on the community, as Woodruff had done throughout his career. In 1996, he answered the question by granting $38 million in Coke stock to the Goizueta Foundation, a charitable trust he had established in his name. It was a sizable gift, certainly. But it did not satisfy critics among Atlanta's philanthropy groups who expected more from someone of Goizueta's wealth and civic stature. At the time of the donation, it represented only around 3 percent of Goizueta's net worth—hardly enough to put him in the league of noteworthy givers like Woodruff, contemporaries like Home Depot founder Bernard Marcus, or headline grabbers like Ted Turner, whose $1 billion pledge to the United Nations seemed motivated almost as much by an appetite for publicity as by the desire to do good.

To OUTSIDERS, THE ESTABLISHMENT OF A CHARITABLE FOUNDATION seemed like a certain sign that Goizueta was migrating toward retirement. Earlier in his career, every major Coca-Cola undertaking bore Goizueta's strong personal imprimatur. Now, as his sixty-sixth birthday approached, two major new undertakings were more closely tied to Doug Ivester than to Goizueta. The effort to develop a "learning culture" at Coca-Cola and an investment in a new information system called "Project Infinity" that started with a $60 million investment both were part of Ivester's personal agenda. An e-mail, voice mail, and systems addict, Ivester had originated the Project Infinity idea and was its chief proponent. And he believed strongly in an efficient and predictable environment for dissemating knowledge—a learning culture—as a competitive advantage in the economy of the future. At the time Goizueta fell ill, little was known outside the company about progress on those two initiatives, but it was clear that whatever came of them would be credited to Doug Ivester.

It did appear that Goizueta was headed toward a retirement of some sort. There seemed to be a part of him, though, that delighted in keeping people inside and outside of Coke guessing about his plans. As much as he made a point of calling Ivester his "partner," just as he had done with Keough, he also continued his habit of occasionally giving his number two an off-the-cuff put-down or rude remark. After the attack on eastern Europe, he boasted to *Fortune* magazine that Ivester "has the nerve of a night prowler." In a locker room or employee rally, such a comment might sound like appropriate braggadocio. But it did not do Ivester any good in the pages of *Fortune*, at a time Ivester was struggling to carve out an image seasoned executive ready to take the reigns at Coke.

Goizueta believed it motivated people when there was some un-certainty about whether they ultimately would get a big promotion, and he felt Ivester was no exception. When asked what he was look-ing for in a chief executive, he explained that he had simple ex-pectations. "Energy is number one," Goizueta said. "Intellectual courage is extremely important too, intellectual courage to go out and do something." It clearly hurt Ivester that Coke USA had not performed better under him, that the new advertising campaigns by Creative Artists Agency had not fared better, that Diet Coke re-mained stuck in the doldrums. But it seemed odd to hear Goizueta question Iveseter's drive and desire for Coke's top job. "He doesn't have enough impetus," Goizueta complained. A lack of impetus was never a shortcoming previously associated with the hard driving Ivester.

To some people, Goizueta's open criticism of Ivester signaled a fail-ing in Ivester that Goizueta seemed to consider insurmountable. Meanwhile, Goizueta himself seemed in no hurry to retire. He regaled friends and Coke executives with the story of a shareholder's comment to him after the 1996 annual meeting. "You should be like the Pope and never retire," he recalled the shareowner saying. To some who heard the complaints about Ivester and the ruminations about Pope-hood, Goizueta had the earmarks of a King Lear, unwilling to step away from his throne, out of the spotlight, and on to a life of much di-minished purpose and power.

Indeed, as much as he had made it clear that people should consider Ivester his heir, Goizueta left the question open by never making a move to leave, and never explicitly stating that Ivester would succeed him. Even until his death, Goizueta never publicly said that Ivester should follow him as Coke's next chairman and chief executive officer. Well aware of his reverence toward Woodruff, some inside the company speculated he might try to keep a hand in Coke's affairs after retire-ment as Woodruff had done, perhaps by staying on as a non-executive chairman. Such thinking did not square with Goizueta's belief in the need for new chief executives to have unfettered reign of their company, without interference from their predecessors. But it did fit with the conception that Goizueta might never be able to release his hold on Coke, the job he loved almost as much as his wife and family.

As Goizueta set plans to leave Atlanta for what would be his last business trip, some executives inside the company speculated that he might be on the verge of making an announcement about succession. He was traveling to Monaco to meet with a group of Coke's largest bottlers, which would be a good audience for such major news. But to most people an announcement on the Monaco trip seemed unlikely. First, Ivester was not making the trip with him. If Ivester was in fact his chosen successor, it would have made no sense to make such an important move without him present. Second, Goizueta would make an announcement like that for maximum effect, in Atlanta, where people would care most. Even so, many inside the company still believed an announcement would have come had Coke's stock not fallen so abruptly beginning in June.

Goizueta had said through the years that he did not want to die behind his desk at Coke. After a career of living his company almost literally every day of the year, he claimed to desire some form of retirement. "I don't want to go directly from here to Arlington" cemetery, he claimed. And retirement was on his mind at one of the last public functions he attended, a dinner honoring Home Depot's Bernie Marcus, who had just announced his own retirement. At the event, Goizueta sought out Marcus and ruminated with one of the few people in Atlanta's business community who was both a contemporary and as close to being a peer of the chairman of Coca-Cola as anyone in Atlanta could get.

The two men agreed that they had become the souls of their companies, and that souls lived on long after the chief executive retires. At the time, there was a metaphysical ring to the conversation worthy of some of Goizueta's most inspired philosophical ruminations. A few weeks later, it proved quite literally true.

Epilogue: The Song at Church

In sixteen years as chairman and chief executive of The Coca-Cola Company, Roberto C. Goizueta never missed a board meeting. He attended his last on July 19, 1997. The night before, he joined the board for an outing to an Atlanta Braves baseball game, and spent the evening with a group of power elite who happened to be his friends. A candid snapshot memorializing the occasion is one of the last photographs of Goizueta, and certainly the last in which he appears with the people who formed his inner circle.

A smiling Don Keough was the man admired throughout Coke and sometimes begrudged by Goizueta because he so naturally fell into the role of "the heart of Coca-Cola." Investor Warren Buffett revered Goizueta because he had the good sense not to muck up the simplicity of Coca-Cola. Investment banker Herb Allen brought Columbia Pictures to Goizueta, awarded him an $86 million pay check for 1991, and later sold him on the advertising switch that led to the creation of "Always Coca-Cola." Attending the game but not in the picture was Jimmy Williams, who stores Coke's secret formula in his vaults at SunTrust Banks, and played a key insider's role in the gloomy game of corporate intrigue that brought Goizueta to the top of Coke, was Goizueta's close neighbor, counselor, and friend.

A few weeks after the board meeting, Goizueta traveled to Monte Carlo, where he met with fifty of Coke's top international bottlers to discuss the continuing game of global conquest in which the bottlers play such an essential role. The bottlers, after all, are the ones who

300

provide the bulk of the capital investment that builds the Coca-Cola system around the world. During his reign, Goizueta had transformed the role of Coke's chairman from someone who carried the bottlers' suitcases, to one who brought them cases filled with cash. They had not trusted him when he first won the job, and now they trusted no one else.

Goizueta added a day trip to Spain to his itinerary, and took a minute to phone Keough with news. The same pair of shoes that had sold for $45 when they had traveled together during the 1980s had jumped to the ungodly price of $50 in late 1997. "They're expensive now," Goizueta wryly joked.

Returning home, Goizueta never quite got over the jet lag from his trip. On Tuesday, September 2, he lunched with Andrew Conway, an analyst from the Morgan Stanley investment firm who once worked as an intern at Coca-Cola. Goizueta handily fielded Conway's questions about Coke's three-year and five-year outlook. He promised that volume growth, the key measure underlying all of Coke's financial numbers, would continue at around 7 percent for at least five years, perhaps ten. "Even in the most difficult economic times, we can manage our portfolio to achieve volume growth," he promised. He reminisced about his sixteen years running Coke, and talked about the importance of focus. He did not say so in so many words, but the gist was simple: Coke is it.

Chatting amiably about his trip, drawing on a True Menthol cigarette, Goizueta made a rare admission for a private man who prided himself on his stamina and meticulous appearance. "Andrew, I'm a little fatigued," he said. "I haven't quite recouped from the trip."

Four days later, Goizueta went to Emory University Hospital. Doctors immediately detected a growth on his lung. Cancer. The Coca-Cola publicity apparatus, complying with securities laws that require immediate distribution of material information, put out a press release, calling it only a "growth" on his lung. They spoke about his vigor, and his plans to return.

For Goizueta's family, the news was a shock, if not a surprise. Goizueta had smoked since preparatory school in Cuba. Rare for a chief executive in these days of virtual prohibition, he routinely lit up his True Menthols during interviews with reporters. He had tried cutting back his smoking a few years earlier, but failed. His children knew better than to try to goad him into quitting. They knew he was too stubborn. Instead, they had set their sites on his wife Olguita, but she kept smoking, too.

For the next two weeks, Goizueta stayed in the Woodruff Suite on the penthouse floor of the Emory hospital. Accessible only with a special elevator key, the wood-paneled suite of rooms was built for Robert W. Woodruff, the longtime Coke chieftain who was Goizueta's mentor and the man most responsible for elevating him to the chairmanship. The suite is not used without clearance from Coca-Cola. Woodruff himself breathed his last there in 1985.

In his week-long stay at the hospital, Goizueta tried to conduct his company's business. Out of habit, he routinely checked Coke's stock price on the machine in the room adjoining his. Two fax machines carried reports from Coke's outposts around the world. He reviewed financial plans with chief financial officer James Chestnut and global strategy with president and chief operating officer M. Douglas Ivester. Doctors and nurses queued behind executives in suits, settling comfortably into the holding pattern that typically applied at Goizueta's office at Coke's North Avenue tower.

The medical team knew quickly that the situation was dire. Within a week, they figured Goizueta had only a few months to live. The Coca-Cola publicists tried to put up a brave front, but that cracked on September 15, when doctors decided they needed to attack the cancer with a combination of chemotherapy and radiation. It sounded ominous. Goizueta returned home after the treatments, but the announcement of the dual regimen marked the point at which the assumption, both inside and outside the company, was that it was only a matter of time.

Goizueta was home on September 21 when he received a get well card signed by 2,000 Coca-Cola employees. Touched, he asked Olguita to read aloud every signature and expression of support. Then he dictated a characteristic reply: "Please let my talented doctors and my terrific family worry about me. You, my Coca-Cola family, just worry about the company." If it sounded like a fairly bald "get back to work," that was not intended. But the private and regal Goizueta could not get comfortable with the thought of his employees feeling sorry for him. On September 26, he was too ill to attend the dedication of a building named in his honor at the Roberto C. Goizueta business school at Emory University. Still, when nurses or doctors asked how he was feeling, he routinely replied with a wry grin and a simple word in his Cuban-inflected baritone, "Fantastic."

Olguita spent her days by her husband's side, alternately buoying him, or being lifted herself by his strong spirit. His children and grandchildren visited frequently. His daughter, Olga, a lawyer-cum-home-maker, drove over from her Atlanta home while his son Roberto S. Goizueta flew down after opening a semester of theology classes at Loyola University of Chicago. The youngest, Javier, took time from his job with Procter & Gamble in Brazil. Goizueta's attention to detail and his authoritarian bearing never wavered. On one occasion, Olguita worked her way through the body of a letter from a business associate, but broke into "et cetera, et cetera" rather than reading obligatory pleasantries at the end. Goizueta looked sharply at her. "Don't et cetera me," he said. "Now start over, from the top."

On October 7, Goizueta returned to the hospital after developing a throat infection and fever as a result of the chemotherapy and radiation treatments. On October 16, 1997, the board of directors met without him for the first time in more than sixteen years. Jimmy Williams chaired the perfunctory meeting, which he adjourned after a discussion of succession but no formal action or proposals. Ivester had been Goizueta's heir apparent since 1993, and Goizueta's refusal publicly to anoint him had given rise to speculation that Goizueta had doubts about Ivester's shortcomings as a leader, corporate statesman, or motivator. "Those who need to know do know," was the best Goizueta ever offered. To those sitting in the pecan-paneled board room, the knowledge was so obvious now it was barely worth discussing. Ivester was the one.

By the time of the board meeting, it was clear that Goizueta had only days to live. At Coke's headquarters, the public relations staff took down reporters' home telephone numbers on October 17, in case there was news over the weekend. *The Atlanta Journal-Constitution* had completed work on a special section devoted to Goizueta. All the paper needed was a front-page headline.

Monsignor Edward J. Dillon of Holy Spirit Catholic Church, Goizueta's parish, shared Olguita's vigil at her husband's side. Roberto and Olguita had grown up together in Cuba, been betrothed since high school, and married immediately after college. They fled Castro together, had four children, and watched helplessly as a son died of leukemia. With Olguita's support, he had risen to the height of corporate America. And with her now, he was ready to die.

Goizueta asked to celebrate a final communion with Olguita late at night on October 18. At ten minutes after midnight, with Olguita cradling his head in her arms, Roberto C. Goizueta breathed his last.

Just after 4 A.M. in Atlanta in the dark early morning of October 18, 1997, Douglas Ivester picked up a telephone receiver and recorded a voice mail for urgent distribution to Coke's employees around the world. "It is with great sadness and a heavy heart that I report to you the passing of our chairman, Roberto Goizueta" Ivester began.

His voice trailed off in grief at the end of the sentence. Then Ivester's south Georgia twang resumed its dirgeful procession. "He loved this company and the associates because of what we were able to accomplish together. He will be sorely missed." Ivester ended the tribute, and the line went dead.

At the funeral service three days later, President Jimmy Carter and his wife Rosalyn headed a group of politicians sitting front left, and the Coke board sat front center, across the aisle from Goizueta's family. A group of American corporate elite headed by George M.C. Fisher, whom Goizueta recruited to head Kodak Corp., sat front right. Roger Enrico, chairman of PepsiCo., also attended. Former civil rights leader and United Nations Ambassador Andrew Young spoke about Goizueta's view of business as a social calling. Then Roberto S. Goizueta eulogized his father. Quoting Goizueta's belief that integrity in business "is the ultimate competitive advantage," the son's voice broke slightly before he could continue. "'Without it,' he said, 'You have nothing.'"

The formal Catholic service came to an end. Members of the Atlanta Symphony Orchestra played Bach's Fugue in G as Goizueta's two sons and four business associates carried the casket down the center aisle of the church. The fugue ended.

Then, quietly and slowly at first, but picking up tempo and volume as the casket moved down the aisle, came a familiar and unmistakable tune. On a hilltop in Europe in the 1970s, a multi-ethnic group of young people had etched the tune into people's minds around the world. No one inside Holy Spirit Catholic Church sang aloud. But almost as one throughout the congregation, the words rose to mind: "I'd like to teach the world to sing, in perfect harmony. I'd like to buy the world a Coke, and keep it company."

Roberto C. Goizueta, who had made it his life's mission to sell the world a simple moment of pleasure, could rest at last.

Notes

For a responsible journalist, any reporting project is an attempt to find and publish the truth as best as possible by interviewing people, reviewing records, researching published information, and locating other sources when available. We must assess the strength of our sources based on the limits of their own experience and knowledge, their biases, and their public and private agendas. My job as a reporter is to synthesize as many accounts as possible into a fair and accurate description of what truly transpired. I have done my best to accomplish this and wish to explain some of my methods and standards for doing so.

I strove in all cases independently to corroborate all comments, especially off-the-record comments, with any parties or records capable of providing relevant information. If an off-the-record remark was contradicted by a single fact, I did not use the remark and held up the remainder of that source's remarks to additional scrutiny. Since many of the people in the story have retired, changed jobs, or even died since the events in question, I did my best to locate their whereabouts through electronic databases, Internet telephone directories, and the like. Where appropriate for purposes of fairness, I have noted when I was unable to locate sources who otherwise might have wanted to comment on a subject in question. Where relevant, I also have noted when people have declined comment.

In cases where sources disagreed, I sought independent corroboration where possible, gave each person an opportunity to comment on the differing accounts of events, and often wound up with a version on which all parties could agree. In a few instances when parties did not agree and no independent means of verification presented itself, I have made a judgment as to the most likely version, and explained the differing interpretation in the chapter notes.

Not long after Mr. Goizueta decided not to cooperate, he requested through his spokesman Randy Donaldson that I stop phoning employees for purposes of this book. I honored this request in the case of people I did not know, but maintained contact with some pre-existing Coke sources. After Mr. Goizueta's death, I again sought cooperation from the company. Doug Ivester declined in writing.

All sources I contacted currently inside Coke and many sources outside the company requested that they make comments only on a not-for-attribution basis. In many cases, sources eventually allowed me to place comments on the record that they originally had made on a not-for-attribution basis. The beverage industry is a small global club, and Coke takes a keen interest in what people say about it, especially in a book that the company's chairman does not want written. In many cases, the generous pensions and severance payments made to ex-employees are done so with a contractual agreement that they not speak about the company without formal permission. Many of these people still do consulting work for Coke, or hope to do business with Coke one day. This does not entirely stop people from talking, of course, but does raise the stakes when they do.

The majority of the quotes attributed to Mr. Goizueta come from previously published articles or unpublished notes from previous interviews with him. In a few cases, I have made minor changes in verb tense to some of his comments, to help the narrative flow of the book. As detailed in the chapter notes, some Goizueta quotes are attributed to him by other sources, both those who would allow attribution and a few who would not.

As with any book, I have relied in some instances on previously published versions of some events. I have in all cases tried to establish through my own reporting the accuracy of the published sources I cite and have introduced new facts, quotes, and nuance to them as warranted. I have cited published sources and unpublished interviews in the notes throughout.

I never stopped hoping that Mr. Goizueta ultimately would find a reason to cooperate with my work. I wish he had. But his decision not to cooperate did not in any way affect my responsibility to the truth of his story, and my duty of diligence in seeking and telling that truth.

The following people granted me interviews:

William Allison
Michael Beindorff
Michael Bellas
John Bergin
Frank Biondi
Alfredo Blanco
Emmett Bondurant
Roy Burry
Harold Burson
Guido Calabresi
John S. Cavelick
Andrew Conway
Richard Cook
Robert Corr
Emilio Cueto
David D'Alessandro
Charlie Donelan

Karl Eller
Gregorio Escagedo
Pierre Ferrari
A.D. Frazier
Marion Glover
Gustavo Godoy
Fred Graham
Nick Gutierrez
Eduardo Hauser
Cassandra Henning
Gary Hite
Bob Holder
Ted Host
Crawford Johnson III
Michael Kami
Don Keough

Joel Koblenz
Jurgen Lens
Fr. Armando Llorente
Luis Mendez
Pedro Menocal
Charlie Millard
Van Myers
Billy Payne
Jack E. Pelo
Richard R. Pelo
Dick Pound
Rob Prazmark
Crawford Rainwater
Stanley Risdon
Bill Schmidt

Peter Sealey
Horace Sibley
Jimmy Sibley
Jeffrey Sonnenfeld
Raymond Southworth
Si Spengler
Roy Stout
Miguel Tarafa
Tony Tortorici
Chaplin Tyler
Ginger Watkins
Bobby Wilkinson
John Wineberg
Richard Yarbrough

In addition, a large number of helpful sources, some in high places at Coke or personally close to Goizueta, agreed to grant interviews or otherwise help. I interviewed 23 people under such circumstances on a not-for-attribution basis.

While Roberto Goizueta and his colleagues currently working at Coke would not cooperate with interviews for this book, I was able to draw from much previously unpublished information from *Business Week* interviews with the following, (with name of interviewer in parentheses):

Ramesh Chauhan (Mark Clifford)
James Chestnut (David Greising)
Gustavo Cisneros (John Pearson)
Ralph Cooper (Maria Mallory)
Doug Daft (Mark Clifford)
Brian Dyson (Walecia Konrad)
Roberto Goizueta (Nicole Harris, Maria Mallory, David Greising)
John Hunter (Maria Mallory)
Neville Isdell (Maria Mallory)

Doug Ivester (Maria Mallory)
James Latimore (Mark Clifford)
B.C. Lo (Mark Clifford)
Miguel Macias (Maria Mallory)
Barry Shea (Mark Clifford)
Suman Sinha (Mark Clifford)
Carl Ware (Maria Mallory)
Sergio Zyman (Maria Mallory, David Greising)

I drew from transcripts of Mark Pendergrast's tape-recorded interviews, in the Pendergrast collection at the Robert W. Woodruff Library at Emory University. On second reference, I refer to these interviews as, for example, "Ayoub to Pendergrast." I draw here from Pendergrast interviews with Sam Ayoub, Bob Broadwater, and Roberto Goizueta.

Abbreviations used are:

Bev. Digest 1988: An exclusive interview with Goizueta covering the entirety of his career to that date.

Goizueta, *Business Week 1995:* An exclusive interview with Goizueta by Maria Mallory, then of *Business Week,* in which he talked at length about his experiences in Cuba. Comments cited with this reference were never published before.

"Macias, *Business Week 1995,*" and other references indicates previously unpublished information from *Business Week* interview with a number of different interview subjects.

"Broadwater to Pendergrast" and other such references refer to transcriptions of interviews donated by Mark Pendergrast from the research of his book, *For God, Country and Coca-Cola,* donated by author Mark Pendergrast to the Emory library. Pendergrast transcribed tape recordings of all his interviews, and only comments he chose not to publish are referenced in this manner. Quotations published in his book are referenced to it.

Woodruff papers: The Robert W. Woodruff collection in the special collections department of the Robert W. Woodruff Library at Emory University..

I have referenced all people by first and last name on first reference, then last name only on all subsequent references.

All correspondence I have listed with names or initials of sender and recipient and date. For example: Goizueta to Woodruff, March 31, 1981. Would be the letter Goizueta wrote Woodruff on March 31, 1981. Unless otherwise noted, all correspondence involving Woodruff as either sender or recipient comes from the Robert W. Woodruff papers in the special collections department of the Robert W. Woodruff Library at Emory University.

While I consulted a broad array of books for background information, I have cited only those from which I directly drew information, and those only in the notes.

In the notes, I have placed quotations marks as a guidepost to indicate key words or phrases that are drawn from actual quotations in the text. Reference words in the chapter notes are condensed, even when they are presented inside quote marks.

Chapter 1   Cuba, Castro, and Coke
Page
1   "Important": *Diario de la Marina,* June 18, 1954.
2   Father an architect and real estate investor: Pedro Menocal, *Business Week* interview with Goizueta, 1995.
2   Made a fortune in sugar mills: *Georgia Trend,* Spring, 1985.
2   Casteleiro businesses: Aurelio Garcia Dulzaides, editor, *Album Azul de Cuba.* Rex Press, Miami, 1965. Gregorio Escagedo Jr., other Cubans.
2   "I was a freshly graduated": *Beverage Digest* interview with Goizueta, September 30, 1988.
2   Family chauffeur: Menocal.
2   Procter & Gamble, etc. Dulzaides, pp. 108–115, and *Cuba, the U.S. & Russia, 1960–1933,* Facts on File, New York, 1963.
3   "Disfruta Coca-Cola": Emilio Cuerto.
3   Olga had enjoyed: *Bev. Digest,* 1988.
3   Earning twice what Coke offered: Goizueta, *Business Week,* 1995.
3   "I want you to work with me": *Bev. Digest,* 1988.
4   "I'll work Sundays": *Bev. Digest,* 1988.

5 "Useful tool": Chaplin Tyler, confidential sources.

5 Woodruff populated: Woodruff papers, various.

6 Basques: P.S. Ormond, *The Basques and Their Country*, London: 1926, p. 118.

6 Baroque mansion: David Tullis photos, Menocal.

7 Grandfather's aphorisms: *Bev. Digest*, 1988, Southpoint Magazine, 1989.

7 Typewriters and air conditioners: Goizueta, *Business Week*, 1995.

7 Compania Industrial, St. Augustin, small-sized: Association of Cuban Sugar Mill Owners, Nick Gutierrez, Alfredo Blanco.

7 Owner of record was Elier and Alfredo Rodriguez: Benito Carbalo, Nick Gutierrez.

7 Exaggerated economic standing: in various interviews—Goizueta, *Business Week* 1995 and others—Goizueta implied outright mill ownership and overstated mill size. Statements of outright ownership were not corrected by Coke's public relations staff.

8 Goizueta's parents belonged to: Menocal, other Cubans.

8 A gregarious yet purposeful man, description of Belen: Fr. Llorente, *Album Azul de Cuba*.

10 A kind of man-child: Fr. Llorente.

11 Exposure to English: Goizueta implied he knew no English when first arrived at Cheshire, Cheshire Academy Commencement Address, 1982, various interviews, but he excelled in English at Belen, and was exposed to the vernacular at summer camp, according to Belen yearbook. Fr. Armando Llorente, other Cubans.

11 Belen sociology, Castro experience: Menocal, Miguel Tarafa, and Tad Szulc, *Fidel: A Critical Portrait*, William Morrow, New York, 1986, pp. 118–130.

11 Belen school day: Menocal, Fr. Llorente.

11 Goizueta studied English, summer camps: Belen yearbook, Fr. Llorente.

12 Boxers: Escagedo, Gustavo Godoy.

12 Olga mixed socially: Fr. Llorente, confidential Cuban source.

12 Casteilero family: Confidential Cuban source.

13 Brigadier: Llorente, Belen yearbook.

13 Father attended Penn, "I didn't know enough English,": Goizueta, *Business Week*, 1995.

14 Cheshire not strong brand name: Guido Calabresi, Si Spengler, others.

14 "Bob" Instead of Roberto: Cheshire yearbook.

14 T.S. Eliot, William Shakespeare, English dictionary: Goizueta Cheshire speech, 1982.

15 Trudged to class: Fred Graham.

15 Study five hours at a stretch, water fights: Dick Cook.

15 Unimpressive student: Raymond W. Southworth, Randolph H. Bretton.

15 Prominent Yale students, visiting politicians: Yale yearbooks, class books, Spengler, Graham, Calabresi.

15 Yale success: Yale class book shows "scholar of second rank" only in junior year. First published Goizueta claim of graduating with "the highest academic honors" came in wedding story in Diario de la Marina, June 16, 1953. Goizueta claims varied, including "top 5% of class at Yale" in Foodline: The Coca-Cola Foods Division, 1980, and 10th in his class. Despite his well-known attention to precise factual accuracy in all published articles (see Chapter 9), Goizueta and the Coke public relations staff did not correct overstatements of academic credentials or claims of outright mill ownership.

16 Never dated another girl: Calabresi, Cook, Spengler, Graham, and Goizueta, *Business Week*, 1995.

16 Singing, nicknames, smoking, fist fight: Cook.

17 Kept in touch only with Calabresi: Cook, Calabresi, Graham, Spengler.

17 "Excellent marriage": Fr. Llorente.

17 Description of ceremony, sister Vivien maid of honor: Fr. Llorente, *Diario de la Marina*, June 16, 1953.

18 Saw Miguel Macias at office: Miguel Macias, *Business Week*, 1995.

18 "Sleeping on sacks of sugar": *Delta Air Lines In-Flight magazine*, September, 1982.
19 First trip to Atlanta: Southpoint, 1989.
19 Rusted bottle research: Goizueta, "A Study of Bottle Washing," presented at meeting of the area chemists and engineers of The Coca-Cola Export Corp., May 1957, Coca-Cola Archives.
20 "It was obvious to us," "They would decide": Goizueta, *Business Week*, 1995.
20 Javier was born, Olga waited, making Coke with sugar, gendarmes check briefcases, in-laws and children to Miami: Goizueta, *Business Week*, 1995.
21 Learned from Coke's intelligence staff: Charlie Millard.
21 Cuba revolution chronology: Facts on File.
22 Friends had left: Menocal and Rick Fagen, et al., *Cubans in Exile: Disaffection and the Revolution*, Stanford University Press, 1968, pp. 120–122.
22 "I am going to go on vacation": Macias *Business Week*, 1995. Goizueta often maintained he considered his trip a vacation from which he expected to return, and he at one point told the *Atlanta Journal-Constitution* he had left in August, but the chronology of events surrounding his departure, the experience of other upper-class Cubans and some of his own statements regarding Sprite launch make that unlikely, and in *Business Week*, 1995 he specifically said October.
22 Needed to launch Sprite, "It was always in the back," $200 in their pocketbooks: *Business Week*, 1995. In a number of interviews regarding Cuba, Goizueta had variously said $20, $40 or $200.

Chapter 2   Flight to the Top
23 Goizueta prepared an inventory: *Business Week*, July 29, 1985.
24 Others carried blueprints, photos: In the Matter of the Claim of the Coca-Cola Co., Claim No. Cu-1743—Decision No. CU-6818.
25 "Unless you lived through it," dreamed of being Coke bottler, $18,000 salary: Goizueta, *Business Week*, 1995.
25 Flat on Venetian Causeway: *Business Week*, July 10, 1995.
26 Met Woodruff: Goizueta, *Bev. Digest*, 1988.
27 Woodruff biography and early history of Coca-Cola from Frederick Allen, *Secret Formula: How Brilliant Marketing and Relentless Salesmanship Made Coca-Cola the Best-Known Product in the World*, HarperBusiness, New York, 1994; also, *Atlanta Journal-Constitution*, March 8, 1985.
29 "Roberto contributed more": Macias, *Business Week*, 1995.
29 Based in Nassau, commuting: *Business Week*, July 10, 1995.
29 Broadwater and 7-Up truck: Mark Pendergrast interview with Broadwater.
29 Broadwater bio: Brad Currey, quoted in *Atlanta Business Chronicle*, Oct. 24–30, 1997.
30 "I love working at Coca-Cola": Roberto S. Goizueta eulogy for Goizueta, Oct. 21, 1997.
31 Austin bio: Nation's Business, June, 1976; Southline, Feb. 1985, and *New York Times*, July 31, 1966.
32 Austin wanted to modernize, Broadwater and Shillinglaw had recommended: Chaplin Tyler.
33 "A curiosity to be looked at": Goizueta, *Business Week*, 1995.
33 "Next great international city": Southpoint, 1989.
33 "He'll go to the top": Currey, *Atlanta Journal-Constitution*.
34 Special assignment: Tyler.
35 Orlando chicken pox: Goizueta to Tyler, May 27, 1992.
36 "Keep in mind how he performs," "They're just ordinary Guccis": Tyler.
37 Pay increase, "At the risk of doing violence": Goizueta, *Business Week*, 1985.
37 Arranging Roy Stout transfer: Roy Stout.
37 Become a citizen: Goizueta, *Business Week*, 1995.
37 "The first obligation implied": Goizueta speech at Monticello, July 4, 1995.

37 Weighing MIT, Harvard and Austin's advice: Goizueta to Tyler, Oct. 31, 1966.
38 Carlos death: Tyler.
39 "I'm at a loss for words": Goizueta to Tyler, Dec. 23, 1970.
41 Shillinglaw fell ill: Joseph W. Jones to Woodruff, Feb. 6, 1974, Woodruff papers.
41 Goizueta tracked down: Mark Pendergrast, *For God, Country and Coca-Cola: The Unauthorized History of the Great American Soft Drink and the Company that Makes It*, Collier Books, New York, 1995, p. 498.
41 Sent Klaus Putter, "state of semi-stupor": Jones to Woodruff, Feb. 7, 1974, Woodruff papers.
42 "I was afraid I'd get caught": Pendergrast, p. 498.
42 Goizueta learns formula, "now full-fledged No. 2": Jones to Woodruff, Feb. 7, 1974, Woodruff papers.
42 Goizueta and May flew to London: Jones to Woodruff, Feb. 7, 1974, Woodruff papers.
42 Expressing "deep appreciation": Goizueta to Woodruff, Feb. 8, 1974, Woodruff papers.
43 "I am most fortunate": Goizueta to Woodruff, Dec. 30, 1974, Woodruff papers.
43 Shillinglaw was shocked: Broadwater to Pendergrast.
43 "I confess to some sadness": Shillinglaw to Woodruff: Dec. 21, 1978, Woodruff papers.
44 Called him "Mr. Woodruff": Goizueta, *Bev. Digest*, 1988.
44 Austin twice tried to acquire American Express: Austin to Woodruff, April 14, 1979, Woodruff papers.
44 Robinson rumors: *Atlanta Journal-Constitution*, July 19, 1979, *Wall Street Journal*, June 10, 1980.
45 "Goizueta was the most astute" Broadwater to Pendergrast.
45 Goizueta increased his courtship: ex-Coke sources.
45 "The duty": Allen, p. 377.
46 "Rogue's gallery": Goizueta to Woodruff, March 3, 1978, Woodruff papers.
46 Speech to chemical engineers: Woodruff papers, Feb., 1978, Woodruff papers.
46 Kentucky Derby: Goizueta to Woodruff, May 2, 1976, Woodruff papers.
47 Churchill bathtub: Goizueta to Woodruff, May 21, 1978, Woodruff papers.
47 Woodruff embarassed himself: Allen, p. 260.
47 Staff at Ichauway was told: Allen, p. 375.
48 Keough the heir apparent: *Wall Street Journal*, March 5, 1980.
48 "We have not performed": *Wall Street Journal*, March 6, 1980.
48 Austin offered Keough presidency: Ex-Coke executive. Keough says there was a discussion, but it was not an outright offer. Keough recognized his mistake: Keough to ex-Coke executive.
49 "I'll never work for the Cuban": Ian Wilson, Keough does not recall conversation but adds, "It was an inelegant time at the Coca-Cola Company, and we all did things we are not proud of today."
49 "It's not time," flabbergasted Collings, "Roberto political": Ex-Coke executive.
50 Raised Woodruff's toilet: Allen, p. 379.
50 "The worst waste of time": *New York Times*, March 4, 1984.
50 "Project Triangle": Stout.
50 Austin killed the project: Keough, Stout.
51 Killeen had warned: Allen, p. 393.
51 "I want you": Wilson. Thank you notes from both Wilson and Williams to Woodruff indicate both men were at Ichauway that weekend. Williams declined comment, but told *Fortune*, June 1, 1981 that he remembered "Mr. Woodruff saying some very nice things about Ian."
52 Seemed Wilson had won: Wilson.
52 Williams persuaded Goizueta and Sibley: Broadwater to Pendergrast, Wilson.
52 "We almost had a disaster": Broadwater to Pendergrast.

52 Wilson to directors: Wilson.
53 "It's either you or me": Keough.
53 Austin called Goizueta, "How would you like to run?" Keough right-hand man: Goizueta to *Bev. Digest*, 1988.
53 "Boss I've got work," Goizueta shook hands: *Wall Street Journal*, June 10, 1980.

Chapter 3 "The Spanish Inquisition"
55 "I would be remiss": Goizueta to Woodruff, June 2, 1980, Woodruff papers.
56 Placed it in a scrapbook: Woodruff papers, green box no. 33.
56 Luke Smith was Woodruff's candidate: Jimmy Sibley, *Atlanta Journal*, July 15, 1980.
57 Directors were shellshocked, "I wish I knew what was going on": Jimmy Sibley, *Wall Street Journal*, June 10, 1980.
57 Lupton lobbying, *Wall Street Journal*, June 10, 1980.
57 Few bottlers met Goizueta, thought Keough a shoo-in: Charles Millard, Bobby Wilkinson, Crawford Rainwater, Crawford Johnson III.
58 Bottlers called and wrote: Wilkinson to Woodruff, June 5, 1980; Cy Chesterman to Woodruff, May 31, 1980; Van Myers to Woodruff, June 3, 1980, all Woodruff papers; Johnson, Millard.
58 "We've got a lot of work": Keough.
58 "This is an American company": Wilkinson to Woodruff, June 5, 1980, Woodruff papers. Wilkinson in interview said he had not met Goizueta when he wrote to Woodruff.
58 Wilson done for, NBC-TV News, Coke response: Wilson, *Atlanta Journal*, June 10, 1980.
59 Keough, not Wilson worried him: *Fortune*, June 1, 1981.
59 Goizueta as new president: *Atlanta Constitution*, June 11, 1980, June 13, 1980.
59 Lead coasters: Allen, p. 383.
60 "My own man," strong nationalism trend: *Wall Street Journal*, June 11, 1980.
60 "Midst of crowd": *Atlanta Constitution*, June 13, 1980.
60 "Finance, technical, marketing," government regulation reason left father's business, "clone the foods division," no new borrowings, domestic 50% of earnings, "The future of the bottlers,": *Wall Street Journal*, June 11, 1980.
62 Fort Worth bottler: *Wall Street Journal*, May 31, 1980.
62 "You must be broke": Goizueta to Pendergrast.
62 Jack Stahl helped: Beverage Industry, July 4, 1980.
63 Hosted a meeting, attendees, menu description: Goizueta to Woodruff: July 11, 1980, Woodruff papers.
63 Recollections of meeting: Johnson, Millard, Crawford Rainwater.
63 Rainwater tickled: Rainwater, Rainwater to Woodruff: July 14, 1980, Woodruff papers.
63 "Meeting was a most auspicious start": Millard to Goizueta, July 15, 1980, Woodruff papers.
64 "Never does any harm": Goizueta to Woodruff, July 21, 1980, Woodruff papers.
64 "They now have me pegged": Goizueta to Woodruff, July 25, 1980, Woodruff papers; Leisure Beverage Insider, July 21, 1980.
65 Trust Co. nomination: Goizueta to Woodruff, June 9, 1980, Woodruff papers.
65 Keough got calls: Johnson, Millard, Keough.
65 Keough talked to Goizueta: Keough.
66 Keough biography: Omaha World Herald, June 16, 1982; Omaha World-Herald, Feb. 18,1996. Buffett pitch to Keough: Roger Lowenstein, *Buffett: The Making of an American Capitalist*, Random House, New York, 1995, p. 66.
66 "At times it's been difficult": Johnson, Millard.
67 "It was the damnedest": Johnson.
67 "It is the curse": Goizueta in Financial Times of London, Oct. 2, 1980.

67 Austin's Alzheimer's: Sibley, Keough, Wilson.
67 Treated Woodruff like grandfather and father: Goizueta, *Bev. Digest*, 1988.
68 Board's new by-laws: Allen, p. 393.
68 Woodruff unhappy over finance committee changes: Jones to Garth Hamby, Sept. 19, 1980, Woodruff papers.
70 "We can't let that happen": Keough.
70 "Mr. Woodruff, you invented debt": Goizueta, *Bev. Digest*, 1988.
71 Goizueta began a study: Keough, ex-Coke executive, Sam Ayoub to Pendergrast.
72 "He'd start by asking questions," "I don't want you to be a yes man": Ayoub to Pendergrast. "Spanish Inquisition," five-year plans, challenge every assumption: Keough.
73 "Facts are facts": Thomas Oliver, *The Real Coke, The Real Story*, Penguin Books, New York, 1987, p. 68.
73 "You saw intestinal courage," "toilet training": Keough.
74 Needed a matrix, "We're liquidating our business," "No sense of direction," "None of our operating executives can read a balance sheet" "You'll get no hearing" "When you start charging": *Fortune*, May 31, 1993, some verb tenses changed.
74 "Some very good news!": Goizueta to Woodruff, May 9, 1980, Woodruff papers.
76 Williams itinerary: Goizueta to Woodruff, Jan. 19, 1981, Woodruff papers.
77 "Thank-you Mr. Goizueta": Sibley.
77 Mission Statement preparation: Keough, ex-Coke source, Sibley.
78 "I wondered how important": Keough.
78 "He didn't know a financial report": ex-Coke executive.
79 Broken job into three parts: Michael Kami, Keough, Tyler.
79 "In a perfect world," "A lot of markets will be opened," "We're a kind of United Nations," "We want to challenge the policy": Kami.
80 Unique role of CEO: Kami, Industry Week, Nov. 1, 1982.
80 Description of March 4 board meeting: Sibley, Keough.
81 Mission statement: Goizueta, Strategy for the 1980s, The Coca-Cola Company.
82 "No sacred cows": Kami, Keough.
82 "Don't take it lightly." Oliver, p. 76.
82 Don't like "strategic planning": Oliver, p. 73.
83 Look at P&G: Keough.
83 "The only company that continues." "Reformulation of our products": Oliver, p. 74.
83 Palm Springs program: Goizueta to Coke board, April 6, 1981, Woodruff papers.
83 "How many times?" Oliver, p. 76.
84 "We're off to a start.": Kami.

Chapter 4   A Break from the Past: Diet Coke and Columbia Pictures
85 Board gave him three years: Sibley.
86 Videotaped a sanitized version: Goizueta to board, April 6, 1981, Woodruff papers.
86 "Flogging in the town square": *Fortune*, Dec. 11, 1995.
87 "Roberto was a tyrant": Ayoub to Pendergrast.
87 "Coke never fires anyone": Tyler.
87 "Not a violinist": *Fortune*, Sept. 8, 1980.
87 Overlooked Jeanne Austin: confidential source.
88 "Insist . . . give 100 percent": *Atlanta Constitution*, Aug. 7, 1980.
89 Charles Navarre bid: Millard, Keough.
89 "You're dead meat": Millard.
90 Hunter for Philippines: Allen, p. 394.
90 Collings opposed: Keough, Ayoub to Pendergrast.
91 "A hell of a lot of money," "I see a great future.": Sibley.
91 Isdell's theatrics: Pendergrast, p. 343.
92 Telegram from China: Goizueta to Woodruff, April 16, 1981, Woodruff papers.
92 "A messenger with no authority": *Atlanta Constitution*, Sept. 3, 1981.

93 "People resent": Lewis Grizzard *Atlanta Constitution*, Sept. 11, 1981.

93 "You end up resenting": William Allison.

94 "I have had an acquaintance": Woodruff to Peachtree Golf Club, July 9, 1981, Woodruff papers.

94 "I hope this board": Woodruff to Peachtree Golf Club, March 31, 1982, Woodruff papers.

94 Locker assignment: Wilson.

94 Golfer tried to order a Coke: Goizueta to Industry Week, Nov. 1, 1982.

95 "Keep my head down" *Wall Street Journal*, June 11, 1980.

95 Details of A.D. Little study, Walt Disney, Shering Plough: Peter Sealey, ex-Coke executive.

96 "You've got to make an acquisition": Keough, ex-Coke executives.

96 Eller and Herbert breakfast, follow up call: Karl Eller.

97 21 Club meeting: Eller, Keough.

98 "Will knock your eyes out": Oliver, p. 84.

98 "We like each other": *Atlanta Journal-Constitution*, Jan. 24, 1982.

98 Little missed television: ex-Coke executive.

98 Allen bio: *Fortune*, Feb. 22, 1982.

99 "I'm a little confused here": Keough.

99 "That's so far off": Oliver, p. 91.

100 "Skip that one Sam": Oliver, p. 92.

101 "You're still the boss," "attend the board meeting": Ayoub to Pendergrast.

101 Built a screening room, "What's this about?" "We're movie moguls": Keough.

102 "I told you so years": *Atlanta Constitution*, Oct. 18, 1982.

102 Zyman's Diet Coke manifesto: Sergio Zyman to Brian Dyson, "The Diet Coke Case," Shreveport Coca-Cola Bottling Co. v. The Coca-Cola Company, No. 83-95 MMS, No. 83-120 MMS, plaintiff's exhibit 23.

103 Zyman bio: *Atlanta Journal-Constitution*, April 1, 1994; *Adweek*, Nov. 6, 1995; Bergin, Stanley Risdon, confidential source; Roger Enrico, *The Other Guy Blinked: How Pepsi Won the Cola Wars*, Bantam Books, New York, 1986, pp. 49–51.

103 Abrupt cancellation shocked: Keough, ex-Coke source.

106 Goizueta launched Diet: Diet Coke case, March 3, 1981, "Lucy" memo.

106 "The Tab company": Pendergrast, p. 341.

106 "Three most important objectives": Diet Coke case, plaintiff's exhibit 1381.

106 "Market testing is to see": *New York Times*, March 4, 1982.

106 Charlie Millard's troops: Millard.

106 Ad cost $1.5 million: Oliver, p. 111.

107 First-year $100 million, "cover-their-ass," Millard.

107 Tab left to die: ex-Coke marketing source.

108 Wine spectrum sale: *Business Week*, Oct. 10, 1983, June 3, 1985.

109 Birthday note to Woodruff: Goizueta to Woodruff, Dec. 6, 1985, Woodruff papers.

Chapter 5 "Give Me Back My Coke!"

110 Stout's team studied: Stout.

111 Met over holidays: Keough, Pendergrast, p. 356.

111 Goizueta summoned Burson, "What is my Achilles heel?": Harold Burson.

112 Stout neglected to ask: Burson, Keough, Stout.

113 "The surest step we've ever made": Goizueta, New Coke press conference, April 23, 1985.

113 "They're going to change": Oliver, p. 75.

113 Gianturco appeared: Goizueta deposition in Diet Coke case, July 5, 1985, in Pendergrast papers. Naming David: Stout.

115 "The last question will be fake," groups went berserk, "I have actually got a formula," "I don't know what you're up to": Bergin.

116   Stout did not ask about taking away: Stout, Bergin, Burson, Oliver p 137.
116   "I'm not going to sit": Oliver, p. 119.
116   "Just because a man is courteous": Allen, p. 403.
116   Dyson bio: Allen, pp. 403–404, *Business Week*, May 26, 1986, Keough.
116   "Explore the possibility": Oliver, p. 121.
118   "Coke is part of landscape": Goizueta at New Coke 10th anniversary celebration, April 10, 1995.
119   "Here's World War II Coke": Bergin.
119   "CFO of the Titanic": Ivester, Coke employees meeting, April 10, 1995.
120   No second-best Coke on market: Oliver, p. 128.
120   Woodruff pointed to White article: Goizueta speech to bottlers, April 22, 1985.
121   The bunker: Bergin, *Advertising Age*, April 29, 1985.
121   "I'm here representing Sergio": Bergin.
122   Allowed Keough and Dyson to inform Millard: Millard, *Atlanta Journal-Constitution*, May 5, 1985.
123   "I caved in": Oliver, p. 136.
124   Zyman personally took charge: Bergin, Oliver, p. 141.
125   "If no one cares?" Bergin.
125   Dry runs: Bergin, Burson.
127   He did not eulogize: *Atlanta Journal-Constitution*, March 10, 1985.
127   Laney's eulogy: Allen, p. 409.
128   Goizueta told his wife: Goizueta at employees meeting, April 10, 1995.
129   "Now we're back in the ball game": Burson.
129   Pollsters: *Wall Street Journal*, May 16, 1985.
130   Press conference: Bergin, Oliver, pp. 158–166.
130   Reporters grimaced: Bergin.
131   Taste test: *Atlanta Journal-Constitution*, April 25, 1985.
131   "I wish the story could be sexier": *Business Week*, July 29, 1985.
131   Dyson publicly contradicted: Beverage World, May 31, 1985.
132   "Why did you take away our Coke?" Oliver, p. 184.
132   "Dad, have patience": Oliver, p. 185.
132   "This is costing us": Johnson.
133   Bellingrath came: *Atlanta Journal-Constitution*, July 12, 1985.
133   "I can put up with flak": Oliver, p. 200.
133   Stout's staff recruited: Stout.
134   "Putting on a hell of an act": Millard.
134   "This is the original": *Atlanta Journal-Constitution*, April 11, 1995.
134   Olguita took her ring off: Millard.
134   "Why are we doing this?" Keough.
135   Goizueta and Burson dreamed up Coca-Cola Classic, "The argument is over," Burson hashed out Goizueta's remarks: Burson.
136   Goizueta concerned for Keough's security: Keough.
136   "Megabrand" concept: Ike Herbert, New York Stock Exchange remarks, Sept. 24, 1985.
137   "If my grandmother had wheels": *Beverage Digest*, July 19, 1985.
137   "Megabrand was layered on": Michael Beindorff.
138   "We get paid to produce results": *Atlanta Journal-Constitution*, Feb. 22, 1988, *Beverage World*, April, 1994.

Chapter 6   Changing the Script: The Bottler Spinoff and Escape from Hollywood
139   Harvest memo: Advert. Age, Dec. 29, 1986.
140   Invited 14,000 guests: *Adweek*, June 17, 1986.
140   "Out of respect," $1.4 billion price, Goizueta immediately approved: Keough.
141   One-on-ones with favored directors: Sibley.

142 "They understand how to work": *Beverage Digest*, Sept. 23, 1983.
143 Discussion they had begun in 1981: Keough, *Bev. World*, July, 1987.
143 Coke would buy part, not all: Keough.
143 "The handshake on the deal," "megabottler": Coke press release, Jan. 27, 1986.
143 "Quite a rain dance": Keough.
144 Looked forward to raising: Goizueta to Woodruff, Dec. 6, 1984, Woodruff papers.
144 Detailed, hands-on approach, $30 million budget, "Business the institution of future," description of centennial layout: ex-Coke executive.
145 Renamed sculpture, selecting marble: *Atlanta Constitution*, May 8, 1986.
145 Olguita on piano: *Atlanta Journal-Constitution*, May 10, 1986.
145 Casting: ex-Coke source, former Coke consultant.
146 Had a shot to buy bottler earlier: Keough.
148 "Participate in rising value": *Beverage World*, September 1986.
149 "It made sense to us": Keough.
149 Ivester bio: Institutional Investor, September 1986; *Atlanta Journal-Constitution*, July 25, 1994.
150 Securitizing television receivables: *Forbes*, Nov. 18, 1985.
150 "The 49% solution": *Wall Street Journal*, Oct. 8, 1987.
151 Allen had virtually no experience: Martin Romm.
151 "Biggest-deal-ever-itis": investment banking source.
152 Goizueta wanted his $24 a share: Keough, Romm.
152 "Spend much less": *Atlanta* Magazine, November, 1982.
153 "Very aloof": Romm.
153 Analysts did not buy: *Wall Street Journal*, Dec. 1, 1986.
153 "Thinking about $15": *New York Times*, Nov. 22, 1986.
154 Investment banking fees: *Atlanta Constitution*, Nov. 25, 1986.
154 "An art, not a science": *Industry Week*, Nov. 1, 1992.
155 Columbia played a part: ex-Columbia source.
156 Terms of Tri-Star: Frank Biondi, *Wall Street Journal*, December 6, 1984.
157 Kick-off management meeting, "We have just acquired,": ex-Coke source, ex-Columbia source. "Put in place the Hollywood crowd": ex-Coke source.
157 "Two of the ten," "The TV business is what you want": ex-Coke source.
157 Vincent bio: *New York Times* Magazine, June 3, 1990.
158 Vincent recognized: ex-Coke source.
158 "Corporate spy": Sealey, Keough.
159 Sealey strategy: *Fortune*, December 1983; Marketing & Media Decisions: August 1984.
159 "Frank Price makes me puke": ex-Columbia source.
160 "Frank Price is a personnel issue": ex-Columbia source, Keough. Frank Price could not be reached for comment.
160 Goizueta despised, first weekend phenomenon: Keough.
161 "You've docked your boat," "There is only one head": *Variety*, Oct. 30, 1984.
161 "Closest I've been to Shields": *New York Times*, March 4, 1984.
161 Visiting "Ghostbusters": ex-Coke source.
161 "Guess we don't get laid": Sealey, ex-Columbia source.
162 "Roberto went through that cycle": ex-Columbia source.
162 "How do you know they'll last?" ex-Columbia source.
163 "Ivester would call": ex-studio chief.
163 "Will always be a soft drink company": Keough, ex-Columbia source, Goizueta: Mission Statement for 1980s.
164 Vincent wants Warner or Time, "Coke has to be a soft drink company": Keough, Columbia source.
164 Vincent flew to Atlanta: ex-Coke source; Sally Bedell Smith, *In All His Glory: The Life of William S. Paley The Legendary Tycoon and his Brilliant Career*, Simon and

Schuster, New York, 1990, p. 584; *Wall Street Journal*, Sept. 12, 1986; Keough says Vincent never asked for permission to look at Columbia, Vincent declined comment.
164 "Is it true": Keough.
165 David Puttnam's "tyranny of the box office," "Hollywood is despicable,"
165 Puttnam's insults: *Variety*, May 18, 1988.
166 Sealey went to "Ishtar": Sealey.
167 Allen's $5 million in fees: *L.A. Times*, May 30, 1989.
167 Looting Columbia: *Business Week*, Jan. 11, 1988.
168 Oscars in 1988: Keough.

Chapter 7   Coca-Colonization
169 Goizueta's grand tour: *Fortune*, May 31, 1993.
170 Flew to Egypt: Sibley.
171 A third of his time: Atlanta Magazine, June 1986.
172 "We haven't grown overseas volume," "Rather than report": *Wall Street Journal*, Dec. 13, 1984.
173 "We don't want to do business": Keough.
175 Polish beer: *Wall Street Journal*, March 13, 1985.
176 "Excursion into high-margin retailing": Berkshire Hathaway annual report, 1989.
176 Keough sent Cherry Coke: *Omaha World-Herald*, Feb. 18, 1996.
176 "It so happens that I am": Lowenstein, p. 323.
177 "Is it her eyes?" *Wall Street Journal*, March 3, 1989.
177 "I like businesses": *Warren Buffett Talks Business*, The University of North Carolina Center for Public Television, Research Triangle Park, NC, 1995.
177 Varsity lunch: Andrew Kilpatrick, *Of Permanent Value: The Story of Warren Buffett*, AKPE, Birmingham, Ala., 1996, p. 234.
178 "If you gave me $100 billion": *Fortune*, May 31, 1993.
178 "People are going to drink": *Buffett Talks Business*.
177 Committed to memory the per-capita: Lowenstein, p. 333.
178 "Look-through earnings": Berkshire Hathaway annual report, 1996.
178 "There was only one question": *Buffett Talks Business*.
179 "Better off if you're in two lousy businesses": *Wall Street Journal*, 1989.
180 Goizueta and Keough had lobbied hard: Keough.
181 "As awkward as tail fins": Goizueta, The Emerging Post-Conglomerate Era: Changing the Shape of Corporate America, mailing to Coke shareholders, January 1988, Coca-Cola archives.
181 Delivery trucks at Berlin Wall: *Wall Street Journal*, April 24, 1990.
181 Ad race with Pepsi: *Atlanta Journal-Constitution*, Dec. 8, 1989.
182 Not distracted by snacks: *New York Times*, Nov. 21, 1991.
183 Keough had pegged Ivester, "Doug, you're going to have to make a decision": Keough.
184 "I suspect you've got your successor": Burson.
184 Hoffman in France: ABC, March 4, 1981.
186 Keough committed $1 billion, "Roberto didn't blink an eye": Keough.
187 "Just ship the product": *Beverage Digest*, March 1, 1991.
187 "Don't need a sign": Keough.
188 "Not the best looking plants": *Atlanta Journal-Constitution*, Nov. 21, 1991.
188 Jumpstart: *Wall Street Journal*, Nov. 1, 1992.
188 Pepsi's $3 billion pact: *New York Times*, April 9, 1990.
189 "Think with mouths open": *New York Times*, Nov. 21, 1991.
190 Spelled out "one million shares": Graef S. Crystal, proxy for Coca-Cola Company's 1991 annual meeting.
190 *New York Times* scooped *Wall Street Journal*: *New York Times*, April 16, 1992, *Wall Street Journal*, March 20, 1992.

190 Allen had pushed, Allen's defense: *Business Week*, Nov. 11, 1996.
191 Jettridge Ave. home value: *Atlanta Magazine*, 1986.
191 Blackland Rd. valuation: Fulton County assessor's office.
191 Country music preference: Goizueta to Pendergrast, Pendergrast papers.
192 Defense at annual meeting: *Atlanta Journal-Constitution*, April 16, 1992.
192 "Who among his shareholders?": *LA Times*, March 20, 1992, Crystal.

Chapter 8 **"Always a Great Shootout"**
193 Coke's $600 million in worldwide ads: *New York Times*, Feb. 8, 1994.
195 Ovitz had a line in: Keough.
195 Goizueta was backing, handled shootout in typical style: Keough.
196 "Go to a hipper source": *Adweek*, Aug. 24, 1992.
196 Ovitz had already approached: former CAA source.
196 Ovitz bio: *Business Week*, Aug. 9, 1993.
197 Featured on the cover: *New York Times Magazine*, July 9, 1989.
197 Keough did not want to approach: Ex-Coke source.
197 Policy against rehiring: Keough.
197 Sealey bio: *Business Week*, March 15, 1993, *Wall Street Journal*, Oct. 26, 1990.
198 "I don't think our advertising," Sealey, Keough.
198 "I don't know if I can": Sealey.
198 "You understand the community": *Business Week*, March 15, 1993.
199 "We got all the back shop in place": *Business Week*, 1994.
199 Busted promotions into three: *Business Week*, Nov. 26, 1990.
199 Coke II, "U.S. is the test market:" *Business Week*, Nov. 26, 1990.
201 Ivester planned to use Sealey as an excuse: ex-Coke source.
201 "I'm not going to negotiate," "shave the beard," "Castro": Sealey.
201 Sealey not talked to Goizueta: Sealey.
202 "Outmoded," "dinosaurs": Ad. Age, Aug. 31, 1992, Sealey.
203 "Greatest star in the world, Coke": Keough.
203 "We need a new direction": Keough.
204 Make CAA and McCann coexist: Bergin, ex-Coke source.
204 "The factory called McCann": Sealey, ex-McCann source, Bergin.
205 "Do what you did for AmEx": *Adweek*, which created a landmark account of the Mc-
      Cann switch in its Feb. 8, 1993 edition. Sources disagreed on precise dates of meet-
      ings and other events. Unless noted otherwise, much factual information and
      chronology of this chapter follows outline of *Adweek*'s article. Interviews with Bergin,
      an ex-Coke source, a McCann source, and an ex-CAA source all also inform this
      version of events.
205 "Agency's last chance": Sealey, Bergin.
205 Bowen's first job: *Adweek*, Feb. 8, 1993.
205 Joint meetings uncomfortable and testy: Bergin, ex-CAA source.
206 Woodruff created "Pause": *Atlanta Journal-Constitution*, March 8, 1985.
206 "They're down to their last": Bergin.
207 "We don't have it yet" *Adweek*, July 26, 1993.
207 Coke sent a plane, "It was high-pressure": ex-CAA source.
208 Ads were world calibre: ex-CAA source.
208 Ovitz introduced: Bergin, Keough.
209 Bergin had sent, "Let the brand be": Bergin.
210 "No taste memory": Goizueta, *Business Week*, 1994, Bergin.
210 Steal-a-matic: Bergin.
211 "Help the blind:" McCann source.
211 "It was marketing 101": Keough."
211 "I am offended": *Adweek*, Feb. 8, 1993, Keough.
211 Bowen followed Keough: Keough.

212 Zyman was working: *Adweek*, Aug. 2, 1993.
213 Tutoring Ivester: *Adweek*, Nov. 6, 1995.
213 Ivester wanted Zyman and Bowen together: *Adweek*, Aug. 2, 1993.
214 CAA team at LAX: ex-CAA source, ex-Coke source.
215 Bergin, Bowen, Geier etc. Keough, Bergin.
216 "Don did not buy in": Sealey.
216 Review panel: *Adweek*, Feb. 8, 1993.
216 "Peter Sealey did good": Goizueta, *Business Week*, 1994.

Chapter 9 The Big Brand Machine
218 "I don't want you to retire": Keough.
218 "Keough" Keough.
218 "I'd like to step down": *Beverage Digest*, Feb. 19, 1993.
219 He had felt uncomfortable; review managers; Ivester succession: Keough.
220 Keough had remained skeptical: Oliver, p. 121.
220 "I went through that door": *Ad. Age*, Dec. 29, 1986.
221 "KO without Keough?": *Beverage Digest*, April 13, 1993.
221 "There was a blind spot": ex-Coke executive.
222 "The chairman can fire the president," one executive called: ex-Coke executive. Keough confirms the remarks, but says they were meant in jest and that he took them that way.
223 Had told Burson about Ivester: Burson.
224 Goizueta called Ivester and Hunter: Goizueta, *Business Week* interview, 1994.
225 "Mello Yellow sells more," "I want it all": Goizueta, *Business Week* interview, 1994.
225 "I don't care if they like the people": Hunter, *Business Week* interview, 1994.
227 Did not want Coke name on Tab Clear: Goizueta, *Business Week* interview, 1994.
227 Get it done fast: *Atlanta Journal-Constitution*, April 10, 1994.
228 Crystal Super Bowl launch: Dec., 1993.
228 Pepsi made huge mistake: Goizueta, *Business Week* interview, 1994.
228 Clears "about to die": *Beverage World*, Dec. 1993.
228 Ivester scrambling to save Diet Coke: ex-Coke source.
230 "This just isn't working out": *Adweek*, July 26, 1993.
230 Goizueta never fired: ex-Coke sources.
230 "Why him?" *Adweek*, Nov. 6, 1995.
230 "enfante terrible": *Atlanta Journal-Constitution*, April 1, 1994.
230 Marketers reporting to Zyman: ex-Coke source.
230 "Get Used to Sergio—GUTS": *Adweek*, Nov. 6, 1995.
231 Zyman considered dumping CAA, Ovitz intervened: Nov. 6, 1995.
231 CAA-Disney raises eyebrows: *Adweek*, Nov. 6, 1995.
232 Goizueta polar bear ties: *Atlanta Journal-Constitution*, April 10, 1994.
232 Sent Ivester to Indiana: *Bev. World*, June 1995.
232 "Some home runs": *Wall Street Journal*, May 13, 1994.
233 "Compete with soup": Goizueta, *Business Week*, 1995.
234 "Fruitopia will be the brand": Goizueta, *Business Week*, 1994.
234 "I'm not the target audience": Zyman, *Business Week*, 1994.
235 Sat on seven boards: *Business Week*, Nov. 25, 1996.
236 Borrowing high-performance Ford cars: *Fortune*, Dec. 11, 1995.
236 Joined Ford hardliners: *Business Week*, Oct. 12, 1992.
237 Goizueta and Phelan led a group: Alecia Swasy, Changing Focus: Kodak and the Battle to Save a Great American Company, Random House, New York: 1997, p. 56.
237 Kodak "very much inbred": *Business Week*, Aug. 23, 1993.
238 Kodak "not been well managed," "If my name leaks": Wineberg.
238 "Our number one candidate was God": *Business Week*, Oct. 20, 1997.
239 Could resort to layoffs: *Atlanta Journal-Constitution*, Sept. 4, 1996.

239 "We're really mad at ourselves": *New York Times*, Nov. 12, 1997k.
239 "No one has inside track," "Until I act": *Wall Street Journal*, May 13, 1994.
240 "Be different . . . agonizing death . . ." "friendly pack of competitors": text of Ivester speech to InterBev, Oct. 25, 1994.
241 "I've got the hose": *Atlanta Journal-Constitution*, July 25, 1994.
241 "He'd walk right by you": ex-Coke executive.
241 "obviously written by hand of an expert": Roy Burry.
242 Threatened to freeze Kaplan out, "you are to analyst reports,": *Wall Street Journal*, Feb. 16, 1996.
242 Terminated relationship with Oliver: Maria Saporta.
243 "So much for predictions": Goizueta to Chris Roush, Dec. 14, 1995.
243 "December *Fortune* . . . December 1938": Goizueta to *Business Week*, 1994.
244 "One, state expectations," "three P's": Goizueta to analysts, March 12, 1996.

Chapter 10 The Games Roberto Played
246 Payne drank cases of Coke, represented good: Billy Payne.
247 Olympics popped into his head: Payne's description of the timing for his inspiration has varied somewhat. In two major articles, *Atlanta Journal-Constitution*, March 3, 1996, and *Sports Illustrated*, Jan. 8, 1996, Payne maintains it was a sudden inspiration, while *Fortune*, July 22, 1996, describes a slightly more drawn out process. While the *Fortune* article's version rings as more likely, Payne now consistently tells the version adopted in the former two articles. We use it here.
247 Candler is great, great, great nephew: *Fortune*, July 22, 1996.
248 Payne wanted a dose of reality, Williams visit: Payne. Williams declined comment on his meeting with Payne.
248 Donaldson stood him up: Payne.
248 Coke was irked by national governing bodies: Gary Hite.
249 Keough ordered internal study, "See if you can change it": Hite.
251 Samaranch meeting: Hite.
251 Race to create TOP program: Juergen Lens, Rob Prazmark, Hite.
252 Goizueta saw an opportunity: Hite.
253 Backing Payne would risk irritating: Hite, Keough, Payne, Bob Holder.
253 Shots of spectators wearing ponchos: Hite.
253 "Not going further in support": Payne.
254 Free corporate jets: Payne.
254 Letter to Manchester: *Atlanta Journal-Constitution*, June 35, 1990.
254 "I was something deeper": Payne.
254 "Try not to read literally": Payne.
255 "Can you drink Coca-Cola": Payne. IOC press office did not respond to requests for interview.
255 "Let's go talk to Roberto": Holder, Payne.
256 "We're not getting involved," remainder of events leading to lunch: Holder.
256 "I really appreciate everybody being here": Holder, Payne.
257 Prazmark congratulated Hite: Prazmark. Hite has no recollection of the conversation.
257 Greeks made themselves nuisance: A.D. Frazier.
258 "Got a pretty big back yard": Keough, *Atlanta Journal-Constitution*, Sept. 19, 1990.
259 Corporate elite met: Payne, Holder, Frazier, and *Fortune*, July 22, 1996, which described Payne's thoughts on the attempted putsch: "Well excuse me, friends. Where were you when I was eating monkey brains in Thailand or blood sausage in Montevideo?"
259 Had Keough in mind: Frazier, other top Olympics sources. Keough says he was not aware his name was floated.
259 Goizueta looked at Billy as puppy: ex-Atlanta Olympics executive. Keough does not disagree, but says the analogy may be overdrawn.

260 Goizueta wanted Payne's finances: Payne.
260 Distrusting Frazier, "How do you know these guys?": Frazier, other Olympics sources.
261 Competed at arriving at work: Frazier.
261 "You will do it at all costs": Payne.
262 "Embarrass us in front of world": *Atlanta Journal-Constitution*, March 18, 1994.
263 Draw plans as if from Goizueta's office: Payne, Frazier, Holder.
263 Goizueta buttonholed governor: *Atlanta Journal-Constitution*, Jan. 22, 1996.
263 "It was antithetical": Frazier.
264 Planning to spend more on Sidney: Hite.
264 "Sports lets you get in dialogue": *Business Week*, July 29, 1996.
265 "Here's a man who has no clue": *Business Week* visit to Big TV in L.A., 1994.
266 "It's our view the relationship is adversarial," freezer of Tab: Frazier.
266 Coke sprang into action: Frazier, *Atlanta Journal-Constitution*, Jan. 22, 1996.
267 "Take the Busch logo off the dais": Frazier.
268 Tried to push through city ordinance: *Atlanta Journal-Constitution*, Jan. 22, 1995.
268 Coke should sign through 2028: David D'Alessandro, Dick Pound.
269 "Cannot be like a doughnut": Text of Goizueta speech, May 20, 1996.
269 Goizueta phoned Jackson re: Rodney King: *Atlanta Magazine*, November, 1992.
269 "Take a nap": Text of Goizueta speech, May 20, 1996.
270 Goizueta's parking pass: Frazier.
271 New contract "didn't make a difference": Frazier.

Chapter 11 **"It's Coca-Cola Heaven"**
272 Sent signed photos, signing deal in Woodruff's office: *Fortune*, Oct. 28, 1996, which first published the definitive account of the Cisneros deal.
273 Russia "turnaround came more quickly": *Atlanta Journal-Constitution*, Aug. 27, 1996.
274 Enrico dancing with Oswaldo's wife: *New York Times*, Aug. 21, 1996.
274 Oswaldo dangled the company before Enrico: *Fortune*, Oct. 28, 1996.
275 "Pepsi never friendly we would grow": *New York Times*, Aug. 21, 1996.
275 Ivester brought Zyman in early: Coke source.
275 Goizueta gave ok after Oswaldo walked, by time Enrico learned was too late: *Fortune*, Oct. 28, 1996.
276 Goizueta did not want distraction from Olympics: Coke source.
276 Chartering jetliner: Coke public relations to *Business Week*, August 19, 1996.
277 Painting trucks: *LatinFinance*, Nov. 1996.
277 "New low, even for Coke": *Beverage Digest*, Sept. 13, 1996.
277 Paid a $2 million fine: *Wall Street Journal*, Dec. 11, 1996. (cq)
278 Ozzie took his silver: *Fortune*, Oct. 28, 1996.
278 "Don't need to beat Coke": *Beverage Digest*, Oct. 11, 1996.
280 "As they've become less relevant": *Fortune*, Oct. 28, 1996.
281 Goizueta flew to UK, "You want to be my partner?": ex-Cadbury source.
282 CCE drops Cadbury brands: *Beverage Digest*, March 28, 1996.
282 Can't work without control: ex-Cadbury source.
283 Parle continued making concentrate: *Wall Street Journal*, Dec. 23, 1994.
283 "ThumsUp so resilient, still outsells Coke": Ramesh Chauhan.
285 Daft met Kuok at Shangri-La, mutual interest in art: Daft.
285 Kuok bio, "offer a cleverer man a joint venture," "gift from heaven": *Forbes*, July 27, 1997.
286 "Beverages not high technology": Chen Bixia.
287 Peter Noland study: Peter Nolan, "Joint Ventures and Economic Reform in China: A Case Study of the Coca-Cola Business System with Particular Reference to the Tianjin Coca-Cola Plant," Cambridge University: 1995.
287 "We're very well liked": Goizueta in *South China Morning Post*, July 2, 1995.
287 "We push hard on discipline": *Atlanta Journal*, July 30, 1995.

288 "Want 10 plants every three years": Goizueta, *Business Week*, 1996.
289 Goizueta introduces Kuok to Warren Buffett: *Forbes*, July 27, 1977.
289 "Soft drink heaven," "No sense marketing if no plant": Goizueta, *Business Week*, 1996.
291 Contour can: *Wall Street Journal*, February 6, 1997.
291 "I consider soup a competitor": Goizueta, *Business Week*, 1995.
292 "Investment banking firms specializing in bottler deals": Keough.
292 "State expectations": Goizueta, Letter to Shareowners, Coke 1995 annual report.
293 Roy Burry led the charge: Roy Burry, April 14, 1997 Oppenheimer & Co. report on Coca-Cola Co.
293 "Coke's raised substantial questions": Burry.
294 Took to heart Michael Novak book: Andrew Young, Goizueta eulogy, Oct. 21, 1997.
294 "While we were once perceived": Goizueta speech to Yale University, 1992.
294 Danger of downsizing": Goizueta to Jeffrey Sonnenfeld, June 17, 1997.
295 "Kept our giving in closet": *Atlanta Weekly*, May 11, 1986.
296 "This initiative is simply about creating value": Goizueta to Boys & Girls' Club convention, 1997.
297 Creates Goizueta Foundation: *Atlanta Journal-Constitution*, Oct. 19, 1997.
297 "Nerve of a night prowler": *Fortune*, Oct. 28, 1996.
298 "Energy is number one": *Fortune*, Oct. 13, 1997.
298 "Be like the Pope," "Don't want to go directly to Arlington": *Atlanta Journal-Constitution*, Oct. 22, 1997.

Epilogue The Song at Church
300 Photo at baseball game: Keough.
301 "They're expensive now": *Beverage Digest*, Oct. 24, 1997.
301 "Andrew, I'm a little tired": Andrew Conway.
301 Went to Emory: Coca-Cola Co. press release.
301 Children knew better: Source close to Goizueta.
302 Description of Woodruff suite: Emory University Hospital source.
303 Met with Ivester, Chestnut: Coke sources.
303 Holding pattern: Msr. Edward J. Dillon, Goizueta funeral, Oct. 21, 1997.
304 "Please let my talented doctors": Coke sources.
304 Jimmy Williams chaired: Coca-Cola press release, Oct. 16, 1997.
304 "Those who need to know": *Fortune*, Oct. 28, 1996.
304 Olga cradling him in arms: Dillon, Goizueta funeral mass, Oct. 21, 1997.
304 "It is with great sadness": Ivester message quoted by Coke source.
304 "Integrity is the ultimate advantage": Roberto S. Goizueta, eulogy, Oct. 21, 1997.

Index